Attitudes and Motivation
in
Second-Language Learning

Attitudes and Motivation
in
Second-Language Learning

ROBERT C. GARDNER

The University of Western Ontario

WALLACE E. LAMBERT

McGill University

NEWBURY HOUSE PUBLISHERS / *ROWLEY, MASSACHUSETTS 01969*

NEWBURY HOUSE PUBLISHERS, INC.

Language Science
Language Teaching
Language Learning

68 Middle Road, Rowley, Massachusetts 01969

Library of Congress Card Number: 72-131120
ISBN: 912066-09-01

Cover design: Holly Nichols

Printed in the U.S.A.   First printing: September,1972

Preface

We take great pleasure in expressing here our gratitude to various people and institutions for making it possible for us to conduct the investigations referred to in this book. First, we want to thank three graduate students who were our collaborators and colleagues for different aspects of the work: Robert Olton, who took a major role in the overall planning of the American studies and the programming and statistical analyses of the results; Kenneth Tunstall, who was of invaluable assistance in planning and conducting the value-orientation study; and Emma Santos, who helped plan and carry out the Philippine Study. Without them and their ingenuity the substance of our work would have suffered immeasurably.

Second, the school superintendents, principals, and teachers in the various settings all helped by sharing our enthusiasm about the importance of the investigations and by making the task of interviewing and testing students as easy and interesting as possible. We are grateful to each of them and to the many students involved, who, in general, seemed intrigued that adults were genuinely interested in their points of view and opinions.

Third, we are deeply indebted to several institutions who have been kind enough to extend financial support for these investigations, enabling many graduate and undergraduate students to become part of McGill's Language Research Group. The Canadian Defence Research Board and the Canada Council have provided small-scale operating grants for a number of years; their assistance has provided a continuity to our research. The U. S. Office of Education, under Title VI of the National Defense Education Act, offered assistance for a one-year period so that two full-time researchers could concentrate their efforts on the American studies. The administrative collaboration with Bruce Gaarder and Alfred Hayes, who were at that time with the Office of Education, was particularly pleasurable. The Ford Foundation provided us the opportunity to visit Manila, one of us (Lambert) for six weeks, the other (Gardner) for a full year, where we got to know certain aspects of that fascinating culture and the educational problems faced by Filipinos. The Ford Foundation also supported Miss Santos's participation in the project.

Finally, we want to thank several colleagues who have forced us to think through the theoretical implications of our work and broaden our often biased interpretations: John B. Carroll, William W. Lambert, Dalbir Bindra, Lee Cronbach, Richard Tucker, and Susan Ervin-Tripp. We thank each of them.

Robert C. Gardner
Wallace E. Lambert

May 1972

The authors' names appear in alphabetical order.

Contents

Tables

Chapter One

Introduction

This book summarizes a twelve-year research interest in what appears to be a very simple question: How is it that some people can learn a foreign language quickly and expertly while others, given the same opportunities to learn, are utter failures? Our interest has centered on this matter of individual differences in skill with foreign languages, and in order to keep as many other influences as possible under control we have so far dealt mainly with adolescents in school settings learning one of the two most prestigious languages in the world, French or English.

Quick answers to this simple question are not that convincing. For example, the notion that "it all depends on how the second language is taught" is not sufficient because some students of languages develop high-level skills relatively easily while others following the same pedagogic procedures show little or no progress. Of course it could turn out in the long run that teaching methods have to be tailor-made for each student, but such a conclusion would be extremely discouraging for teachers and school administrators, since certain students would be asked to follow audio-lingual presentations, others programmed instruction, and still others the old-fashioned grammar-translation procedures, etc.

Another quick answer is that "some people have a knack for languages, others do not," but it is very difficult to determine just what the knack is. In fact our twelve-year study has been for us a fascinating search for that knack. From the start, we were persuaded that it would turn out to be something more than "having an ear" for languages—one of the well-entrenched myths often used to explain one's own failures and other's success—because, we argued, everyone learns a first language and thus everyone must have some basic ear or capacity for learning languages. And yet we were impressed with John Carroll's (1956, 1958) work on the development of standardized measures of language-learning aptitude. Individual differences in such an aptitude might very well account for the individual to individual variability in achievement in language study. Still we were not convinced that aptitude was the complete answer. In research where measures of aptitude were correlated with grades received in language courses, sometimes the relationship was very high, while in other situations the relationship was surprisingly low (Carroll, 1956).

One also wonders about the aptitude factor if he looks back into history a bit. When everyone had to know a second language, it seems that everyone, regardless of aptitude, learned it. Take France as an example. Many grandparents or even parents of today's generation spoke regional languages such as Basque, Breton, Provençal as home languages and learned French at school only, and apparently with no handicaps (Delaunay, 1970). Similarly, when Latin was the major literary language, educated people from all over Europe learned it as a matter of course. It shocks us to realize that Seneca, Vergil, Livy, and Cicero—those we read as models of the Latin language—learned Latin only as a second language (Mackey, 1967). It seems then that when the social setting demands it, people master a second language no matter what their aptitudes might be. What then is it to have a knack for learning a foreign language?

We have approached this absorbing question not as linguists or language teachers but as behavioral scientists—in particular, social psychologists—interested in the matter of learning. When looked at from a sociopsychological perspective the process of learning a second language takes on a special significance. Over and above aptitude, one would then anticipate that a really serious student of a foreign or second language who has an open, inquisitive, and unprejudiced orientation toward the learning task might very likely find himself becoming an acculturated member of a new linguistic and cultural community as he develops a mastery of that other group's language. Advancing toward biculturality in this manner could have various effects on different language learners. For some, the experience might be seen as enjoyable and broadening. For others, especially minority group members, it could be taken as an imposition, and learning the language would be accompanied by resentment and ill feeling. In other cases, it could be accompanied by deep-seated and vague feelings of no longer fully belonging to one's own social group nor to the new one he has come to know. At another extreme, a learner with a less democratic orientation might consider the language learning task as a means of becoming more cultured (in the superficial sense of the term) or as equipping him with a skill or tool useful for some future occupation, with little genuine regard for the people or the culture represented by the other language. In certain circumstances, the learner might be anxious to develop skill in another group's language as a means of getting on the "inside" of another cultural community in order to exploit, manipulate, or control, with personal ends only in mind. Thus, there are various forms the language-learning process could take, at least theoretically, and if sociopsychological factors can have such varied and dramatic impact on the more serious, advanced student of languages, one wonders whether the debutant might not be similarly affected, because his attitudes, his views of foreign people and cultures, and his orientation toward the learning process might well determine or limit his progress in developing second-language competence.

A series of studies carried out by a small group of us at McGill University and the University of Western Ontario over the past twelve years has been concerned with such topics, and the findings of these investigations have gradually permitted us to construct the beginnings of a sociopsychological theory of second- or foreign-language learning. This theory, in brief, maintains that the successful learner of a second language must be psychologically prepared to adopt various aspects of behavior which characterize members of another linguistic-cultural group. The learner's ethnocentric tendencies and his attitudes toward the members of the other group are believed to determine how successful he will be, relatively, in learning the new language. His motivation to learn is thought to be determined by his attitudes toward the other group in particular and toward foreign people in general and by his orientation toward the learning task itself. The orientation is said to be *instrumental* in form if the purposes of language study reflect the more utilitarian value of linguistic achievement, such as getting ahead in one's occupation. In contrast, the orientation is *integrative* if the student wishes to learn more about the other cultural community because he is interested in it in an open-minded way, to the point of eventually being accepted as a member of that other group. Variance in outlooks is recognized: some may be anxious to learn another language as a means of being accepted in another ethnolinguistic group because of dissatisfactions experienced in their own culture, while others may be as interested, in a friendly and inquisitive way, in the other culture as they are in their own. However, the more proficient one becomes in a second language, the more he may find his place in his original membership group modified since the new linguistic-cultural group is likely to become for him something more than a mere reference group. It may, in fact, become a second membership group for him. Depending upon how he makes his adjustment to the two cultures, he may experience feelings of chagrin or regret as he loses ties in one group, mixed with the fearful anticipation of entering a new and somewhat strange group. Thus feelings of social uncertainty or dissatisfaction which often characterize the immigrant and the bilingual may also, we believe, affect the serious student of a second language.

Theories are very useful devices because they help explain complicated phenomena, such as language learning, and because in testing out implications, new and unanticipated implications are nearly always brought to light, thereby forcing the researcher to continue probing. The theory just presented in a summarized fashion has evolved from a long run of research studies. Thus, various critical aspects of it have been tested, but only in a superficial and limited fashion. In fact, at this point in time, it is clear to us that only a start has been made, and it is hoped that much more research will follow from this start. But because this is a new look at language learning and one with potentially valuable suggestions for teachers of foreign languages and language program directors, it seems wise to present the evidence now available in some detail. With the aim of presenting that evidence, spotty as it is, and of introducing our research approaches, each of the basic studies involved will first be summarized and integrated, and then the major research referred to will be presented in its entirety as a separate *Reading* in Appendix C. We hope the whole set of readings referred to in various chapters will be useful not only to those who want to follow our arguments in detail, but also those who may want the details in order to take some of the next research steps that will become obvious as we proceed.

The first studies (Gardner and Lambert, 1959; Gardner, 1960; placed in Appendix C as Readings Number One and Number Two) were carried out with English-speaking high school students in Montreal who were studying French. These students were examined for language-learning aptitude and verbal intelligence as well as for attitudes toward the French community and intensity of motivation to learn French. Our measure of motivational intensity was similar to Jones's (1949 and 1950) index of interest in learning a language, which he found to be important in his research with students in Wales. A factor analysis of these indices indicated that aptitude and intelligence formed a single factor or cluster which was independent of a second made up of measures of motivation, type of orientation toward language learning, and social attitudes toward French Canadians. Teachers' ratings of achievement in French were reflected equally prominently in both factors. In this case, then, French achievement was dependent upon both aptitude and intelligence as well as upon a sympathetic orientation toward the other group. It was the orientation that apparently provided a strong motivation to learn the other group's language. In the Montreal setting, students with an integrative orientation were more successful in second-language learning than those who were instrumentally oriented. In our research to date, we have not tried to measure or treat separately the manipulative orientation mentioned earlier, and we are aware that a certain amount of error in classifying students may occur until attention is given to this separate form of orientation. The recent work on Machiavellianism by Christie and Geis (1970) suggests an intriguing mode of studying this type of outlook and its possible role in foreign-language learning.

A follow-up study (Gardner, 1960; Reading Number Two) confirmed and extended these findings, using a larger sample of English Canadian students and incorporating various measures of French achievement. In this case it was difficult to dissociate aptitude from motivational variables since they emerged in a common factor that included not only French skills stressed in standard academic courses but also those skills developed through active use of the language in communication. Apparently in the Montreal context, the intelligent and linguistically gifted student of French is more likely to be integratively oriented, making it very likely that he could become outstanding in all aspects of French proficiency. Still in the same study, the measures of orientation and desire to learn French emerged as separate factors, independent of language aptitude, and in these instances it was evident that they alone play an important role, especially in the development of expressive skills in French. Further evidence from the intercorrelations indicated that this integrative motive was the converse of an authoritarian ideological syndrome, opening the possibility that basic personality dispositions may be involved in language-learning efficiency.

In the follow-up study, information had been gathered about the attitudes of the students' parents toward the French community. These data supported the notion that the student's orientation toward the other group is likely developed within the family. That is, students with an integrative disposition to learn French had parents who also were integrative in outlook and sympathetic to the French community. The students' orientations were not, however, simply a reflection of their parents' skill (or lack of it) in French or to the number of French acquaintances the parents had. That is, the integrative motive is not simply the result of having more experience with French at home. Rather it seems to depend on the family's attitudinal disposition.

A study by Anisfeld and Lambert (1961; Reading Number Three) extended the experimental procedure to samples of Jewish high school students who were studying Hebrew at parochial schools in Montreal. They were administered tests measuring their orientations toward learning Hebrew and their attitudes toward the Jewish culture and community as well as tests of verbal intelligence and language aptitude. Intercorrelations among these tests and measures of achievement in the Hebrew language at the end of the school year were carried out. The results indicated that both intellectual capacity and attitudinal orientation affect success in learning Hebrew. However, whereas intelligence and linguistic aptitude are relatively stable predictors of success, the importance of the attitudinal measures varies from one school district to another, depending upon the social class of the neighborhood. For example, the measure of a Jewish student's desire to become more acculturated into the Jewish tradition and culture was a sensitive indicator of progress in Hebrew for children in a particular district of Montreal, one where, in the process of adjusting to a North American gentile environment, Jews were concerned with problems of integrating into the Jewish culture. In another district where Jews who were recent arrivals in North America lived in relatively poor circumstances, the measure of desire for Jewish acculturation did not correlate with achievement in Hebrew, whereas measures of pro-Semitic attitudes or pride in being Jewish did.

To follow up these ideas, students undergoing an intensive course in French at McGill's French Summer School were tested for changes in attitude during the six-week study period (Lambert, Gardner, Barik, and Tunstall, 1962; Reading Number Four). Most were American university students or secondary school language teachers who, in their orientations to language learning, referred themselves more to the European French than to the American French community. In this study, it became apparent that feelings of social uncertainty were markedly increased during the course of study. As students progressed to the point that they thought and even dreamed(!) in French, it was noted that their feelings of social unrest also increased. At the same time, they tried to find occasions to use English even though they had pledged to use only French for the six-week period. The pattern suggests—and this is only an hypothesis to be tested independently—that American students experience feelings of social disorganization when they concentrate on and commence to master a second language and, as a consequence, develop stratagems to control or minimize such feelings.

The final study in the original series (Peal and Lambert, 1962; Reading Number Five) compares ten-year-old monolingual and bilingual youngsters on measures of intelligence. Of relevance here is the clear pattern of results showing that bilingual children have markedly more favorable attitudes toward both language communities than do monolingual children, who definitely favor one cultural group over the other. Furthermore, the parents of bilingual children are viewed by their children as holding the same strongly sympathetic attitudes, which was not the case for the parents of monolingual children. This finding also suggests that linguistic skills in a second language, extending to the point of bilingualism, are controlled by family-shared attitudes toward the other ethnolinguistic community.

The home influence has been carefully examined in the recent study of Feenstra and Gardner (1968). They surveyed the attitudes of parents directly and included in their analysis the parental data along with a complete battery of aptitude, achievement, motivation, and attitude measures of adolescents studying French at high school in an Ontario setting. Not only did they replicate the earlier findings by demonstrating again the relation of an integrative motive to achievement in the second language, but they also showed a marked correspondence of attitudes between the two generations (cf. Gardner, Taylor, and Feenstra, 1970). Furthermore, parents with positive attitudes toward the other language community more actively encouraged their children to learn that language than did parents with less favorable attitudes.

These results appear to be consistent and reliable enough to be of general interest. Methods of language training could perhaps be strengthened by giving major consideration to the social and psychological implications of language learning. Because of the possible practical as well as theoretical significance of this approach, it seemed appropriate and necessary to test its applicability in cultural settings other than Canadian ones. The studies to follow were accordingly conducted in various regional settings in the United States, two of them also bicultural and a third more representative of "typical" urban American cities. The bicultural settings permitted an examination of attitudes working two ways: attitudinal dispositions of American students toward linguistic minority groups in their immediate environment, and attitudes of members of the cultural minority group toward the general American culture in which they function. After looking more deeply into the nature and function of attitudes, stereotypes, and value systems, and the role they play in second-language learning, we finally tested out the same set of ideas in a very complex and interesting foreign setting, that of the Philippines, where learning foreign languages plays a vital role in most students' lives.

It is to these extensions of the ideas summarized here that we will turn in the following chapters. First, though, there are preliminary discussions about research plans and about the work of others interested in the same questions as we are that will occupy us in the next chapter.

Chapter Two

Background Ideas and the Research Procedures

Although we are primarily interested in the roles of attitudes and motivation in the acquisition of a foreign or second language, we realize, of course, that there are many other types of individual differences of language students that could affect students' progress and achievement in the study of languages. Thus, it is necessary to plan investigations and choose methods of analysis that take these potentially important other characteristics into account. The research reported here should throw light on the role played by selected other variables as well as the motivational ones.

Carroll (1962) suggests that second-language achievement varies as a function of three learner characteristics: aptitude, general intelligence, and motivation, and two instructional variables: the opportunity the student has for learning and the adequacy of presentation of the material to be learned. Since our own research is concerned with students learning French in high school settings, it is reasonable to assume that for any given sample, the adequacy of presentation and opportunity for learning are essentially the same for all students—fixed as they are by the selection of teachers and the curriculum. Of course teaching techniques and teachers' personalities can certainly affect the attitudes and motivation of students, but these important factors have been ruled out or reduced as much as possible in this investigation. Still, there is no question that students differ in language aptitude, intelligence, and motivation and consequently these attributes were assessed. The approach used in the studies to be presented consists of testing or measuring a reasonably large sample of students and examining the relationships among all of a large number of measures. The resulting correlation matrices were factor analyzed in order to discover through the patterns of intercorrelations the major dimensions or underlying factors that account for the correlations. By including measures of language aptitude, intelligence, attitudes, motivation, and second-language achievement, we are able to determine the effects of motivational variables, for example, on achievement relative to the influence of language aptitude and intelligence.

Factor Analysis

A statistical technique known as "factor analysis" is used in all the investigations described in this book. It is an extremely useful research tool, especially for exploratory investigations such as ours. For those unfamiliar with it, we will introduce the technique in nontechnical language. (A more complete introduction can be found in Cronbach, 1970, who also suggests appropriate follow-up readings.) The aim of factor analysis is to simplify and classify the meaning of a set of interrelated variables. Typically one begins with a correlation matrix, i.e., a table that lists the correlations or degrees of relationship between each and every other variable introduced into an investigation. In our case we start with 41 variables, which when intercorrelated make a correlation matrix of 820 correlation coefficients. (The rule is that N variables produces a matrix of $N(\frac{N-1}{2})$ correlation coefficients.) If one were dealing with a small number of variables, say 4 or so, no fancy methodology would be needed; one could collect into separate groups all variables that correlate substantially with each other but not with others in the matrix. As the number of variables increases, however, this becomes progressively more difficult to do and highly subjective, because there are no hard-and-fast rules to decide when one variable is clearly related to some but not other members of a set. To circumvent this problem factor analysis permits one to tease apart sets of related variables in a very objective manner. The trick is to test the relationship of each variable with one of a number of independent (i.e., uncorrelated or orthogonal) dimensions or factors. If a set of variables shows a substantial degree of relationship to one of these reference factors which is made to be independent of any of a number of other factors, then it is assumed that the members of the set are truly related to each other.

We can illustrate these notions with an example from our own research. We use factor analysis to help us determine what sorts of personal characteristics or dispositions (the variables) influence proficiency in acquiring a second language. Our interpretations and explanations are determined and limited by the ways in which the variables align themselves on the various factors. In our Canadian studies, for instance, we were "told" that something more than verbal intelligence and language learning aptitude is involved because a completely independent, separate attitudinal-motivational factor emerged from the analysis that proved to be as important in accounting for proficiency as the intelligence-aptitude factor. More than that, the composition of the factors tells us whether attitudes form a set with motivation or with ethnocentrism, etc., or whether in some settings they pull apart to form separate clusters.

In conducting a factor analysis, the investigator first obtains the matrix of relationships among variables (i.e., the correlation matrix), and then performs a fixed set of operations on this matrix to produce a new matrix (the factor matrix) which contains as many rows (variables) as the correlation matrix, but fewer columns. The reduction in the number of columns results because the more basic relationships among all variables are more abstract and thus can generally be accounted for by a smaller number of dimensions than the total number of variables. There are many different ways of obtaining the factor matrix, each method producing a somewhat different type of factor matrix. In this book two different types of matrices are obtained, a centroid factor matrix and a principal axis factor matrix. These matrices are obtained by specifiable and objective mathematical procedures. Typically, these matrices are then subjected to one further arithmetical operation known as a "rotation" and the resulting matrix is referred to as a rotated factor matrix. The purpose of rotating the matrix is to provide a new matrix with reference dimensions that make it more meaningful psychologically than is possible with the original matrix, which varies according to the mathematical model used. The rotated factor matrix, however, is derived from the relationships existing in the original correlation matrix, and there is nothing in the rotation procedure that modifies these relationships. In fact, the rotation procedure employed almost uniformly throughout this book—the normalized varimax procedure—is a completely objective and arithmetical procedure.

To interpret the meaning of a factor matrix, one considers each factor separately, directing attention to those variables that receive substantial "loadings" on a factor, that is those measures with networks of intercorrelation pervasive enough to establish the nucleus of the factor under scrutiny. Then the researcher examines the pattern of high loadings from every possible angle so as to discover the underlying dimension or theme that brings a particular set of measures together in that fashion. This is the discovery and fun aspect of the analysis. To reduce the personal biases that can affect the interpretations, it is valuable, we have found, to have two researchers working independently, and to check with a third party whenever a difference of emphasis occurs. There is a question about how large a loading must be to merit attention. We were guided by the research of Cliff and Hamburger (1967) who estimate that with samples as large as ours a loading of $\pm.30$ is noteworthy. In technical terms, the standard error of a factor loading is approximately equal to $1/\sqrt{N}$; thus, in our case, this would correspond to a Z score of 3.05, p < .002.

Motivation and Attitudes in Learning

Comparatively little past research has looked into the motivational aspects of second-language achievement, though the concept is often used as an explanation of differences in attainment. One reason for this may be the inherent difficulty in conceptualizing and measuring those motivational variables that would likely determine success in second-language learning. Our initial speculations grew out of theoretical explanations of first-language development, particularly those of Mowrer (1950). Mowrer suggests that the parents' activities and, indeed, their mere presence are reinforcing or rewarding because such activities are regularly associated in the infant's mind with satisfaction of basic biological and social needs. Since this reinforcement is generally accompanied by verbalization on the part of the parents, the language sounds themselves can acquire "secondary" or derived reinforcing properties. When the infant is alone and utters a sound sequence like one in the language of the parents, this act, through auditory feedback, is in itself reinforcing for him. The tendency of the child to imitate the parents in this way Mowrer calls "identification." Such a scheme may not explain the whole of first-language acquisition, since much of language learning takes place through subtle forms of perceptual learning where the role of reinforcement is much less obvious (see Hebb, Lambert, and Tucker, 1971) or through direct forms of reinforcement, as when the parent withholds a reward until the child makes the appropriate language response. Mowrer argues, however, that a good deal of instrumental learning of various forms—including perceptual learning itself—is based on an emotionally toned dependence between infant and parent.

We reasoned that some process like identification, extended to a whole enthnolinguistic community and coupled with an inquisitiveness and sincere interest in the other group, must underlie the long-term motivation needed to master a second language. Other motivations such as a need for achievement or a fear of failure seem appropriate for short-term goals such as passing a language course, but seem insufficient to account for the persistence needed in the laborious and time-consuming task of developing real competence in a new language. The notion of identification as used in the second-language learning situation differs in degree and substance from Mowrer's use of the term in his explanation of first-language learning. As a consequence, we introduced a new term, "an integrative motive." For Mowrer, identification derives from the reduction or satisfaction of basic biological needs, while in most second-language learning situations more interpersonal or social motives are obviously brought into play. (These social needs are referred to technically as secondary or derived drives by Miller and Dollard, 1941.) In both the first- and second-language cases, however, language is a means to an end rather than an end itself, in the sense that languages are typically learned in the process of becoming a member of a particular group, and the sustaining motivation appears to be one of group membership, not of language acquisition per se. We will, therefore, reserve the term identification for the first-language condition, and when it is a question of second-language learning refer to a willingness to become a member of another ethnolinguistic group as an integrative motive. This distinction is useful since it emphasizes the desire for integration (common in both situations) but distinguishes it from identification and the antecedent conditions which promote such a motive.

Numerous observations suggested to us that some integrative-like process plays an important role in second-language acquisition. In an early study of bilingualism, for example, Lambert (1955) discussed the case of an English-speaking American graduate student who when measured with psychological tests proved to be clearly dominant in his use of French over English. Interviews indicated that this particular student had a distinctive pattern of attitudes; he was disillusioned with the American scene, reacted against anything that was not European, and read only French newspapers and other reading material. He claimed that he had recently been to France and was returning as soon as possible, apparently to stay. This somewhat dramatic case typifies an extreme form of what we mean by an integrative motivation. Less striking but similar cases are reported by Whyte and Holmberg (1956). They found that among numbers of Americans working in Latin America those who believed that they shared physical attributes with Latin Americans and who wanted to interact with them as social equals learned the local language and became much more fluent than workers who could not or would not make this identification.

Other studies report attitudinal differences associated with second-language achievement which are consistent with this interpretation. For example, Lambert, Hodgson, Gardner, and Fillenbaum (1960), found that bilingual subjects obtained significantly lower scores than monolinguals on the California F-Scale (Adorno et al., 1950). Similarly, Gardner (1958) found that adults enrolled in advanced French classes in evening-school language programs had lower F-Scale scores than adults in more elementary French courses. Since the F-Scale purportedly measures authoritarian and prejudiced attitudes, these findings suggested to us that second-language achievement might be facilitated by a favorable and accepting orientation toward ethnolinguistic groups different from one's own.

Finally, Nida (1956) presented a case history that illustrates the influence of a factor like identification in second-language achievement, but in this instance one sees how an overemotional desire to be integrated in one linguistic group can deter the acquisition of another group's language. Nida describes a missionary who had extreme difficulty in acquiring a usable command of a foreign language despite good teachers, a great deal of effort, and a high level of intelligence. Under study, it turned out that this man's parents had immigrated to the United States, and as a boy he had dissociated himself from his foreign cultural background and insisted on speaking English exclusively at home. His desire for integration into the American culture was so intense that he denied knowing the parental language. Nida suggests that this person was unable to overcome his intense emotional reaction to a "foreign" non-English language.

The notion of an integrative motive implies that success in mastering a second language depends on a particular orientation on the part of the learner, reflecting a willingness or a desire to be like representative members of the "other" language community, and to become associated, at least vicariously, with that other community. Hence the acquisition of a new language involves much more than mere acquisition of a new set of verbal habits. The language student must be willing to adopt appropriate features of behavior which characterize members of another linguistic community. The words, grammatical patterns, mode of pronunciation, and the sounds themselves should have a significance for the successful learner that goes beyond simple translations or equivalences given by a teacher, a grammar book, or a dictionary. Instead these come to be regarded as distinctive aspects of the behavior of the other cultural group. The student's attitudinal orientation toward that group, we argue, will influence his progress and efficiency in adopting these novel and strange linguistic habits into his own repertoire.

We felt one could estimate or measure the value orientation of a prospective student of a foreign language by means of structured interviews or carefully planned questionnaires. If a student when questioned about his interest in foreign-language study and the potential value it held for him assigned high priority to learning more about the other ethnolinguistic group as a people (be it the ancient Greeks or Spanish-speaking immigrants from Cuba), or to meeting and becoming acquainted with the members of that community, this we would take as a reflection of an integrative orientation. Hence when the rationale for studying a foreign language reflected an inquisitiveness and genuine interest in the people comprising a cultural group, be it an interest in an ancient people or a contemporary one, or a desire to meet with and possibly associate with that group, we take it to be a symptom of an integrative outlook. Of course, an intelligent manipulator of people would pass this filter, too, since he would also realize the need to know about and associate with the other group in order to exploit them. No attention was given to this manipulative form of motivation in the studies presented here, but the fascinating work of Christie and Geis (1970) on Machiavellianism provides researchers with a valuable means of measuring manipulative personality dispositions. Future research on foreign-language learning could well profit from a consideration of this form of motivation.

The contrasting form of orientation we did give attention to is referred to as an *instrumental* orientation toward the language-learning task, one characterized by a desire to gain social recognition or economic advantages through knowledge of a foreign language. The perspective in this instance is more self-oriented in the sense that a person prepares to learn a new code in order to derive benefits of a noninterpersonal sort. This notion is a simple extension of Skinner's (1953) and Parsons' (1951) uses of the concept "instrumental." The contrast we have drawn, then, has at one extreme an integratively oriented learner who in considering the learning task is oriented principally towards representatives of a novel and interesting ethnolinguistic community, people with whom he would like to develop personal ties. At the other extreme the instrumentally oriented language learner is interested mainly in using the cultural group and their language as an instrument of personal satisfaction, with few signs of an interest in the other people per se. Our index of these two forms of motivation for language learning is, at this stage, crude, since in categorizing students, we pay attention only to the order of priority—instrumental reasons given priority over integrative ones, or the converse—labeling each student with one or another form of orientation. It is time now that this very useful index be expanded and elaborated in order that a genuine dimensional scale or continuum may be used to explore more comprehensively this aspect of motivation.

There is another important form of orientation to language learning that could come into play, but again we have only superficially touched on it in our analyses. This is the resentment members of one linguistic group (usually the minority group) can have toward another group whose language or dialect they are forced to learn through social or economic pressure. We will see the influence of this orientation on certain French-American students studying through English in the United States and among certain Filipino students who also study through English. Comprehensive modes of analyzing this outlook could of course be developed and the topic certainly merits special consideration in research.

When behavioral scientists talk about motivation they usually make a distinction between the goal toward which concerted activity is directed and the effort or persistence demonstrated in the process of striving for the goal. Dunkel (1948) suggested that this dichotomy was useful for the case of second-language learning, where attention should be given both to the objectives or purposes of second-language acquisition and the intensity of motivation shown by the language learner. In our work, we see the major motivational goal—from the point of view of the learner—to be a general orientation or outlook toward the learning process which can take either an integrative or an instrumental form. As for the persistence or intensity of motivation, we reasoned that a first-level index could be developed through questioning each student about his interest in and attitude toward the work required for his foreign-language course, his spontaneous attempts to improve his skills outside of class requirements, and his personal interest in continuing the study of the language. In this fashion, a motivational intensity scale was formed which permits us to rank students, from those with strong and persistent motivation to those with few or no signs of interest, effort, or persistence.

There is no reason to expect to find a relationship between one form or the other of motivational orientation and motivational intensity, since the instrumentally oriented learner could be as intense or more so than the integratively oriented student. Still, we felt that the integratively oriented learner might be better motivated because the nature of his goals is more likely to sustain the long-term effort needed to master a second language, especially when one starts only at the high school age level. This becomes one of the working hypotheses in our studies and we will return to it at several points in the chapters to follow.

Other Sociopsychological Variables of Interest

Other learner characteristics were examined as well. We reasoned that the type of orientation toward the task of learning a foreign language very likely develops from a deep attitudinal base. Learners who have strong ethnocentric or authoritarian attitudes or who have learned to be prejudiced toward foreign peoples are unlikely to approach the language-learning task with an integrative outlook. To check on this possibility and to examine how the orientation index itself relates to these fundamental attitudes, standardized measures of ethnocentrism and authoritarianism were taken from the publications of Adorno, Frenkel-Brunswick, Levinson, and Sanford (1950). To measure attitudes toward specific foreign groups, new measures were developed or old ones were revised. Each of these measures and others designed to test out various hunches we had are described in detail in the chapters to come.

We had two major reasons for measuring feelings of societal dissatisfaction or social uncertainty. First, it seemed possible to us that certain students with an integrative orientation toward another cultural group might have developed along the way a basic dissatisfaction with their own society and were thus perceiving language study as a way of examining a potentially better way of life, much as the more sensitive student activists were in the 1968-70 period when they expressed their dissatisfaction with the social system in a much more transparent and open way. Second, we felt that regardless of his attitudes toward society at the start of the language-learning process, the more advanced student of language might well find that his new skills permitted him to leave his own cultural group and become a member of the new group whose language he had nearly mastered. Thus, the new option opened to him might create disillusionment, a feeling of being lost somewhere between two cultures. With these ideas in mind, we developed a measure of each student's relative satisfaction with his own cultural group in contrast to the other, and adapted Leo Srole's scale of *anomie* (Srole, 1951) as an index of social incertitude. The concept anomie comes from the writings of the French sociologist Emile Durkheim (1897), whose research dealt with feelings of normlessness or not belonging (literally, anomie means being without norms or social ties). Durkheim saw a deep significance in feelings of this sort because for him they were symptoms of adjustment difficulties faced by most people in urban, industrialized communities. It was our hunch that this important notion, as relevant today as it was in the era of the industrial revolution, could be extended beyond the case of the marginal man lost in a large anonymous community. The immigrant as well as the bilingual person must also struggle against tremendous odds to keep and maintain comfortable contacts with two cultural traditions and retain full membership in both. Here again we have only started, because in order to stay close to Durkheim's line of thought we made only a few changes in the original version of Srole's scale. It seems particularly appropriate in the light of our overall results to now go further in the development of a comprehensive measure of the full range of feelings of alienation or personal disorganization experienced by bilingual and bicultural individuals.

The Plan of the Chapters to Follow

Each of the variables discussed plays a role in the working hypotheses that underlie our research. This is evident in the readings already referred to and in the studies we present next. In the next chapter we try out these hypotheses in a non-Canadian setting, the United States. In the first case we turn our attention to English-speaking American high school students studying French in bicultural communities, Louisiana and Maine, where the French language and traditions are still alive. These groups of young people are thus similar to those we investigated in the greater Montreal setting. We then report on a more typically American community in Connecticut, where the students studying French at school have as a reference group the European French people, three thousand miles away rather than in their own neighborhoods. Then we focus our sights on French-American high school students in Louisiana and Maine because they are members of a cultural minority group. These young people come from homes in which French is used as a means of communication but attend English language schools where they too are studying French. Finally, we apply the same analytic scheme in a totally different cultural setting—that of Manila in the Philippines—where English is the predominant language of instruction but hardly ever a home language. In this instance English is a cultural import, and our theoretical notions of how attitudes and motivation affect language learning skill—in this case, English—are given a solid test.

Before we proceed, we should say a word about the presentation of our results and discussion. For some readers, certain parts may seem quite technical and if they become discouraged, they should realize that interpretations and summaries are provided at regular intervals so that the technicalities can be passed over. However, in writing this book we also have in mind the psychologists and educationists who will want to understand and evaluate for themselves the details of the arguments and discussions presented, especially since a new line of approach with important pedagogical implications is involved.

These readers may be tempted to replicate our findings in different contexts or take the next research steps that are called for. It is to be hoped that many language teachers will also be prompted to return and reread the technical details, perhaps with the help of a colleague from the behavioral sciences, so that they—the ones best situated to judge the educational possibilities of the approach and to envisage next research steps—can participate in the development and improvement of second-language learning and intercultural understanding.

Chapter Three

Extensions to American Settings:
The Louisiana, Maine, and Connecticut Studies

How far can one generalize the findings just discussed and the theory they suggest? The pattern of results obtained in our Canadian studies may be peculiar to Montreal or to bilingual and bicultural settings only. The Montreal students began their formal training in French in elementary schools, and thus a really serious student of language could develop high-level skills by the end of his high school years, enough in fact to permit him to interact smoothly with members of the other language community. Perhaps environmental supports of that sort are necessary for the integrative-instrumental distinction to have a relevance. In essentially unilingual settings, types of orientation might not play a role at all. It could be that in the United States, for example, different views of the utility or value of learning foreign languages would override the theoretical distinctions we have found important in Quebec and Ontario. Similarly, would we likely find the same relationship of ethnocentrism and second-language achievement in other communities?

It was with questions of this sort in mind, and with a serious desire to test the generalizability of our notions about the language-learning process, that we crossed the border. The regions we selected after a good deal of thought and search were a community in the state of Louisiana, another in Maine, and a third in Connecticut. The first two we saw as interesting comparisons because in one (Maine) there is an active minority subculture of French-Americans, making it somewhat similar in that respect to the bicultural Quebec scene. Louisiana has a reputation too of having a French-American subculture of some importance and even though we had our doubts about its state of vivacity, we realized that the non-French community would very likely have a relatively clear stereotype of

French people and French ways of life. Thus the Louisiana and Maine sites were meant to be somewhat like the Montreal community with regard to students having personal experience (first- or second-hand) with French people as they begin their study of French. These settings *should* provide a relatively easy test for the generalizability of earlier Canadian results.

The choice of Connecticut was meant to be a stiffer test because there, we reckoned, the foreign reference group for high school students studying French should be more vague, possibly based on stereotypes of France and its populace. In that sense, it might be a more "typical" American region—if there really is any such region in the United States—and the findings based on Connecticut students could be particularly instructive, whether they supported or set severe limits on our theoretical notions.

We will describe each of the three American settings in more detail in separate sections to follow. But first we want to introduce the general procedure we followed and the various measures we developed for all three American sites.

The Measuring Instruments

Over fifty separate tests or indices were included in the battery given to each student. Our plan here is to describe each of these instruments briefly so that the reader can get a feeling for our means of eliciting information relevant to the various psychological processes we suspect may play a role in the development of second-language competence. To get an even fuller understanding, complete copies of all the questionnaires and ratings scales used are presented in Appendix A. Standardized measures taken from already published works are not reproduced again because they are easily available.

It is very apparent as one examines these fifty-odd scales and rating instruments that they cover a vast domain. We see each of them as a potentially instructive clue that might help clarify some of the mystery about individual differences in success in foreign-language study. As this is meant to be an exploratory investigation, we worked on the principle that it was best to probe broadly, to include even those tests that had only a low probability of revealing a relationship, rather than being selective at the start. We relied on the statistical procedure to decide which variables ultimately prove to be important and which show little promise.

Motivation and Attitudinal Measures

1. *Orientation Index.* This scale was taken from the first study by Gardner and Lambert (1959; see *Reading Number One*) and provides the student with four alternative reasons for studying French (see Appendix A, item 1). The student was asked to rank the four as to their relevance for him personally. Scoring of

this index uses a simple two-way classification: if either of the two integratively worded reasons was seen as most personally relevant a score of 2 was assigned and if either of the two instrumentally worded reasons was chosen as most relevant, a score of 1 was given.

2. *Student's Orientation.* This is a variant of the above and is taken from an earlier study (Gardner, 1960; see *Reading Number Two*). On the basis of a student's responses to three questions dealing with his views of the advantages and personal satisfactions associated with a mastery of French, he was classified as integratively (2) or instrumentally (1) oriented. This variant, which was separated from the first in the testing order, requires the student to supply reasons rather than reacting to reasons provided to him.

3. *Rating of Integrative Orientation.* This is a further variant: the student was asked to rate, using 7-point scales, the extent to which each of four integrative reasons for studying French was descriptive of his own feelings. An integrative reason is one which places emphasis on learning a second language in order to learn more about or meet members of the other language group. For example, "It will enable me to make good friends more easily among French-speaking people." The higher a student's score on this measure, the more integrative his orientation is presumed to be.

4. *Rating of Instrumental Orientation.* Again, using 7-point scales, the student in this case was asked to judge his own reasons for studying French with reference to four instrumentally oriented statements, i.e., statements that emphasized the utilitarian values of second-language achievement, with no sign of interest in the people whose language was being studied. For example, "I think a knowledge of French will some day be useful in getting a good job." The higher the student's score the more his motivation fits the instrumental type.

5. *Anomie.* Srole's (1951) anomie scale was used along with several new items developed specifically for adolescents. The combined scale is meant to measure personal dissatisfaction or discouragement with one's place in society.

6. *Authoritarianism.* Thirteen items were selected on the basis of their discriminatory power from Forms 45 and 40 of the California F-Scale (Adorno et al., 1950). The scale was designed as a measure of authoritarian or antidemocratic ideologies, reflecting a generalized prejudice of foreign peoples.

7. *Ethnocentrism.* Seven items from the E-Scale of Adorno et al. (1950) were slightly reworded to make them more appropriate for high school students. This scale purports to measure ethnocentrism and suspicion of foreign people and ideas.

8. *Preference for America over France.* Nine items were constructed which make invidious comparisons between the French and American ways of life. Agreement with the items reflects a personal preference for American society, while disagreement indicates a comparative dissatisfaction with the American in comparison to the French way of life. An example item is, "The French way of

life seems crude when compared to ours."

9. *Attitudes toward French-Americans.* Sixteen positively worded statements about "French-Americans" were presented, and students indicated on a 7-point scale how much they agreed or disagreed with each. A sample item is, "French-Americans set a good example for us by their family life."

10. *Motivational Intensity.* Six multiple-choice statements were developed as an index of intensity of motivation to learn French. They asked about work done for assignments, future intentions to study and make use of the language, amount of practice of the language outside school, and the importance attributed to a knowledge of the language. The students were asked to choose, in each case, an alternative most descriptive of themselves.

11. *Desire to Learn French.* Eight multiple-choice statements were developed to reflect the extent to which a student wants to learn the language. The items dealt with the student's preference for French over other school courses, his eagerness to do assignments and his degree of attention in class, his interest in the French course and in using the language. These items, in contrast to those in the Motivational Intensity scale, focus more on the student's attitude toward learning French than on the amount of effort spent in acquiring the language. Whether they in fact are different will become apparent when the correlations are examined.

12. *Social Inquisitiveness.* This scale was constructed as an estimate of the student's likelihood of actively seeking out interpersonal contacts and social interaction in contrast to being socially passive. Eight stories were presented in which two individuals. are contrasted, one socially active, the other passive. Students were asked to state, in each case, which character was most like themselves. Our hunch in developing this scale was that the more socially and mentally inquisitive person might be more integratively oriented or more motivated and skilled at learning the audio-lingual components of a second or foreign language. We will see if there is any merit in this notion.

13. *Sensitivity to Others.* This variable consisted of eight statements describing how much or little attention one gives to the feelings of others. The student indicated how characteristic each statement was of his own behavior. A sample item is: "I often do things my own way, without thinking about how it will affect others." The idea underlying this scale was that the more socially sensitive or empathic person might be more integratively oriented or more gifted for learning the oral-aural features of a foreign language.

14. *Parental Encouragement to Learn French.* Students indicated on a 7-point rating scale the extent to which their parents encouraged them to study French. In this instance, we were interested in knowing what role, if any, parents played in the student's desire and motivation to learn French.

15. *Parents Favor Student Learning French.* Students estimated how their own parents felt about their (the students) study of French. The item was scored

as favorable or indifferent. This rating was included in order to assess the effect, if any, of a slightly different form of parental support on the student's motivation and achievement.

16. *Parents' French Friends.*   Students were asked whether their parents had any close friends who were French-speaking. The score was based on a yes-no division. Again, we wanted to assess the effect of parents' roles as models on the attitudes and orientations of the students.

17. *Student's French Acquaintances.*   Students were asked whether they knew any French-speaking people. Here we reasoned that students' attitudes (favorable or unfavorable) would be more salient if based on interpersonal experience.

18. *Student's French Friends.*   Students were asked whether any of these French people were really good friends. The item was scored as a yes-no question and became a further measure of attitudes, in this case, based on more intimate experience.

For variables 19-24, each student was asked to evaluate the following people using a series of twenty-three 7-point rating scales such as *sincere* . . . insincere, dependable . . . undependable, etc. (see Appendix A, items 19-24). An overall score was assigned for each group rated, which was the average ratings over the twenty-three scales. The higher the score, the more favorable the opinion.

19. *French People From France;* 20. *Me;* 21. *Americans;* 22. *Me, As I'd Like to Be;* 23. *French-Americans;* 24. *My French Teacher.*

Variables 25 and 26 reflect students' stereotypes toward French and English-speaking people. Students listened to tape recordings of nine "speakers" reading a short descriptive passage, some readers using English, others French, actually a translated version of the same paragraph. The first recording (an English guise) was used only to introduce the rating procedure, and responses to this voice were not analyzed. The remaining eight "speakers" were, in reality, four fluent English-French bilinguals who read the passage once in one of their languages, and further along on the tape, again in the other language. Students rated the personality of each guise on twenty 6-point evaluative scales provided for that purpose. Each student's comparative evaluations of the French and English guises of the speakers were compared statistically. Two of the speakers were chosen so that their French was "European" in style while the other two spoke with a North American style and accent. Two scores were obtained for each individual, one for his evaluations of European French speakers, the other for his comparative views of American-French speakers. This technique is described in Lambert, Hodgson, Gardner, and Fillenbaum (1960), and in Lambert, Anisfeld, and Yeni-Komshian (1965), and is discussed more fully in Chapter 5. It is meant to measure stereotypes people hold of speakers of a foreign language.

25. *Comparative Evaluation of European French and English Speakers.*   The

mean difference between the evaluative ratings assigned to the two European guises and their corresponding English guises was calculated for each student. Positive scores reflect a favorable evaluation of the American-English over the European-French guises, while negative scores reflect a favorable evaluation of the European-French over the American-English guises.

26. *Comparative Evaluation of French-American and English Speakers.*   The mean difference between the evaluative ratings given to two American-French guises and two corresponding American-English guises was calculated for each student. Positive scores reflect a preference for American-English over American-French guises.

Language Aptitude Measures

Variables 27-31 are the five subscales of the Carroll-Sapon *Modern Language Aptitude Test* (1959). The manual describes each subscale as follows:

27. *Number Learning*: Measures both memory and general auditory alertness.

28. *Phonetic Script*: memory for speech sounds, and the ability to associate speech sounds with orthographic symbols.

29. *Spelling Clues*: knowledge of English vocabulary and sound-symbol associations.

30. *Words in Sentences*: sensitivity to grammatical structures.

31. *Paired Associates:* rote memory ability.

French Language Achievement Measures

Variables 32-35 are the four subscales of the *Cooperative French Listening Comprehension Test* (Form A) taken from Brooks (1955). These are described in the manual as follows:

32. *Phonetic Discrimination:*   measures the ability to make auditory distinctions (e.g., in consonant or vowel sounds) in aural comprehension of French.

33. *Answering Questions:*   comprehension of isolated questions asked in French.

34. *Completion of Statements:*   ability to complete French sentences when presented aurally.

35. *Comprehension of Passages:*   ability to comprehend and retain descriptions presented in short passages of French.

Variables 36-38 are the three subscales of the *Cooperative French Test, Elementary* (Form Q) taken from Greenberg and Spaulding (1940).

36. *Reading:*   ability to choose appropriate alternatives to complete written French sentences.

37. *Vocabulary:*   knowledge of English equivalents to French words.

38. *Grammar:*   ability to complete French translations of English sentences.

39. *Midyear Grade in French.* The school authorities provided us with each student's overall grade in French as of the midyear evaluation.

40. *Other than School Experiences with French.* Students were asked whether they learned their French in school; if not, they were asked to describe what other learning opportunities they had. For example, they might mention that they had learned French from their parents, had lived in a French community, had learned it through friends, etc. Subjects were given a low score if they had learned their French primarily in school, and a higher score if outside social situations played a part in their proficiency.

41. *Self-rating of French Skills.* Each student rated himself, using 4-point scales, as to how well he could *speak, read, write,* and *understand* (spoken) French. Scores for speaking French were doubled in calculating the total score because it was felt that speaking ability in French was most indicative of overall achievement in these schools where the audio-lingual aspects of French were stressed to one degree or another, and because of its importance in interpersonal communication.

42. *Rating of Mother's French Skills.* Using a 4-point scale for each attribute, students rated their mother's ability to *speak, read,* and *understand* French. Again, the rating for speaking French was doubled in calculating the total rating. These variables are seen as both indicies of parental support and of outside school experience.

43. *Rating of Father's French Skills.* Using a 4-point scale for each attribute, students rated their father's ability to *speak, read,* and *understand* French. Again, the rating for speaking French was doubled in calculating the total rating. These variables are seen as both indices of parental support and of outside school experience.

Variables 44-49. Each student was asked to read a short prose passage and his oral production was recorded on tape. The tapes were later analyzed and scored by a linguist on the following variables: Phonetic Accuracy, Linking, Stress, Rhythm, and Absence of Nasalization. For each of these variables, ratings were made on a 6-point scale ranging from 0 to 5.

44. *Phonetic Accuracy* measured the student's ability to give a correct phonemic rendering of the printed word. In the word *quinze*, for example, the digraph *qu* should be pronounced as /k/ and not as /kw/; similarly in *ans, un* and *maison*, the combinations *an, un* and *on* should be rendered as one nasal vowel, not as a vowel followed by a nasal consonant. Other examples are the pronunciation of *t* as /s/ in *nationale, 11* as a /y/ in *Bastille, e* as an open /e/ in the second syllable of *Nevers;* in the word *observatoire* the *b* is unvoiced, that is pronounced almost as a /p/, and in all plural words the final *s* is silent as is also the *p* in *sept.*

45. *Linking* is a device peculiar to French which causes the last consonant of

a word to be pronounced as the first sound of a word beginning with a vowel, under certain conditions. For instance, *sept ans* is pronounced as if it were one word. In certain cases, linking is obligatory, in others it is forbidden and finally in some cases it is facultative. Only the first two cases were considered in calculating the subscore.

46. *Stress* consists of accentuating a given syllable by increasing the duration and intensity of its vowel, and sometimes by altering the pitch. In French, stress does not affect a particular syllable, as it does in English, but always falls on the last syllable of a group of words, known as a phonetic word. The phrase *Je m'appelle Claude* is such a word and is stressed on *Claude,* pronounced /Klod/.

47. *Rhythm* affects the whole sentence, which should be pronounced as a series of phonetic words and not as a list of unconnected grammatical words. Thus, if a student pauses in the wrong places he is said to ignore the rhythm of the language. Unusually slow reading and halting reading were also considered breaches of rhythm.

48. *Absence of Nasalization* is a term used to describe the fact that in French a nasal consonant such as /m/ or /n/ should not cause the surrounding vowels to become nasalized. In the word *nationale* the vowels /a/, /o/ and /a/ should remain entirely free of nasalization despite the proximity of the consonant /n/.

49. *Correctness and Complexity of Free Speech.* For this test, two flash cards were used, one bearing the words *Je vais,* the other *Si nous* and the student was asked to complete each sentence. As before, his responses were tape recorded. Subscores were obtained in each case by considering the complexity of the response pattern, and its correctness. Scales from 0 to 3 were used in each case, the maximum score being 12.

Complexity of Pattern

With one exception (*Je vais bien*), responses to *Je vais* fell into three categories. In order of increasing difficulty these are: (a) a noun or nominal expression such as *au restaurant, au tableau noir;* (b) a verb or verbal phrase such as *étudier, faire une promenade;* (c) a compound or complex clause sometimes elaborated into a full sentence, for example *Je vais à la ville parce qu'il y a une fête nationale, Je vais au laboratoire pour parler français avec mon professeur dans ma classe de compréhension.* Responses to *Si nous* also fell into three categories: (a) a clause in the present tense followed by a clause in the future tense: *Si nous allons au théâtre nous nous amuserons;* (b) a clause in the imperfect tense followed by a clause in the conditional tense: *Si nous allions chez vous nous pourrions faire de la musique;* (c) a single clause in the imperfect in which the intonation used clearly indicated that the speaker was making a suggestion: *Si nous allions au cinéma?* (how about going to a movie?). This last pattern, although shorter than the previous two, is far more sophisticated or "advanced" since it is taught much later in the course of French instruction and since it differs more markedly from the corresponding English pattern. It is generally employed only by those speakers who feel at ease in French. Hence, in our opinion, it deserved the highest score.

Correctness.

Grammatical accuracy was considered independently from the complexity of the response pattern chosen by the student. One point was taken off for each mistake. However, spoken French as the French themselves speak it, and not literary French as it is taught in books, was considered the standard. Thus, if a student said, *Si nous avions de l'argent, on pourrait aller au cinéma,* he was not penalized for switching from *nous* to *on* in the same sentence, since so many French people do it in the course of informal conversation.

50. *Reading Fluency*. Two experts in standard and American French independently rated the oral productions of each student, on a 7-point scale, in terms of their fluency in reading French. These two ratings were totalled to produce an estimate of each student's fluency.

51. *Pronunciation Accuracy*. Each student's oral production was also rated on 7-point scales in terms of the accuracy with which he pronounced the French words in their context. The emphasis in this rating was on the total impression of the accuracy, rather than on the adequacy of pronouncing various key words.

52. *Type of Accent*. The judges rated the extent to which the oral productions reflected a French-American accent, or a European-French accent. The categories used were as follows: 1. (definite French-American), 2. (moderately French-American), 3. (slight French-American accent characteristics) , 4. (no trace of either French-American or European accent), 5. (slight European-French accent), 6. (moderately European-French), 7. (definite European-French accent). The ratings of two judges were totaled to produce scores ranging from 2. (French-American) to 14. (European).

Personal Characteristics

53. *Measured Intelligence*. The school authorities provided intelligence test scores. In Louisiana the IQs were based on Thurstone's test of Primary Mental Abilities while those from Maine and Connecticut were based on the Otis Self-Administering Intelligence Test.

54. *Sex*. This classification was treated as a separate variable in order to determine any boy-girl differences in performance, attitudes or motivation.

General Procedural Matters

Once the responses of the students were collected and scored, the process of checking out the degrees of association among the various measures was started. The first step involved equating or "standardizing" the raw scores for students with differing amounts of training in French within each of the three geographical areas. For example, the English-speaking students in Maine were in their first, second, or third year of French study; the Connecticut students were in their first and third year of French study; and the Louisiana students were in either their first or second year of French. In order to combine the responses of students who had different amounts of training, we had to standardize the French achievement scores for each regional setting, that is, remove the effect of different lengths of training on achievement. Since other possibly important variables (e.g., attitude, intelligence, aptitude, motivation) might also vary systematically from one level of training to another, it was decided to standardize students' scores on *all* variables before combining across levels. If in actuality there were differences attributable to degree of training, this standardization procedure would have no effect on any student's relative position in the distribution. In the interpretation of the correlations, emphasis is placed on the performance of students relative to others at their own level of training. For example, a positive correlation between aptitude and a particular French achievement measure indicates that those students with considerable aptitude do better on that French achievement test than do others with less aptitude who are at the same level of training.

Because this procedure may be helpful for others contemplating related research, a bit more detail may be appropriate. Midterm French grades were standardized twice, first with regard to teacher differences, in order to remove the effects of different standards of grading, and then with respect to level of training. In other cases, no equating was called for. For example, the scores for the two French-American samples (to be discussed later) were not standardized. In Louisiana, all but three of these students had had one year of formal training in French, making the correction unnecessary. In Maine, by way of contrast, the French-American students had a mean of 9.91 years of formal French instruction at parochial and high schools, but since over 82 percent of this sample of students had studied French for ten years, we decided the training was essentially the same for all.

All of the fifty-four variables listed for the English-speaking samples of students were intercorrelated, using Pearson product-moment correlation co-efficients. Because of the storage limits of the IBM 650 computer at our disposition (4,060 words of drum and core storage on the augmented machine) we could only use a 41 x 41 variable matrix for determining centroid factors. Consequently, for each regional sample, thirteen variables were deleted from the total fifty-four variable correlation matrix on the basis that those eliminated would not contribute substantially to any factor pattern. The prime consideration for deletion of a variable was its lack of significant correlations with other variables in the matrix. In those few instances where choices had to be made between two equally promising variables, attention was given to the ease and usefulness of interpretation, the measure with less possible ambiguity being retained.

This necessity of deleting tests explains why the measures used are not identical from one setting to another. For each, however, there is a common core of "reference variables" and the basic factor structures do not vary substantially, as we shall see.

The deletion of variables of course places some restrictions on the comparability of interpretation from sample to sample, but these are of only minor importance. We will be concerned with general relationships—intellectual and linguistic aptitudes, specific outgroup attitudes (toward French people), generalized other-group attitudes (toward foreigners), motivation of various forms, and measures of French achievement—and measures of all of these will be included in the matrices of each sample of students. Where interpretation of other variables is stressed, or where attention is paid to relatively low factor loadings, cautionary statements are made. Thus, this study does not apply one particular test battery in a number of social situations; rather it is an exploratory study of variables suspected to be pertinent for students in a particular sociocultural setting. Where attempts are made to integrate the results from the various settings, they are intended as general summaries of findings which reflect similar or contrasting configurations of student characteristics.

On the more technical side, the centroid factor analyses were continued until it was obvious that the residuals contained no outstanding common variance. Tests of significance of the residuals were performed when there was any doubt (from visual inspection) about when one should stop factoring. In certain ambiguous cases, we turned to Humphreys' rule (Fruchter, 1954, p. 79) to help define a factor. In general, more factors were extracted in using a visual inspection than in applying Humphreys' rule. The basic criterion used with the visual inspection technique was: a) a reduction in all residuals to a value less than 0.10; and b) no consistent pattern in the reflected values.

Each of the obtained factor matrices was rotated using Kaiser's "normalized varimax criterion" (1958). This rotational scheme is completely objective, producing successive rotations until the "variance" of squared factor loadings does not increase by a specified amount. Pretesting a series of matrices indicated that if the acceptable "specified amount of increase" was less than .002, the resulting rotated matrix was stable. This, then, was the criterion finally accepted as an index of when to stop rotating, and it was obvious from the rotational solutions produced that "factor simplicity" was achieved.

The next three sections of this chapter cover the results of the factor analyses for American students in Louisiana, Maine, and Connecticut. They will be examined one at a time and in each case we will list the forty-one variables finally used in each regional analysis, and then present the final rotated factor matrix. To save space, we have not included the centroid factor loadings, but the tables of intercorrelations of all variables are placed in Appendix B. In the discussion of results, we will refer to the patterning of variables and to the structure of each factor on the basis of which we will draw our inferences about the language-learning process.

The Louisiana Study

Our plan was to search for two communities in the United States where Americans and French-Americans would have social contacts close enough to assure that both cultural groups would have formed stable attitudes toward one another, but not so fixed that within each group individual differences in favorableness and unfavorableness of attitudes would not be apparent. Thus, our plan was to study bicultural communities where attitudes toward members of the other group would likely vary from one extreme to another. For purposes of comparison, a third setting that would not be bicultural in this sense was also included in our design in order that we might determine if students' attitudes toward a clearly foreign linguistic-cultural group — the French people of France rather than a local Americanized group — would also play a role in the language-learning process.

Lafayette Parish in Louisiana was chosen as one bicultural community after consultation with Dr. Vernon J. Parenton, Professor of Sociology at Louisiana State University. Dr. Parenton specializes in the sociology of French-American people. In his correspondence with us, he strongly recommended "Southwest Louisiana as the area best suited for the study, specifically in the parishes (counties) of St. Landry, St. Martin, Lafayette, Iberia, and Vermilion where there are several communities which meet your specifications. The city of Lafayette, population about 50,000, is the hub of the Acadian subculture ... The majority of the French-speaking people of Louisiana live within a radius of about fifty miles from this city." Dr. Parenton also noted that the French-speaking society which formerly existed along Bayou Lafourche about twenty years ago "has undergone extensive changes and is no longer as representative of Acadian subculture as is the Southwest Louisiana area."

Mr. Robert L. Browne, Superintendent of the Lafayette Parish School Board, and Mr. Ray W. Miles, Director of Guidance Services, were contacted and they responded in the most friendly fashion possible, inviting us to carry out the study in Lafayette. Mr. Miles helped us in numerous ways at every stage of the study.

The sample of Louisiana American students was made up of seventy-two white boys and girls studying French in their first year and twenty-four in their second year at the high school level. The total sample numbered ninety-six.

Representatives of all the high schools in the parish were included in the sample. A student was considered American (in contrast to French-American) if he came from an English-speaking home where he would have had no experience with the French language. Many of these students may have been of French ancestry, but no selection was made on that basis.

We were anxious to complete the major testing as early as possible in the year so as to maximize the time elapsed before the achievement testing took place in the spring. In this fashion, we tried to throw some light on the predictive capacities of the test battery. Accordingly, the first testing was carried out in early December 1960, when a four-hour period was arranged with all students meeting in a large auditorium at the Lafayette school. The testing session took a full school day with several rest breaks and a lunch period. The students' midyear grades in French were provided by the teachers. Then in late April 1961, the various tests of achievement in French were administered both in group settings for standardized tests and individually for the oral production measures. The analyses of data had unfortunately to be started before final French grades were available.

Variables Included for the Louisiana Sample of American Students

The following 41 measures were kept as the most promising ones, after analyzing the intercorrelations of the 50-odd possible candidates. The 41 x 41 correlation matrix is placed in Appendix B as Table 1-B. Table 1 is the final rotated factor matrix and it follows next in the text.

1. Anomie Scale
2. F-Scale
3. Ethnocentrism Scale
4. Preference for America over France
5. Attitudes toward French-Americans
6. Student's French Friends
7. Motivational Intensity
8. Desire to Learn French
9. Parental Encouragement to Learn French
10. Student's Orientation
11. Parents' French Friends
12. Student's French Acquaintances
13. Orientation Index
    Modern Language Aptitude Test (MLAT)
14. Number Learning; 15. Phonetic Script; 16. Spelling Clues;
17. Words in Sentences; 18. Paired Associates
19. Sex

French Listening Comprehension Test (FLCT)
20.   Part I; 21.   Part II; 22.   Part III; 23.   Part IV
24.   Parents Favorable to Student Knowing French
   Cooperative French Test (CFT)
25.   Reading; 26.   Vocabulary; 27.   Grammar
28.   Self-rating of French Skills
29.   IQ (PMA)
30.   Midyear French Grade
   Average Ratings on Semantic Differential Scales
31.   "Me as I'd Like to Be"; 32.   "French-Americans"
33.   English-speaking Guises versus French-American Guises
   Oral Production Ratings
34.   Phonetic Accuracy; 35. Linking; 36. Stresses; 37. Rhythm;
38.   Free Speech (Correctness and Complexity); 39. Fluency in
Reading Aloud in French; 40. Pronunciation Accuracy; 41. Type of
Accent.

Results for the Louisiana American Students

Factor I* represents a broad dimension of language aptitude and second-language proficiency. The presence of all the aptitude and intelligence measures (Vs. 14-18; 29) indicates that the dominant feature of this factor is verbal intelligence and aptitude. One's standing on this verbal aptitude dimension is a very good indication of how he will achieve in French grammar, vocabulary, and reading (Vs. 25-27), in his French course (V. 30), but is somewhat less predictive of performance in French comprehension (Vs. 20-22) and barely predictive of proficiency in spontaneous expression, reading fluency, or pronunciation (Vs. 38, 39, and 40). The different magnitudes of the factor loadings for different measures of French achievement suggest that the academic program stresses the development of certain skills more than others. Reading, vocabulary, and grammar are commonly emphasized in the first two years of foreign-language instruction, whereas the ability to make fine aural discriminations in pronunciation and to respond to questions presented aurally, although taught in school, are probably given a lower priority. The same is true for oral skills; it is unlikely that equal attention is given to grammatical and pronunciation accuracy in spontaneous speech. From this point of view, Factor I appears to circumscribe the dominant intellectual components associated with the conventional introductory program of instruction in French. To the extent that particular French skills are stressed in the academic program, the more

---

*The reader can follow the discussion best by noting which variables have high loadings on each factor, starting with Factor I in the first column of Table 1. These sets of highly interrelated measures constitute the empirical basis for the interpretations and conclusions that follow. Note that the factors are not necessarily discussed in numerical order.

intelligent students perform well, relatively, as they would in any other school subject.

Table 1

Final Rotated Factor Matrix for the *Louisiana* Study

Variables	I	II	III	IV	V	VI	VII	VIII	IX	X	h²
1. Anomie	-.18	-.10	.02	.02	-.48•	-.10	.12	.10	-.05	.06	.32
2. F-Scale	-.17	.07	-.06	.01	-.62•	.07	-.08	-.15	-.13	.01	.47
3. Ethnocentrism	-.17	.12	-.27	.12	-.43•	.13	-.21	-.02	.08	-.16	.41
4. Prefer. America	-.10	-.02	.00	-.05	-.57•	-.16	.01	.08	.10	-.26	.45
5. Att. to Fr. Am.	-.05	-.07	-.77•	.00	.00	.04	.05	.22	-.04	-.10	.67
6. French Friends	-.02	.03	-.67•	.03	.03	-.20	.03	-.06	-.30•	-.02	.58
7. Motiv. Intens.	.14	-.06	-.05	.51•	.09	-.09	.02	-.03	-.09	.00	.32
8. Desire Learn Fr.	.16	-.06	.05	.75•	.07	-.01	.03	-.06	-.09	.04	.61
9. Parent. Encour.	.06	.03	-.08	.56•	-.15	.08	.02	.14	.10	.09	.39
10. Orientation	.06	.06	-.13	-.17	-.13	-.08	-.05	-.01	.00	-.63•	.49
11. Parents' Fr. Friends	-.15	.07	-.06	.18	-.10	.20	.04	.00	-.68•	-.08	.59
12. S's Fr. Acquaintances	-.07	-.10	-.23	-.04	.01	.00	-.08	.01	-.57•	.08	.41
13. Orient. Index	-.07	.10	-.22	.04	-.03	-.03	-.04	.47•	.00	.00	.29
14. No. Learning (MLAT)	.49•	.16	-.02	.06	.02	-.03	.46•	-.09	.08	.15	.52
15. Phon. Script (MLAT)	.64•	.22	.05	-.01	.14	.02	-.04	.03	.09	-.04	.50
16. Spell. Clues (MLAT)	.66•	.07	.09	.04	-.06	.14	-.03	-.19	-.07	-.08	.53
17. Wds. in Sent. (MLAT)	.73•	.15	-.11	.14	.11	-.18	.00	-.26	.20	-.02	.75
18. Pd. Assoc. (MLAT)	.64•	.10	.05	.02	.04	.13	.24•	-.14	.11	.17	.56
19. Sex (Girls/Boys)	.13	.17	.17	.12	.08	.41•	.11	-.05	-.03	.20	.32
20. FLCT - I	.43•	.23	-.07	.04	.22	-.06	-.07	.11	.18	-.05	.35

Table 1 (continued)

Final Rotated Factor Matrix for the *Louisiana* Study

Variables	I	II	III	IV	V	VI	VII	VIII	IX	X	h²
21. FLCT - II	.42•	.13	-.05	-.13	.10	.02	-.03	.27	-.22	.24	.40
22. FLCT - III	.39•	-.05	.15	.22	.32•	.18	.00	.15	-.07	-.29	.48
23. FLCT - IV	.17	-.05	-.09	-.19	-.06	.57•	-.03	.00	-.12	.06	.43
24. Par. Fav.	.13	.05	-.11	.41•	-.22	.12	-.23	.00	-.03	.32•	.43
25. CFT - Reading	.72•	.04	.18	.26	.10	.29	-.01	.23	.05	-.08	.78
26. CFT - Vocabulary	.66•	.22	.10	.24	.10	.35•	.04	.30•	.04	-.12	.80
27. CFT - Grammar	.69∘	.11	.11	.26	.24	-.07	-.13	-.10	.14	-.02	.69
28. Self Fr. Skills	.07	.03	-.12	.21	.28	.39•	-.03	-.13	-.17	-.13	.37
29. IQ	.51•	.15	.05	.04	.01	-.04	.19	.10	-.25	.20	.45
30. French Grade	.52•	.18	-.05	.35•	.32•	.03	.25	-.04	.03	-.10	.61
31. Me	.04	.24	-.41•	.06	-.09	.12	.00	-.28	-.04	-.05	.34
32. French-Am.'s	-.13	-.06	-.80•	.07	-.09	-.10	-.03	.15	-.06	-.03	.72
33. Voice: Eng.-Fr. Am.	.04	.04	.29	-.01	-.28	-.34•	.19	-.06	-.12	-.03	.34
34. Phon∘ Accuracy	.09	.81•	-.02	-.00	.04	-.11	.12	.22	.02	-.01	.74
35. Linking	.05	.75•	.17	.04	.16	-.11	-.21	.03	-.03	.00	.68
36. Stress	.14	.87•	-.05	-.12	.08	.08	-.20	.02	-.08	.13	.87
37∘ Rhythm	.24	.86•	-.02	-.09	-.02	.04	-.10	.04	.00	.13	.83
38. Free Speech	.31•	.60•	.06	-.02	-.27	.08	-.15	-.07	-.03	.07	.58
39. Reading Fluency	.26	.81•	-.05	.12	.03	.13	.35•	-.06	.10	-.11	.90
40. Pron. Accuracy	.29	.84•	-.02	.09	.00	.12	.22	.00	.08	-.16	.90
41. Accent	-.05	.72•	-.08	-.04	-.12	-.02	.35•	-.11	.01	-.12	.71

Various other aspects of achievement in French are not related to this intellectual component, possibly because they too were not stressed in the academic learning situation. For instance, intellectual capacity does not appear to play an important role in one's ability to pronounce French accurately (V. 34), to speak with correct linkings, stress, and rhythm (Vs. 35, 36 and 37), to acquire a characteristic French accent (V. 41), or to comprehend complex discussions in French (V.23). If these features of French achievement are given a low priority in the school program, they will not likely be given any special attention by intellectually capable students, who may be more likely to center their interests on matters that count for good grades. Of course it could also be that the intellectually brighter student may not have any special ability in the expressive components of foreign-language study (see *Reading Number Six*).

Factor II is composed of the various measures of linguistic proficiency in oral French: phonetic accuracy, linking, stress, rhythm, correct usage of French in free speech, reading fluency, pronunciation accuracy, and mastery of the French accent (Vs. 34-41). The oral skills reflected in this factor are not related to the other measures of French achievement found in Factor I, or to aptitude or intelligence, since these variables do not emerge on Factor II. This separation of French oral skills (Factor II) from the more passive ones represented in Factor I is of interest. Although we presume that less emphasis is given to the development of oral skills in the Louisiana schools included in our study, this does not explain the individual differences among Louisiana students that do show up on the measures of oral skill. In fact, there are no reasons for such proficiency suggested by Factor II.

One substantial clue, however, comes from the interesting pattern of tests loading on Factor VII. Here the Number Learning subtest of the MLAT (V. 14) appears in a cluster with the measures of reading fluency and type of French accent (Vs. 39 and 41). The pattern suggests that these two aspects of oral skill — reading fluency and a European accent — depend on some type of ability to differentiate foreign sounds and hold them in memory (Carroll, 1958).

Factor III is a dimension of attitudes toward French-Americans. The loadings of Variables 5, 6, and 32 all reflect negative evaluations of French-Americans, and Variable 33 reflects a perceptual bias favoring English over French-American speakers. The high loading of Variable 31 is of interest; it means that students with negative attitudes towards French-Americans and French-American culture have a generally negative view of themselves. The converse also holds, that is, those who appreciate French-Americans have favorable self views.

What role does motivation play in French proficiency for our Louisiana students? Factor IV tells that story: motivation and desire to learn French (Vs. 7 and 8), when supported by the student's family (Vs. 9 and 24), are associated with a high level of achievement in French course work (V. 30) and, to a lesser extent, achievement in reading, vocabulary, and grammar (Vs. 25-27). This pattern indicates that achievement in these school-taught features of French depend not only upon intelligence (Factor I), but also—and quite independent of intelligence—upon a motivation and desire to learn the language. Thus, regardless of intelligence, the motivated student with encouragement from his family can do well in school-taught French.

Factor V is an ethnocentric cluster, comprising measures of anomie, authoritarian prejudice, ethnocentrism, and preference for American over French ways of life (Vs. 1-4). Those with an ethnocentric ideology have trouble with French comprehension (V. 22) and in the French course generally (V. 30).

The loadings on Factor VIII are generally small, but the relatively large loading of Variable 13 indicates that the factor measures some aspects of an integrative orientation toward French study. Since the Vocabulary test (V. 26) also appears on this factor, we see another instance of the integrative orientation affecting certain aspects of French proficiency.

Factor IX reflects a family-wide friendship for French people (Vs. 11, 12, and 6), but in this instance it bears no relation to any of the achievement or aptitude measures.

The composition of Factor X indicates that Louisiana students with an instrumental orientation toward the learning of French (V. 10) and who have parental support for studying French (V. 24) nonetheless lack skill in French comprehension (V. 22).

The constellation of variables forming Factor VI is of special interest: skill in comprehending complex French discussions (V. 23), having a good French vocabulary (V. 26), and feeling personally adequate in French (V. 28) are positively related to a favorable evaluation of French-American in contrast to English speakers (V. 33). The pattern is especially characteristic of girls (V. 19). This factor is noteworthy for two reasons: it points out which features of second-language study girls find easy at the same time that it highlights the relationship between the ability to understand complex discussions in a second language and a favorable attitude towards native speakers of the other language. The fact that it is girls who are particularly attracted to the speech of members of the other group and that girls also excel in vocabulary and French comprehension is instructive in itself. It would now be worthwhile to probe in depth the reasons why girls and boys differ in attitudes and rate of development of second-language skills in the Louisiana setting.

Summary

In the Louisiana setting several independent determinants of achievement in French were discovered. Intellectual capacity (including measures of intelligence and language-learning aptitude) seems to play an essential role in the development of competence in French grammar, vocabulary, and reading, i.e., those components typically emphasized in standard high school programs of language study. The language aptitude subtests are particularly powerful predictors of proficiency in these components, more so than the IQ measure used. Intellectual capacity, however, appears to have little to do, in this setting, with the ability to speak French properly, to read fluently, to acquire a characteristic accent, or to comprehend complex discussions in French.

This independence of oral skills from other aspects of proficiency has two or more possible meanings: the Louisiana schools involved in this investigation may neglect the development of audio-lingual skills, or it may be that a distinct set of aptitudes are required for oral-aural proficiency. It is puzzling that oral skills are not accounted for by attitudes either in this case. Thus we have no explanation for the fact that Louisiana students do vary greatly among themselves in French oral competence. It may be that students have differential access to model speakers of the language, through differences in travel experiences or contacts with French speakers at certain periods of their linguistic development, but these are only guesses. Certain clues from an independent factor (Factor VII) suggest what type of aptitude may underlie oral skills. We found that a student's reading fluency and mastery of a French accent appear to derive from an aptitude for making phonemic distinctions and memorizing foreign sounds as these are measured by the Number Learning subtest of the MLAT. But this too is only a flimsy lead. If a similar separation of oral skills turns up in the other American settings, it would be worthwhile to direct attention to this matter in future research so as to delineate in detail the bases of oral skill in a foreign language. The MLAT would be one useful instrument among others for such a study.

We also found (Factor IV) that grades in French—quite independent of intellectual capacity—are dependent on the student's motivation to learn the language. This personal motivation to do well, which affects how well one actually succeeds in school French and various aspects of reading, vocabulary, and grammar, likely stems from a home atmosphere where parents encourage and in turn are encouraged by their children's progress in learning the language.

Grades in French and one aspect of French comprehension ability also appear to depend on a democratic, unprejudiced attitude toward foreign peoples and a favorable evaluational reaction to French-speaking people (Factor V). The student who has ethnocentric attitudes and who denigrates the French way of life is likely to do poorly in school French and in certain aspects of comprehension, independent of his intellectual capacity or motivation to do well in French.

It is of particular interest that we find French grades contributing to Factors I, IV, and V. This means that grades are assigned by teachers for several different reasons: because the student is bright (Factor I), because he is highly motivated

(Factor IV), or because he has nonethnocentric attitudes (Factor V). Specific attitudes toward the French-American people are not related to French achievement (Factor III), and an integrative orientation toward learning French plays only a small role in language achievement (Factor VIII).

A separate and independent cluster of measures appeared on Factor VI: skill in comprehending complex French discussions, having a good French vocabulary, feeling personally adequate in the language, and holding favorable views of French-speaking people. Girls in this setting fall on the favorable side of this dimension and boys on the unfavorable side. Although we were not able to explain this sex difference in outlook, the factor nonetheless is a very important one. The relatively high loadings of several achievement measures tell us that one's attitude and feelings toward the representatives of the group whose language is being studied are essential factors in language learning, independent of intelligence or of motivation.

Finally, as is seen in Factor X, parents of these Louisiana students are apparently more ready to encourage their children to learn French for instrumental than integrative reasons.

This then is the general picture for the Louisiana academic setting. In the next sections we will see if the same patterns appear in the other American communities. In any case, we have already uncovered interesting contrasts with the Canadian patterns discussed earlier. In Montreal, for example, there was no mystery underlying individual differences in expressive skills in French. Intelligence and language aptitude as well as attitudes and motivation were all clearly involved. Students could use the language outside school and develop expressive competence in real life situations if they wanted to. Apparently the Louisiana communities we are dealing with are more bicultural than they are bilingual in the sense that few opportunities may actually exist outside school to use the spoken language. Thus, even if students with favorable dispositions toward French wanted to they might not have opportunities to communicate in the language. We will develop this idea further in Chapter 4 as we examine the ways in which French-American young people in these communities use French. But it remains a mystery so far why some American students in the Louisiana setting are very competent in French expressive skills while others are very poor.

Do these patterns and trends hold in other American settings?

The Maine Study

The second bicultural setting was chosen with the assistance of Gerald Brault and Dean Allen of Bowdoin College, Maine. Dr. Brault had directed several French-American Summer Institutes at Bowdoin, the purpose of which was to train French-American secondary school teachers, many from the state of Maine, in modern methods of teaching French. He suggested that the region between the cities of Brunswick and Lewiston would be a very appropriate setting since the French-American communities there had kept alive a French atmosphere and maintained the use of the language. Furthermore, the French-American subgroup was well-known to American students in the areas. With an introduction from Dr. Allen, principals of several public high schools in this region were contacted and we were cordially invited to carry out the study in their schools.

As in Louisiana, we sought out American students—those from English-speaking homes—who were studying French in school. Those finally selected attended high schools from communities that provided many opportunities to encounter French-American families and to develop attitudes toward French-Americans. Since the public schools in the area offer three years of French training at the high school level, the final sample included 75 students at the first-year level, 36 at the second, and 34 at the third, making a total of 145 students.

The initial testing took place in early December 1960 and was conducted in various high schools in the area. Midyear grades in French were supplied by the teachers, and the French achievement tests were administered in group and individual sessions in late April, 1961.

Variables Included in the Maine Study

The following measures were selected as the most promising ones from a preliminary analysis of intercorrelations. The 41 x 41 correlation matrix for these variables is placed in Appendix B as Table 2-B. The final rotated factor matrix, Table 2, follows next in the text.

1. Anomie Scale
2. F-Scale
3. Ethnocentrism Scale
4. Preference for America over France
5. Attitudes toward French-Americans
6. Attitudes toward French Friends
7. Motivational Intensity
8. Desire to Learn French
9. Sensitivity to Others
10. Student's Orientation
11. Parents' French Friends
12. Student's French Friends
13. Orientation Index

Modern Language Aptitude Test(MLAT)
14. Number Learning; 15. Phonetic Script; 16. Spelling Clues;

17.   Words in Sentences; 18. Paired Associates
19.   Sex

French Listening Comprehension Test (FLCT)
20.   Part I;   21. Part II; 22. Part III;   23. Part IV

Cooperative French Test (CFT)
24.   Reading;   25. Vocabulary; 26. Grammar
27.   Self-rating of French Skills
28.   IQ (Otis)
29.   Midyear French Grade

Average Ratings on Semantic Differential Scales
30.   "French People from France";   31. "Me";   32. "Americans";
33.   "Me as I'd Like to Be"; 34. "French-Americans"; 35. "My
       French Teacher"

Oral Production Ratings
36.   Phonetic Accuracy; 37. Linking;   38. Stress; 39. Rhythm;
40.   Nasalization;   41. Free Speech (Correctness and Complexity)

Results for the Maine Sample of American Students

The composition of Factor I (the first column in Table 2) defines a dimension of broad ability in French verbal expression including phonetic accuracy, use of appropriate linkings, stress, rhythm, and nasalization, and skill in speaking accurately in a free speech testing situation (Vs. 36-41). For the Maine students, these oral production skills are associated with achievement in French reading and vocabulary and, of special interest, with the student's own perception of competence (Vs. 24, 25, and 27). Other measures of French achievement including school grades in French are not represented in this cluster. Apparently teachers in these high schools grade on other bases than expressive skill, while students judge their own progress in French, at least in part, in terms of expressive competence. One MLAT subtest, Phonetic Script (V. 15) is related to oral skill in French, and this relationship would be expected on the basis of the construction of the MLAT (see Carroll and Sapon, 1959).

In Factor X we have a clue as to the basis of teachers' evaluations of French competence. Here, school French grades (V. 29) are clearly associated with achievement in French reading, vocabulary, and grammar (Vs. 24-26), and are dependent upon aptitudes in English vocabulary and grammar (Vs. 16-17) as well as intelligence (V. 28). As was also true in Louisiana, it seems that the more apt pupil will profit most from the language instruction programs in the schools.

Table 2

Final Rotated Factor Matrix for the *Maine* Study

Variables	I	II	III	IV	V	VI	VII	VIII	IX	X	h²
1. Anomie	-.01	-.58*	-.24	.00	.07	.18	.09	.03	-.12	.02	.46
2. F-Scale	-.03	-.01	-.29	-.04	-.02	.56*	-.09	-.02	-.13	.10	.43
3. Ethnocentrism	-.07	.02	.03	.01	.00	.66*	-.08	.00	-.06	-.08	.46
4. Prefer. Am/France	-.07	-.01	-.07	.00	.10	.59*	.13	.02	.02	-.14	.41
5. Att. to Fr. Am.	-.05	.61*	.01	.03	.03	-.03	.00	-.03	-.23	-.09	.44
6. S's Fr. Friends	-.02	.73*	-.14	.20	.12	.06	-.07	.18	-.01	-.01	.65
7. Motiv. Intensity	.08	.11	.11	.61*	-.06	-.12	-.08	.08	.11	.21	.50
8. Desire Learn Fr.	.00	.08	-.01	.78*	.00	.02	-.07	-.04	-.10	.17	.67
9. Sens. for Others	.13	.18	-.01	.35*	-.13	-.16	-.27	.15	.11	-.12	.34
10. S's Orientation	-.13	.24	-.15	-.10	-.14	.05	.07	.10	-.43*	.02	.33
11. Parents' Fr. Friends	.09	.07	.07	-.03	-.12	-.23	.21	.09	.40*	.22	.35
12. S's Fr. Acquaintances	-.11	.35*	.02	.12	.01	.13	-.13	.35*	-.07	-.08	.32
13. Orient. Index	-.10	.05	-.08	.23	.01	-.30*	-.08	-.10	-.20	-.22	.27
14. No. Learning (MLAT)	.15	-.03	.72*	.12	.04	-.02	.03	.00	-.07	-.01	.56
15. Phon. Script (MLAT)	.41*	-.07	.45*	.14	.15	-.15	.01	-.09	-.07	.24	.51
16. Spell. Clues (MLAT)	.27	.02	.25	.11	.19	-.19	-.03	.41*	.09	.31*	.50
17. Wds. in Sent. (MLAT)	.18	.03	.54*	.17	.01	-.01	.06	-.22	.20	.43*	.63
18. Pd. Assoc. (MLAT)	.12	.10	.60*	.01	.03	-.07	-.21	.13	.03	.05	.47
19. Sex (Girls/Boys)	.11	-.02	.16	.37*	-.01	.15	-.26	.14	.06	-.18	.33
20. FLCT - I	.14	.12	.17	.06	.59*	-.07	.04	-.10	.03	.03	.43

Table 2 (continued)

Final Rotated Factor Matrix for the *Maine* Study

Variables	I	II	III	IV	V	VI	VII	VIII	IX	X	h²
21. FLCT - II	.10	-.01	-.08	-.03	.75*	.10	-.05	.06	.06	.23	.65
22. FLCT - III	.06	.03	-.01	-.11	.78*	-.06	.16	-.08	.05	.04	.67
23. FLCT - IV	.07	-.05	.03	-.03	.65*	.16	.04	.27	-.12	-.03	.55
24. CFT - Reading	.33*	-.13	-.11	.12	.20	-.03	.07	.16	.01	.51*	.48
25. CFT - Vocab.	.42*	-.11	.15	.16	.24	.03	.00	.15	-.04	.43*	.50
26. CFT - Grammar	.28*	.04	.19	.11	.16	-.09	.05	-.05	.10	.69*	.66
27. Self Ratings Fr. Skills	.43*	.12	.02	.13	-.03	-.25	.15	-.25	-.10	-.15	.40
28. IQ	.18	.01	.49*	-.06	-.06	-.28	.23	.28	-.09	.36*	.64
29. French Grade	.22	-.05	.32*	.43*	-.02	-.11	-.05	.21	.12	.52*	.69
30. Fr. People France	.13	.33*	-.17	-.06	-.05	-.10	-.44*	-.01	-.10	.06	.38
31. Me	-.05	-.15	.05	-.16	-.00	-.10	-.70*	.06	-.01	-.05	.56
32. Americans	.10	-.22	.09	-.05	-.08	.28	-.55*	-.15	-.06	.05	.49
33. Ideal Me	.02	-.01	.06	.07	.07	-.01	-.62*	.11	.07	-.10	.42
34. French-Am.'s	-.04	.76*	.01	.00	.00	.09	-.36*	-.08	.05	.05	.73
35. French Teacher	-.11	.34*	-.12	.30*	.02	.12	-.46*	-.17	-.05	.15	.51
36. Phon. Accur.	.72*	-.01	.06	-.05	.10	-.04	.03	.05	.04	.25	.61
37. Linking	.55*	-.06	.08	.02	-.03	.02	-.05	.04	.35*	.23	.49
38. Stress	.77*	-.02	.17	-.03	.22	.12	-.14	.02	.22	.23	.49
39. Rhythm	.64*	-.09	.21	.02	.17	.04	-.25	.00	.36*	.00	.76
40. Nasalization	.57*	-.07	.02	.06	.09	-.15	.13	.01	-.08	.03	.69
41. Free Speech	.52*	.03	.18	.13	.15	-.05	-.12	.01	-.04	.14	.38

Factor II is made up of various measures of attitudes toward French people, both French-Americans and European French (Vs. 34, 5, 6, 30). This favorable attitude toward French people is associated with a sense of satisfaction with one's own culture (low anomie, V. 1), and appears to generalize to the French teacher (V. 35) and to friendship contacts with French people (V. 12), but it is not related to any of the French achievement measures. Thus this favorable outlook toward French people does not affect the development of skills in French.

Factor III represents a general intellectual aptitude cluster since both aptitude and IQ measures (Vs. 14, 15, 17, 18, 28) are congregated on the dimension. This intellectual capacity is important for school grades in French (V. 29) but *not* for the other French achievement measures. Although less pronounced, this factor also includes Variable 2, meaning that measured IQ and language-learning aptitude plus a nonauthoritarian value system work together to promote high grades in French. Thus, those children who have the intellectual and linguistic capacity and who profess a democratic orientation toward other peoples are more likely to obtain good grades in French, even though other measures of achievement in the language are not similarly affected.

Factor IV indicates that students with a strong motivation and desire to do well in French (Vs. 7, 8) coupled with a sensitivity for the feelings of others (V. 9) do well in course work in French (V. 29), quite independently of their intellectual capabilities. This motivation, mainly characteristic of girls (V. 19), is apparently generated in some fashion by the relations established with French teachers, since "favorable attitudes to the French teacher" (V. 35) is part of this network of variables.

Factor V shows that in Maine the Listening Comprehension subtests (Vs. 20-23) congregate into a single group and are not associated with other achievement measures, with aptitude or IQ or with attitudinal or motivational variables.

Factor VI consists of measures of an ethnocentric attitude. It demonstrates that students with authoritarian and ethnocentric attitudes and with a preference for the American over the French way of life (Vs. 2, 3, 4) are likely to be instrumentally oriented toward French study (V. 13). This ethnocentric syndrome is not directly related to any of the French achievement measures, as it was both in the Louisiana and the Montreal studies. For some reason left unexplained, Maine students are neither hampered nor helped in their study of French by this form of ethnocentrism. This interesting outcome may be due to the fact that they are nonetheless motivated to learn French, albeit instru-mentally, in spite of their ethnocentrism. Furthermore, the ethnocentrism expressed here does not include negative attitudes toward the French-American or European French people (Vs. 5, 6, 30, 34). This important finding deserves further study in follow-up research.

Factor IX permits us to examine further the Maine students' instrumental orientation toward French study. The parents of the students who express an instrumental orientation have many French-American friends (note loadings of Vs. 10 and 11), suggesting that the young people have social contacts with the French community through their families and are alerted to the practical value of French in outside-school activities. The factor also indicates that these students do particularly well in two aspects of oral skill: making proper linkings and having appropriate rhythm in their French expression (Vs. 37 and 39). Thus, experience with French people enhances expressive skills, as one would expect.

Factors VII and VIII are less relevant. Factor VII reflects the ways students rate various peoples on the evaluative scales of the semantic differential (Vs. 30-35), and these patterns of responding are generally unrelated to any other variables in the matrix. Factor VIII is defined by only two variables. Students with an ability to use symbols in a creative fashion, as measured by the Spelling Clues subtest of the MLAT (V. 16), claim to have a number of French-speaking acquaintances (V. 12). The absence of other variables argues against any attempt to provide a meaningful interpretation of this configuration.

Summary

In this analysis, we noted that the aptitude-intelligence measures are not powerful indicants of achievement in French as they were in the Louisiana setting. Nevertheless, certain MLAT subtests are fairly strong predictors of grades received in French, and two subtests (Word in Sentences and Spelling Clues) are fairly good indicators of achievement in French grammar, vocabulary, and reading.

In Maine, as in Louisiana, motivation and desire to learn the French language are important accompaniments of proficiency in school-taught French. In Louisiana, motivation to learn the language was supported by a favorable parental attitude toward learning French, while in Maine motivation appears to stem from a favorable view of the French teacher and a sensitivity for the feelings of others.

The teachers in Maine apparently assign grades in French courses with reference either to the student's intellectual ability and his mastery of grammar and vocabulary, or in terms of the student's ideology (democratic in contrast to authoritarian) and his sensitivity for others. In neither the Maine nor Louisiana settings do teachers pay much attention to the student's oral skill in French in determining grades. However, the Maine students feel they are progressing well in the language (are self-reinforced, so to speak) when they feel they have developed oral skills. This discrepancy between teachers and students as to which components of language are more important has many implications and could form the basis of a valuable follow-up study.

In Maine, in contrast to Louisiana, an ethnocentric syndrome of attitudes is linked with an instrumental orientation to learn the French language, but not with negative attitudes toward French people. We feel that the ethnocentrism shown by the Maine students does not affect negatively their achievement because it is linked with an instrumental motive toward French study and because it does not include a prejudiced attitude toward French people. In the Maine setting, an instrumental orientation apparently is generated in homes where parents have many French friends, and this familial experience with French people appears to assist the Maine students in certain aspects of oral skill in French.

Perhaps the most noteworthy outcome of the investigation to this point is the fascinating setting contrasts in the patterning of variables that has emerged. The complex networks of student reactions in Louisiana and Maine reflect fundamental differences in the social structures of the two communities, especially in the degree to which French-Americans have been assimilated into American communities. We have seen that young people growing up in these two settings have quite distinctive views of French-American people and culture, and their perceptions appear to influence how they approach the task of learning the French language. Certain subtle clues suggest that in Louisiana the French fact is something of the past while in Maine the impression is that the French influence is more vital and contemporary. We will have a chance to examine this notion more carefully when we study the French-American youngsters themselves and compare just how French and/or American they really are. The point here is that a large multiethnic nation such as the United States likely permits linguistic minority groups within its communities to make many different types of social adjustments. The intensity of the heat under the melting pot seems to vary from one community to another and probably in some settings the melting process may never have really started. The sociocultural background of American communities—although not the focus of this investigation—nevertheless becomes relevant because we see the impact of background differences even on the attitudes and motivations of students involved in learning a foreign language.

It follows that in order to understand the process of education—including the learning of languages and the ways of life of other peoples—we now need more comprehensive follow-up studies that take sociocultural factors more into account. It also follows that these two bicultural settings are particularly appropriate candidates for such comprehensive investigations since during the past ten years both have started to regenerate a serious interest in the cultural and linguistic heritages of their citizens. For example, the recent Bilingual Education Act has provided financial support to Maine and Lousiana to develop the rich potential of their French-American citizenry. It would be instructive and extremely valuable to use this investigation as a base to compare changes that may well take place over the next few years.

We turn next to a third American setting, one somewhat more typically American—if there is such a thing in the United States. Our question now becomes: What patterns of variables will characterize students learning French in a large industrial New England site where no special French-American influence is involved?

The Connecticut Study

The third American study was made possible through the cooperation of the principals and French teachers of several public high schools in Hartford, Connecticut. Students at either the first or third year level of high school French study were included, 74 at the first level and 68 at the third, making a total of 142 students.

The Hartford community was interesting to us for several reasons. First, the school system had recently incorporated modern methods of language training into its curriculum, including an emphasis on the oral-aural approach to teaching, the use of taped materials, and some laboratory facilities for oral practice. Second, compared to the bicultural settings of Louisiana and Maine, it was more representative of large urban American communities. The greater Hartford Area comprises Americans of various linguistic and cultural backgrounds as do most large American cities on the eastern coast, and there is a sizable subgroup of French-Americans in the area. The Connecticut students, therefore, were very much aware of linguistic and ethnic differences in the community, including French-Americans, but they did not have concentrated experience with French-Americans exclusively, as was the case for the American students in Louisiana and Maine. We presumed that their conception of French people and culture would refer mainly to French people from France, the focus of their French courses at school.

The major part of the testing in this case was carried out only in mid-February and the French achievement tests were administered in mid-April. Thus, there was less time spread between initial and final testings than there had been in Louisiana and Maine.

Variables Included in the Connecticut Study

The following 41 variables were selected as the most promising from a preliminary analysis of the larger set of intercorrelations. The 41 x 41 correlation matrix for these variables is placed in Appendix B as Table 3-B. The final rotated factor matrix, Table 3, follows here in the text.

1. Rating of Integrative Orientation
2. Rating of Instrumental Orientation
3. Anomie Scale

4. F-Scale
5. Ethnocentrism Scale
6. Preference for America over France
7. Attitudes toward French-Americans
8. Motivational Intensity
9. Desire to Learn French
10. Social Inquisitiveness Scale
11. Parental Encouragement to Learn French
12. Orientation Index

Modern Language Aptitude Test (MLAT)
13. Number Learning; 14. Phonetic Script; 15. Spelling Clues;
16. Words in Sentences; 17. Paired Associates
18. Sex

French Listening Comprehension Test (FLCT)
19. Part I; 20. Part II
21. Parents Favorable to Student Knowing French

Cooperative French Test (CFT)
22. Reading; 23. Vocabulary; 24. Grammar
25. Other Than School Experiences in French
26. Self-rating of French Skills
27. Rating of Mother's French Skills
28. IQ (Otis)
19. Midyear French Grade

Average Ratings on Semantic Dffferential Scales
30. "French People from France"; 31. "Me as I'd Like to Be"
32. "French-Americans"

Oral Production in French Linguistic Ratings
33. Phonetic Accuracy; 34. Linking; 35. Stress; 36. Rhythm;
37. Nasalization; 38. Free Speech (Correctness and Complexity);
39. Reading Fluency; 40. Pronunciation Accuracy; 41. Type of Accent

Results for the Connecticut Study

Factor I for the Connecticut students comprises the measures of intelligence
(V. 28), language learning aptitude (Vs. 13-17), certain features of French
achievement (reading, vocabulary, and grammar) and grades received in French
(Vs. 22-24, 29). Thus individual differences in French grades and progress in

reading, vocabulary, and grammar are presumably based at least in part on differences in intelligence and linguistic aptitude. As was apparent in the Louisiana study, we find in Connecticut too that different types of French achievement have different weights on this factor, very likely reflecting the emphasis given to the development of the various component skills by the French teachers in the classroom learning situation. Thus, grammar and reading have the greatest weight on the factor, followed by vocabulary, and then by different aspects of expressive skill in French, particularly type of accent and rhythm (Vs. 41, 36), but also pronunciation accuracy and phonetic accuracy (Vs. 40, 33). Factor I then is essentially similar in makeup to the intelligence-aptitude factor found with the Louisiana students.

Factor I has another interesting characteristic. Note the negative loading of Variable 25 (other than school experiences with French) on the factor. The direction and magnitude of this loading indicates that the student who does well in school-taught French has had little or no experience with French outside of school, or alternatively that those who have had extensive experience with French in other than school settings score relatively low on intelligence and aptitude measures, and receive low grades in French. This may well be a social class phenomenon in the sense that low IQ and relatively limited aptitude are standard characteristics associated with lower social class backgrounds, and it appears to be children with these characteristics who come more in contact with French people and the French language outside of school. Unfortunately little credit seems to be given for this extracurricular French experience, at least as far as school grades are concerned.

Factor III is dominated by the loadings of all the measures of oral proficiency (Vs. 33-41). The composition of this factor helps us delineate some of the major components of oral skill. On one hand, phonetic coding ability, as measured by the Phonetic Script and Spelling Clues tests (Vs. 14 and 15), is evidently important in the development of oral skill, as Carroll (1960, pp. 46-47) would expect. On the other hand, experiences with French outside of school (V. 25) and with family members who know French (V. 27) are equally important and one cannot tease apart the influences of aptitude and outside school experience in this case. In any event, students who have developed oral skills feel that they know French (V. 26).

Subjective feelings of progress in French (V. 26) also appear on Factors IV and VII for Connecticut students, indicating that there are several independent bases for these self-ratings of achievement in the language. Factor IV demonstrates that certain students feel they are progressing in French as a function of their aural competence (Vs. 19 and 20) and the development of their French vocabulary (V. 23). Factor VII reveals another basis for feelings of progress in the study of French, namely that one is receiving good grades in the

Table 3

Final Rotated Factor Matrix for the *Connecticut* Study

Variables	I	II	III	IV	V	VI	VII	VIII	IX	X	h²
1. Integrative	.04	.15	.15	.14	.12	.09	.37	-.30	-.02	-.12	.34
2. Instrumental	-.20	.00	-.11	-.17	.26	-.19	.32	-.02	.23	-.02	.35
3. Anomie	-.20	-.02	.01	.01	.52	.05	.00	-.02	-.08	-.00	.33
4. F-Scale	-.10	-.09	-.21	.04	.47	.09	.00	.04	.14	.25	.38
5. Ethnocentrism	-.20	-.03	-.19	.13	.27	-.12	.04	.04	.18	.48	.46
6. Prefer Am./France	-.17	-.27	.09	.00	.24	-.12	-.27	.20	.23	.31	.45
7. Att. to Fr.Am.	.06	.12	-.20	-.10	.06	.42	.07	.02	.10	-.03	.26
8. Motiv. Intens.	.13	.24	.20	.07	-.18	-.01	.63	.09	.00	.10	.57
9. Desire Learn Fr.	.16	-.07	.19	.11	-.06	.03	.71	-.08	.05	.11	.61
10. Social Inquis.	.18	.09	-.05	.17	-.02	-.04	-.03	.02	.07	-.57	.40
11. Parent. Encour.	-.02	.71	.10	.11	.03	.05	.08	-.02	.02	-.08	.54
12. Orientation Index	.06	.13	.06	.14	.22	.06	.40	.10	-.16	-.08	.30
13. No. Learning (MLAT)	.65	-.04	.11	.07	-.13	.04	.08	-.24	-.03	-.02	.53
14. Phon. Script (MLAT)	.59	-.09	.41	.14	-.19	-.10	.08	-.18	.08	.02	.64
15. Spell. Clues (MLAT)	.66	-.02	.30	-.03	-.03	-.06	-.19	-.12	.14	-.16	.60
16. Wds. in Sent. MLAT	.74	.02	.20	.07	-.10	-.23	.04	.00	.04	-.08	.66
17. Pd. Assoc. (MLAT)	.68	.16	.08	.04	-.08	.07	.11	-.00	-.10	-.02	.53
18. Sex (Girls/Boys)	.16	.06	-.01	-.25	-.06	.45	.28	-.02	.15	.10	.41
19. FLCT - I	.17	.10	.05	.85	-.02	-.05	.07	.04	-.08	-.09	.79
20. FLCT - II	.12	.05	.08	.84	.03	.02	.11	-.04	.03	-.03	.74

Table 3 (continued)

Final Rotated Factor Matrix for the *Connecticut* Study

Variables	I	II	III	IV	V	VI	VII	VIII	IX	X	h²
21. Par. Favorable	.07	.83*	.08	.01	-.10	.09	.09	.01	.10	-.05	.74
22. CFT - Reading	.69*	-.05	.27	.18	-.17	.11	.13	.35*	-.03	.04	.76
23. CFT - Vocab.	.56*	.07	.26	.30*	-.20	.14	.15	.22	.04	-.09	.63
24. CFT - Grammar	.70*	.16	.24	.22	-.06	.04	.13	.31*	.17	.06	.78
25. Non-School Exp.	-.32*	-.06	.31*	.15	.03	.00	-.04	.47*	.21	.11	.51
26. Self Fr. Skills	.01	.00	.33*	.38*	.22	.17	.30*	.13	.11	.03	.46
27. Mother Fr. Skills	-.06	.20	.30*	.02	.01	-.07	.06	.30*	.10	-.16	.27
28. IQ	.80*	-.05	.21	-.05	.03	-.05	.00	-.12	.03	-.19	.76
29. French Grade	.44*	-.14	.27	-.21	-.27	-.05	.40*	.20	-.04	.03	.61
30. Fr. People France	-.20	.11	.01	.05	.04	.55*	-.07	-.05	.04	-.26	.43
31. Ideal Me	.07	.08	.09	-.02	.00	.08	-.01	.07	.45*	.00	.23
32. French-Am.'s	-.06	.02	.07	.16	.04	.64*	-.03	-.01	-.09	.11	.46
33. Phon. Accur.	.29	-.10	.79*	.03	-.06	-.14	.11	.07	-.02	-.03	.76
34. Linking	.16	.16	.61*	.00	.01	.03	.15	.00	-.16	.29	.55
35. Stress	.26	.00	.73*	-.07	-.15	.10	-.00	.15	.02	-.12	.68
36. Rhythm	.30*	.09	.72*	.19	.02	-.04	.12	-.02	.00	-.08	.67
37. Nasalization	.11	.09	.58*	-.15	.21	.05	.14	.06	-.04	-.02	.46
38. Free Speech	.20	-.22	.40*	-.14	-.23	-.06	.08	.33*	.03	.40*	.60
39. Read. Fluency	.26	.02	.72*	.23	-.27	-.03	.10	-.02	.34*	-.02	.86
40. Pron. Accur.	.29	.10	.68*	.23	-.25	.03	.12	.06	.34*	.07	.82
41. Accent	.31*	.14	.64*	.25	-.05	-.19	.04	.02	.09	.03	.65

course (V. 29), even though there are no other symptoms of outstanding oral skill or of any other type of proficiency in the language. This agreement between students and teachers concerning language competence is furthermore related to the student's motivation and desire to learn French (Vs. 8 and 9). Motivational zeal of this sort characterizes students who are both integratively (Vs. 1 and 12) and instrumentally (V. 2) oriented. Pervasive motivation of this sort then has as strong an impact on French grades as do the intellectual-aptitude characteristics noted in Factor I, although motivation does not affect other aspects of French achievement (such as oral competence) as much as intelligence and language aptitude do.

In this setting, the motivational and attitudinal variables do not congregate on the same factor as they did in the Montreal studies. Instead, the various attitude measures congregate on separate dimensions. Factor V, for example, suggests that an authoritarian ideology is coupled with a disenchantment with one's society (Vs. 4 and 3). Although there are indications that authoritarian attitudes are associated with poor language performance (Vs. 29, 38, 39, and 40), the relationships are not strong. Furthermore, specific attitudes toward French-speaking people are independent of French achievement. Factor VI indicates that favorable attitudes toward French people from Europe or America (Vs. 30, 7, and 32), mainly characteristic of girls (V. 18), have no influence one way or another on French proficiency of any sort. These favorable attitudes are free-floating in the sense that no other personal characteristics accompany them. Apparently if they are to count in the language-learning process, attitudes must touch either one's ideology (e.g., authoritarianism, as was the case in Factor V) or one's motivational system (e.g., form of orientation, motivational intensity, or desire, as was the case in Factor VII).

On the other hand, certain unexpected combinations of attitudes and personality dispositions can have an influence on French competence. Factor X provides an interesting illustration. Students who lack social inquisitiveness (who tend to seek out the routine, V. 10) and who are ethnocentric and biased toward American ways (Vs. 5, 6) are nonetheless likely to show out-of-the-ordinary expressive skills in French in the form of free speech accuracy, and proper linking (Vs. 38 and 34). We would need a much more extensive set of personality and attitude indices to adequately interpret this complex cluster, though there are indications in this setting at least that the development of certain expressive skills calls for some type of constricted personality structure.

Factor IX is equally complex, and it also outruns our capacities of interpretation since we have too few indices of personality dispositions to work with. It indicates that students whose ideal self-image is inordinately attractive (V. 31) are likely to read French fluently and with an outstanding pronunciation (Vs. 39 and 40).

The analysis of the Connecticut data points to other influences that bear on second-language achievement. Consider the composition of Factor VIII, which reveals the importance of outside school contacts with French. Those students who have such experiences with French (Vs. 25 and 27) tend to reject the integrative reasons for studying a foreign language (V. 1) at the same time as they show above average competence in French reading and grammar tests and in free speech (Vs. 22, 24, and 38). Apparently for certain students extracurricular experience with French enhances achievement quite independently of attitudes, motivation, intelligence, or language learning aptitude. The potential importance of this isolated and "cold" experience is worth further study in its own right. Perhaps it is through this route that the mechanical and drill aspects of second-language instruction sometimes have an impact on achievement.

Finally, we note in Factor II that students who report that their parents encourage them to study French (V. 11) also report that their parents favor this activity (V. 21). Since no other variables contribute to this factor, it seems that parental encouragement alone has no effect on students' progress in the language. In fact, Factor VII suggests that to be effective, motivation must be self-generated and essentially independent of parental support.

Summary

With this third American investigation, conducted in a large urban center, we become all the more confident of the essential roles played by attitudes and motivation—quite apart from intelligence and language aptitude—in the development of second-language competence. Evidence supporting this conclusion has appeared in all three of the American studies even though we have been fascinated by each community's unique and distinctive patterns of influence on language proficiency. For example, in all three settings, we have found that students' grades in French derive from a strong motivation and desire to learn the language. Only in the Connecticut study, however, does this motivation appear to be based on an integrative orientation toward the French people and their culture, that is, an interest in adopting French modes of thinking and behaving while learning the language (Factor VII). We also find in the Connecticut setting that students who have authoritarian and anomic attitudes are very likely to do poorly on several measures of French achievement (Factor V). Still, free-floating favorable attitudes toward French people (Factor VI) are not a sufficient basis for enhancing achievement in the study of the language, nor are favorable attitudes toward the French culture which are encouraged (and possibly sustained) by parents. To be effective, attitudes must it seems be pervasive and deep enough to seriously involve the student and his ideologies. It is through his own self-generated motivation that attitudes can have an impact on progress in language study.

We realize, of course, that one must be careful in drawing causal inferences when working with correlational data of this sort. From the statistics alone, it is just as correct to conclude that when achievement in French is above average, the student will then derive a pleasure from language study which in turn will enhance his attitudes toward the language and the people it represents as well as his motivation and desire to learn. We choose to set this alternative aside because it begs another question: Where did the above average achievement come from in the first place? We would expect that those who have the potential for high achievement—those with above average results on the MLAT—would be the ones with the most favorable attitudes and strongest motivation. However, in all three American studies the intelligence and language aptitude factor has few loadings of an attitudinal or motivational sort. Thus, the attitudinal-motivational factors (in the Connecticut study, Factors VII, V, X. and VI) are *independent* of intelligence and aptitude, and we therefore feel confident in interpreting the causal direction of events as we have. The problem touched on here is nonetheless still open for experimental verification; without actual experiments, the issue can never be finally settled.

This is certainly not to say that intellectual and linguistic capacity are not important predictors of achievement in their own right. The Connecticut study demonstrates clearly how intelligence and language aptitude—independent of attitudes and motivation—affect proficiency, especially in the standard school-taught aspects of French. In Connecticut, the Otis intelligence measure is a very good predictor of French grades, reading, vocabulary, and grammar skills, complementing the MLAT measures. For the Connecticut students, this general intellectual capacity also predicts how well oral skills will be developed, particularly phonetic accuracy, proper rhythm in French speech, and the acquisition of a standard French accent. Since a strong emphasis is placed on the development of expressive skills in the Hartford schools, we presume this accounts, at least in part, for the relationship of grades and expressive skills seen in two separate factors (Factor I, III). It is worth emphasizing this point because some educators have perhaps been skeptical of the real value of the MLAT battery, presuming it was only a special type of intelligence test that predicts grammar-translation achievement mainly. It now appears that in schools that train for expressive skills, the MLAT is a potentially very valuable instrument for predicting achievement in these domains as well.

This analysis also reveals a good deal about a student's subjective feelings of progress toward mastery of the language, a more subtle but nonetheless basic motivational force in its own right. The Connecticut students can have a sense of accomplishment in their study of French for any of several reasons: by realizing that their expressive skills are improving (a reaction we noted in the bicultural settings as well); by realizing that their aural competence is improving; and by being strongly motivated, both integratively and instrumentally, to learn the language and to identify with the other group. Interestingly enough, it is the student with this motivational base to his feeling of satisfaction who evokes a similar satisfaction on the part of the teacher, since the grades she assigns correspond to the student's degree of motivation and interest.

The Connecticut study also demonstrated the significant influence extra-curricular contact with French can have on one's achievement. Students who have outside school experiences with the language and whose mothers are relatively skilled in French are advantaged in certain forms of achievement (Factor VIII). We were intrigued to find that students with this outside experience were completely neutral in their attitudes toward the people involved. Apparently proficiency in a language can be enhanced by "cold" experience which is unrelated to intelligence, language aptitude, attitudinal orientation, or motivation. If students who fit this pattern were examined separately and tested further, we might learn more about the type of motivation needed for success with the more mechanical, programmed types of language training experiences, which are also often seen as efficient but "cold."

Finally, we had certain indications in this analysis that it might be worthwhile to extend research into the personality sphere in order to assess the notion that certain personality types may be more gifted for language than others. Since this was not a major interest when we designed our studies, we have only hints to work with. For example, we noted that a lack of social inquisitiveness (as we measured it) appeared to have an indirect effect on achievement in French (Factor X). This suggested a way-out idea: perhaps some type of constricted personality configuration contributes to the development of certain expressive skills. Similarly we noted that an exceptionally attractive image of one's ideal self might have a favorable influence on the development of reading fluency and pronunciation skills (Factor IX), but this notion too is only a hunch, and is meant to suggest next research steps that could be valuable.

Overview of the Louisiana, Maine, and Connecticut Studies

All three American studies provide further evidence for the complex nature of second-language achievement. At least two independent sources of influence have emerged in each setting, an intelligence-aptitude and an attitudinal-motivational source. Thus these investigations, conducted in a variety of sociocultural contexts, provide reassuring replications of the general notions we started with in Montreal. At the same time, we have been amazed to find in each setting distinctive and unique patterns of interrelated variables, making it evident that each community, American or otherwise, has its own complex network of social influences.

We have stressed repeatedly that the sources of influence on second-language proficiency are "independent." From a statistical point of view, this simply means that certain clusters of highly associated variables form into units or factors that have no correlation with one another. From a sociopsychological point of view, however, this independence tells us a good deal about the psychological processes that underlie the various factors. For instance, because our two major sources of influence are found in independent factors, this means one cannot predict from a knowledge of a student's intelligence or language-learning aptitude scores what his attitudes or motivations would be, or vice versa. Nor can one predict what a student's total range of achievement skills are likely to be from a knowledge of either source of influence alone. To do so, one needs information about *both* the intelligence-aptitude and the attitudinal-motivational characteristics, or more generally, information from any number of independent factors that might emerge in a more comprehensive analysis.

This last point is important because we may be dealing here with only two of many possible independent dimensions that affect achievement in language study. In one analysis, for example, we stumbled onto the idea that configurations of personality traits might prove in time to be another independent dimension of importance. The dimensions we are working with then may someday be seen as relatively inconsequential compared to others that may be discovered. But as we look back into the history of the problem we are addressing, it seems we have made substantial progress. At least we are now confident that the knack of learning languages is something more than simply having an ear for languages, or simply having experience with the language in question, or having a certain pattern of language-learning aptitudes. Those conceptions had missed a totally independent dimension that in our eyes seems to be as powerful a source of influence and in certain regards a more powerful one.

We are intrigued with the attitudinal-motivational domain because one sees a challenge in changing and improving the attitudes and motivations of the potential language learner. This does not mean that changing attitudes and motivations is an easy proposition, for that is not true. But there is a good deal of optimism among social psychologists about our present state of knowledge and know-how in this domain (see Lambert and Lambert, 1964; Triandis, 1971). Nor are we saying that linguistic aptitude and intelligence are necessarily rigidly fixed by heredity (see Hunt, 1965, for an alternative view we find more convincing). Instead we are of the opinion that once we know more about the ways in which the finer subfeatures of aptitude and intelligence affect the language-learning process, attention can then be directed to developing these intellectual capacities as much as possible and as early as possible. Because they have started the search, we are indebted to Carroll and his associates and to Pimsleur (1966) for their work on language-learning aptitudes.

The Role of Aptitude and Intelligence in French Achievement

It is evident in these three studies that the subtests of the Modern Language

Aptitude Test (MLAT) are generally highly correlated with measured intelligence. The MLAT battery and the one intelligence measure used in each study turn out to be strong predictors of achievement in reading, vocabulary, and grammar as measured by the Cooperative French Test (CFT) in two of the settings, although somewhat less powerful in the third (Maine). But in addition to predicting CFT scores, intellectual and linguistic capacity are also reliable indicants of grades received in French, accuracy in French speech, and of proper use of rhythm in oral French when the school's language program gives serious attention to the oral-aural features of French, as was the case in Connecticut.

The subtests of the MLAT, apart from the intelligence component, are differentially sensitive to the various components of French proficiency. In general, our findings support Carroll's way of conceptualizing language aptitude, and tend to validate the Carroll-Sapon Modern Language Aptitude Test. Thus, in the Louisiana study, the Number Learning subtest appeared to predict well a student's reading fluency and his development of a good accent in French. The Phonetic Script and Spelling Clues subtests were strong indicators of expressive skills in both the Maine and Connecticut studies. Also in the Maine study, Spelling Clues, along with an index of the number of the student's French friends, predict skill in comprehending complex passages of French as measured by Part IV of the French Listening Comprehension Test (FLCT).

Because this topic may be of special interest to certain readers, we present in *Reading Number Six* (Appendix C) a detailed examination of how the MLAT subtests relate to measures of intelligence and to second-language achievement.

The Role of Attitudes and Motivation in French Achievement

In all three studies we find that students with a strong motivation and desire to learn French obtain good grades in their French courses at school. In each setting, however, there is apparently a different social or attitudinal foundation for this motivation. In Louisiana, the motivation appears to derive from a strong parental encouragement and personal satisfaction for the student himself in his attempts to learn the language. In Maine, the motivation is apparently fostered by the student's identification with his French teacher, and depends in part on the student being sensitive to the feelings of other people. In Connecticut the strong motivation to learn French seems to stem from the student's integrative orientations toward the study of the language as well as a realization of the potential usefulness of the language.

In two settings it was found that an ethnocentric syndrome (comprising high scores on the F-Scale and on the measures of Ethnocentrism, Anomie, and Preference for America over France) was clearly associated with poor grades in French as well as with poor comprehension or poor oral reading skills. In the

Maine setting, low F-Scale Scores, indicating a democratic outlook, interacted with measures of intellectual capacity and aptitude as associates of above average grades in French.

Other findings were specific to settings. For instance, in Louisiana, it was found that stereotyped negative feelings toward French-Americans are associated with poor comprehension of complex French passages and poor vocabulary development. At the same time, an integrative orientation toward learning French and favorable attitudes toward French-Americans appears to enhance the development of vocabulary in French and, to a lesser extent, skill in French comprehension. In Maine we noted that the number of French friends the student has determines in part (along with measures of intellectual capacity and aptitude) his comprehension of complex French passages. Furthermore, Maine students who are instrumentally oriented in their study of French and whose families have a number of French-speaking friends are likely to develop above average expressive skills in the language.

Student's Own Estimates of Progress in the Language

One other matter came to light which merits special consideration. We noted several instances where students' own estimates of how well they were doing in their mastery of French was at variance with the teachers' estimates as reflected in the grades assigned. This became salient in the cases of students who showed above average expressive skills. They were personally satisfied with their progress, but the teachers apparently gave little weight to expressive skills in their grading. Since the student's personal view of what it means to learn a language can deeply affect his motivation to learn, student-teacher discrepancies can be extremely serious matters. Research directed specifically towards this topic would be of great value.

The Connecticut data indicated that students may feel they are progressing in language study for various reasons: if their expressive skills are above average; if their aural skills are above average; or if their motivation is strong in both its integrative and instrumental forms. The third case is particularly interesting because it is this type of student—highly motivated and integratively oriented— who reaches consensus with the teacher on what it is to do well in language study. The trouble is that the other two types do not reach a consensus with their teachers.

Chapter Four

The French-American Students Approaches
to the Study of French

How might members of a linguistic minority group in the United States
approach the learning of their "own" language at school? In considerating this
question, we would be just plain wrong to come to any of the following hasty
conclusions: (1) any minority group member would welcome enthusiastically
the opportunity to study his own language at school; (2) none of them would
care much about it because English is the necessary language for getting ahead in
America; (3) most of them speak the language at home so they really do not
need to study it at school; (4) none of them speak the language at home any
more so they would be starting at scratch with other students.

It is more reasonable to expect a variety of different reactions, ranging from
enthusiasm through indifference to suspicion, embarrassment, and rejection.
There would also likely be differences in reactions from one regional setting to
another in the United States, since in certain communities minority languages
have died out while in others foreign languages are very much alive. And within
each setting some families would have been able to maintain the foreign language
while others would not.

Our purpose in this chapter is to actually examine the reactions of
French-American high school students in the same Louisiana and Maine
communities we have just surveyed. Judging from the variety of attitudes the
American students in these regions displayed, we can be quite certain that the
French-American young person would be well aware of the social significance
attached to his heritage and the reactions he might elicit from others, no matter
how carefully he walks the fine line dividing his French and his American
backgrounds. As we shall see, a fascinating series of approaches to the study of
the French and English languages emerge in this analysis, many of which appear
to be disruptive or dysfunctional. A few, however, seem to promote the full
potential of the bicultural person.

We, of course, are still interested in how attitudes, motivation, and aptitude affect the language-learning process even in this special case. We had to increase the scope of the measures used to assess attitudes and motivation, but certain of the basic measures and indices were retained. Thus, in addition to the already familiar indices of attitudes, motivation, orientation, and aptitude, we try now to measure such factors as the French-American student's "desire for French identity," or his tendency "to think in French." We had certain questions in mind from the start. For instance, how well will the MLAT aptitude measures work with those who have learned French at home as infants? What would an "instrumental orientation toward French study" mean for a French-American studying his own language at school? As we shall see, there were numerous surprises in store.

General Procedure

The two samples of French-American high school students were administered a battery of tests designed to assess their proficiency in various French language skills, their motivation and desire to master French, their degree of language aptitude, and their attitudes towards the French-American, European French, and American cultures. The Maine students had a mean of 9.91 years of French instruction in their schools while the Louisiana students had only 1.05. This large discrepancy reflects a difference in educational policies in the two communities. In the Maine area studied, courses in French started at grade 1 whereas in the Louisiana public schools they started at grade 10. Furthermore, the French-American students in Maine were essentially segregated in the sense that they obtained their education in a Catholic parochial school—with separate schools for boys and girls—while in Louisiana the French-American students attended public high schools.

The home language of these students is not standard or European French, and there are differences in the dialects of French used in the homes of Louisiana and Maine students (cf. Tisch, 1959; Read, 1963). We will assume nonetheless that neither variety of French hampers the mastery of the standard form taught in the schools of both regions, although we will encounter signs that local varieties of French are not always appreciated by teachers. Our own linguistic analysis of French expressive skills, however, does not penalize the nonstandard speaker in any way.

For the French-American students, seventeen additional indices were devised. These unfamiliar measures are described briefly below, and the complete form of each one is given in Appendix A.

1. *Comparative Preference for English over French Acquaintances.* The Students were asked to rate, on one 7-point scale, how much they liked their own English-speaking acquaintances, and on a second scale how much they liked

their own French-speaking acquaintances. The final score used in the analysis was the English rating minus the French; the higher the score the more preference is shown for English-speaking acquaintances. A constant of 10 was added to each difference score to eliminate minus entries.

2. *Desire for French Identity.* The students were asked to respond to eight items asking about their desire to have more experiences with French people and culture in various situations outside school. High scores indicate a pervasive desire to identify with a French cultural tradition.

3. The three subscales of the *Cooperative French Test, Advanced Form Q* (Greenberg and Spaulding, 1940) were used with the French-American students. Although similar in format to the elementary form given to the English-speaking students, the level of this test is much more demanding. The subscales are: Reading, Vocabulary, and Grammar.

4. *Number of Years Studying English.* The number of years each student had studied English was asked, and this number was included as a separate variable.

5. *Thinking in French More than English.* Students were given a 7-point scale, one end of which was labeled "Always (think) in English," and the other "Always (think) in French." They were asked to place a check mark somewhere along the scale to indicate in which language they felt they did their thinking. A student who checked midway between the two extremes would signify that he had no dominant language, or that he used both languages equally often in thinking. Those with a low rating showed a dominance of thinking in English and those with a high rating showed a dominance in French.

6. *Prefer Speaking French More than English.* Each student rated on a 7-point scale the extent to which he preferred to speak in English (1) or French (7). A rating of 4 indicated no preference.

7. *Self-rating of English Skills.* Four-point scales were provided to indicate what the student thought his ability was in *speaking, reading,* and *understanding* (spoken) English. Scores for speaking English were doubled in the total because we felt this skill was especially important for interpersonal communication.

8. *Word Completion.* Students were given forty-five seconds to complete each of four two-letter sequences, thereby making them into meaningful words. They were instructed to make as many words, either French or English, as possible from the sequences "li-----," "va-----," "su-----" and "te-----." Two raters familiar with both English and French classified the completed words as either "English," "French," or "both English and French." The score on this test was taken as the number of English minus French words. To eliminate negative numbers, a constant of thirty was added to each score. Thus, high scores indicate a dominance of English responses, and low scores a dominance of French.

9. *Word Detection.* They were also presented with four nonsense strings: *Pintonightresoisle, takinozzlesew, patomenstle,* and *calmaistueacheery.* They

were instructed to find as many English and French words as they could in each. The time allotted was one minute for each; the scoring system was the same as for number 8 above.

10. *Word Associations.* Three English words and their translated equivalents in French were presented one at a time; students were instructed to write as many associated words, using the same language as the stimulus word, as they could in a one-minute time period. The words were presented in the order: *maison, idea, pauvre, house, idée,* and *poor.* The same scoring system as for number 8 was used here also. The rationale for the use of these last three tests can be found in a paper by Lambert, Havelka, and Gardner (1959).

11. *Nationality When Asked by English-speaking Person.* These students were requested to indicate whether they would say they were American (scored 1), French (2), or French-American (3), if questioned about their nationality by an English-speaking individual.

12. *Nationality When Asked by French-speaking Person.* They were also asked to indicate whether they would say they were American (scored 1), French (2), or French-American (3), if questioned by a French-speaking individual.

13. *Reinforcements for Speaking European French.* Each student was asked to specify the reaction of each of six different groups of people to his adopting the European French style of speech. The six groups were: parents, brothers and sisters, close French-American friends, French teacher, French-speaking schoolmates, and English-speaking schoolmates. Their responses for each type of interlocution were classified as "favorable" (scored 3), "tolerant" (2), "unfavorable" (1), or "no answer" (0). The scores were totaled to produce an estimate of the amount of social reinforcement a student would receive for speaking a European-style French.

14. *Desire to Live in France.* They were asked to rate on 7-point scales how much or how little they would like to live in France, either "for a short time," or "permanently." The ratings for both statements were totaled to provide an estimate of desire to live in France.

15. *Rating of Integrative Orientation to Learn English.* The same items used to index an integrative orientation to learn French were rated by the French-American students, but this time with the English language specified.

16. *Rating of Instrumental Orientation to Learn English.* The same items indicating an instrumental orientation to learn French for the American students were rated, but this time with English substituted for French.

17. *Phonetic Discrimination.* The students listened to a series of thirty sets of speech sounds, chosen to represent phonetic differences between standard and French-American styles of French. For each set, they heard one speech sound followed by another. After approximately thirty seconds had elapsed, a third speech sound was presented which was identical to either the first or

second sound heard, or to both. (For five of the sets, the three speech sounds were identical.) They were instructed to indicate whether the third sound was identical to the first or the second one presented, or whether all three sounds were identical. The total score was the number of correct classifications.

The Louisiana French-American Study

As was mentioned earlier, Lafayette Parish is the hub of the French society in Louisiana. With the help of Mr. Raymond Miles, Director of Guidance Services for the Lafayette Parish School Board, we asked all high school teachers of first- and second-year French in the parish to determine how many of their students came from homes where one or both parents regularly use the French language in communication, that is, where students would have had the opportunity to learn at least to speak French from their parents and siblings. These students we refer to as "French-Americans."

A total of eighty French-American first and second-year high school students were available for testing in late February, 1961. They came from all the high schools in the parish and met in a large auditorium of Lafayette High School for a group test lasting three and one-half hours. In late April, they came together again for the achievement tests.

From preliminary interviews with a number of these students and their teachers, we realized that there was no need to translate our testing materials into French, since most French-American young people in the area had little or no reading experience in French. Teachers advised us, however, to use the advanced form of the Cooperative French Test (rather than the elementary form used with the American students) since there would likely be a great range of proficiency in French.

Variables Included in the Louisiana French-American Study

The following 41 variables were selected as the most promising ones after a preliminary analysis of the full table of intercorrelations. The 41 x 41 correlation matrix for these variables is placed in Appendix B as Table 4-B. The final rotated factor matrix, Table 4, follows here in the text.

1. Rating of Integrative Orientation
2. Anomie Scale
3. F-Scale
4. Ethnocentrism Scale
5. Preference for America over France
6. Attitudes toward French-Americans
7. Voice Study: English Guises/Standard French Guises

8.   Motivational Intensity
9.   Desire to Learn French
10.   Sensitivity to Others
11.   Type of Accent
12.   Desire for French Identity
13.   Voice Study: English Guises/French-American Guises
   Modern Language Aptitude Test (MLAT)
14.   Number Learning; 15. Phonetic Script; 16. Spelling Clues;
17.   Words in Sentences; 18. Paired Associates
19.   Free Speech (Accuracy and Complexity)
   French Listening Comprehension Test (FLCT)
20.   Part I; 21. Part II; 22. Part III; 23. Part IV
24.   Fluency in Reading Aloud
   Cooperative French Test (CFT)
25.   Reading; 26. Vocabulary; 27. Grammar
28.   Pronunciation Accuracy
29.   Self-rating of French Skills
30.   Sex (Girls/Boys)
   Oral Production: Linguist's Ratings
31.   Phonetic Accuracy; 32. Linking; 33. Stress; 34. Rhythm;
35.   Nasalization
36.   Thinks in French versus English
37.   Preferred Language for Speaking (French/English)
38.   Self-rating of English Skills
   Language Dominance Measures
39.   Word Completion; 40. Word Detection; 41. Word Associations

Results for the Louisiana French-American Students

In this instance, Factor I represents a dimension of French oral skill (Vs. 24, 28, and 31-35), but it includes as well French reading and vocabulary proficiency (Vs. 25 and 26). For these students, however, oral competence in French is not dependent upon language aptitude, motivation, or attitudes. The loadings of Variables 7, 10, and 29 (a more favorable attitude toward English-speaking than European French guises, a sensitivity for others, and a rather high self-rating in French competence) are suggestive, but they make relatively small contributions to the configuration. They are therefore not the major determinants of the individual differences in French oral skill that do exist in the group. Instead, it is more likely that experiences at home and in the community are more critical. We learned in our discussions with these students that some converse in French only with family members while others are addressed in French by their parents but they respond in English and use English only with other children in the family.

Factor II demonstrates that language aptitude (Vs. 14-18) is associated with listening comprehension skill (V. 20) and with proficiency in French reading, grammar, and vocabulary (Vs. 25-27).

The pattern of variables forming Factor III depicts a type of French-American student who is more spontaneous and expressive in French than in English (V. 41), who is confident of his proficiency in French (V. 29), who is above average in aural and oral French achievement (Vs. 23 and 35), even though somewhat deficient in auditory memory and alertness (V. 14). What does this marked degree of French language dominance signify for a French-American adolescent in Louisiana? Our only clue comes from the relatively strong preference this type of student shows for America over France (V. 5). The interesting question is why do these students who are so very French themselves exaggerate the merits of the American relative to the French way of life? One possibility is that a young French-American growing up in this American setting may encounter personal conflicts of allegiances when his proficiency in French goes beyond some average or normative level.

Factor VIII has a similar overall profile, but since it forms an independent complex of variables, it represents the reactions of a different type of student. In this instance, the student type in question is more perceptually alert in French than in English (V. 40) and somewhat above average in his proficiency with certain features of French (Vs. 20 and 28). As before, the pattern is characteristic of those who show a strong preference for the American over the French way of life (V. 5), with some deficiency in an English-based test of aptitude (V. 16). In this case, too, there is no clear pattern of associated characteristics to help us get to the roots of this apparent ambivalence. Nonetheless both Factors III and VIII point to some type of personal confusion of cultural allegiances when French language skills go beyond some average point.

There are interesting differences in the ways male and female French-Americans react to their bicultural and bilingual heritage. These differences are depicted in Factors V and X where sex (V. 30) plays a prominent role in the constellation of variables. In Factor V, the profile for girls has these components: low anomie (V. 2), a preference for France over America (V. 5), a pronunciation accent that is relatively more European than French-American in style (V. 11), a poor control of French phonemes (V. 31), but also a tendency to think more in English than French (V. 36), a preference for speaking English rather than French (V. 37), and a favorable self-view of one's competence in English (V. 38). This complex pattern can be interpreted in many different ways, but the interpretation we find most consistent with the findings is the following: certain French-American girls in the Lousiana setting are well

Table 4

Final Rotated Factor Matrix for the *Louisiana French-American* Study

Variables	I	II	III	IV	V	VI	VII	VIII	IX	X	XI	XII	h²
1. Integ. Rating (Fr.)	.18	-.01	.21	.49*	.07	.20	.09	-.01	.15	.27	.18	.21	.54
2. Anomie	-.03	-.14	.15	.05	-.55*	-.09	.23	.18	-.10	-.20	.02	-.03	.49
3. F Scale	.18	.15	-.08	.13	.03	-.03	.71*	-.01	.12	.11	.14	.10	.64
4. Ethnocentrism	-.08	-.15	.11	.01	-.05	-.10	.58*	.07	-.05	.04	-.15	-.13	.44
5. Prefer. Am/France	.14	-.28	.35*	.05	-.30*	.09	.24	.36*	-.13	.03	.28	-.05	.60
6. Att. to Fr. Am.'s	-.02	.02	.13	.26	.16	.31*	.32*	-.20	.39*	.17	.13	.39*	.70
7. Voice: Eng/Eur. Fr.	.27	.01	-.05	-.14	.13	-.60*	.07	-.15	-.11	.01	-.02	.04	.51
8. Motiv. Intens.	.07	.07	.09	.67*	.11	-.06	-.02	.15	.24	.08	.04	.08	.58
9. Desire Learn Fr.	.10	.11	-.13	.80*	.06	.15	.05	-.05	-.09	.00	-.06	.17	.75
10. Sens. for Others	.25	-.04	-.19	.35*	-.06	.03	-.06	.22	-.14	.23	.14	.04	.35
11. Accent: Eur/Fr.Am.	.10	.09	.01	.14	.60*	-.06	.06	-.06	.00	-.06	.09	.04	.44
12. Des. Fr. Ident.	.08	.08	.03	.15	.07	.00	.03	.03	.06	.12	-.01	.71*	.57
13. Voice: Eng./Fr.Am.	.03	-.15	.09	-.09	-.13	.09	-.01	.02	-.01	-.05	-.50*	-.04	.32
14. No. Learn. (MLAT)	.03	.39*	-.41*	.11	.20	.23	.25	-.21	-.06	-.13	.08	.03	.55
15. Phon. Script (MLAT)	.05	.60*	-.15	.23	.26	.07	.15	-.04	.14	-.04	-.05	-.20	.60
16. Spell. Clues (MLAT)	.12	.34*	.23	.01	-.12	-.05	-.11	-.29	.36*	-.05	-.08	.11	.45
17. Wds. in Sent. (MLAT)	.03	.72*	-.01	-.07	.10	.06	-.08	-.05	.03	.12	.21	.09	.62
18. Pd. Assoc. (MLAT)	.15	.29	-.28	-.06	.16	.20	-.25	.18	.16	.27	.21	-.04	.49
19. Free Speech	.27	.15	.06	.02	.03	.66*	-.01	-.09	.06	-.05	-.15	.04	.57
20. FLCT - I	.10	.67*	-.03	.03	.10	-.06	.04	.30*	.18	.13	-.09	.25	.68

Table 4 (continued)

Final Rotated Factor Matrix for the *Louisiana French-American Study*

Variables	I	II	III	IV	V	VI	VII	VIII	IX	X	XI	XII	h²
21. FLCT - II	.13	.06	.25	.11	.11	.13	.05	.04	.02	.62*	.05	.14	.54
22. FLCT - III	.05	.10	.04	.06	-.13	-.18	.00	-.19	.16	.58*	-.02	.09	.47
23. FLCT - IV	.11	.27	.29	.04	-.16	.02	-.11	.11	.04	.37*	.09	.28	.44
24. Reading Aloud	.68*	.06	-.05	-.04	.23	.12	.04	.14	.42*	.18	.11	.10	.80
25. CFT - Reading	.34*	.34*	.09	.15	.06	.17	-.09	.03	.67*	.26	.12	.04	.83
26. CFT - Vocab.	.31*	.34*	-.01	.17	-.06	.18	.03	.08	.53*	.23	-.05	.13	.64
27. CFT - Grammar	.12	.49*	.03	.25	-.14	.22	-.01	.20	.29	.39*	.06	.03	.66
28. Pronunciation	.68	-.03	-.15	.13	.16	.02	.17	.28	.29	.17	-.09	.00	.77
29. Self Fr. Skills	.27	-.14	.38*	.29	-.07	.00	.13	-.03	.20	.13	.37*	.18	.57
30. Sex (Girls/Boys)	.15	.04	.00	.08	.44*	-.12	.06	-.03	.05	.48*	.01	-.12	.48
31. Phon. Accur.	.68*	-.08	-.08	.17	-.29	-.14	-.01	-.06	.11	.01	-.10	.08	.64
32. Linking	.46*	.12	.15	.24	.22	.01	.25	.03	-.05	.10	-.52*	.07	.71
33. Stress	.73*	.24	.07	.05	.08	.08	.13	-.03	-.02	.20	.01	-.03	.67
34. Rhythm	.75*	.06	.07	.02	.18	.01	-.16	.01	-.01	.01	-.03	.12	.65
35. Nasalization	.54*	.06	.30*	.23	-.24	-.01	.05	-.18	.09	-.08	.13	-.14	.59
36. Think in Fr./Eng.	.03	.13	.18	.14	-.55*	.05	.12	-.06	-.07	.01	.18	.60*	.79
37. Prefer. Speak Fr./Eng.	.09	.00	-.22	.15	-.51*	-.06	-.11	.20	.14	.01	-.18	.59*	.76
38. Self Eng. Skills	.03	.16	.05	.21	.54*	-.04	.19	.07	.30*	-.14	.09	-.07	.53
39. Word Compl. (Eng./Fr.)	-.02	.05	-.16	-.15	.18	.09	.48*	-.21	-.08	-.17	-.02	.00	.40
40. Word Detection (Eng./Fr.)	-.02	-.11	.00	-.07	.11	.02	.08	-.60*	-.01	.09	.05	-.07	.41
41. Word Assns. (Eng./Fr.)	.00	.03	-.62	.03	-.04	.12	.03	.04	-.05	-.19	.14	-.02	.46

adjusted to their society (low anomie score), making them comfortable as English-speaking Americans. They are nonetheless favorably oriented toward their French background and have apparently responded enthusiastically to the academic study of French which is definitely European oriented. Although well adjusted to the American scene, one has the impression that this type of student could be easily encouraged to change her language preferences, at least to the point of no preference, if given opportunities and social reinforcements for being more French.

For boys, there seems to be more of a personal conflict involved. To see their profile, we reverse the poles of all variables that contribute to Factor V. The profile then suggests this sketch: a subgroup of Louisiana French-American boys are ill at ease with their society (high anomie), prefer America to France, have more of a French-American than European pronunciation style and differentiate the two styles well, at the same time as they think more in *French* than in English, prefer to speak French to English, and downgrade their competence in English. In other words, this subgroup of adolescent boys may have pronounced feelings of social disorganization as a consequence of their linguistic dominance in French. Their preference for speaking French is apparently based on their generally greater facility with French and a feeling of incompetence in English. The personal conflict they seem to encounter could be reduced by switching the language preference to English, but that would apparently require more competence in English than they now have. Thus they seem to feel socially handicapped by their French language dominance.

It is interesting to speculate about a more general type of solution that would affect both boys and girls who fit this pattern: if greater societal supports for being French were provided, then both boys and girls could become more at ease by being themselves, i.e., both French and American. We may well be looking in here at a personal predicament faced by many members of linguistic minority groups. The attempts currently underway to revive the French language and traditions in Louisiana provide an excellent opportunity to check for changes in the reactions of French-Americans. It would be extremely valuable to repeat this study in Louisiana in the 1970's to see if these patterns of conflict are reduced in intensity or eliminated.

In Factor X, other aspects of French competence are associated with sex (V. 30). In this case it is aural skills (Vs. 21, 22 and 23) and proficiency in French grammar (V. 27). For this separate subgroup of French-American girls, above average competence in these more passive aspects of French achievement has no clear association with any other variables, attitudes included. This factor suggests that girls may have an easier time than boys with the development of passive skills in French, regardless of intellectual, attitudinal, or motivational characteristics.

Attitudes do play prominent roles in the composition of Factors VI, IX, and

VII. In Factor VI there is a very strong suggestion that competence on measures of French free speech (V. 19) is determined by favorable reactions toward speakers of European French (V. 7) and favorable attitudes toward French-Americans (V. 6). Favorable attitudes toward one's own ethnic group appear to contribute to a different constellation of abilities in French, as seen in Factor IX. Here a positive view of one's own group (V. 6) coupled with a skill in English vocabulary (V. 16) and a feeling of competence in English (V. 38) contributes to outstanding performance on tests of expressive skills in French (reading aloud, V. 24, and pronunciation, V. 28) as well as the more passive skills (reading, vocabulary, and grammar, Vs. 25-27). This profile is especially interesting because it implies that French-American young people who have an appreciation for their cultural and linguistic background are psychologically free to become fully bilingual.

Favorable attitudes toward French-Americans are nonetheless no guarantee of competence in the French language. Note the composition of Factor VII, which indicates that French-American students who have a favorable attitude toward their own ethnic group (V. 6) but who are at the same time authoritarian and ethnocentric in outlook (Vs. 3 and 4) show no outstanding competence in French. If anything they seem to be perceptually more alert in English than French (V. 39).

Apparently some balance or restraint is needed if the French-American adolescent is to make the optimum adjustment to his bicultural inheritance. Factor XII reveals that too strong a desire for French identity (V. 12) coupled with a favorable attitude towards one's own ethnolinguistic group (V. 6) may influence one's preference for speaking French over English (V. 37) and one's tendency to think more through French than English (V. 36), but this pro-French mental outlook does not necessarily promote competence in the language. In fact, there is no evidence in Factor XII that students with this very favorable French attitude have any out of the ordinary skill in French. The composition of Factor XI tells a similar story: students can have a sense of confidence in their competence in French (V. 29) and a very favorable evaluation of French-American style speech (V. 13) with no signs of being talented in the language (note, in fact, the large negative loading of Variable 32).

The now familiar pattern of motivational variables define Factor IV. Students who are integratively oriented in their study of French (V. 1) are highly motivated to learn French (Vs. 8 and 9), and are sensitive to the feelings of others (V. 20). There is a slight indication in the pattern of loadings on this factor that such students have favorable attitudes toward French-Americans (V. 6), feel competent in French (V. 29), and are somewhat skilled in French grammar (V. 27), but these relationships are not as strong here as in the other settings investigated.

Summary

For the French American students in the Louisiana setting, oral skills fall out as a separate independent dimension having no association with language aptitude, motivation, or attitudes (Factor I). It is our speculation that individual differences in oral competence are attributable to different amounts of experience with French in the home and neighborhood. Individual differences in French listening comprehension and in reading, grammar, and vocabulary are, however, likely determined by language aptitude (Factor II). The importance of motivation appeared in Factor IV where it was evident that a strong motivation and desire to learn French, especially for integrative reasons, contribute to subjective feelings of being competent in French and to above average performance on measures of French grammar.

Other findings from this analysis point to the roles played by one's cultural background and one's reaction to being both French and American in the development of language proficiency. In fact, we have uncovered a fascinating range of French-American student reactions, each of which merits further investigation on its own.

First, for those who have maintained French as the more dominant and spontaneous language in their thinking, we have seen (in Factors III and VIII) an uncertainty or ambivalence as to which language they prefer to speak, and which cultural tradition they want to align themselves with.

Second, there are fundamental differences in the ways male and female French-Americans respond to the bilingual and bicultural requirements of their world (Factor V). In the Louisiana setting, French-American girls appeared well adjusted to society and were apparently comfortable in English, preferring to speak it to French, at the same time that they showed a preference for the French over the American culture. The boys seem to face more of a personal conflict because they were less at ease with society, preferring the American culture to the French, and yet thinking more in French than English and preferring to speak French, possibly because they worry about their competence in English. The profile suggests that these boys felt socially handicapped because of their French language dominance. Thus, for both boys and girls there is a discordance between proficiency in the two languages and identification with the two cultures.

Finally we have seen how certain clusters of attitudes can have an impact on the development of language competence while others have either no effect or act as a hindrance (Factors VI, VII, IX, XI, and XII). For instance, positive attitudes towards the French-American culture coupled with favorable reactions to speakers of European French were prominently associated with skill in French free speech (Factor VI). Likewise, positive attitudes towards one's own ethnic group coupled with a feeling of confidence in one's proficiency in

English had a pervasive association with various types of French skills (Factor IX), suggesting that French-American students who are content and comfortable with both their cultural and linguistic backgrounds are thereby psychologically free to become fully bilingual. Other attitudinal clusters, although favorable and positive in part, prove to be dysfunctional, indicating that the optimal adjustment for the French-American young person is a delicate one, calling for a balanced and thoughtful personal outlook. Thus, Factor VII made it plain that favorable attitudes toward one's own cultural group when coupled with authoritarianism and ethnocentrism showed no association with competence in French. Furthermore, in Factors XII and XI we saw that too strong a desire for French identity linked with a positive attitude towards one's own group appeared to influence the student's preference for speaking French and his tendency to think more in French, but did not promote any noteworthy competence in the language.

The Maine French-American Study

The French-American students in Maine attended Catholic parochial schools—separate schools for boys and girls—in the same communities as those we described in the Maine study. Although all course work in these schools was conducted in English, French-American students would normally have taken a French course each year throughout their elementary and secondary school training. The sample consisted of ninety-eight students in their first and second years of high school, all enrolled in French courses. They came from homes where French was the main (but not exclusive) language of communication.

From preliminary interviews with students and teachers, it was apparent that most of the French-American students were bilingual and had many opportunities to interact with English-speaking Americans in their communities. Thus there was no need to translate the test materials into French, since all students had much greater experience reading and writing English than French. Still we were advised to use the advanced form of the Cooperative French Test, as was done for French-Americans in Louisiana.

We soon realized through our visits to the region that the two schools had quite different approaches to teaching French. In the girls' school, emphasis was placed on the development of audio-lingual competence with much attention being given to laboratory work and free expression in French. In sharp contrast, the teachers in the boys' school focused on the more conventional skills of reading, translation, and grammar. This difference we felt might make for interesting contrasts in the outcomes.

Group tests were administered in February 1961 and the French achievement tests were given in late April 1961 during the testing period arranged for the American students.

Variables Included in the Maine French-American Study.

The following 41 variables were selected as the most promising after a preliminary analysis of the intercorrelations of all variables used. The 41 x 41 correlation matrix for these variables is placed in Appendix B as Table 5-B, and the final rotated factor matrix, Table 5, follows here in the text.

1. Rating of Integrative Orientation
2. Rating of Instrumental Orientation
3. Anomie Scale
4. F-Scale
5. Ethnocentrism Scale
6. Preference for America over France
7. Attitudes toward French-Americans
8. Motivational Intensity
9. Desire to Learn French
10. Sensitivity for Others
11. Parental Encouragement to Learn French
12. Sex
13. Desire for French Identity
14. Orientation Index

Modern Language Aptitude Test (MLAT)
15. Number Learning; 16. Phonetic Script; 17. Spelling Clues;
18. Words in Sentences; 19. Paired Associates
20. Free Speech in French (Accuracy and Complexity)

French Listening Comprehension Test (FLCT)
21. Part I; 22. Part II; 23. Part III; 24. Part IV

Cooperative French Test (CFT)
25. Reading; 26. Vocabulary; 27. Grammar
28. Self-rating of French Skills
29. Rating of Mother's French Skills

Oral Production Ratings
30. Phonetic Accuracy; 31. Linking; 32. Stress; 33. Rhythm
34. Thinks More in French than English
35. Preferred Language (French/English)
36. Self-rating of English Skills
37. Word Completion
38. Word Detection
39. Word Associations
40. Desire to Live in France
41. Phonetic Discrimination Test

Results for the Maine French-American Study

The positive loadings of all the subtests of the MLAT (Vs. 15-19) define Factor I (first column in Table 5) as a language aptitude dimension. However in this case, language aptitude does not have an important influence in French achievement except for the students' own feelings of competence with the language (V. 28). In contrast to the Lousiana case, the language aptitude subtests are not associated with achievement in reading, vocabulary, and grammar (Vs. 25-27). Instead the MLAT battery for these students seems to be more closely associated with proficiency in English (Vs. 36 and 38). This outcome is reasonable if we assume that the Maine French-American students are much more French than those from Louisiana and have used French more from infancy on. We would then expect language aptitude to reflect their skill with English since the MLAT is based on English competence.

Factor I is more complex, however. Note that Variables 5 and 6 also contribute strongly to the pattern, i.e., a nonethnocentric outlook and a preference for the French culture over the American. This intricate combination of language aptitude, English competence, and a nonethnocentric pro-French attitude appears to give these students a confidence in French as well as English, but curiously they do not excel in any of the various French tests of competence. One has the impression that they may have a false sense of how skilled they are in French.

The dominant theme of Factor II is attitudes, but in this case we find a strange mixture: strong endorsement of both integrative and instrumental reasons for studying French (Vs. 1 and 2), a favorable attitude towards one's own ethnic group (V. 7), strong ethnocentric and authoritarian attitudes (Vs. 4 and 5), coupled with poor language aptitude, especially on one subtest calling for competence in English (Vs. 17), and poor aural skill in French (V. 21). We have seen earlier that ethnocentrism and authoritarianism are typically symptoms of poor language achievement even when they appear in combination with otherwise favorable attitudes. It appears that an undemocratic suspicion of foreign ideas and people either hampers the language-learning process, or that such attitudes are adopted as a means of justifying one's poor performance in language study. In the present case, this suspicious world view is associated with a failure to develop competence in either French or English. In this example we have two possible interpretations: either these students cannot develop language competence because of their view of foreign peoples, or they lack the aptitude and justify their poor performance with a suspicious world view.

Factor III describes a quite different type of student, one who thinks in French and prefers to speak French to English (Vs. 34 and 35), who has a very strong desire to learn the language and to develop a French identity (Vs. 9 and 13), and who has a sense of assurance in his French competence (V. 28).

Table 5

Final Rotated Factor Matrix for the *Maine French-American Study*

Variables	I	II	III	IV	V	VI	VII	VIII	IX	h²
1. Integ. Rating (Fr.)	.05	.70*	.04	.09	-.16	-.19	.28	-.18	.05	.68
2. Inst. Rating (Fr.)	-.09	.72*	.06	-.05	-.16	-.22	-.01	-.31*	.20	.74
3. Anomie	-.20	.03	.04	-.18	.21	.13	-.28	.20	.01	.25
4. F Scale	-.18	.59*	-.13	-.14	.08	.18	.09	.23	.13	.53
5. Ethnocentrism	-.45*	.40*	-.18	-.09	.13	.00	.20	.03	.06	.47
6. Prefer. Am/France	-.46*	.28	-.09	-.23	.32*	-.14	.01	.35*	.06	.60
7. Att. to Fr. Am.'s	-.03	.71*	.01	.07	.04	.12	.16	.06	.03	.55
8. Motiv. Intens.	-.07	.27*	.19	.09	-.14	.19	.64*	-.16	.16	.65
9. Desire to Learn Fr.	-.02	.22	.44*	.16	-.19	.04	.63*	-.07	.05	.71
10. Sens. for Others	.01	.21	-.13	.04	-.21	.16	.24	-.23	-.04	.25
11. Parent. Encour.	.20	.13	.18	.03	.00	.09	.15	-.16	.44*	.34
12. Sex (Girls/Boys)	.15	.01	.06	.25	-.46*	.51*	.19	-.23	.12	.66
13. Desire Fr. Ident.	.16	.09	.61*	.17	-.01	.10	.02	-.12	-.09	.46
14. Orient. Index	.13	-.16	-.04	-.16	.11	.03	.07	-.09	-.60*	.46
15. No. Learning (MLAT)	.69*	.05	.11	.04	-.17	.02	-.02	.00	.01	.53
16. Phon. Script (MLAT)	.64*	-.13	-.04	.29	-.06	.12	.02	.03	.05	.54
17. Spell. Clues (MLAT)	.35*	-.46*	.00	.09	.04	.05	.24	.06	.15	.43
18. Wds. in Sent. (MLAT)	.38*	-.23	-.11	.09	-.11	.15	-.27	.02	.40*	.48
19. Pd. Associates (MLAT)	.69*	-.09	.05	.08	-.08	.22	.06	.08	.06	.56
20. Free Speech	.11	.05	.11	.35	.04	.24	.21	-.05	.50	.51

Table 5 (continued)

Final Rotated Factor Matrix for the *Maine French-American Study*

Variables	I	II	III	IV	V	VI	VII	VIII	IX	h²
21. FLCT - I	.18	-.31*	.13	.29	-.26	.24	.17	-.10	.22	.44
22. FLCT - II	.25	.02	.25	.10	-.16	.74*	.09	-.03	.05	.72
23. FLCT - III	.12	.03	.20	.27	-.24	.51*	.18	.02	.47*	.70
24. FLCT - IV	.27	.04	-.06	.30*	-.30*	.63*	.16	-.11	.15	.71
25. CFT - Reading	.15	.03	-.02	-.06	.85*	-.17	-.13	-.01	-.12	.82
26. CFT - Vocab.	.04	-.04	-.11	-.07	.83*	-.02	-.11	.01	-.04	.72
27. CFT - Grammar	.18	-.10	-.04	-.09	.80*	-.16	-.07	.05	-.03	.73
28. Self Fr. Skills	.33*	-.28	.36*	.08	-.03	.15	.15	-.37*	.31*	.60
29. Mother Fr. Skills	.07	.04	.02	.03	-.10	.12	.16	-.50*	-.02	.31
30. Phon. Accur.	.22	.20	.15	.55*	-.10	.35*	.26	.03	.19	.65
31. Linking	.09	.17	.11	.57*	-.25	.02	-.13	-.27	.10	.53
32. Stress	.09	-.09	.11	.82*	-.16	-.01	-.02	-.09	.16	.76
33. Rhythm	.20	.02	.06	.62*	.07	.19	.05	.09	.14	.49
34. Think in Fr./Eng.	.05	-.03	.71*	.03	-.08	.15	.15	.14	.16	.61
35. Prefer Speak Fr./Eng.	.04	-.13	.71*	.09	-.06	.02	.25	.03	.13	.62
36. Self Eng. Skills	.46*	-.06	-.08	.00	.04	-.06	.01	-.36*	.32*	.46
37. Word Compl. (Eng./Fr.)	.02	-.04	-.18	.11	.08	-.14	-.48*	.04	.02	.30
38. Word Detec. (Eng./Fr.)	.34*	.19	.11	-.12	-.15	.00	-.01	.51*	-.12	.48
39. Word Assns. (Eng./Fr.)	.07	.08	.29	.04	.00	-.42*	-.04	.35*	-.05	.40
40. Des. Live Fr.	-.06	.27	.02	.25	-.13	.14	-.01	-.22	-.07	.24
41. Phon. Discr.	.25	-.05	.01	.13	-.20	.11	-.03	-.07	.25	.21

Although the motivation system depicted is clearly pro-French, there are no indications (other than the self-ratings) that there is any special competence in French involved. Thus, a strong pro-French bias does not guarantee outstanding competence in French.

It is also true that a strong motivation and desire to learn French are no guarantee of outstanding performance. Factor VII, for instance, is dominated by large loadings of motivational intensity and desire to learn French (Vs. 8 and 9) and dominance in French over English (V. 37). None of the other indices of French achievement contributes to this factor, however.

Similarly, Factor IV makes it evident that certain students can develop outstanding proficiency in French without any particular attitudinal support. In Factor IV all of the linguistic measures of oral proficiency have heavy loadings (Vs. 30-33, 20) along with three tests of aural competence (Vs. 21, 23, and 24). This pattern of an out of the ordinary audio-lingual capacity is not related in any substantial way to measures of aptitude, attitude, or motivation.

Interestingly enough, an English-dominant, pro-American frame of mind is also no assurance of outstanding performance in English for these French-American young people, and seems to result in feelings of uncertainty concerning their competence in French. Factor VIII makes this point clear: those students with a strong English dominance (Vs. 38 and 39), whose family has little competence in French (Vs. 28 and 29), who see little instrumental value in studying French (V. 2), and who prefer America to France (V. 6) nonetheless feel incompetent in English (V. 36).

The several styles of adjusting to a bicultural heritage examined so far are essentially dysfunctional. What does account for individual differences in language competence for these French-American young people from Maine? Certain clues are found in Factors V and VI. Note that sex (V. 12) plays a prominent role in both factors. As we had suspected after our visits to the two parochial schools involved, the differences in approach to teaching French manifest themselves in the different skills developed by boys and girls. Factor VI displays the pattern of achievement skills of girls while Factor V reveals the achievement profile of boys. It is obvious in Factor VI that girls excel in aural skills (Vs. 22-24), phonetic accuracy (V. 30), and associational fluency in French (V. 39). Boys, in rather sharp contrast (see Factor V) excel in reading, vocabulary, and grammar (Vs. 25-27), but do poorly on at least one test of aural competence (V. 24). The boys characteristically prefer America to France (V. 6). Since this boy-girl contrast is independent of any of the MLAT subtests, we attribute the sex differences in performances to the teaching approaches emphasized in the two schools. The magnitude and clarity of the difference is highly instructive, and yet one wonders if the mode of instruction itself is the only influence at work or if the programs in the respective schools were adopted specifically to the interests of boys in one case and girls in the other. In other words, perhaps girls respond well to an audio-lingual form of language instruction because they are interested in interpersonal use of the French language, while boys may respond well to a more conventional type of instruction because they are interested mainly in developing passive skills in the language rather than making public their French background through audio-lingual use of the French language.

Factor IX presents us with a final set of clues as to the determinants of individual differences in language competence for the Maine French-American students. Factor IX is characterized by a motivation to learn French which is mainly instrumental rather than integrative in form (V. 14) and one that has strong parental support (V. 11). This family-wide realization of the social usefulness of French appears to have a particularly favorable impact on the young person's language competence and, ultimately, on his adjustment to the two cultures. Note that the profile includes a superior knowledge of English grammar (V. 18), a high level of proficiency in French free speech (V. 20), an above average competence in French aural skills (V. 23), and a feeling of confidence *both* in French (V. 28) *and* in English (V. 36).

Summary

This analysis was highly instructive for us. As we tried to sort out the various relationships between aptitude, attitudes, and achievement in French, we were continually struck by the way the attitudes and motives of these bicultural young people appear to influence the development of skills in both French and English. There is in other words substantial evidence here that the French-American's attitudes towards his own ethnolinguistic group and the surrounding American way of life can influence his French and English language development, in some cases resulting in a dominance of French over English, in other cases, a dominance of English over French, and in some cases full bilingual competence.

First we saw that the MLAT measures of language aptitude take on a different meaning when used with linguistic minority groups who have kept their native language alive. Thus the language aptitude tests for the Maine French-Americans became more sensitive as predictors of competence in English than in French (Factor I). But Factor I was complex because in the constellation attitudes were linked with aptitude, forcing the conclusion that the French-American adolescent with a good deal of language aptitude, demonstrated competence in English, and a nonethnocentric pro-French outlook will have a sense of confidence both in English and in French. Still we were somewhat apprehensive that these students might have more confidence than they should in their French skills, since there were few signs, apart from self-ratings, that they were above average in any of the features of French language competence tested.

Next, we saw that a particular configuration of attitudes can be dysfunctional to the language-learning process. Even though a French-American adolescent may be oriented to learn French for both integrative and instrumental reasons, he may actually do poorly in both French and English if he holds negative views of foreign peoples and ideas (Factor II). Because certain aptitude variables enter the cluster, it is not clear what the actual causal sequence is: whether the negative attitudes to foreign peoples hamper his language development in English and French or whether he lacks the necessary aptitude and then rationalizes his incompetence by adopting an undemocratic and ethnocentric outlook. It is evident in either case that the adjustments of allegiances involved are stressful ones.

Several types of adjustment were brought to light that seem to restrict the potentials of the French-American student. For example, a strong pro-French bias (including a tendency to think in French, to prefer speaking in French, to want to be identified as French) does not promote outstanding competence in the French language (Factor III). Nor does a strong motivation and desire to learn French necessarily promote language proficiency (Factor VII). Likewise, a strong pro-American frame of mind (including signs of English dominance over French, preference for American culture over France, and a lack of interest in learning French) does not automatically promote outstanding skill in English (Factor VIII). This type of French-American student, we found, felt insecure in his English competence. Thus, several modes of dealing with the bicultural demands made upon them were not effective for these French-Americans. We then re-asked the major question: What modes of adjustment do appear effective?

Several interesting and illuminating answers were suggested. One had to do with the style of language training emphasized in the two schools included in the Maine study: a girls' school that built its program around an audio-lingual philosophy of education, and a boys' school with a conventional language program, i.e., one that emphasized the development of the more passive skills. The profiles of Factors V and VI demonstrate the marked contrast in types of competence developed in the two cases. Girls have outstanding audio-lingual proficiency in French (Factor VI) while boys are above average in reading, vocabulary, and grammar proficiency (Factor V). Unfortunately, in this case, we cannot unravel the sex factor from the type of training emphasized, but this could easily be done in follow-up research. Our hunch is that the language programs at the two schools may have been arranged to satisfy different interest patterns of girls and boys. That is to say, French-American girls may want to keep the French language alive and active, while boys may be encouraged to develop the more passive (and less public) aspects of the language (boys we found stated a preference for the American culture over the French). The major point, however, is that some combination of the type of language instruction offered and the sex of the student seems to play a very important role in developing quite different profiles of skills in French.

Finally with Factor IX we saw perhaps the most efficient approach to a bicultural heritage: in this instance, the French-American student with a determined instrumental orientation toward French study who has strong parental support to do well appears to have demonstrable skill in various features of French proficiency and to feel confident of his competence in both French *and* English. It should be kept in mind that the instrumental form of motivation also takes on a different meaning when applied to a member of a linguistic minority group studying his own language (see *Reading Number Three*). For such a person an instrumental orientation means that he would find French useful in his work, in his schooling, etc. Thus, instrumental signifies practical or useful in this context, as it did for the Jewish students learning Hebrew in the Anisfeld-Lambert (1961) study. This point is important because a family-shared realization of the potential utility of French study seems to provide a comfortable adjustment to an otherwise disruptive cultural dilemma. Of all the various approaches that are attempted by these students, this one emerges as the most hopeful and encouraging. Compared to overplaying their Frenchness on the one hand or their Americanness on the other, both of which seem to be personally unsatisfactory, the family-supported instrumental approach seems to be much more than a simple compromise solution. Instead it provides a genuine opportunity to become both French and American.

The French-American Students: Comparisons and Contrasts

Many questions about the two French-American groups of students are still unanswered. For instance, we have had several indications that there are important differences in the degree of French competence between the Louisiana and Maine groups and in the opportunities each group has to be part of an active French community. Even though both groups, by definition, come from homes where French is a major language of communication, we have no idea as yet just how well the language is maintained from infancy on either in the home or in the subculture. One wonders too if there really is a French-speaking subculture in the Louisiana and Maine communities under study.

These are matters of major importance for anyone who is serious about revitalizing the linguistic resources of the country, or who sees the value of helping ethnic minority groups develop a sense of pride in their cultural background. To provide tentative answers to questions of this sort, we have reworked the data collected for the main analysis so that mean (or average) scores on the various measures can be compared. Although mean scores eradicate the vast differences among various subgroups of students, they do permit us to make a series of interesting and enlightening comparisons. First, we will compare the two French-American groups on each of the measures, and then each French-American group with the corresponding group of American students living in the same Louisiana and Maine communities. These comparisons will give us a different look at how far French-Americans have come in capitalizing on opportunities to be bicultural, and how far they have yet to go.

Comparisons of Louisiana and Maine Groups

There is no doubt that important differences do exist between the two groups of French-Americans not only with respect to training in the French language and degree of bilinguality but also with regard to the degree of assimilation. The comparisons of the two groups on the various measures are given in Table 6. Note first (in Comparison 1, Table 6) that the Maine group not only has a great deal more formal instruction in French, but it also has more opportunities to learn and use French in the home, since the parents in Maine are generally better skilled in French and give more encouragement to their children to learn French (Comparisons 19, 20, and 51). Although the two groups have similar numbers of French-speaking friends (Comparison 55), it is very likely that more French is spoken among friends in Maine than in Louisiana. Furthermore, the Maine students enjoy being with other French-Americans more than do those from Louisiana (Comparison 52).

Still there is no difference in attitudes towards French-Americans (Comparison 45) or toward the American culture (Comparison 44), meaning that neither group shows a real preference for America over France. They also are alike in their desire and motivation to learn French (Comparisons 47 and 48) and neither shows a preference for speaking French over English (Comparison 32). There are also no differences between Louisiana and Maine groups in authoritariansim, ethnocentrism, or anomie (Comparisons 41-43). The major contrast appears to center on the social atmosphere of the two settings, the Maine community being apparently more actively French. It is noteworthy in fact that the Louisiana community has been able to sustain a strong motivation to learn French and a favorable attitude toward their own group with relatively less family and subculture support.

The Maine students see much more clearly the instrumental value of knowing French (Comparison 40), are more confident in their proficiency in the language (Comparison 18), and do more of their thinking in French (Comparison 31) even though they do not receive more reinforcements for speaking French (Comparison 33). The evaluative reactions to European French-speaking people are also more favorable in Maine (Comparison 46), though the Maine students are no more interested in living in France (Comparison 36).

Table 6

Comparisons of French-American Students from Louisiana and Maine

Variables	Louisiana French-Americans Mean	Variance	Maine French-Americans Mean	Variance	df	t-tests*
1) Years of French Study at School	1.05	0.11	9.91	0.36	186	-124.81
2) MLAT, Number Learning	19.82	73.22	19.08	93.21	183	0.34
3) MLAT, Phonetic Script	17.73	14.48	20.07	17.63	183	-3.95•
4) MLAT, Spelling Clues	6.20	13.77	6.71	17.78	178	-0.86
5) MLAT, Wds. in Sentences	13.42	33.56	15.35	37.29	182	-2.19•
6) MLAT, Paired Associates	12.42	24.90	13.35	36.50	183	-1.13
7) Phonetic Discrimination (r = 0-30)	17.02	13.25	18.38	11.33	183	-2.62•
8) Free Speech in French (r = 0-12)	6.01	4.37	7.72	4.42	161	-5.18•
9) FLCT, Part I	4.55	3.04	8.25	1.94	182	-16.13•
10) FLCT, Part II	5.61	3.72	8.28	1.67	184	-11.17•
11) FLCT, Part III	5.58	3.04	8.36	2.98	180	-10.73•
12) FLCT, Part IV	4.45	4.86	8.88	4.96	184	-13.45•
13) Reading Fluency (ms = 14; np = 8)	4.96	2.30	6.82	4.74	112	-3.59•
14) CFT, Reading	17.51	67.96	33.00	67.28	176	-12.48•
15) CFT, Vocabulary	14.51	25.54	28.67	42.18	176	-16.00•
16) CFT, Grammar	12.88	17.34	22.61	25.15	176	-13.90•

Table 6 (Continued)

Comparisons of French-American Students from Louisiana and Maine

Variables	Louisiana French-Americans		Maine French-Americans			t-tests*
	Mean	Variance	Mean	Variance	df	
17) Pronunciation Accuracy (ms=14; np=8)	5.49	2.96	6.61	2.33	112	-5.62•
18) Own French Skills (n=5-20)	14.54	5.71	16.66	7.35	178	-5.49•
19) Mother's Fr. Skills (n=4-16)	12.40	4.69	14.54	7.35	169	-5.61•
20) Father's Fr. Skills (n=4-16)	12.14	5.51	13.81	10.61	154	-3.60•
21) Type of Accent European/Fr. American (Eur. ms=14; Fr. Am. ms=2)	7.75	1.24	3.32	1.40	112	20.18•
22) Phonetic Accuracy (ms = 5)	1.96	.75	4.19	.37	170	-19.50•
23) Linking (ms = 5)	1.59	.39	2.70	.27	170	-12.61•
24) Stress (ms = 5)	1.80	.23	2.81	.20	170	-14.25•
25) Rhythm (ms = 5)	1.37	.31	2.56	.40	170	-12.97•
26) Nasalization (ms = 5)	1.42	.29	1.87	.12	170	-6.55•
27) Own English Skills (n = 5-20)	17.87	4.83	18.00	4.18	173	-0.41
28) Word Completion (Eng/Fr) (np = 30)	36.47	42.40	36.44	51.83	174	0.03
29) Word Detection (Eng/Fr) (np = 30)	39.53	23.73	36.46	27.19	177	4.04•
30) Word Association (Eng/Fr) (np = 30)	37.13	49.74	35.74	24.19	168	-1.51
31) Thinking in Fr/Eng (n = 1 (Eng) 7(Fr))	2.08	1.81	3.37	2.17	172	-5.95•
32) French Pref. Language (r = 1(Eng), 7(Fr))	2.63	3.47	3.11	2.89	171	-1.77

Table 6 (Continued)

Comparisons of French-American Students from Louisiana and Maine

Variables	Louisiana French-Americans		Maine French-Americans			t-tests*
	Mean	Variance	Mean	Variance	df	
33) Reinforcements for Speaking Standard French (r = 0-18)	11.92	7.99	11.87	7.24	128	0.10
34) Reference to Self as French, for English people (1=Am; 2=Fr; 3=Fr.Am)	1.43	.59	2.32	.84	174	-6.90•
35) Reference to Self as French, for French people (1=Am; 2=Fr; 3=Fr.Am)	1.57	.61	2.38	.80	175	-6.29•
36) Desire to Live in France (ms=14; np=8)	7.97	11.62	7.95	11.07	166	0.05
37) Integrative Orientation to Learning English (ms=28; np=16)	23.11	20.77	23.13	17.37	173	-0.03
38) Instrumental Orientation to Learning English (ms=28; np=16)	22.23	21.74	22.79	19.59	173	-0.80
39) Integrative Orientation to Learning French (ms=28; np=16)	22.21	23.65	21.39	21.92	170	1.11
40) Instrumental Orientation to Learning French (ms=28; np=16)	18.19	31.04	21.66	22.78	171	-4.39•
41) Anomie (ms=84; np=48)	43.07	125.56	41.37	14.61	164	0.92
42) F-Scale (ms=91; np=52)	56.30	93.79	67.09	100.09	164	-0.51

Table 6 (Continued)

Comparisons of French-American Students from Louisiana and Maine

Variables	Louisiana French-Americans		Maine French-Americans			t-tests*
	Mean	Variance	Mean	Variance	df	
43) Ethnocentrism (ms=49; np=28)	32.45	69.58	34.18	43.00	164	-1.48
44) Preference for America/France (np = 36)	34.97	11.76	37.07	78.17	164	-1.36
45) Attitudes to French-Americans (ms=112; np=64)	87.69	23.44	86.28	20.95	149	0.58
46) Voice Study: Eng./Eur. French (np = 0)	0.28	0.05	0.03	0.04	184	2.51*
47) Motivational Intensity (ms=18; np=12)	13.38	4.58	12.89	5.61	173	1.42
48) Desire to Learn French (ms=24; np=16)	21.51	18.66	21.31	20.73	170	0.28
49) Social Inquisitiveness (ms=32; np=20)	19.70	10.26	19.35	11.81	170	0.69
50) Sensitivity for Others (ms=56; np=32)	33.45	44.13	37.30	29.18	180	-2.06*
51) Parental Encouragement to Learn French (ms=7; np=4)	5.41	3.23	5.93	1.86	176	-2.18*
52) Liking Eng. Friends vs. Liking Fr. Friends (np = 10)	9.76	0.94	10.08	0.69	174	-2.36*
53) Desire for French Identity (r = 8-44)	37.61	58.81	34.46	45.59	175	2.89*
54) Voice Study: English/ Am. French (np=0)	0.14	0.04	-0.03	0.03	184	1.91
55) Number of Fr. Friends	1.96	0.04	1.96	0.04	176	0.17

*Positive entries mean that Louisiana Ss Score higher, minus means Maine Ss score higher. Entries of 2.00 or more are reliable at the .05 level of confidence, or better.

Note: r = range of possible scores; ms = maximum score possible on measure; np = neutral point on scale.

The Louisiana students are more anxious for French identity (Comparison 53), suggesting that by comparison they miss not being part of a vital French subculture. Compared with the Maine students, they are much less likely to refer to themselves as French when asked about their ethnic background by either English-speaking or other French-speaking people (Comparisons 34 and 35). In addition, their style of French speech is markedly less French than is that of the Maine group. In fact, their accent (Comparison 21) has no French characteristics to speak of (whereas the Maine group has a distinctive French-American accent) and, from a linguistic point of view, their speech in French is notably poorer in phonetic accuracy, proper linking, stress, rhythm, and nasalization (Comparisons 17 and 22-26).

It is not only the speech style that differentiates the two groups, however. The free speech and reading fluency of the Maine students (Comparisons 8 and 13), their skill in the more passive aspects of French (Comparisons 14-16), and their comprehension of spoken French (Comparisons 9-12) are all significantly better than those of the Louisiana French students. This superior skill in French has not apparently made them feel any less proficient in English, for they rate themselves as highly competent in English skills (Comparison 27) and they value a knowledge of English to the same degree as the Louisiana students (Comparisons 37 and 38). They apparently are more balanced in their bilingual skills than are the Louisiana students, who show more of an English language dominance on one of our measures of bilinguality (Comparison 29). The Maine students have had more varied experiences in languages (standard French at school from an earlier age, American French at home, and English in the community), and this may well have contributed to their better performance in making phonemic distinctions in French and in sensing grammatical differences in English-based tests, as noted in Comparisons 7, 3, and 5 even though there are no differences in language aptitude tests that do not depend on particular English skills (Comparisons 2 and 6).

Summary

In summary, these comparisons indicate that the French-American students from Maine are participants in a subculture which transmits its linguistic and cultural legacy more effectively than the French community in Louisiana has been able to do. In fact, the pattern of comparisons suggests that the French tradition in Louisiana is merging more rapidly with the general American culture than is the case for the Maine communities studied. There are important historical factors that contribute to this regional difference. For example, Maine continues to be a New England receiving center for French-Canadians who immigrate to the United States, and its proximity to French Canada means that they can keep a communication link with French Canada through television and radio. Louisiana in contrast is more outside the French-Canadian and European. French orbits of influence. This fact makes it all the more striking that the Louisiana students' motivations to learn French and their attitudes toward their cultural background remain stubbornly favorable.

Being a visibly cohesive subculture, however, must have an impact on the community as a whole. We sense this, because the attitudes of the English-speaking American students in Maine are not as favorable as those of the Louisiana Americans (see Comparison 7 in Tables 7 and 8). This implies that in the Maine communities investigated here, English-speaking people may view the French-Americans with somewhat more suspicion, perhaps because they seem so determined to maintain their identity. At the same time, the attitudes in the Louisiana communities studied appear to be very favorable for any attempts to revive the French tradition, it would seem.

Nonetheless, there are many factors working together in the Maine setting. There is stronger family support for the transmission of the culture, and a school system providing more extensive experience with the language. As a consequence, the Maine French-American students are more skilled in all aspects of French and more ready to think of themselves as French, as though they were more proud of their ethnic background. And what is most important, they are at the same time more confident and apparently more competent in English than their counterparts in Louisiana.

Comparisons of French-American and American Students

We have just seen that the Maine group of French-American students are far superior to the Louisiana group in French proficiency. One wonders, in fact, if those from Louisiana are actually any different in French skills from the non-French students with only school training in French. Likewise, just how good are the Maine students compared to non-French students from the same area?

To answer these questions, comparisons were made between French-American and American students on those measures common to both groups. In Table 7, Louisiana French-American students are compared with American students studying French at the first and second year high school levels and in Table 8, Maine French-Americans are compared with American students finishing their first, second, or third year of high school French. (In Maine, it will be recalled, three years of French are offered at high school while in Louisiana only two years are offered.)

First we notice certain consistent differences between both groups of French-American students and their American counterparts. In both regions, the French-American students are definitely more aware of the integrative and the instrumental value of learning French (Comparisons 1 and 2 in Tables 7 and 8) since for them French proficiency means maintaining ties with family, community, and linguistic birthright. Nevertheless, they do not show any greater motivation or desire to learn French (Comparisons 8 and 9) nor do they receive any more parental encouragement to learn the language (Comparison 12) than do American students. This discrepancy between the value placed on a knowledge of French and the degree of motivation to learn the language merits special attention in future research. For the French-American students, the value of knowing the language seems to outweigh the motivation to learn it. This may mean that they foresee the possible social conflicts that could arise if French became their dominant language. For the American students, the value of knowing the language is more in line with the motivation to learn, both falling about at the neutral point.

Both groups of French-American students also differ from the American students in attitudinal dispositions. For instance, the French-Americans are significantly more anomic, authoritarian, and ethnocentric (Comparisons 3, 4, and 5 in Tables 7 and 8). They are also definitely more favorable to the French-American culture than are American students, at the same time as they show a stronger preference for the American to the European French way of life (Comparisons 7 and 6), suggesting that they may be confused about their real allegiances. The fact that they show a stronger preference for America over France than the American students is of particular significance. The overall pattern of the French-Americans' attitudes, when compared to that of the American students, is one of ethnocentric anomie and confusion of allegiances.

Although the French-Americans express as much sensitivity for others as do American students (Comparison 11) they are noticeably less outgoing and socially inquisitive than Americans (Comparison 10). This social reserve is consistent with our hypothesis that they may be self-conscious about their ethnic distinctiveness.

Most of the comparisons on the Modern Language Aptitude Test (Comparisons 19-23) show that both French-American groups perform much more poorly than the American students. This very pronounced difference is likely due to the form and content of the MLAT which presupposes a native facility with English. It also demonstrates how cautious one must be in attempting to measure the intellectual or verbal abilities of linguistic minority groups with tests developed and standardized for use with monolingual subjects.

With regard to oral and aural proficiency in French, however, one reads a different story. From Table 8 we see that the Maine French-Americans are way ahead of all three American subgroups on all measures of oral skill (Comparisons 13-18), with one exception, while in Louisiana, the French-American students generally perform no better or poorer than the American students (Table 7, Comparisons 13-18 and 28-30). The Louisiana French-Americans, for example, perform no better than the American students on tests of phonetic accuracy, linking, and stress, or reading fluency. Even their accent is judged as no more French in style than is that of the American students. They are in fact

Table 7

Comparison of Louisiana French-Americans and Louisiana American Students
With One or Two Years of French Training

	French-American Students		American Students Level I		Level II		t-tests*			
	Mean	Variance	Mean	Variance	Mean	Variance	A-B	df	A-C	df
	(A)		(B)		(C)					
1) Integrative Rating (ms=28; np=16)	22.21	23.65	16.79	22.93	16.92	27.08	6.79•	147	4.54•	100
2) Instrumental Rating (ms=28; np=16)	18.19	31.04	12.44	16.30	13.21	20.08	7.12•	148	3.97•	101
3) Anomie (ms=84; np=48)	43.07	125.56	31.42	95.32	30.13	44.53	6.58•	142	5.31•	97
4) F-Scale (ms=91; np=52)	66.31	93.79	61.59	82.36	58.96	131.88	2.99•	142	3.06•	97
5) Ethnocentrism (ms=49; np=28)	32.45	69.58	29.17	40.72	28.08	42.16	2.61•	142	2.32•	97
6) Preference for Am/Fr. (np=36)	34.97	117.62	29.48	69.61	27.13	71.94	3.36•	142	3.21•	97
7) Attitudes to French-Americans (ms=112; np=64)	87.69	234.40	78.63	226.47	80.91	256.72	3.41•	131	1.75	85
8) Motivational Intensity (ms=18; np=12)	13.38	4.58	12.54	4.90	12.88	6.69	2.38•	150	0.96	103

Table 7 (Continued)

Comparison of Louisiana French-Americans and Louisiana American Students With One or Two Years of French Training

	French-American Students		American Students Level I		Level II		t-tests*			
	Mean (A)	Variance	Mean (B)	Variance	Mean (C)	Variance	A-B	df	A-C	df
9) Desire to Learn Fr. (ms=24; np=16)	21.51	18.66	21.96	10.07	20.96	13.46	-0.72	148	0.56	101
10) Social Inquisitiveness (ms=32; np=20)	19.70	10.26	21.04	7.65	21.29	7.54	-2.72*	149	-2.18*	102
11) Sensitivity for Others (ms=56; np=32)	35.45	44.13	37.10	41.32	38.09	29.04	-1.55	153	-1.74	106
12) Parental Encouragement to Learn French (ms=7; np=4)	5.41	3.23	5.35	2.81	4.88	4.44	0.21	151	1.21	103
13) Phonetic Accuracy (ms=5)	1.96	.75	1.96	.51	2.00	.21	0.00	148	-.18	98
14) Linking (ms=5)	1.59	.39	1.49	.42	1.63	.44	.95	148	-.24	98
15) Stress (ms=5)	1.80	.23	1.76	.24	1.89	.20	.43	148	-.75	98
16) Rhythm (ms=5)	1.37	.31	1.71	.26	1.78	.27	-3.84*	148	-2.97*	98
17) Nasalization (ms=5)	1.42	.29	1.03	.09	1.11	.09	5.33*	148	2.42	98

Table 7 (continued)

Comparison of Louisiana French-Americans and Louisiana American Students With One or Two Years of French Training

	French-American Students		American Students Level I		American Students Level II		t-tests*			
	Mean (A)	Variance	Mean (B)	Variance	Mean (C)	Variance	A-B	df	A-C	df
18) Free Speech (r = 0-12)	6.01	4.37	4.85	5.60	7.47	3.93	3.05*	139	-2.70*	89
19) MLAT, Number Learning	19.82	73.22	19.64	80.12	21.46	49.16	0.13	158	-0.86	110
20) MLAT, Phonetic Script	17.73	14.45	20.18	17.31	22.63	15.57	-3.87*	158	-5.50*	110
21) MLAT, Spelling Clues	6.20	13.77	10.24	39.12	15.96	61.04	-5.02*	157	-8.57*	109
22) MLAT, Wds. in Sentences	13.42	33.56	20.49	64.99	27.63	62.82	-6.40*	158	-9.69*	110
23) MLAT, Paired Associates	12.42	24.90	15.92	34.99	19.17	26.47	-4.03*	158	-5.78*	110
24) FLCT, Part I	4.55	3.04	5.94	4.66	7.89	1.88	-4.40*	152	-7.59*	104
25) FLCT, Part II	5.61	3.72	2.84	2.29	4.25	2.40	9.59*	152	2.83*	104

Table 7 (continued)

Comparison of Louisiana French-Americans and Louisiana American Students
With One or Two Years of French Training

	French-American Students		American Students				t-tests*			
			Level I		Level II					
	Mean	Variance	Mean	Variance	Mean	Variance	A-B	df	A-C	df
	(A)		(B)		(C)					
26) FLCT, Part III	5.58	3.04	3.52	2.86	4.56	3.02	7.32*	152	2.25*	104
27) FLCT, Part IV	4.45	4.86	2.63	1.90	5.01	3.78	5.86*	152	-0.99	104
28) Pronunciation Accuracy (ms=14; np=8)	5.49	2.96	5.82	4.32	6.73	5.98	-1.03	137	-2.38*	87
29) Reading Fluency (ms=14; np=8)	4.96	2.30	4.88	2.71	5.47	3.20	.30	137	-1.19	87
30) Accent: Eur/ Fr. Am. (Eur, ms=14; Fr. Am, ms=2)	7.75	1.24	8.04	1.52	7.68	3.58	-1.45	137	.19	87

*Positive entries indicate that the French-American Ss obtained the higher scores on the variable when compared with each of the groups of English-American Ss. With degrees of freedom (df) of these magnitudes, a t-test entry of 2.00 or greater is reliable at the .05 level of confidence, or better.

Note: r=range of scores; ms=maximum score possible; np=neutral point on scale.

Table 8

Comparison of Maine French-American and Maine American Students
With One, Two or Three years of French Training

	French American Students		American Students Level I		Level II		Level III		t-tests*		
	Mean (A)	Variance	Mean (B)	Variance	Mean (C)	Variance	Mean (D)	Variance	A–B	A–C	A–D
1) Integrative Rating (ms=25; np=16)	21.39	21.92	15.07	27.77	15.86	23.67	15.14	21.71	8.20*	5.86*	6.25*
2) Instrumental Rating (ms=25; np=16)	21.66	22.78	13.17	30.41	13.40	11.44	10.34	16.92	10.65*	9.32*	11.42*
3) Anomie (ms=84; np=48)	41.37	146.12	32.37	61.32	34.80	106.78	32.69	58.56	5.49*	2.82*	3.61*
4) F-Scale (ms=91; np=52)	67.10	100.08	60.47	81.02	56.00	184.57	56.66	73.81	4.42*	4.98*	5.02*
5) Ethnocentrism (ms=49; np=28)	34.18	43.00	29.96	63.45	25.66	82.91	24.18	45.29	3.72*	5.78*	6.95*
6) Preference for America/France (np=36)	37.07	78.17	26.03	68.78	23.70	50.88	22.79	40.58	8.15*	7.75*	7.99*
7) Attitudes to Fr.-Americans (ms=112; np=64)	86.28	209.50	74.07	259.38	70.57	230.04	68.85	258.42	4.97*	5.01*	5.26*
8) Motivational Intensity (ms=18; np=12)	12.89	5.61	12.68	5.06	12.15	6.98	12.33	5.63	0.60	1.49	1.07

Table 8 (continued)

Comparison of Maine French-American and Maine American Students
With One, Two or Three Years of French Training

	French American Students		American Students Level I		Level II		Level III		t-tests*		
	Mean (A)	Variance	Mean (B)	Variance	Mean (C)	Variance	Mean (D)	Variance	A–B	A–C	A–D
9) Desire to Learn French (ms=24; np=16)	21.31	20.73	20.97	15.60	20.94	17.25	20.83	16.56	0.50	0.41	0.51
10) Social Inquisitiveness (ms=32; np=20)	19.35	11.81	20.82	8.69	21.81	9.64	20.68	6.93	-2.91•	-3.50•	-1.87•
11) Sensitivity for Others (ms=56; np=32)	37.30	29.18	37.77	31.83	36.49	61.56	32.28	43.44	-0.56	0.67	-0.80
12) Parental Encouragement to learn French (ms=7; np=4)	5.93	1.86	4.92	2.97	5.51	3.05	5.41	2.45	4.23•	1.41	1.71
13) Phonet. Accuracy (ms=5)	4.19	.37	1.75	.73	2.41	.79	3.09	.78	20.85•	11.98•	6.94•
14) Linking (ms=5)	2.70	.27	1.41	.54	1.72	.61	2.34	.23	12.74•	7.63•	2.93•
15) Stress (ms=5)	2.81	.20	1.52	.46	1.66	.36	2.39	.33	14.37•	11.07•	3.80•
16) Rhythm (ms=5)	2.56	.40	1.26	.32	1.52	.39	2.26	.45	13.21•	7.70•	1.98
17) Nasalization (ms=5)	1.87	.12	1.04	.13	1.27	.20	1.43	.25	14.55•	7.49•	4.90

Table 8 (continued)

Comparison of Maine French-American and Maine American Students With One, Two or Three Years of French Training

	French-American Students		American Students Level I		Level II		Level III		t-tests*		
	Mean (A)	Variance	Mean (B)	Variance	Mean (C)	Variance	Mean (D)	Variance	A–B	A–C	A–D
18) Free Speech (r=0-12)	7.72	4.42	4.37	5.82	7.06	5.65	7.21	3.47	9.24•	1.41	1.05
19) MLAT, Number Learning	19.08	93.21	25.13	92.92	28.20	87.53	33.97	61.21	-4.05•	-4.79•	-7.53•
20) MLAT, Phonetic Script	20.07	17.63	21.01	15.77	23.29	9.58	24.48	14.66	-1.48	-4.11•	-5.02•
21) MLAT, Spelling Clues	6.71	17.78	10.53	34.44	11.86	35.89	19.45	66.04	-4.87•	-5.40•	-10.98•
22) MLAT, Words in Sentences	15.35	37.29	21.40	54.11	23.86	44.12	29.97	49.96	-3.84•	-6.83•	-10.78•
23) MLAT, Paired Associates	13.35	36.50	14.05	29.94	16.11	29.07	18.66	25.74	0.78	-2.37•	-4.26•
24) FLCT, Part I	8.25	1.94	5.63	4.20	6.40	2.86	8.29	2.28	9.70•	6.17•	-0.13
25) FLCT, Part II	8.28	1.67	2.17	3.45	3.56	3.12	5.92	3.83	24.94•	16.11•	7.38•
26) FLCT, Part III	8.36	2.98	2.04	2.62	3.62	3.29	4.95	5.40	23.58•	16.99•	8.26•
27) FLCT, Part IV	8.88	4.96	2.84	3.21	3.56	2.18	6.70	5.88	18.58•	12.55•	4.39•

*Positive entries indicate that the French group scores higher on any particular variable and minus entries indicate the converse. In general, at t-value of 2.00 or larger is reliable at the .05 level of confidence. Degrees of freedom range from 155 to 170 for A–B comparisons, from 118 to 130 for A–C comparisons, and from 111 to 124 for A–D comparisons.

poorer on measures of rhythm and accuracy of pronunciation, and the one case where they perform better than the American students is on the measure of nasalization.

The one exception referred to above has to do with measures of French free speech. Both groups of French-Americans are rated at about the same level or below the American students on this test. Our hunch is that this apparent inadequacy is due to the social reserve noted in Comparison 10, and to a feeling of embarrassment when asked to speak naturally—that is, in their French-American style—while in a school setting. The examiners in both settings commented on this "shyness" or "embarrassment" when French-Americans were asked to complete the sentences for the free speech test. J. L. Tisch (1959) also refers to the French-Americans' "sense of shame" about their style of French.

Both groups of French-Americans perform better than the American students on the tests of French Listening Comprehension (Comparisons 24-27) except for Part I, which measures a form of phonetic discrimination. This general superiority in listening comprehension, however, is again more pronounced for the Maine than the Louisiana French-Americans. In fact, the more advanced American students in Louisiana score at about the same level as the Louisiana French-Americans on Part IV of the FLCT, that part which measures comprehension of complex discussions in French.

Two facts about the American students are noteworthy: (1) they show definite stepwise increases in proficiency from year to year on the oral and aural tests, and (2) they have more of an integrative than an instrumental orientation to the study of French.

Summary

In summary, these comparisons highlight important differences in attitudes of French-American and American students. We found that the French-Americans are more anomic, authoritarian, and ethnocentric than American students, and although more sympathetic to the French-American culture, they nevertheless express a strong preference for the American over the European French way of life. The pattern gives one the impression again that French-American young people are caught up in a very meaningful conflict of allegiances involving the two facets of their cultural background.

Both groups of French-Americans are decidedly poorer than the American students on the MLAT, indicating once more how difficult it is to get a true reading of the aptitudes of ethnic minority groups when one uses tests standardized for monolingual and monocultural subjects.

Both French-American groups, however, are generally superior to American students in French comprehension skills even though the Maine group of

French-Americans is superior to the Louisiana group in this respect. In French oral proficiency, the Maine group is markedly superior to American students, whereas the Louisiana group is no better than and in some respects inferior to the American students. The superiority of French-Americans in oral skills, however, does not include spontaneous speaking in French. On our test of free speech (which measures the complexity and accuracy of spontaneous speech), neither group of French-Americans showed any superiority over American students. This we interpret as likely due to their shyness and embarrassment in using their own style of French in a school setting.

Thus, it has become even more evident in this analysis that it is not easy to grow up being both French and American in an American community. Still we have seen throughout this investigation a very healthy resistance to giving up one's identity, even part of it. The ingenuity of French-Americans in making various sorts of adjustments to their dual nationality has been the highlight of the investigation. Many of these adjustment strategies prove to be ineffective and unsatisfying while others appear to be extremely comfortable and functional, especially those that permit these young people to be themselves in all respects, French *and* American, skilled in French *and* English.

The fact that the attitudes of the American students toward the French-American people and their culture are favorable is especially encouraging. Perhaps we can place our hope in the current adolescent group who want so desperately to improve and change the American society. They may be more prone to share our belief that French-Americans will be better Americans if they have social support for being French as well. However, as we shall see in the next chapter, American students still hold pejorative stereotypes about French-speaking people that counteract their favorable attitudes. Thus, there is little place for complacency it seems; the recognition, understanding, and social support so important to ethnic minority groups cannot yet be taken for granted.

Chapter Five

Students' Stereotypes of French-Speaking People

We have just seen certain signs of hope for the maintenance of the languages and cultures of American ethnic minority groups. The measured attitudes of the young people in all three American settings appear to be open and friendly toward French-Americans. Standard attitude measures, however, have well-recognized limitations in the sense that the true feelings of a respondent are tempered by what he feels one should express publicly about private feelings. This is not to belittle their usefulness or their validity, quite to the contrary (cf. Triandis, 1971). In the present studies we have found wide variations in measured attitudes and the attitudes fall into consistent relationships from setting to setting. But because attitude measures are known to be affected by group norms of opinion or standards of expected reactions, and because the issue at hand is so important, we decided to look more deeply into the stereotypes students have of French-speaking people. Programs aimed at improving the status of minority groups require as full an understanding as possible of how members of that group are actually thought of and perceived. Programs of language training could also be made more effective in light of such information, we believe.

The method we chose for this purpose was developed in an earlier research study (Lambert, Hodgson, Gardner, and Fillenbaum, 1960) and is referred to as the "matched-guise" technique of eliciting stereotypes (see also Anisfeld and Lambert, 1964; Anisfeld, Bogo, and Lambert, 1962; Lambert, Tucker, and Frankel, 1966; Preston, 1963; Lambert, Anisfeld, and Yeniyk-Komshian, 1965; Lambert, 1967). The basic study is presented as *Reading Number Seven* in Appendix C.

The procedure stems from a very simple notion: hearing the flow of a foreign language evokes in the mind of the listener certain attitudinal reactions that have become associated with the particular foreign people who habitually use that language. The association may have been established through direct experience with members of the group or indirectly through attitudes picked up from important people in one's social environment who in turn may have had little or no direct experience with the group in question. If we were to ask listeners to give spontaneously their evaluations of the person whose voice is being heard we would likely capture their stereotypes of the language-group represented, that is to say, their attitudinal reactions associated with those people who characteristically use that language. This is especially likely if, unbeknown to the listeners, they also gave their reactions to the *very same speaker* who on another occasion presented the identical message in English. Thus, if we could compare the reactions to the matched guises of bilingual speakers, we would have a fairly good view of the stereotypes involved.

In the present case, of course, we are interested in how American high school students react to and perceive French-speaking in comparison with English-speaking people. With that purpose in mind we asked all three groups of American students and the two French-American groups to participate in the following way. They listened to tape recordings of the voices of "eight speakers," all male, some reading in English and others in either standard French or Canadian-style French. Linguists advised us that the Canadian-style French was very similar to that spoken by certain French-Americans in Louisiana and by most French-Americans in Maine. We will, for convenience, refer to this as the French-American style from here on. As they listened to a speaker reading a passage, the students were asked to ignore the language being used and the content of his talk and instead to imagine what type of person the speaker was, whether tall or short, good-looking or not, dependable or not, intelligent or stupid, likable or unlikable, etc., as we all do when we hear a strange voice over the telephone or hear someone talking outside our line of view. Listeners were asked to rate the personality traits of each speaker, using 6-point rating scales that ranged, for example, from very little generosity to very much, etc. The first speaker might be English-speaking and the second French-speaking with a European French accent, reading a French translation of the same passage. Separate rating sheets were provided for the evaluation of each speaker's personality characteristics.

In order to control for real personality differences between speakers, perfect English-French bilinguals played the roles of two speakers so that actually the voices of only four *people* were used in the recordings, each speaking once in American-style English and once in one or the other of the two styles of French. We were then able to compare the estimates of personality traits evoked by each speaker as he used alternately his English and French guises.

Of major concern to us at this point are the types of stereotypes American young people have of people who normally speak French. If our aim is to encourage students to learn another cultural group's language and if attitudes toward the other group can appreciably affect one's motivation to learn that language, than an investigation of students' stereotypes of speakers of that language may illuminate some of the troubles encountered in developing second-language proficiency. In Tables 9 and 10 we present the average evaluations ascribed to the two French-American speakers in one case and to the two standard French speakers in the other. Each entry in the table is a t-test result, reflecting the downgrading or upgrading of the French relative to the English guises. When the entry is positive, it indicates that the English guises are rated higher (i.e., more favorably in most cases) on a particular trait. Negative entries indicate that the French guises are rated higher on that trait. When underlined, the entry is statistically significant at beyond the .05 level of confidence, using two-tailed tests of significance.

Results for the American Students

The American students from Louisiana view the speakers of standard French as less honest, less dependable, and less reliable than speakers of English. There is also a trend to perceive them as shorter, less intelligent, and less stable than when they speak in English. At the same time, the standard French speakers are considered more humorous and entertaining. For the Louisiana students, American-French speakers are seen as shorter, less thoughtful, less honest, less generous, and less kind, at the same time as they are thought to have somewhat more leadership qualities, more self-confidence, more ambition, more character, and to be more nervous. In this context, these apparently complimentary traits may signify a type of bossiness or cockiness in the minds of the listeners, making it difficult to determine whether or not they meant to balance negative traits with positive ones.

The American students in Maine view persons speaking standard French as shorter, less leaderlike, less thoughtful, less intelligent, less honest, less self-confident, less dependable, less generous, less kind, less reliable, less ambitious, less stable, and with less character than English Speakers (Table 9). Although we are generalizing here from only two representatives of standard French speakers, there is, nonetheless, an unmistakably pejorative set of stereotypes of European French people in the thinking of these students. The only exception is that the standard French speakers are viewed as having more humor and in this context, humor may signify ridiculous or comical. However, no reliable differences emerged between the French and English guises for attractiveness, friendliness, entertainingness, nervousness, sociability, or general likability.

Table 9

American Students' Evaluations of Speakers of French and English*

Trait Judged	Louisiana Students' Judgments of Speakers of		Maine Students' Judgments of Speakers of		Connecticut Students' Judgments of Speakers of	
	Stand. Fr. (n=101)	Am. Fr. (n=101)	Stand. Fr. (N=144)	Am. Fr. (N=68)	Stand. Fr. (N=118)	Am. Fr. (N=114)
Height	1.93	2.14•	5.35•	2.42•	1.31	2.49•
Good Looks	0.16	1.23	0.16	4.67•	-1.85	-0.48
Leadership	0.88	-1.95	3.75•	-2.80•	1.40	-2.66•
Thoughtfulness	1.69	2.62•	5.37•	1.61	4.21•	0.40
Sense of Humor	-4.50•	-0.91	-4.58•	0.97	-3.62•	-1.44
Intelligence	1.92	-1.15	5.63•	-1.17	2.58•	-1.80
Honesty	4.04•	4.31•	6.90•	2.01•	5.29•	2.60•
Self-confidence	-0.99	-4.87•	2.09•	-4.60•	0.38	-5.77•
Friendliness	-1.34	1.49	-0.63	1.63	-0.99	1.61
Dependability	3.68•	1.71	7.16•	0.91	3.79•	-0.75
Generosity	1.19	2.06•	3.91•	1.56	2.84•	2.23•
Entertainingness	-3.71•	-1.97	-0.86	-1.34	-3.91•	-2.46•
Nervousness	-0.12	-3.54•	1.32	-3.00•	-1.35	-4.85•
Kindness	0.44	2.12•	3.63•	2.12•	3.92•	2.78•
Reliability	2.18•	-0.46	5.82•	0.59	2.79•	0.84
Ambition	0.80	-2.39•	4.82•	-1.86	0.50	-1.63
Sociability	-1.33	-1.58	0.56	-0.44	-2.61•	-1.65
Stability	1.86	-1.69	3.88•	-1.01	3.18•	-1.58
Character	0.47	-2.20•	2.53•	0.32	3.35•	0.69
General Likability	0.59	-0.16	1.37	1.29	0.11	0.39

*Entries are t-values derived from the application of the t-test, a statistical procedure used to test the significance of differences between group means. Values that are marked with a black dot (•) are statistically significant. A positive value means that the English guises of speakers are rated more extreme on the dimension in question, i.e., the speakers are thought to be comparatively taller, more intelligent, more honest, more nervous, more ambitious, etc., when speaking English than when speaking French. For example, the first entry indicates that the Maine American students judge the English guises as significantly taller than either the standard French or Franco-American guise. Similarly, a negative value means that the French guise is rated more toward the extreme.

The Maine students hold a quite different set of stereotypes about French-American speakers. People speaking with this style of French are seen as shorter, less attractive, less honest, and less kind than when speaking English. At the same time, they are perceived as having more leadership qualities, more self-confidence, more nervousness, and slightly more ambition and intelligence. The meaning of leadership in this context also very likely reflects a bossiness quality, suggesting that the general stereotype of French-Americans is that of a relatively short, unattractive, dishonest, unkind, bossy, self-confident, nervous, intelligent, and ambitious person.

There is a striking similarity between the Maine and Louisiana American students in their perceptions of French-American speakers. In both settings, the French-American speaker is seen as a short, selfish, unkind, bossy, somewhat brash, nervous, and ambitious person who is also entertaining, possibly in the sense that he is ridiculous or comical.

The Connecticut students view the speakers of standard French as less thoughtful, intelligent, honest, dependable, generous, kind, reliable, stable, and as having less character. At the same time, French speakers are seen as somewhat more physically attractive, as having more humor, and as being more entertaining and sociable than the English controls. Thus, in terms of more basic personality traits such as dependability, kindness, honesty, or intelligence, the continental French person is viewed by the Connecticut sample as clearly inferior to the English-speaking person even though he is considered to be more physically attractive, sociable, and entertaining.

The Connecticut students' perspective of the French-American guises is of interest because of its striking similarity to the stereotype held by Louisiana and Maine students, who come from areas where more opportunities exist for direct experience with speakers using the American style of French. Even in Connecticut, however, the French-American speaker is seen as shorter, less honest, less generous, and less kind although more leaderlike, somewhat more intelligent, more self-confident, more entertaining, and more nervous.

Results for the French-American Students

It is of particular interest that French-American young people in our Louisiana sample have the same stereotypes about French speakers as do their English-speaking neighbors, as can be seen in Table 10. The standard French speaker is seen as less good-looking, less of a leader, less thoughtful, less intelligent, less honest, less friendly, less dependable, less reliable, less stable, and less likable than his English-speaking counterpart. The French-American speaker is also perceived as shorter, less good-looking, less of a leader, less kind, and less likable. At the same time, however, he is seen as more nervous, and there is the familiar trend, although not so pronounced in this case, for the French-American to be seen as more humorous and self-confident.

Table 10

French-American Students' Evaluations of Speakers of French and English*

Trait Judged	Louisiana French-American Students' Judgments of Speakers of		Maine French-American Students' Judgments of Speakers of	
	Standard French (N=86)	American French (N=86)	Standard French (N=96)	American French (N=96)
Height	1.75	3.18•	3.08•	1.03
Good Looks	3.76•	5.36•	0.08	2.04•
Leadership	3.71•	3.04•	1.00	-0.07
Thoughtfulness	2.93•	1.64	1.08	0.02
Sense of Humor	0.17	-1.31	0.04	0.05
Intelligence	3.56•	1.75	-0.03	-2.08•
Honesty	3.76•	0.84	-1.00	-0.05
Self-confidence	1.03	-1.56	-0.03	-2.01•
Friendliness	2.14•	0.25	1.03	1.05
Dependability	2.53•	0.37	-0.05	-1.03
Generosity	1.81	1.54	1.04	-1.03
Entertainingness	1.59	-0.18	-0.02	1.03
Nervousness	1.95	-2.19•	-0.04	-0.08
Kindness	0.56	2.41•	-1.01	0.03
Reliability	2.13•	1.61	0.00	-0.01
Ambition	1.09	1.03	-0.06	-2.09•
Sociability	0.67	1.16	1.02	0.02
Stability	2.05•	0.40	-1.02	-1.01
Character	1.49	1.23	-0.05	-0.01
General Likability	2.28•	2.70•	0.04	-0.01

*Entries are t-values; those marked with a black dot (•) are statistically significant. A positive entry means that the English guises are rated more extreme on the dimension (e.g., taller, more intelligent, more honest, more nervous, more ambitious, etc.). For example, the Louisiana French-American students view the English guises as significantly taller than the French-American but not significantly taller than the standard French guise. Negative entries mean that the French guise is rated more extreme for the trait in question.

The pattern of results for the French-American students in Maine is distinctively different from all the rest. As stressed in earlier chapters, these students have closer ties with both their linguistic and cultural background than do the French-Americans in Louisiana. Perhaps as a consequence of striving to remain French, the French-Americans in Maine show more of a sense of affection and attraction for people who are French. For them, the standard French speakers are perceived as comparatively short, but no other invidious comparisons are made with the English guises. Thus, there is no downgrading of the basic personality features of European French people.

The picture is of even more interest when attention is directed to the stereotypes French-American students in Maine have of French-Americans. They are judged to be less attractive physically but more intelligent, more self-confident, and more ambitious. Thus, the French-American students in Maine see their own linguistic-cultural group as being at least on a par in terms of basic personality characteristics although inferior in physical traits.

Summary

In summary, we have found that American students who are engaged in the study of French have a generally negative set of stereotypes of French-speaking people. Typically, they see the European French speaker as being less thoughtful, less intelligent, less honest and dependable, less generous, less kind, less reliable, less stable, and as having less character than the same person speaking English. At the same time, the European French person is seen as being more humorous and entertaining as though he were thought of mainly as a comic or a jester.

The American students have different but also clearly negative stereotypes of the French-American person. He is perceived as being comparatively short, less honest, less generous, and less kind, although with more leaderlike traits, more self-confident, more entertainingness, clearly more nervousness, more ambition, and somewhat more stability, sociability, and intelligence. In general the stereotyped French-American is relatively unkind, dishonest, short, nervous, self confident, bossy, and ambitious. The fact that he is also seen as entertaining may mean that even with his ambition and leadership potential he is not taken too seriously.

The reactions of the French-American students from Louisiana are very similar to those of the American students, suggesting that they may have adopted community-wide stereotypes about their own group, a characteristic reaction of various minority groups (see Lambert et al., 1960). The French-Americans from Louisiana give the impression that they identify with the "American" image of French people. No such pattern is apparent among the French-American students from Maine, however. In fact, there is strong evidence in their case of a basic attraction to the French image, even though American standards of physical attractiveness and sociability seem to be more highly valued. We have no convincing explanation for this difference in perceptions between Louisiana and Maine French-American students. It may be due to the greater French enculturation the Maine students have had, but this is only a guess. Certainly, the whole matter deserves to be carefully studied for its own sake.

These findings reveal dramatically one of the difficulties students have in orienting themselves favorably to the cultural-linguistic group whose language they are supposed to learn. It is also suggested here that teachers of French must work at a great disadvantage in their attempts to teach the language of a people who are thought of in such negative terms. Since it is our contention that the learning of another group's language would be greatly facilitated if negative stereotypes of the sort surveyed here could be changed to favorable and friendly dispositions, it would now be of interest to devise means of systematically modifying these images. But even as such attempts at change go on, there is a need for both Americans and French-Americans to realize that they have much to do themselves to change these images, biased and distorted as they undoubtedly are.

Chapter Six

Student Views on the Value of Language Study

Up to now we have focused on the way students' attitudes and motivation affect performance in standard programs of language study. Using that frame of reference, we have seen the important roles these factors play in the development of second- or foreign-language proficiency from one North American setting to another. In this chapter we broaden our line of regard to enable us to get perspective on the place foreign-language study holds in the overall hierarchy of values of American students. Thus the questions we ask ourselves here are more general and philosophical. Just how relevant is the study of a foreign language for an American adolescent? Does it ever compete with the major preoccupations of adolescents, such as preparing for future occupational roles or finding one's place in society? Are foreign peoples and their languages given special consideration by American young people, nearly all of whom have foreign origins of their own?

We believed that the major competition of interests would likely come from social and personal concerns such as finding oneself as a person, developing skills for the future world of work, and preparing to get along in an achievement-oriented society. To develop means of assessing students' value systems we turned to the research work of David McClelland and his associates (1961; 1969) on achievement needs for one source of ideas, and to the social psychological research on value systems for another. From these, we either selected available measures or devised new ones we thought would help elucidate the questions we had in mind. Rather than looking for any one set of values, we expected to find a whole series of approaches to life, to academic work, and to foreign-language study. Factor analysis, we felt, would be a particularly useful method for discovering the whole range of possible value hierarchies.

Although we tried to make this investigation as extensive as possible, we still had to restrict the number of variables to a manageable size. Thus, we decided to bypass the various attitude and orientation measures used earlier but to keep the indices of motivational strength and desire to learn French. With regard to achievement measures, we could not use the time-consuming projective techniques McClelland has found so valuable (McClelland, 1961) and instead contented ourselves with substitute procedures (Gough, 1956). Likewise for values, the more comprehensive measures suggested by Kluckhohn and Strodbeck (1961), Vogt (1955), and Morris (1956) were simplified and adapted to provide us with very straightforward indices of values and social motives.

Since we are interested here in students' values and how they affect school achievement in general and the study of a foreign language in particular, we included in this battery measures of value orientations toward life, school work, and toward French study, considered separately. We also included more comprehensive measures of intellectual capacity and aptitude, tests of diligence in homework, indices of socioeconomic background of the family, school grades in all courses, and the basic measures of French achievement already familiar to the reader.

The analysis was carried out on data collected from the Louisiana English-speaking American students only. The testing was integrated with that of the major studies discussed earlier except that in this case final grade averages were obtained from teachers and school officials at the end of the school year. In the following section, brief descriptions of each test used are presented along with the scoring procedures. The scores on all tests were correlated and factor analyzed using the same procedures as described in Chapter 3.

Description of Variables Used in the Value Orientations Study

1. *Socioeconomic Status (SES) of Family.* Roe's (1956) classification system was selected as an index of general socioeconomic level of the family as well as the intellectual capacity required for the fathers' occupations. The higher the score, the more demanding the job and presumably the higher the socioeconomic background of the family.

2. *Average School Grade.* The final grades in all academic courses except French (excluding typewriting and home economics) were averaged. The higher the score, the better the average grade.

3. *Final French Grade.* The higher the score, the better the French grade.

4. *Cooperative French Test.* Standard group test of grammar, vocabulary,

and reading ability in French. The higher the score, the better the competence in these elements of French.

5. *French Listening Comprehension Test.* Standard group test, demanding ability to understand spoken French. The higher the score, the better the student's French aural skills.

6. *Oral French: Linguistic Quality.* A linguistic analysis was made of the tape-recorded speech of each student reading a prepared passage. A total score comprised accuracy in pronunciation, proper linking, stress, rhythm, and absence of nasalization on vowels surrounding nasal consonants. The higher the score, the more linguistically accurate the speech.

7. *Oral French: Skills.* Students were asked to complete two sentences given the starting words "Je vais . . . ." and "si nous . . . ." Their responses were graded for accuracy of vocabulary and grammar, and for degree of complexity of the completion. For example, "Je vais bien" was scored lower than "Je vais à la ville parce qu'il y a une fête nationale." Higher scores reflect a more accurate and complex oral response.

8. *Primary Mental Abilities Test (PMA).* Standard group-administered intelligence test (see description given in Appendix A.).

9. *Test of Educational Ability, Grades 9-12 (Thurstone and Thurstone, 1958).* A group test designed to provide an estimate of aptitude for current school work. It is a power test consisting of 110 items with a time allotment of twenty-seven minutes. The test provides five subscores: language, reasoning, quantitative, total, nonreading total score. The total scores (used here) can also be converted into percentile ranks or an "ability quotient" (AQ). There are two subtests which form the "language" score: *word grouping,* twenty items of the multiple-choice type, such as, "find the word that does not belong," and *synonyms,* thirty items. The "reasoning" score is based on thirty *letter-series* items, for example, "What letter should come next in this series, abx, cdx, efx, ghx, ...? (taken from PMA, ages 11-17). The "quantitative" score is based on thirty *number judgment* items. These use the multiple-choice technique involving simple arithmetical computations, numerical skills, and judgments concerning numerical relationships. The high scorers on the total test are likely to have high aptitude for school work of all sorts, verbal as well as nonverbal.

10. *Modern Language Aptitude Test, (MLAT), Total Score.* Standardized test of aptitude for languages, described in Appendix A.

11. *Achievement via Independence, from the California Psychological Inventory (CPI) (Gough, 1956).* Students were asked to indicate whether they agree or disagree with thirty-two descriptions of personal opinion; for example, "I look up to my father as an ideal man" (disagree); "I seem to be about as capable and smart as most others around me" (agree). The statements were designed to identify "those factors of interest and motivation which facilitate achievement in any setting where autonomy and independence are positive behaviors." A high

score means that a student is "mature, forceful, strong, dominant, demanding and foresighted, independent, and self-reliant and having superior intellectual ability and judgment." A low score means that the student is "inhibited, anxious, cautious, dissatisfied, dull and wary, is submissive and compliant before authority and lacking in self- insight and self-understanding."

12. *Achievement via Conformance (Gough, 1956).* Students were asked to indicate whether they agree or disagree with thirty-eight descriptions of personal opinion such as, "I have a strong desire to be a success in the world" (agree), "I am said to be hotheaded" (disagree). The statements were designed to identify "those factors of interest and motivation which facilitate achievement in any setting where conformance is a positive behavior." A high score means that the student is "capable, cooperative, efficient, organized, responsible, stable and sincere, is persistent and industrious, valuing intellectual activity and intellectual achievement." A low score means that the student is "coarse, stubborn, aloof, awkward, insecure and opinionated, is easily disorganized under stress or pressures to conform, and pessimistic about his occupational future."

13-20. *Social Motives.* Students were asked to indicate how characteristic it was of themselves to strive earnestly for particular social goals. The following social goals were referred to in Variables 13-20: (to strive for) success in life (*success*); a life free from worry and uncertainty (*security*); to seek out things of interest and challenge (*cognitive*); to win approval of friends, family, and teachers (*sociality*); to seek excitement and pleasure (*pleasure*); to improve oneself morally and help others (*morality*); to develop one's body and improve one's health (*physical*); to develop talent and appreciation for the various arts (*artistic*). Each question permitted a range of scores from 1 indicating a lack of relevance for the student answering, to 7 indicating an exact description of the student in question. Five questions were included about the success dimension and an average score was derived. One question only was used for each of the other social motives.

21-28. *Social Values.* Eight descriptive phrases referring to different values in life were presented to each student and he was asked to rank each as to how much he would like it to apply to himself. The list was: ambitious and a success; secure and free from worry; intelligent and imaginative; important and popular; leading a life of excitement and pleasure; kind and good; healthy, with fine body and face; having talent and appreciation for the arts. The same values were presented in negative form (e.g., ambitious became lazy) and rankings of how much one would *dislike* to have them apply to himself. Rankings were transformed so that a high score on a particular value dimension means it was considered both a desirable trait to have and, in its negative form, a particularly undesirable trait to have.

29. *Information about Expected Future Occupation.* Students were asked to indicate, along 7-point scales, how sure they were of what is demanded of them

in their expected occupation, and how much they knew about the actual day-to-day features of that occupation. The higher the score, the more information the student has accumulated about his future occupation, presumably reflecting an interest.

30. *Certainty of Realizing Occupational Goal.* Students were asked to indicate how certain they were of realizing their expected occupation and how difficult they felt it would be to realize this occupation. The maximum score was given to the student who was very certain of realizing an occupational goal that he, nonetheless, felt would take a great deal of time and effort. This variable, therefore, reflects a self-assurance of realizing a challenging occupational goal.

31. *Expectation of Good Grades.* Students were asked what average grade they were striving for in their courses for the current year. Their expectations were corrected for appropriateness by comparing the student's expected average for the previous academic year with what he actually received. Striving for an A+ was assigned a score of 9 while striving for a C- was given a 1. If a student was working for an A average and if in the previous year he also expected an A and actually got it, his score would remain 9 (no correction would be needed). If he were an overestimator (expected an A last year but actually got a B), his final score was reduced by the correction. Likewise, if he were a conservative estimator (expected a B but got an A average in the previous year), then his score would be raised by the correction. This variable, therefore, is an index of a realistic expectation of obtaining good grades.

32. *Diligence in Homework.* This variable reflects a student's willingness to do more than he feels is absolutely necessary to receive good grades. They were asked how much homework they usually devote to school work and also how much they felt they should work at home to receive an A average, a B average, or a C average. If a student was actually working above what he felt was necessary to get an A average, he would have a very high score. He would have a relatively low score if he was doing about what was required for a C average. Thus, a high score indicates a serious concern with homework, or diligence in studying.

33. *Family-wide Aspiration for Good Grades.* Students were asked how satisfied or dissatisfied they would be to obtain average grades ranging from A+ to F and how pleased or displeased their parents would be if they received each average. High scores reflect a great deal of likely dissatisfaction (on the part of the student and his parents) if the student did not receive very high grades.

34. *Ease of Scholastic Attainment.* Students were asked to estimate how many weeks or days before the final exams they would have to study diligently to receive all A's, a B average, a C average, etc. If a student mentioned he would *not* have to work for long to get good grades, he received a *higher* score. Thus, this variable reflects the ease of attaining a high scholastic average.

35. *Study Efficiency.* Students were given higher scores if they could refrain from letting their minds wander in class, could concentrate on homework for a long period, refrain from daydreaming while studying, could easily determine what is important in an assignment, and if extracurricular activities did not keep them from completing homework.

36. *Grade Aspirations in French.* Students indicated what grade they were trying to get in French study. The higher the grade sought for, the higher the score.

37. *Ease of Attaining "A" Grade in French.* Students were asked how much homework they would regularly have to do to achieve an "A" average in French. The *less* time needed on homework, the higher the score.

38. *Motivational Intensity Scale.* See description in Chapter 3. The higher the score, the more the effort put into French study.

39. *Desire to Learn French.* See description in Chapter 3. The higher the score, the stronger the student's desire to learn the language.

40. *Value of Success in French.* Students were asked to state how important doing well in French was for them. The higher the score, the more importance they attributed to doing well in French study.

41. *Enjoyment of French Homework.* Students were asked how much they enjoyed studying and doing written homework in French. The higher the score, the more favorable their attitude toward French homework.

Variables Included for the Value Orientations Study. The 41 x 41 correlation matrix for these variables is placed in Appendix B as Table 11-B. The final rotated factor matrix is given in Table 11 which follows here in the text.

1. Socioeconomic Status of Family (Roe's classification)
2. Average School Grade (excluding French)
3. Final French Grade
4. Cooperative French Test (Total)
5. French Listening Comprehension Test (Total)
6. Oral French: Linguistic Quality
7. Oral French: Skills
8. IQ: Primary Mental Abilities Test (Total)
9. Test of Educational Ability, Grades 9-12 (Total)
10. Modern Language Aptitude Test (Total)
11. Achievement via Independence (CPI)
12. Achievement via Conformance (CPI)
13. Success Motive; 14. Security Motive; 15. Cognitive Motive;
    16. Sociality Motive; 17. Pleasure Motive; 18. Morality Motive;
    19. Physical Motive; 20. Artistic Motive
21. Success Value; 22. Security Value; 23. Cognitive Value;
    24. Sociality Value; 25. Pleasure Value; 26. Morality Value;

27. Physical Value; 28. Artistic Value
29. Degree of Information about Expected Future Occupation
30. Certainty of Realizing Occupational Goal
31. Expectation of Good Grades
32. Diligence in Homework
33. Family-wide Aspiration for Good Grades
34. Ease of Scholastic Attainment
35. Study Efficiency
36. Grade Aspirations in French
37. Ease of Attaining an "A" in French
38. Motivational Intensity to Learn French
39. Desire to Learn French
40. Value of Success in French
41. Enjoyment of French Homework

Results of the Value Orientations Study

An unusually large number of variables have substantial loadings on Factor I, and it becomes an interesting task to find the underlying characteristics these various measures have in common. To help reduce the number, two large classes of variables can be isolated. First, the aptitude or ability measures are all represented: IQ, Educational Ability, and MLAT (Vs. 8, 9, and 10). Likewise all the achievement variables are included in the complex: school grades and French grades (Vs. 2 and 3) as well as all aspects of French proficiency, passive as well as audio-lingual skills (Vs. 4-7). Furthermore, self-assurance about achievement in all school work, French included, is represented; school work is seen as easy (Vs. 34 and 37) and expectations of doing well run high (Vs. 31 and 36). Factor I, therefore, describes a general ability-achievement dimension, telling us that students' success in academic matters depends on intellectual abilities. This, of course, is not at all surprising, but what is particularly relevant to our interests is the finding that French proficiency—academic aspects as well as audio-lingual ones that call for social support outside school—falls in the pattern just as proficiency in mathematics, history, or geography very likely would, had we included these in our analysis.

Assuming then that intellectual ability is one important determinant of academic achievement, what is it that lies behind individual differences in abilities and helps them to develop? Difficult as it is to unravel the real causal chain of events, we nevertheless do have certain important clues offered here. First, the socioeconomic status of the family plays a principal role (V. 1) as do parental support and expectations (V. 33). The loadings of the two measures of achievement orientation (Vs. 11 and 12) and the one of success motive (V. 13)—the

Table 11

Final Rotated Factor Matrix for the Value Orientation Study

Variables	I	II	III	IV	V	VI	VII	VIII	IX	X	h²
1. SES Background	.54•	.04	.04	-.08	.02	-.04	-.07	.32•	.07	-.06	.42
2. School Grades	.68•	-.07	.43•	.14	-.04	-.00	.08	.08	.03	-.02	.68
3. French Grade	.67•	-.13	.29	.30•	-.14	.06	.23	-.02	-.09	.06	.72
4. CFT	.74•	.02	-.10	.31•	-.07	.12	.11	-.02	-.18	.15	.75
5. FLCT	.55•	.08	-.36•	.04	-.03	.14	.01	-.01	-.14	.15	.50
6. Oral Fr. Quality	.53•	-.10	-.05	.02	-.05	.11	-.10	.09	-.08	-.22	.38
7. Oral Fr. Skills	.44•	-.08	.14	-.02	.02	.21	-.21	.16	-.09	-.04	.35
8. IQ (P.M.A.)	.58•	-.20	-.08	.18	.19	.01	-.17	.34•	.07	.01	.61
9. Educ. Abil.	.61•	-.06	-.14	.19	.34•	.06	.08	.36•	.10	-.09	.70
10. MLAT	.76•	-.05	-.06	.15	.11	-.01	.02	-.09	.12	.07	.64
13. Success Mot.	.32•	.47•	-.01	.11	.56•	.15	.13	.13	.06	.08	.72
11. Achieve. by Ind.	.45•	-.07	-.14	.09	.25	-.14	.16	-.09	-.05	.45•	.55
12. Achiev. by Conf.	.35•	.01	.10	.01	.22	.04	.03	.03	-.08	.48•	.43
14. Security Mot.	-.03	.51•	.11	.02	.16	.47•	.21	.24	.00	.22	.67
15. Cognitive Mot.	.05	.54•	.14	.11	.10	.01	-.19	.12	-.07	-.23	.44
16. Sociality Mot.	-.16	.70•	-.18	.06	.13	.05	.12	.21	.10	.08	.65
17. Pleasure Mot.	.05	.63•	-.12	-.12	-.05	-.13	-.01	-.10	-.02	-.11	.47
18. Morality Mot.	-.09	.50•	.11	.01	.30•	.23	-.07	.06	-.38•	.23	.61
19. Physical Mot.	-.14	.54•	.15	.14	-.11	.14	-.20	-.18	.11	.05	.47
20. Artistic Mot.	-.04	-.00	.16	.14	.49•	.12	.03	-.28	-.06	-.03	.39

Table 11 (Continued)

Final Rotated Factor Matrix for the Value Orientation Study

Variables	I	II	III	IV	V	VI	VII	VIII	IX	X	h^2
21. Success Val.	-.15	.14	.53*	.07	.13	.03	-.07	.03	.17	.16	.41
22. Security Val.	.08	.01	.21	-.01	-.34*	.33*	-.20	.14	.15	.28	.43
23. Cognitive Val.	-.06	-.08	.03	-.09	-.08	-.37*	-.04	.08	-.09	.09	.19
24. Sociality Val.	.01	-.17	-.08	-.06	.02	.11	.55*	.02	.23	-.28	.49
25. Pleasure Val.	.11	.06	-.11	-.12	-.01	.03	.12	.03	.03	-.55*	.36
26. Morality Val.	.04	.09	-.05	-.07	-.08	-.18	-.05	.15	.54*	.29	.45
27. Physical Val.	-.11	.08	-.65*	.10	-.02	-.00	.02	.08	.13	-.06	.48
28. Artistic Val.	.02	-.14	.02	.20	.23	.06	.01	.08	-.08	.07	.51
29. Info. Fut. Occup.	.07	.05	.06	-.00	.52*	.01	-.09	-.02	.12	.13	.32
30. Realiz. Occup. Goal	-.05	-.10	.01	.04	-.03	-.03	-.07	-.20	-.46*	-.10	.28
31. Expec. Grades	.42*	.16	-.07	.24	.36*	-.05	.23	.04	-.25	.01	.51
32. Dilig. Homework	.49*	.06	.13	.11	.01	-.18	-.16	-.13	.08	.29	.44
33. Famil. Aspir.	.53*	.02	-.02	.14	.19	-.08	.04	-.14	.28	-.07	.46
34. Ease School. Attain.	.65*	.23	.08	.19	.02	-.41*	.10	.13	.08	.13	.73
35. Study Effic.	.22	.16	-.02	.34*	.09	.10	-.19	.14	.03	.03	.27
36. Grade Aspir. in Fr.	.53*	.01	.14	.52*	-.01	-.04	.37*	.12	-.04	.04	.73
37. Ease Attain French	.42*	.17	-.04	.33*	.01	-.30*	.29	-.04	-.00	.03	.49
38. Mot. Inten. Fr.	.03	.07	-.08	.59*	.33*	.04	.09	-.08	.15	.18	.54
39. Desire Learn Fr.	.14	.04	.05	.74*	-.04	-.07	.07	-.14	-.13	-.05	.62
40. Value Succ. Fr.	.20	.02	-.05	.77*	.01	-.02	-.12	-.04	-.01	.10	.67
41. Enjoy Fr. Hmwk.	.18	-.06	.01	.77*	.07	.15	-.03	-.01	.07	.00	.66

only motive having salience for the widely successful student—are of particular significance. Judging from McClelland's work on individual differences in achievement need (McClelland, 1961; 1969), this emphasis on achievement or success very likely stems from the attitude and value atmosphere of the family, which in turn affects the parents' approach to child training. From this point of view, the constellation of variables in Factor I makes good sense. One certain way to develop broad proficiency in school work, French study included, is to have the good fortune of coming from a well-to-do family, one that encourages and expects good results at school, and one that instills a motivation system focused on achievement and success. Mix these background factors with good intellectual aptitude and ability and the young person is very likely to excel in all academic work, language study included. No special motivation or desire to learn French seems needed (note insignificant loadings of Vs. 38 and 39), although general diligence in homework apparently is (V. 32). Since a dimension is involved, one can read another, more serious version of the story told by Factor I by taking the opposite pole of the dimension as a reference point. Thus, the young person from a less advantaged background, without parental support, with relatively poor abilities and low achievement orientations is very likely to do poorly in academic work, including the study of language.

Several very important implications follow from this patterning of variables. First, we are intrigued by the value orientations and social motives of successful students. We noted that they had *no* particular value system, that is, none of the value variables (Vs. 21-28) loaded on this factor. This does not mean that this type of student is without values, but only that no one or no restricted set of values typify the academic powerhouse. With regard to social motives, however, it is obvious that he (or she) is single-minded in his motive to succeed and no other social motives (not even cognitive or artistic ones) get in the way. We may have our finger here on the academic "grind," talented and successful as he or she may be.

Second, we find that the MLAT measures get lost in the intelligence and educational ability configuration and it is difficult to determine the distinctive contribution made by the language aptitude subtests. In the Louisiana, Maine and Connecticut studies it was also difficult to assess fully the independent importance of the MLAT because it usually was linked with intelligence. Because this topic could be of special interest to those readers who want to understand the relationships of language aptitude, intelligence, and second-language achievement, we conducted a separate analysis of the American students from Louisiana (Gardner and Lambert, 1965), which demonstrated that measures of intelligence are relatively independent of both language aptitude and second-language achievement. Furthermore, each of the MLAT subtests appears to underlie independent aspects of French achievement. This more technical report is reproduced as *Reading Number Six* in Appendix C.

Third, the patterning of variables in Factor I shows us that a subgroup of our most talented students of foreign languages has no special regard for the language per se nor any special motivation or desire to do well in language study. Rather than being a central goal for this type of student, French study is incidental to a more general goal of preparing oneself for getting ahead in the world. The point is that French training, even for some of the most gifted students of the language, fits into a much broader frame of reference. It is one of the tests of success in academic life and passing these tests is necessary in order to make a better place in one's social environment.

There is, however, another route one can follow to obtain good school grades and above average achievement in French that does not call for a privileged home background or outstanding intellectual aptitudes. This approach is apparent in Factor III, where a strong value placed on success (V. 21) and a rejection of physical values (V. 27) is associated with school grades in general and French grades in particular (Vs. 2 and 3). There is something mysterious about this student type because he (or she) also seems to do well mainly through a success orientation, not through ability or special interest in French (note insignificant loadings of Vs. 8 and 9, and Vs. 38-40), and although the grade in French may be above average no other measures of French proficiency made an appearance in the constellation. In fact, there is a substantial indication in Factor III that this type of student will do very poorly in aural French (V. 5). Nonetheless, it seems that "thinking" success is a pretty powerful substitute for ability when it comes to getting good grades. Again we find that French achievement is simply drawn into the overall academic success pattern; language study is not of special interest to this type of student, who manages nevertheless to get good grades in French, too.

Factor IV reveals quite a different student type, one with an overriding interest in French (Vs. 36-41), who excels in French grades and in French vocabulary, reading, and grammar (Vs. 3 and 4) but not necessarily in other school grades (note the insignificant entry for V. 2). The orientation of this subgroup of students is also independent of family background and aptitude (note the insignificant entries for Vs. 8, 9, and 10). It appears then that earnestness for French proficiency can substitute for language aptitude or academic potential if the student has high aspirations for this goal (V. 36) and shows an ability to stay at it (V. 35). Some American students then are aficionados of French and they can achieve well in all but the audio-lingual features of the language, regardless of intellectual ability or home background. Note that there are no patterns of social motives or values (not even the success orientation) that characterize this student type. If anything, the social motives of these students are generally at a low level of intensity.

Another type, depicted in Factor VII, also has a flair for French (independent of intelligence or language aptitude) and also a very prominent value peak, that of sociality (V. 24). Students fitting this pattern expect good grades in French (V. 36) and find it easy to obtain good grades in French (V. 37), although the evidence that they are above average in French is not strong (V. 3). These students have no special encouragement from parents, nor any socioeconomic privileges at home that contribute to the pattern. It is possible then that those who value social approval and popularity may have other personality characteristics that specifically enhance progress in French. The picture is not clear, however, since the loading of French grades is not large, and none of the aural or oral skills enter the configuration. Still this finding merits separate attention in follow-up research.

Too many motives and values are of questionable usefulness and may in fact even hamper in some mysterious manner a student's academic progress. Consider the. makeup of Factor V, for example. The student type represented in this pattern has a set of strong social motives—success, artistic, morality(Vs. 13, 20, and 18)—and a rejection of the security value (V. 22). He has above average educational ability (V. 9) though not necessarily a high IQ (insignificant entry of V. 8), is well set on his future occupation (V. 29), expects good grades (V. 31), and has a strong motivation to learn French (V. 38). Nonetheless, there is no indication that he will do well either in general school work or in French. There are alternative interpretations possible here. It may be that the success motive should not be diluted by competitors in the artistic and morality spheres; the high achiever depicted in Factor I had nothing but success in mind. Or it could be that a success orientation without abilities is ineffectual. More research is needed to decide between these and other possible alternatives. What is evident at the moment though is that success orientation is not necessarily a certain formula for academic proficiency in general, nor is strong motivation to learn French a guarantee of success in that single domain.

A very similar conclusion about the ineffectual nature of motivation without' concomitant abilities is also suggested by the composition of Factor II. Here we find students with a variety of social motives (Vs. 13-19), but there is no evidence that they are successful in any academic or linguistic pursuits.

Factor VI isolates other patterns of values and motives that also have no favorable influence on academic achievement. Here we find a type of student with a strong security motive and security value (Vs. 14 and 22) who at the same time rejects cognitive values(V. 23).This pattern has no direct effect one way or the other on academic achievement (French included), although it appears to create an impression in the student that it is difficult to get ahead in all forms of academic work, French included (Vs. 34 and 37).

Similarly, Factor IX depicts a group of students who reject morality values (Vs. 18 and 26) and who have low expectations with regard to occupational goals (V. 30). There are no signs that academic achievement, including French, is affected one way or another by this orientation.

Factor X tells a similar story, this time about the hard worker who has little to show for it. Students fitting this pattern have strong achievement strivings (Vs. 11 and 12), and reject pleasure values (V. 25). There is also some evidence that these students are diligent in homework (V. 32), value security and morality (Vs. 22 and 26), and reject sociality (V. 24). The trouble is that their academic achievement, including French, is not outstanding in any respect.

Finally, the story suggested by Factor VIII is of special importance because it deals with the socioeconomically disadvantaged student (negative loading of V. 1) who is nonetheless talented (Vs. 8 and 9). The value profile is characterized by a strong rejection of artistic values (V. 28). In this case there are no signs of general academic proficiency or of success in French. Certain questions come to mind about this profile. Might these students be able to captitalize on their abilities if they were oriented to success? Why should students with this level of ability not think in terms of success? Does the socioeconomic background of the family have such a determining role? Judging from the contrast with Factor I, where high ability students from privileged homes are so successful, one has the feeling that parental support for academic work and the instilling of achievement values may, by their presence, be the important determiners of academic success for the youngster from a privileged home and, by their absence, limit the academic performance of the talented youngster from a less advantaged background.

Summary

This analysis has uncovered an instructive and potentially very useful set of facts about the place of language study in the overall value hierarchies of typical American students. Descriptions of various student types emerged from the analysis, each type with distinct approaches to life, the academic world, and the study of a foreign language. Judging from their influence on school performance and on the development of foreign-language skills, we begin to realize that certain life styles are productive and efficient while others seem to disrupt the learning process and restrict the student's full potential. Although we have barely scratched the surface here, still very valuable messages for language teachers, educators, and parents are unmistakeably present in the patterns.

One subgroup of students (Factor I) has everything at its disposition: intelligence, academic abilities, language aptitude, advantaged socioeconomic background, parents who care and encourage, and a value system geared for success and achievement. These students really cannot miss in life, and at the high school level, at least, it is very clear that they do not. They excel in all aspects of school work, including second-language training, not only those aspects emphasized in the school's training program but also the more socially based audio-lingual skills as well. For them, trying to prepare one's way for the future is a central goal and French study is incidental in the sense that it is simply another school subject. They are good at estimating how much effort is required to do well in school and they realize they do not have to strain in order to succeed. However, they have such a broad-ranged competence, extending beyond school requirements, that they constitute an interesting challenge to teachers who are themselves clever enough to channel these abilities into more socially worthwhile directions than the success-achievement route that appears to be a preoccupation. For such students, language training could certainly be made a much more personally and socially significant enterprise than "just another" high school course.

Having such an array of things in one's favor is not the only route to proficiency in French, however. We found that another subclass of students who are not outstanding in intellectual abilities or favored as to home background can nonetheless excel in school work and in selected features of French achievement as well. What seems to be called for in this case is a value system focused on success (Factor III). For them, thinking in terms of success seems to be a fairly good substitute for ability in getting ahead in academic work. Here, too, French achievement is not of special interest but is an incidental concomitant of academic work. There are surely ways teachers could also develop a separate and strong interest in language study for this type of student as with the privileged subgroup just described. Perhaps in this case an instrumental orientation could be stimulated with a view toward broadening the student's motivation system.

Perhaps the most disturbing case is the subgroup of students who are intellectually talented but disfavored by a socioeconomically restricted home background (Factor VIII). The trouble is that these gifted youngsters show no signs of academic proficiency (French study included). Our feeling is that they lack the parental support that seems to determine whether a youngster will have an optimistic outlook on life and a desire to achieve. Students who fit this pattern constitute the most important educational challenge, and deserve urgent and serious consideration because they can become not only disheartened but also embittered.

Another student type was of particular interest (Factor IV) because it suggested that young people can develop a passion for language study, regardless of family background, intelligence, or value orientations, and excel in it but not necessarily in other school work. Another type depicted in Factor VII, although less pronounced, also suggests that students can become above average in French proficiency without the benefits of high aptitudes or favorable socioeconomic status if their values have a certain structure, in this case a focus on popularity and social approval.

We also found that too many social motives and values or specific combinations of values may limit or even hamper students' progress in academic work in general, and in foreign-language study in particular. One student type (Factor V) has a diversity of strong social motives including success, artistic, and morality, an above average educational aptitude, achievement, motivation, and desire to do well in French study. This pattern, however, is not associated with proficiency in French or in general school work. Success and achievement orientations, therefore, do not guarantee academic success. Neither does a strong security orientation (Factor VI), nor one that denigrates moral values (Factor IX), nor a broad system of social motives (Factor II). Even a pattern composed of a strong achievement motive coupled with low pleasure and sociality values (Factor X) has no influence one way or another on school performance.

Each of these configurations that includes values and motives is intriguing. Since certain patterns are generally successful ones and others unsuccessful, they provide insights for educators as to the types of students who can be more or less easily excited by academic programs that are currently in style. They can also serve as guides for renovating the makeup of language programs so as to interest a wider array of student types. At a more theoretical level, the contrasts in value patterns can be used as guides or hypotheses for research into the motivational bases of academic success and failure.

Chapter Seven

The Philippine Study

So far, so good. We have taken some ideas about second-language learning that first took shape in bilingual and bicultural Montreal and tried them out in three widely different American settings, one essentially "all-American" and the other two American as well as French-American in makeup. In all of these social contexts we have increased our confidence in the ideas because the role of attitudes and motives in the second-language acquisition process has been unmistakable. At the same time, however, we have learned that each setting and each ethnolinguistic group has its own fascinating pattern of sociopsychological influences that change in unexpected ways the manner in which attitudes and motivation play their roles.

In this chapter, we take the same set of notions out of the North American context to the Philippines, where their generalizability and universality are given a very demanding test. Why the Philippines? There are several reasons why this choice was a particularly valuable one. First we switch in this case from a focus on French as the target language to English, calling for new forms of tests, not only proficiency tests but language aptitude subtests as well. This switch also forced an important change in attitude scales since America rather than France becomes the society in focus. Second, the societal, economic, and ultimately personal importance of English as a second language for Filipinos is of a different order than French for English-speaking North Americans. Over sixty languages are spoken in the Philippines and partly because of this diversity, English has become the major language of instruction from the early years on, is rapidly becoming the language of the business world, and according to an important investigation by Tucker (1968) is currently the most prestigious language of all. Thus success in mastering this second language (it is hardly ever used as a home language) determines one's upward mobility and one's future—a sharp contrast to the value attributed to French by English-speaking North Americans. The Philippines, then, where there is such a high instrumental value placed on English language proficiency, was an excellent choice to test one of our hypotheses, namely that the integrative motive plays a substantial role in the acquisition of a second language. Finally, this Asian setting is one example of a large number of developing nations throughout the world that have imported a language of worldwide recognition as one of its ways of becoming an integral part of a worldwide community. Thus, the test of our notions in the Philippines could be instructive for other developing nations as well.

Subjects, Variables, and Procedure

The subjects for this study were 103 senior high school students living in a suburb of Manila. They had completed about six years of formal training in English as a subject matter, and from the third grade on the medium of instruction had been English. Still there is a wide range of proficiency in English language skills, both audio-lingual and the more passive features. It is with this interindividual variance that we, of course, are mainly concerned.

Forty-seven variables were included in the study and all of the test materials, except those measuring English achievement, were written in Tagalog (Pilipino), the language of the region in which the testing was conducted and the home language of all students involved in the study.

The group testing was conducted in three sessions. The first required forty minutes during which time the students completed the questionnaire containing various attitude and motivation measures. During the second session, also forty minutes, the language aptitude measures were administered. In the final session (thirty minutes) the students completed the tests of English achievement. Subsequent to the group testing, each student was tested individually on the three measures of oral proficiency in English. At the end of the final testing session students were asked to take a related questionnaire home for their parents to complete.

The Variables Used in the Philippine Study.

Variables 1-6 are ratings made by the students themselves of their proficiency in various language skills. Scores were the sum of the ratings on 4-point scales (ranging from "not at all" to "fluently") for ability to speak, read, write, and understand various languages.

1. *Student's Knowledge of English;* 2. *Parents' Knowledge of English;* 3. *Student's Knowledge of Tagalog;* 4. *Parents' Knowledge of Tagalog.*

5. *Student's Mean Proficiency in Nonvernacular Languages* (e.g., training in Spanish or some other major language other than English is required at high school and university levels).

6. *Student's Mean Proficiency in Vernacular Languages Other than Tagalog.* Variables 7-19 are adaptations of the familiar attitudinal and motivational measures.

7. *Orientation Index.* The students were presented with four possible reasons for studying English, two instrumental (e.g., it will some day be useful in getting a good job), and two integrative in content (e.g., it will allow me to meet and converse with more and varied people). Responses were classified as being instrumentally (1) or integratively (2) oriented according to the alternative chosen.

8. *Instrumental Orientation.* Students rated the extent to which each of four instrumental reasons for studying English described their feelings. A high score indicates an intense instrumental orientation.

9. *Integrative Orientation.* Students rated the extent to which each of four integrative reasons for studying English described their own feelings. Scores were the sum of these four ratings.

10. *Motivational Intensity.* Six multiple-choice items adapted from the original Motivational Intensity scale were used. The items assess the average amount of English homework done each night, future intentions to study and make use of English, and the importance attributed to knowing English. For each item, they indicated the alternative most descriptive of themselves. High scores reflect a high degree of motivational intensity to learn English.

11. *Desire to Learn English.* They were presented with eight multiple-choice items adapted from the original Desire to Learn French scale. Items dealt with a student's eagerness to do assignments, ability to pay attention in class, etc. High scores reflect a strong desire to learn English.

12. *Parental Encouragement.* Using an 8-point scale, students answered six questions dealing with the encouragement they receive from their parents to do well in English. These items were taken from Feenstra and Gardner (1968).

13. *Interest in Foreign Languages.* Seven multiple-choice items measured each student's general attitudes toward learning foreign languages. Items were positively worded statements concerning interest in being proficient in a foreign language; students indicated agreement or disagreement with each item on a 5-point scale. A high score indicates a strong interest in foreign languages.

14. *Study Habits.* Twenty-five multiple-choice items selected from the Brown-Holtzman Survey of Study Habits (1953) were provided. High scores on this questionnaire indicate effective study habits.

15. *Attitudes toward Americans.* Seven positive and seven negative statements about Americans; students were asked to either agree or disagree with

each item. A high score on this scale reflects a positive attitude towards Americans.

16. *Authoritarianism.* Eleven items selected from the California F-Scale (Adorno et al., 1950) that were considered appropriate for the Philippine setting.

17. *Ethnocentrism.* Five items adapted from the Ethnocentrism Scale (Adorno et al., 1950).

18. *Anomie.* Five items designed to measure an individual's disenchantment with society.

19. *Cultural Allegiances.* Eight items adapted from the scale used for the French-American students. Statements compared American and Filipino ways of life; a high score indicates a preference for the Filipino culture.

Variables 20-24 were adaptations of the MLAT (Carroll and Sapon, 1959).

20. *Number Learning.* In translating this test every attempt was made to follow the directions, time limits, and item content in the original test. The test was designed to measure both memory and general auditory alertness.

21. *Phonetic Script.* This test followed the same format as the corresponding test in the MLAT; it is a measure of both memory for speech sounds and ability to learn the correspondence between the speech sounds and orthographic symbols.

22. *Disarranged Letters.* An adaptation of a test developed by Carroll (1958); students were given six groups of five disarranged letters with instructions to rearrange the letters into meaningful words.

23. *Paired Associates.* In the translation of this test, the same format as that used in the MLAT was maintained. It is a measure of rote memory ability.

24. *Words in Sentences.* Rather than translating the original MLAT items, twenty-five pairs of sentences were constructed to be similar in intent to those used in the MLAT. In its original form, this test measures sensitivity to grammatical structures.

25. *Vocabulary.* This measure was taken from Form A of the Cooperative English Test.

26. *Reading Comprehension.* Also taken from Form A of the Cooperative English Test.

27. *Grammar.* A test developed at the Philippine Normal College by Maurity Plaza (1964) as a measure of English grammar for college freshmen.

28. *Listening Comprehension.* A test developed at the Philippine Normal College by Adoracion Halili (1965), consisting of five selections, each read aloud twice. Following the second reading, students were asked five questions on the content of the selection.

Variables 29-35 were measures obtained from the school records.

29. *General Average for the Previous Three Years in School;* 30. *Academic Average for the Previous Three Years in School;* 31. *Average Grade in English*

for the Previous Three Years in School; 32. *Average Grade in Pilipino for the Previous Three Years in School;* 33. *Average Grade in English for the Current Year;* 34. *Average Grade in Pilipino for the Current Year;*

35. *Intelligence.* The Philippine Mental Ability Test, consisting of seventy-two items which measure mathematical ability, vocabulary, and the ability to perceive number and figure relations, etc.

Variables 36-43 were indices obtained from the *parents* of the students under study. They were similar to those administered to the students. For Variables 36-39, parents indicated their estimates of how their children felt; Variables 40-43 assessed characteristics of the parents themselves.

36. *Orientation Index;* 37. *Instrumental Orientation;*
38. *Integrative Orientation;* 39. *Parental Encouragement;*
40. *Attitudes toward Americans (P);* 41. *Authoritarianism (P);*
42. *Ethnocentrism (P);* 43. *Cultural Allegiances (P);*
44. *Anomie (P).*

Variables 45-47 are tests of the student's oral proficiency in English.

45. *Oral Reading Fluency.* Two judges rated each student's fluency in reading a standard English passage, using 7-point rating scales. The sum of these two ratings constituted the index of oral reading fluency.

46. *Pronunciation Accuracy.* The same two judges rated the accuracy with which each student pronounced words in context. The total score served as an index of pronunciation accuracy.

47. *Free Speech Fluency.* Using stimulus words as cues, students produced orally three or four sentences involving the idea suggested by the cues. Responses were scored for complexity of response pattern and correctness by two judges using 7-point rating scales.

Results for the Philippine Study

Pearson correlation coefficients were computed among the forty-seven variables. (This study is the most recent one and there are now fewer limitations on the number of variables that can be factor analyzed by computers.) The resulting correlation matrix (Table 12-B in Appendix B) with communality estimates based on the highest absolute correlation for a variable, was factor analyzed using the principal axis solution. Seven factors were extracted and rotated by means of the normalized varimax solution. The rotated factor matrix is presented in Table 12.

Factor I receives appreciable loadings (that is, ones greater than ± .30) from fifteen variables. These include three standard measures of English achievement (Vs. 25, 26, and 27), three indices of oral English proficiency (Vs. 45, 46, and 47), all measures of academic performance (Vs. 29-34), the Philippine Mental Ability Scale (V. 35), the Words in Sentences subtest (V. 24), and the Cultural

Allegiances scale administered to the parents (V. 44). Except for the Cultural Allegiances measure, the overall nature of this factor is academic achievement based on performance measures, including indices of general academic standing as well as proficiency in Pilipino and English. Because of the importance of English in the educational system of the Philippines, it makes sense to regard English achievement as an essential aspect of academic achievement. Thus, since English is the language of instruction, academically superior students would also be expected to be superior in English language skills.

The other two measures loading on this factor give us insights into the sources that influence or promote academic achievement in the Philippine context. First, the Words in Sentences subtest, a measure of grammatical skill, has a high loading, suggesting that this feature of linguistic aptitude is necessary for academic achievement since even the language of instruction is a second language for all students involved. Second, the presence of the measure of Parental Cultural Allegiance suggests another important correlate of academic achievement. The negative loading means that students whose parents prefer the American to the Filipino way of life are more successful in this American-based curriculum. Apparently, these parents provide important incentives to their children to do well in the all-English curriculum.

Factor II comprises eight attitudinal and two oral measures of English proficiency, indicating that the basic nature of the factor has to do with an integrative motive for learning English. The configuration of loadings shows that integratively oriented students (Vs. 7 and 9) show considerable motivation and desire to learn English (Vs. 10 and 11), express an interest in foreign languages (V. 13), have good study habits (V. 14), report considerable parental encouragement to learn English (V. 12), and appear satisfied with society and their role in it (V. 18). It is of interest that this pattern includes most of the components that characterize the integrative motive, but differs in certain fundamental ways from the integrative motive described in previous studies, mainly because of the attitudinal variables that fall into the cluster. In three previous studies (Gardner and Lambert, 1959; Gardner, 1960; Feenstra and Gardner, 1968), the integrative motive included positive attitudes toward the other language community, while in other studies (see Gardner, 1966; also Chapter 3 of the present volume) it included a nonethnocentric outlook. In the present case we find the various indices of the integrative motive associated with a lack of anomic feelings. A similar pattern turned up with the French-American students from Louisiana (see Chapter 4 of the present volume) where anomie became part of the integrative motive.

What might this mean in the Philippine setting? One possibility is that the urban culture of the Philippines is becoming Americanized to the extent that a strong motivation to master English, the language of schooling and business, becomes an endorsement of the culture and a contentment with it. An

Table 12

Final Rotated Factor Matrix for the Philippine Study

Variables	I	II	III	IV	V	VI	VII
1. Student's Knowledge of English	.13	.10	.55	-.11	-.02	-.08	-.04
2. Parents' Knowledge of English	.12	.17	.46	.04	-.51	.06	.12
3. Student's Knowledge of Tagalog	.10	-.07	.27	-.18	.02	-.13	.18
4. Parents' Knowledge of Tagalog	.05	.12	.21	-.18	-.42	.22	.36
5. Student's Knowledge of Non-Vernacular Languages	.14	-.11	.03	.00	-.33	-.10	.06
6. Student's Knowledge of Other Vernacular Languages	.09	.03	.07	.03	-.09	-.38	-.04
7. Orientation Index	.00	.36	-.05	-.30	.17	.01	-.09
8. Instrumental Orientation	.15	.23	.24	.12	.25	.08	.11
9. Integrative Orientation	.11	.36	.12	-.03	.33	.19	.07
10. Motivational Intensity	.16	.68	.08	.16	.05	.09	-.08
11. Desire to Learn English	.08	.79	.02	-.05	-.05	-.04	-.07
12. Parental Encouragement	.09	.44	.12	.08	-.17	.13	-.01
13. Interest in Foreign Language	.07	.58	-.28	.06	.14	.12	-.08
14. Study Habits	.15	.49	.31	-.15	.04	.11	-.01
15. Attitudes Toward Americans	.16	.19	-.14	-.04	-.26	.29	-.09
16. California F-Scale	.06	.27	-.11	.37	.27	.03	.03
17. Ethnocentrism	.00	.02	.00	-.06	.45	-.06	.11
18. Anomie	.04	-.44	-.01	.08	.29	.27	.11
19. Cultural Allegiance (Filipino/Am.)	.10	-.10	.19	.23	.43	.03	.10
20. Number Learning (MLAT)	.28	-.20	.12	.01	-.03	.19	.04
21. Phonetic Script (MLAT)	.18	-.19	.28	.03	-.14	.02	-.10
22. Disarranged words (MLAT)	.21	.00	.09	.06	.01	.15	-.25
23. Paired Associates (MLAT)	.25	.02	-.05	.09	-.06	-.14	-.10
24. Words in Sentences (MLAT)	.51	-.03	.00	-.07	-.28	.12	.01
25. Vocabulary (CET)	.62	.15	.23	-.03	-.11	.03	-.11
26. Reading (CET)	.54	-.12	.33	.04	-.08	.10	-.06
27. Grammar (PNC)	.72	.03	.27	.16	-.11	.17	-.24
28. Listening Comprehension	.20	.06	.50	.22	.05	-.06	.05
29. General Average (1st-3rd-Year)	.89	-.02	.05	-.19	.09	-.05	-.06
30. Academic Average (1st-3rd Year)	.91	.02	.04	-.18	.06	-.05	-.04
31. Average Grade in Eng. (1st-3rd Yr.)	.88	.10	.03	-.02	.01	-.02	-.07
32. Average Grade in Filipino (1st-3rd Yr.)	.85	.09	-.06	-.11	.07	-.11	.11
33. Average Grade in Eng. (4th Yr.)	.86	.15	.06	.12	-.15	.02	-.12
34. Average Grade in Filipino (4th Yr.)	.80	.05	-.02	-.01	.02	-.10	-.02
35. Philippine Mental Ability (IQ)	.64	-.03	.04	-.33	-.04	.17	-.21
36. Orientation Index (Parent)	.13	.08	-.11	-.64	-.09	.02	-.06
37. Instrumental Orientation (P)	.07	.04	.59	.13	.10	.06	-.08
38. Integrative Orientation (P)	.09	.15	.21	.27	.08	.32	.06
39. Parental Encouragement (P)	.04	.11	.19	-.07	-.19	.54	.20
40. Attitudes toward Americans (P)	.02	.17	-.13	.11	-.03	.57	.25
41. California F-Scale (P)	.02	-.09	-.01	.17	-.06	.04	.64
42. Ethnocentrism (P)	.11	-.07	-.08	-.12	.08	-.10	.66
43. Anomie (P)	.14	-.12	.08	.21	.34	.13	.55
44. Cultural Allegiance (P) (Filip./Am.)	.30	.01	.20	.25	.41	-.18	.46
45. Oral Reading Fluency	.56	.35	.11	.46	-.22	.04	.18
46. Pronunciation Accuracy	.59	.45	.04	.30	-.24	.10	.15
47. Free Speech Fluency	.67	.11	.00	.05	-.19	.04	.05

interesting account of such feelings and the more general conflict of American and Asian sources of influence in the Philippines is given by Farwell (1967).

The presence of two measures of English achievement (Vs. 45 and 46) on Factor II gives further support to our contention that an integrative motive, independent of intelligence and language aptitude, is important for second-language achievement. As we have noted in previous studies, the integrative motive affects oral skills primarily. The consistency of this finding across cultures provides convincing evidence for the validity of the underlying theory.

Factor III is composed of six main variables: students' ratings of their own and their parents' proficiency in English (Vs. 1 and 2); the instrumental value attributed by the parents to English achievement (V. 37); the students' study habits (V. 14); and two measures of students' proficiency in English listening and reading comprehension (Vs. 28 and 26). The composition of this factor suggests that parents who see the instrumental value of knowing English develop skills in the language themselves and make sure that their children do the same. Apparently they use the language with the children and provide opportunities for them to read in English. It is noteworthy that this relationship of parental instrumental orientations and students' achievement had not appeared in the Canadian studies of Gardner (1960) or Feenstra and Gardner (1968) although it did for the French-American students in the Maine setting (see Chapter 4 of this volume). Apparently when parents see the instrumental value of a language, they can favorably influence their children's progress in the language.

Factor IV describes another, independent, form of instrumental orientation that enhances oral proficiency. In this case, parents who are instrumentally oriented with respect to their children learning English (V. 36) appear to pass this orientation on to their children (V. 7) at least in the case where the children have below average intelligence (V. 35) and an authoritarian personality disposition (V. 16). Of special interest is the fact that these children are relatively superior in oral reading skills (Vs. 45 and 46). This factor complements Factor III, since both suggest that parents who see the utilitarian value of a mastery of English can transfer this view to their children and thereby improve the children's proficiency. The Philippines, then, have provided us with intriguing contrasts with regard to the development of audio-lingual skills in a second language. We have traced out an integrative route to oral proficiency (Factor II) and two instrumental routes to aural and oral proficiency (Factors III and IV).

The remaining three factors do not encompass any of the measures of English achievement, yet they do reveal important patterns of parental and student attitudes. The major theme of Factor V is reminiscent of the French-American cultural conflict discussed in Chapter 4. In the Philippine case, symptoms of a cultural conflict present themselves at both the parental and student levels. This subgroup of parents is socially disorganized or anomic (V. 43) and yet favors the

Filipino to the American way of life (V. 44). Their children also favor the Filipino over the American form of life (V. 19) and are ethnocentric in outlook (V. 17) at the same time as they approach the study of English with an integrative orientation (V. 9). It is of special interest that both parents and their children seem to have trouble with languages, or at least the young people think this is the case; the students see their parents as being poor in both English and Tagalog (Vs. 2 and 4) and themselves as being poor in a school-taught nonvernacular such as Spanish (V. 5). We cannot unscramble the causal sequence here; it could be that the linguistically ungifted person is especially prone to problems of adjusting to the social atmosphere of Manila, or it could be that the anomic feeling is basic and interferes with the development of necessary language proficiencies. In either case, the problem merits closer study on its own because language competence appears to be intimately linked here with personal allegiances to a native culture and an imported one.

The theme of Factor VI is a strong pro-American orientation on the part of a subgroup of Philippine parents. They hold favorable attitudes towards Americans (V. 40), encourage their children's study of English (V. 39), and are under the impression that their children have a pronounced integrative outlook toward learning English (V. 38). The deception comes in the fact that the offspring do not endorse an integrative orientation (note Vs. 7 and 9) nor do they show any out of the ordinary proficiency in either English or Tagalog. The fact that they are particularly poor in other Philippine languages (V. 6) is of significance. In view of the current nationalistic sentiment in the Philippines, it appears that these pro-American parents have not been successful in fostering outstanding achievement in English, although they may have inhibited their children's development of competence in Philippine vernaculars.

Factor VII concerns the attitudes and perceptions of parents and gives us a peek into the value conflicts that may characterize contemporary Philippine society. The pattern of variables includes a marked sense of anomie (V. 43), ethnocentric and authoritarian attitudes (Vs. 41 and 42), a preference for Filipino over American culture (V. 44), and outstanding skill in Tagalog (V. 4). The configuration suggests that in the Philippines today those who have a strong pride and affection for their own cultural traditions encounter anomie perhaps because such a world view is not necessarily socially supported. Apparently the American influence must be reckoned with or accepted to some degree at least.

Summary

In summary, the Philippine results are particularly encouraging because they permit us to make statements about certain aspects of the second-language learning process that have relevance outside North American settings. At the same time as this analysis revealed cross-culturally stable relationships, it also brought to light others that seem tied to special cultural contexts.

English has a very special status in the Philippines. Not only is it the world language adopted by the Filipinos as the language of economic life, it has also become the sole or major medium of instruction in this multiethinic nation, although rarely is it a home language. With this as background, we found that students who approach the study of English with an instrumental outlook and who receive parental support in their views are clearly more successful in developing proficiency in the language than are those who fail to adopt this orientation. The importance of an instrumental form of motivation for progress in language study was also evident in our analysis of the French-Americans and their orientations to learning English. This type of relationship, interestingly enough, has not turned up in our studies of American and Canadian students learning French. Apparently when there is a vital need to master a second language, the instrumental approach is very effective, perhaps more so than the integrative.

However, with another subgroup of Filipino students we also discovered the by now familiar relationship between an integrative motivational system and progress in second-language development, especially in the oral-aural features of proficiency. This cross-cultural validation greatly strengthens our confidence in the theoretical notions that originally got us going on the problem. It seems all the more evident now that learners who identify with the cultural group represented by a foreign or second language are very likely to enjoy an advantage in attempts to master that language. Their motivation to learn the language appears to stem from and be sustained by the desire to identify.

The message for teachers and directors of language programs is clear: in North American settings, students of *foreign* languages will profit more if they can be helped to develop an integrative outlook toward the group whose language is being studied. An instrumental approach has little significance for them, and little motive force, it seems. For members of ethnic minority groups in North America or citizens in developing nations where imported foreign languages become one of the national languages, the story is different. Learning a *second* language with national and worldwide recognition is for them of vital importance, and both instrumental and integrative approaches to the learning task must be developed. The fascinating challenge for these groups however is to keep their own cultural and linguistic identity while mastering the second language. What has been most encouraging to us throughout these investigations is the fact that one can with the proper attitudinal orientation and motivation become bilingual without losing one's identity. In fact, striving for a comfortable place in two cultures seems to be the best motivational basis for becoming bilingual.

Chapter Eight

Attitudes and Motivation in Second-Language Learning: In Perspective

This book started with a simple question we asked ourselves about twelve years ago, and in our attempts to come up with a simple but believable answer, we have been led from one question to another, each one forcing us to search wider and deeper for answers. Since research is in large measure nothing but a question and answer process, perhaps we can best recapitulate the story and put it into proper perspective by collecting the questions that guided the venture and summarizing briefly the part answers we have found.

How is it that some people can learn a second or foreign language so easily and so well while others, given what seem to be the same opportunities to learn, find it almost impossible? With this as a start, we began to wonder about the more general question of what it is to have a knack for languages. To say that one has to have "an ear for languages" is to give an excuse rather than an answer, since it is too easy to transfer mysteries to biology, either as the source of one's linguistic difficulties or as the source of one's linguistic genius. Perhaps then the knack for languages lies in a profile of abilities or aptitudes that develop differently from person to person, some profiles favoring the language-learning process more than others. This idea makes good sense, but there is likely something more to it than aptitudes. Everyone or almost everyone learns his native language painlessly, so why would not everyone have at least a minimally adequate aptitude profile? And history makes it clear that when societies want to keep two or more languages alive, and learning more than one is taken for granted, everyone seems to learn two or more as a matter of course.

We believed that there was something more involved because we looked at the language-learning process with the eyes of social psychologists. From that perspective, learning a foreign language takes on a somewhat special significance. Social psychologists would expect that success in mastering a foreign language would depend not only on intellectual capacity and language aptitude but also on the learner's perceptions of the other ethnolinguistic group involved, his attitudes towards representatives of that group, and his willingness to identify enough to adopt distinctive aspects of behavior, linguistic and nonlinguistic, that characterize that other group. The learner's motivation for language study, it follows, would be determined by his attitudes and readiness to identify and by his orientation to the whole process of learning a foreign language. We saw many possible forms the student's orientation could take, two of which we looked at in some detail: an "instrumental" outlook, reflecting the practical value and advantages of learning a new language, and an "integrative" outlook, reflecting a sincere and personal interest in the people and culture represented by the other group. It was our hunch that an integrative orientation would sustain better the long-term motivation needed for the very demanding task of second-language learning, and here we had in mind students in North American contexts studying the popular European languages. For the serious student who really masters the foreign language, we saw the possibility of a conflict of identity or alienation arising (we used the term "anomie") as he became skilled enough to become an accepted member of a new cultural group. His knowledge of the language and the people involved would both prepare him for membership and serve as a symptom to members of the other group of his interests and affection. Thus the development of skill in the language could lead the language student ever closer to a point where adjustments in allegiances would be called for.

The American Studies

The details of how this theoretical overview developed and how it was tested with research conducted in the Montreal setting are given in Chapters 1 and 2, and in a set of readings placed in Appendix C. But then we wondered how far one could generalize the results of Canadian-based studies and how relevant the theory they suggested would be in other settings. Perhaps they are only meaningful for a bilingual and bicultural setting like Montreal. Suppose the same notions were put to test in the United States where, it is said, there is a different set of attitudes and a different social policy toward ethnic minorities who attempt to maintain their languages and their identities. Would attitudes and motivation have the same influence on American young people studying foreign languages? Would the instrumental-integrative distinction make sense, and would the ethoncentric syndrome play as prominent a role as it appeared to in Montreal?

In Chapter 3 the results of three American studies—one conducted in Louisiana, one in Maine, and one in Connecticut— are presented in detail, each setting having its own fascinating set of influences on young people studying a foreign language. Over and above the setting-to-setting diversity, however, we find in all three social contexts substantial evidence for the separate roles played by intelligence and aptitude and by attitudes and motivation in the development of second-language competence. For example, in all three studies it became evident that students with strong motivation and desire to learn French obtain good grades in French at school. And yet in each context there was a distinctive attitudinal basis for this motivation. In Louisiana, parental support and encouragement seemed to underlie the motivation. In Maine, the important factors were the student's identification with his French teacher and his sensitivity to other people's feelings. In Connecticut, it was an integrative orientation toward the language-learning process and a realization of the usefulness of knowing the language. Ethnocentric attitudes also affected students' progress in all three settings. In two cases, those with an ethnocentric ideology do poorly in French course work as well as on measures of aural and oral competency, and in the third case (Maine) ethnocentrism played its role in combination with measures of intelligence and language aptitude. Other patterns of attitudes and motivation were also found to determine achievement in particular manners from one setting to another.

At the same time, the American studies also provided impressive evidence for the importance of language-learning aptitude and intelligence in second-language proficiency, quite separate from attitudes and motives. Measures of language aptitude and intelligence were powerful predictors of achievement in French reading, vocabulary, and grammar in two of the three settings although somewhat less so in the third (Maine). But in addition to predicting progress in these more passive aspects of French language study, the intelligence and aptitude measures were also reliable barometers of grades received in French, and in settings such as Connecticut where the oral-aural skills are stressed in the language program, they become accurate predictors of these features of French proficiency as well. We also found that the subtests of the MLAT, quite apart from the intelligence factor, are differentially sensitive to various components of French proficiency, supporting Carroll's conceptualization of the nature of language aptitude.

The American studies also brought to light the different ways teachers and students view the development of proficiency in a foreign language. For example, students with outstanding expressive proficiency in French felt they were progressing well with the language, but teachers, judging from the grades assigned, often gave no credit for this form of competence. In other cases, it was the student with marked ability in French comprehension who felt he was doing well, but again the teachers did not agree. Other students who were highly motivated to learn the language for both integrative and instrumental reasons felt they were doing well and, interestingly enough, in this case teachers were more prone to agree. Since teacher-student discrepancies of these sorts can have an enormous dampening effect on the student's motivation, we suggested that research attention now be given to this matter.

Thus our confidence in the general notions that underlie these investigations has been increased greatly since we have found that factors of an attitudinal and motivational sort play very important roles in the acquisition of a second or foreign language in a variety of North American contexts. Instructive and interesting as this may be to language teachers and those concerned with theories of teaching, what is the message for the educational psychologist? We view these studies as attempts to clarify the factors at play in learning, and the results as suggestions for liberalizing current theories of learning. In the first place, our conception of attidues as an essential component of motivation is similar to that of Cook (1969), who in an important theoretical paper incorporates attitudes, values, and personality traits as "motivelike constructs" of major significance in determining behavior. Then we see our work as an expansion of Miller and Dollard's now classic interpretation of social learning (1941). For Miller and Dollard, learning takes place when the learner wants something, notices something, does something, and receives something. Thus in their view, learning requires the interplay of four essential components: motivation (the wanting aspect), perception (the noticing aspect), responding (the doing aspect), and reward or reinforcement (the receiving aspect). If any component is neglected, learning will not take place, that is to say, if motivation were set to zero, for example, or if no reward were forthcoming for responses made, learning would be disrupted.

In this book, we have been exploring the motivational system and the part it plays in second-language learning. But as we examine the many ramifications of the language learner's motivation, we see that it can affect and be affected by the other essential components of learning as well. Thus, we find that an integrative and friendly outlook toward the other group whose language is being learned can differentially sensitize the learner to the audio-lingual features of the language, making him more perceptive to forms of pronunciation and accent than is the case for a learner without this open and friendly disposition. If the student's attitude is highly ethnocentric and hostile, we have seen that no progress to speak of will be made in acquiring any aspects of the language. Such a student not only is perceptually insensitive to the language, but apparently is also unwilling to modify or adjust his own response system to approximate the new pronunciational responses required in the other language. His unwillingness likely stems from the fact that he derives no personal reinforcement in trying to assimilate the new linguistic system. Even the highly motivated student who does make the appropriate adjustments and develops skill in differentiating foreign sounds and incorporating them into his own repertoire often fails to receive the anticipated reinforcements from the teacher, who may have quite different criteria of progress in mind.

We have also found it very profitable to think of second-language learning in much the same way as Mowrer (1950) views the child's learning of the first language. His fascinating "autistic" theory of first-language learning differs in an essential way from Skinner's (1953) more mechanical approach to the problem. This is not to say that Skinner's notion of instrumental conditioning has no place in explaining language learning, which is clearly not true. It is rather a matter of emphasis and of trying to go deeper into the acquisition process itself. For Mowrer, word learning for both children and talking birds takes place when the *sounds* of words gradually come to carry a reinforcement power in themselves so that ultimately the learner *wants* to produce the sounds on his own. The sounds become reinforcing agents through the association the infant makes between the pleasantness of those who are nurturant towards him and various characteristics of their behavior, including the linguistic sounds they make. Learning the sounds, of course, also satisfies the basic social needs of the infant, for example, the need to communicate with valued people in his environment and to become similar to and belong with such people. Thus, in order to learn the rudiments of a language, the infant must come to identify with language users and want to be like them. Learning their code and the distinctive way they use it is one of the infant's means of expressing his identification. In this view it is not a simple case of the child emitting approximations to real words and having them shaped up through reinforcement, as Skinner seems to suggest. Mowrer believes that the reinforcing quality of sounds promotes a tendency in the child to play with sounds, to imitate adult utterances and in general serves as the base for the acquisition of the more complex features of the language. It is from this base too that the process of perceptual learning, so important in first-language acquisition, may have its start (see Hebb, Lambert, and Tucker, 1971, for a more complete development of this idea). We see a very similar developmental sequence in the case of learning a foreign language which is incidentally easier to study because the learning process unfolds more slowly. The learner, we argue, must be willing to identify with members of another ethnolinguistic group and to take on very subtle aspects of their behavior, including their distinctive style of speech and their language. Throughout these studies we have focused attention on individual differences in willingness to make this type of identification and the motivational implications of these differences. In doing so we hope we have thrown some new light on both the learning and teaching processes.

The French-American Studies

How might members of a linguistic minority group in America approach the school learning of their own language? As expected, we found among the French-American young people in the Louisiana and Maine communities a variety of different reactions ranging from suspicion and embarrassment to enthusiasm. We also found important differences in reactions between the Louisiana and Maine social contexts.

The two investigations presented in Chapter 4 demonstrate convincingly that the attitudes of French-American adolescents towards their own ethnolinguistic group and the American way of life can influence their linguistic development in both French and English, leading in some instances to a dominance of French over English, in other cases of English over French, and in still others bilingual competence. The outcome seems to be determined, in part at least, by the way the young French-American handles the conflicts of allegiances he is bound to encounter. For instance, we found in Louisiana that positive attitudes towards the French-American culture coupled with favorable stereotypes of the European French were highly associated with certain expressive skills in French. Other types of outlook, however, seem to restrict the potential development of these young people. Thus, a very strong pro-French attitudinal bias or an exceptionally strong motivation and drive to learn French do not automatically promote outstanding competence in the French language. Nor does a strong pro-American outlook assure proficiency in English.

Certain modes of adjustment were especially interesting because they provide the young French-American with models of how best to capitalize on his bicultural heritage. In Louisiana, for example, students with particularly favorable attitudes towards their own cultural group coupled with a competence in English were outstanding on various measures of proficiency in French. This pattern suggests that French-Americans who are content and comfortable with both facets of their cultural and linguistic heritage are psychologically free to become full bilinguals. In Maine we noted a somewhat different adjustment of equal social significance: French-American students with a strong instrumental orientation toward French study who receive parental encouragement to do well in French demonstrate outstanding skills in various aspects of French and feel assured of their competence in both French and English. Realizing that "instrumental" has a quite different meaning for students learning their own language, this family-supported instrumental approach offers the French-American a real chance of being both French and American.

The issue here is an extremely important one since most linguistic minority groups in North America remain in conflict and too often fail to make satisfactory adjustments. Take the Spanish-American as an example. In the United States, many Spanish-American parents find it logical to suppress the amplification of Spanish culture and the use of Spanish at home in order to better prepare their children for life in the English-speaking world of America. This type of logic is now being seriously challenged. For example, Padilla and Long (1969) are convinced that early bilingualism has a facilitating rather than a depressing effect on academic success. They found that Spanish-American students who were successful at college (i.e., those who completed a graduate program of study) typically came from homes in which both Spanish and English were used whereas Spanish-American college dropouts typically came from homes where English only was spoken. The important point here is that a minority group's feelings of marginality are not eliminated by switching off one of the competing cultural influences. The study of Peal and Lambert (1962) makes the same point even more emphatically. They found that French-Canadian ten-year-old children who came from homes where both French and English language skills were nurtured from infancy on had many advantages over a comparable group of children from homes where only French was used. Not only were the bilinguals far superior in English skills and at the same level in French, but they were also ahead in school grade level, and much advanced on various measures of intelligence. As more information of this type accumulates, members of minority groups will begin to realize that a much more rewarding mode of adjusting to the American scene is available to them, namely, the nurturance of two linguistic and cultural traditions.

There is an interesting parallel between the reactions of the French-American young people we studied and those of Italian-Americans described by Irving Child (1943). In 1943, Child studied the dilemma faced by second-generation Italian-Americans in a New England community; they too wondered what they were: Italian or American. From childhood on they had learned that they would likely be jilted by other youngsters in the community if they displayed too many signs of their Italian background. Still, they also realized that if they rejected this background they could lose the many satisfactions they enjoyed by belonging to a warm and cohesive Italian subgroup. Child found three typical modes of adjusting to this conflict. Some rebelled against their Italian background and made themselves as American as possible. Others rebelled in reverse, rejecting American ways as much as they could while proudly associating themselves with things Italian. The third type displayed an apathetic withdrawal from thinking of themselves in ethnic terms of any sort; this type tried unsuccessfully to escape the problem by avoiding situations where the issue of cultural background might come up, or by denying that there were any basic differences between Italians and Americans. In short, some tried to belong to one group or the other exclusively, and some, because of strong pulls from both sides, were unable to belong to either.

The parallel with the French-Americans is very close, except for one important difference. In Chapter 4, we have seen examples of French-American young people who had a strong preference either for the American or the French way of life, and in either case we noted that they were inadequate, relatively, in one language or the other. We also found subgroups who remained in conflict and showed an inadequacy in both languages, much like the ambivalent type Child described. In his study, however, Child did not find a subgroup corresponding to those French-American young people who have identified with both American and French traditions and who apparently have freed themselves to become fully bilingual. It is this subgroup, we believe, that has really surmounted the conflict of allegiances. The difference between Child's study and ours may be due to several factors: Child may have restricted his focus to those in conflict, excluding those who had made a satisfactory adjustment; there may be essential differences in the social pressures to adjust faced by Italian-Americans and French-Americans; or there may have been important changes in the social policy of maintaining minority languages in the period between 1943 and 1960 when we conducted our study in New England. It would certainly be worthwhile to replicate both of these studies in the 1970's since so many efforts are currently being directed toward bilingual and bicultural education in North America. Can an individual belong to two cultural groups simultaneously, that is, can he develop a bicultural identity? Our belief is that he certainly can. In fact we have the feeling that the bilingual-bicultural approach is the one most likely to help ethnic minority groups find a better and more comfortable place in American society.

A new question then comes to mind: Just how French are French-American young people? Have they really maintained a French tradition? We examined this issue in Chapter 4 also by comparing the Louisiana and Maine French-American samples on a series of measures, and by comparing both samples with English-speaking American young people from the same locales.

The interregional comparisons indicated convincingly that French-Americans in the Maine communities we studied are more effective in transmitting their linguistic and cultural legacy than those in Louisiana. The French tradition in Louisiana in fact seems to be fusing more rapidly with the American culture. Still the attitudes of Louisiana students toward their cultural background and their motivation to learn French are at the same high level as in Maine. The Maine communities nevertheless enjoy many cultural advantages: e.g., strong family support for staying French, and a school system that provides training in French from the elementary grades on. Consequently the Maine students were found to be much more skilled in all aspects of French, more ready to think of themselves as French, and, perhaps most important, more confident of their proficiency in English than their counterparts in Louisiana.

When compared with English-speaking Americans, both groups of French-American students are more anomic, authoritarian, and ethnocentric, and although more sympathetic to French-American culture, they still show a strong preference for the American over the European French way of life. This pattern of attitudes and feelings supports our contention that these young people do have serious personal conflicts of identity. Both groups are also much poorer on the English-based Modern Language Aptitude Test, but perform much better than American students on tests of French comprehension, although the Maine group is decidedly better. In French oral proficiency, the Maine group is clearly superior to the American students while the Louisiana French-Americans are at about the same level and in certain respects inferior to the English-speaking Americans. In short, we find here a very stubborn resistance to cultural erosion, especially in the Maine communities included in the investigation. This finding incidentally squares with Lemaire's (1966) sociohistorical study of French-Americans. Although the Louisiana setting is more outside the sphere of French influence from Canada and France, there too we were struck by the strong desire and motivation of young people to remain French.

Stereotypes and Language Learning

What types of mental images are evoked in the thinking of American students as they study French? The stereotypes students have of French people is an important matter because it could be a stumbling block not only for English speakers studying French but for French-Americans as well. The attitudes students hold of French people seemed favorable enough (Chapter 4), but we still wondered if part of the favorable attitude might only be a tendency to appear democratic and fair toward minority groups. In order to look a little deeper into their feelings, we examined students' stereotypes of French people by means of the "matched-guise" procedure, described in detail in Chapter 5 and in Reading Number Seven in Appendix C. This technique gets at the more private attitudes and mental images people have of foreign ethnolinguistic groups. What we found in brief was that American adolescents studying French at school generally have negative stereotypes of French people. For instance, they see representative European Frenchmen as being less honest, dependable, intelligent, kind, reliable, generous, and stable than Americans. At the same time, they see the typical Frenchman as more humorous and entertaining, as though he were taken to be a comic. The stereotypes of French-Americans are just as negative although they take a slightly different form: in the eyes of American students, French-Americans are shorter, less honest, generous, and kind but somewhat more bossy, self-confident, and nervous than Americans.

What is just as discouraging is the fact that French-American students from Louisiana have stereotypes of French people very similar to those of the English-speaking American students, suggesting that they have adopted the American image of French people. This is not the case, however, for French-

Americans from the Maine communities. At least they have favorable images of both European French and American-French people, suggesting that they have a deeper pride in being French.

The major point is that students of French appear to have pejorative and biased images of typical representatives of the ethnolinguistic group whose language they are supposed to master. One can imagine the difficulties a French-teacher would have in her attempts to penetrate and modify these images. The need to systematically modify these images, distorted as they certainly are, becomes very evident, since negative stereotypes of this sort, if accepted by a majority of students, could sabotage any educational effort to teach the language of the group in question.

Student Views on the Value of Language Study

Just how relevant is the study of a foreign language for an American adolescent? That is to say, where does it stand in a student's overall hierarchy of values? We wondered for instance if American young people, preoccupied as they are with preparing for future occupational roles and finding themselves socially, ever take time out to consider the intended purposes of language study and the peoples and cultures represented by such programs. To get a first-level look at the value hierarchies of the typical American student, we conducted a separate study with the Louisiana English-speaking students, focusing on their values and interests in various aspects of life. In addition to measures of social values, we also included in the battery a comprehensive assessment of scholastic aptitude, indices of the family's socioeconomic background, and certain of our standard measures of motivation to learn French and of language aptitude.

The analysis, described in full in Chapter 6, was extremely profitable because it provides important guidelines not only for language teachers but also for educators, parents, and adolescents. Different life styles came to light, some of which were productive and valuable in the young person's development while others were disruptive and restrictive. One subgroup of students, for example, had everything in its favor: intelligence, academic talent, language aptitude, advantaged home background, parents who care and encourage, and a value system built around success and achievement. Students with this profile excelled in all types of school work, language study included. For them getting ahead in life was a central goal and the learning of French was incidental, just another school subject they could master with ease. It seemed to us that these broadly talented young people could, with a different approach from parents and teachers, be oriented toward more socially valuable goals than the success-achievement style that preoccupies them. Similarly language study could be made something more significant than just another subject matter.

Other life styles are also conducive to proficiency in French. Certain students who were not favored with intellectual ability or home advantages still excelled in French, apparently because their value systems were also focused exclusively on success. Success at school was their current concern and French for them also was just another academic challenge. Another type of student presented a very disturbing picture: these young people came from less privileged homes but nevertheless had outstanding intellectual talent. However, they did not excel in any academic work, French study included, apparently because they lacked the parental encouragement needed for success motivation. The student who fits this pattern is especially likely to become discouraged and embittered.

Another student type was of special interest because the students involved had developed a passion for language study and excelled in it but not in other academic work. Still others were outstanding in French without the benefits of aptitudes or home background apparently because their values were focused on popularity and social approval. Thus, various student types came to light each with its own pattern of values and each providing clues about life styles that favor academic work in general and foreign-language study in particular.

The Philippine Study

In Chapter 7 we took our original set of ideas about attitudes and motivation out of the North American context entirely. The final question took this form: Will these research results and the theory underlying them hold up in really foreign settings? For example, will the general scheme be relevant in the Philippines, where a foreign language, English, has become not only a second national language but also the medium of instruction from the early grades on and an essential language for economic advancement and success?

For the Philippine study we had to shift attention from French to English and from France to America. It also meant reworking the content of many of our measures and changing our expectations about student reactions, for in this case the language being offered has enormous instrumental value. The results of this investigation brought to light certain cross-national stable relationships and certain others that are tied to cultural contexts. For example, we found that Filipino students who approach the study of English with an instrumental orientation and who receive parental support for this outlook were clearly successful in developing proficiency in the language. Thus, it seems that in settings where there is an urgency about mastering a second language—as there is in the Philippines and in North America for members of linguistic minority groups—the instrumental approach to language study is extremely effective. Nevertheless, for another subgroup of Filipino students an integrative orientation toward the study of English had a striking effect on proficiency, especially the audio-lingual aspects. This cross-cultural support for the importance of motivational and attitudinal dispositions strengthens greatly our confidence in the basic notions we started with. But still the Philippine investigation changed our perspective on the instrumental-integrative contrast. We see now that the typical student of *foreign* languages in North America will profit more if he is helped to develop an integrative outlook toward the group whose language is being offered. For him, an instrumental approach has little significance and little motive force. However, for members of ethnic minority groups in North America as for those living in nations that have imported prestigious world languages and made them important national languages, the picture changes. Learning a *second* language of national or worldwide significance is then indispensable, and both instrumental and integrative orientations towards the learning task must be developed. The challenge for these minority groups or those who import languages is to keep their own linguistic and cultural identity while mastering the second language, and in this regard various findings indicate that becoming bilingual does not mean losing identity. In fact, we are now convinced that striving for a comfortable place in two cultural systems may be the best motivational basis for becoming bilingual which in turn is one's best guarantee for really belonging to both cultures.

Looking Ahead

Throughout the discussions, we have mentioned various next steps in research that seem to us to be worthwhile. Of course, each reader will have his own ideas about which lines of thought are worth following up, which should be examined again from a different perspective, and which should be questioned and challenged. We will be most satisfied if we have been able to provoke an inquisitive frame of mind. Still it is appropriate for us to conclude with a brief overview of what we feel remains to be done.

It would be wrong to leave the impression that we have established the cross-cultural validity of the basic notions introduced in these investigations. That is certainly not the case. In fact what has been most impressive in this array of studies is the setting-to-setting contrasts that have emerged and the basic distinctiveness of each sociocultural context. Not only should other settings be studied in their own right, but these same settings should be revisited and reexamined with improved versions of the same instruments and measures and with newer, more searching instruments.

These have been exploratory studies only and we have moved swiftly and superficially from one important matter to another. That may be a good research strategy for exploration, but to be of permanent value, the follow-up work must be much more precise and comprehensive. For example, many of the measures used were not pretested, item analyzed, or checked for reliability and validity. Examples of how these instruments can be improved are available in the works of Madelaine Cooke (1967) and Jones and Lambert (1959, 1965, and 1967).

Our studies are limited too because they compressed the time between the measurement of cognitive abilities and attitudinal dispositions and the testing of language performance. It would now be valuable to shift to longitudinal investigations in which information about cognitive abilities as well as attitudes, stereotypes, values, and motivational orientations was gathered from students and parents *before* the language training is started (see the procedure described by Hayes, Lambert, and Tucker, 1967). This change is needed in order to disentangle attitudes and proficiency so that one can follow more clearly the casual sequence. For example, one could argue that doing well or poorly in a program of language study could influence attitudes toward the people and culture represented. We feel justified in drawing the opposite conclusion—that attitudes are a more stable personal characteristic which influence and determine one's progress in mastering a foreign language—for several reasons. First, attitudes and motivation are usually related to language achievement *independent* of aptitude and intelligence, making it difficult to argue that achievement determines attitudes or motivation since that tack raises a question about what, other than aptitude, determines the level of achievement in the first place. Second, the strong relationship we find between parents' and children's attitudes (see *Reading Number Two*) suggests that attitudes are developed in the home, before language training starts. Third, when we have attempted to measure attitudes before language training actually starts (see Feenstra and Gardner, 1968), the same general outcomes appeared.

At the same time as one extends the investigation to new contexts with improved methods, it would be equally valuable to concentrate on *experimental* studies of the roles of attitudes and motivation in learning. It is here that we make contact with current research and theory in the social psychology of attitudes, as illustrated in a recent study by Kanungo and Dutta (1966, 1969). Their research was conducted in Calcutta with Bengali college students as the experimental subjects. Bengalis were chosen because they "were known to have strong feelings of pride and group identification." Each student was asked to memorize a list of forty adjectives, twenty of them pleasant and twenty unpleasant. Two groups matched on learning ability were formed, one led to believe that the adjectives were actually attributes of Bengalis, the other that the adjectives described a purely fictitious people from another country. What is relevant is that the first group remembered many more of the adjectives believed to describe their own people, especially the favorable ones, in contrast to the comparison group that recalled more unfavorable than favorable ones. Furthermore when asked to rate the intensity of meaning of the adjectives, the groups differed reliably: the favorable adjectives were rated more pleasant when they referred to one's own group while the unfavorable ones were more unpleasant when ascribed to a foreign people. There is no question in this example that attitudes affect not only learning and memory but also the basic meaning of words themselves. Their 1969 study went further and established that attitudes affect the initial storage in memory of the adjectives as well as their retrieval from memory.

The experimental model could be used in various ways to throw more light on the operation of attitudes. For instance, using an unknown or an artificial language, one could have matched groups of subjects memorize or learn various components of the language (e.g., vocabulary glosses or properties of inflection or syntax) when the language is ascribed to two fictitious foreign peoples, one described in complimentary terms, the other negatively. Research of this sort with youngsters at various age levels would be especially valuable to help us determine when attitudes have their most powerful influence.

In a similar fashion, one could examine the instrumental integrative contrast in finer detail. Suppose two groups of students who have the same French teacher were matched on language aptitude and on several aspects of ethnocentrism. In the Montreal scene, prominent bilingual adults who are known to children (e.g., Jean Beliveau, a hockey star, and Giselle MacKenzie, the actress) could be asked to talk to both groups of children periodically, stressing with one group the instrumental advantages and with the other group the integrative advantages of knowing both languages. This difference in treatment could then be related to progress in second-language achievement over the course of a year or two.

There is still another phase of research, however, that calls for attention as well, namely the troublesome matter of *changing* attitudes, stereotypes, values, and motivation. There were numerous occasions in the preceding chapters where we saw how ethnocentric and prejudiced views held students back in various ways, where widely shared negative stereotypes of certain peoples appeared to make the work of a language teacher almost impossible, and where particular profiles of values and motives seemed to make the difference between success and failure at school work in general and language study in particular. Changing these basic elements of personality, however, is a delicate matter. Children often bring the attitudes of their parents or closest friends to school with them and educators wonder if these private matters are really the business of education. Our feeling is that much can be done by sympathetic and skillful teachers in calling these private views out and examining them through discussion. Children, fortunately, can unlearn almost as rapidly as they can learn, and they can be counted on for seeing what is fair and what is not. To help teachers and parents to effectively modify the attitudes of children, there is now available a growing body of knowledge in the social psychology of attitude change (see for example the excellent overviews of Triandis, 1971; Zimbardo and Ebbesen, 1969; Fishbein, 1967). To take a single example, Zimbardo and Ebbesen (1969) mention a technique which they believe is one of the most effective in changing perceptions and attitudes or increasing tolerance of contrary ideas: namely, to have the person involved "publicly espouse a set of opinions with which he strongly disagrees" (p. 57 f.). In this scheme, the person is made an active participant rather than a passive receiver of persuasive communications. A good deal of research shows that thinking about and publicly defending the other person's point of view, much as a debater or lawyer does, has a tremendous impact on stubborn attitudes and stereotypes. Talented teachers could make good use of this and related insights from psychology.

The language teacher often must work through just such stubborn points of view. For example, suppose that in the course of studying Swahili or French as used in an African setting, students learn that Africans eat and apparently enjoy eating grasshoppers. (This happens incidentally to be a real example; Stanley Thom, 1971). It takes little imagination to see what nasty effects this knowledge might have on the sympathetic feelings the teacher may have been able to develop among her students up to that point. Interestingly enough, the "grass-hopper eating" problem has received a good deal of research attention recently (Smith, 1961; Zimbardo, Weisenburg, Firestone, and Levy, 1965). Techniques are described for inducing adults to actually eat fried grasshoppers for the first time (about 50 percent of the subjects ate two or more in the experiment) and to basically change their attitudes toward grasshopper eating! Most teachers incidentally would not have anticipated that the changes were greater when the experimenter presented himself as a relatively unattractive person than when he was seen by the subjects as a really nice fellow.

Other valuable and instructive procedures for changing attitudes are less dramatic but also effective (see Staats and Staats, 1958; Lott and Lott, 1960). Likewise, McClelland's ongoing studies of the modification of basic value and motivation systems (1961, 1969) are extremely important developments for those in language pedagogy who realize the necessity of going far beyond the teaching of another code.

In any attempts to change students' outlooks, attention also must be given to age differences. For example, a cross-national study of children's views of foreign peoples by Lambert and Klineberg (1967) suggests that the age of ten or so may be the most receptive and friendly developmental period for introducing cultural differences. Perhaps language training should be adjusted to capitalize on this age level, for it is then that children are more likely to see foreign peoples as different but interesting, whereas before and after the age of ten or so they tend to link "different" with "bad." This issue of ethnocentrism has always been a national sickness, and a handicap for those teaching foreign languages. Still we see a real hope in the thinking of young people who, in all parts of the world today, are no longer sure that their own ways of life are the best, and are inquisitively searching everywhere for better, fairer ways.

Appendix A

I. Procedures Used with English-Speaking American Students

II. Procedures Used with French-American Students

I. PROCEDURES USED WITH ENGLISH-SPEAKING AMERICAN STUDENTS

1. Orientation Index

The following instructions were given to Ss: "Following is a statement with four possible answers given. You are asked to read the statement and then rank the alternatives from '1' to '4' as they refer to you. Mark '1' for the alternative most applicable in your case, '2,' the next most applicable, and so on.

It may be that you have some reason which has not been included among the alternatives. Item 'e' is therefore left blank to allow you to include your own personal reason. Insert your reason in the space provided and include it anywhere in the ranking that you think it belongs. If item 'e' is included, the ranks will run from '1' to '5.' If two alternatives appear to be equal, give them the same ranking."

I AM STUDYING FRENCH BECAUSE:

____ a. I think it will someday be useful in getting a good job.
____ b. I think it will help me to better understand French people and their way of life.
____ c. It will allow me to meet and converse with more and varied people.
____ d. A knowledge of two languages will make me a better educated person.
____ e. Any other personal reason.

2. Student's Orientation

Ss were asked to reply in writing to the following questions:

a. What advantages do you think there are for being able to speak French?____

_____

b. What disadvantages are there for not being able to speak French? _____

_____

c. What type of personal satisfactions do you think you would experience if you could speak French well?_____

_____

Motivational and Attitudinal Measures

3. *Rating of Integrative Orientation;* 4. *Rating of Instrumental Orientation*

Ss were presented a list of eight reasons frequently given by students for studying French. They were asked to read each reason carefully and indicate the extent to which it was descriptive of their own reasons for studying French. Endorsement of one of the following reasons was interpreted as indicating an *Integrative orientation*:

a. It will help me to understand better the French people and their way of life.

b. It will enable me to gain good friends more easily among French-speaking people.

c. It should enable me to begin to think and behave as the French do.

d. It will allow me to meet and converse with more and varied people.

Endorsement of one of the following reasons was interpreted as indicating an *instrumental orientation:*

a. I think it will some day be useful in getting a good job.

b. One needs a good knowledge of at least one foreign language to merit social recognition.

c. I feel that no one is really educated unless he is fluent in the French language.

d. I need it in order to finish high school.

The rating scale below each question had the following form:

Not my feeling   Definitely
   at all   ____: ____: ____: ____: ____: ____: _____ my feeling

5. *Anomie;*   6. *Authoritarianism;*   7. *Ethnocentrism;* and 8. *Preference for America over France*

Ss were given a series of forty-one statements representing opinions often expressed by students of their own age, accompanied by the following instructions:

"The following statements are opinions which have often been expressed by students about your age. They cover a wide range of topics and it has been found that many people agree with each statement and many disagree. There are no right or wrong answers. You are asked to mark each statement in the left-hand margin according to your agreement or disagreement as follows:"

+1: slight support, agreement

+2: moderate support, agreement

+3: strong support, agreement

-1: slight opposition, disagreement

-2: moderate opposition, disagreement

-3: strong opposition, disagreement

The forty-one statements from all four scales were given in random order. They are classified below to correspond to the scales. Note that certain items are "reversed," i.e., their content is the opposite of that reflected by the name of the scale. For example, items 2 and 8 are reversed with regard to anomie.

5. Anomie Scale:

1. In the U.S. today, public officials aren't really very interested in the problems of the average man. (Modified Srole [1951] item.)

2. Our country is by far the best country in which to live. (Disagreement reflects anomie.)

3. The state of the world being what it is, it is very difficult for the student to plan for his career.

4. In spite of what some people say, the lot of the average man is getting worse, not better. (Original Srole item.)

5. These days a person doesn't really know whom he can count on. (Original Srole item.)

6. It is hardly fair to bring children into the world with the way things look for the future. (Original Srole item.)

7. No matter how hard I try, I seem to get a "raw deal" in school.

8. The opportunities offered young people in the United States are far greater than in any other country. (Disagreement reflects anomie.)

9. Having lived this long in this culture, I'd be happier moving to some other country now.

10. In this country, it's whom you know, not what you know, that makes for success.

11. The big trouble with our country is that it relies, for the most part, on the law of the jungle: "Get him before he gets you."

12. Sometimes I can't see much sense in putting so much time into education and learning.

6. *F-Scale* (There are no reversed items here; they all reflect antidemocratic ideology.)

1. Obedience and respect for authority are the most important virtues children should learn.
2. What youth needs most is strict discipline, rugged determination, and the will to work and fight for family and country.
3. Nowadays when so many different kinds of people move around and mix together so much, a person has to protect himself especially carefully against catching an infection or disease from them.
4. What this country needs most, more than laws and political programs, is a few courageous, tireless, devoted leaders in whom the people can put their faith.
5. No weakness or difficulty can hold us back if we have enough will power.
6. Human nature being what it is, there will always be war and conflict.
7. A person who has bad manners, habits, and breeding can hardly expect to get along with decent people.
8. People can be divided into two distinct classes: the weak and the strong.
9. There is hardly anything lower than a person who does not feel a great love, gratitude, and respect for his parents.
10. The true American way of life is disappearing so fast that force may be necessary to preserve it.
11. Nowadays more and more people are prying into matters that should remain personal and private.
12. If people would talk less and work more, everybody would be better off.
13. Most people don't realize how much our lives are controlled by plots hatched in secret places.

7. *Ethnocentrism Scale* (No reversed items)

1. The worst danger to real Americanism during the last fifty years has come from foreign ideas and agitators.
2. Now that a new world organization is set up, America must be sure that she loses none of her independence and complete power as a sovereign nation.
3. Certain people who refuse to salute the flag should be forced to conform to such a patriotic action, or else be imprisoned.
4. Foreigners are all right in their place, but they carry it too far when they get too familiar with us.
5. America may not be perfect, but the American way has brought us about as close as human beings can get to a perfect society.
6. It is only natural and right for each person to think that his family is better than any other.

7. The best guarantee of our national security is for America to keep the secret of the nuclear bomb.

8. *Preference for America over France Scale* (No reversed items)

1. Compared to the people of France, Americans are more sincere and honest.
2. Family life is more important to Americans than it is to people in France.
3. Compared to Americans, the French are an unimaginative people.
4. Americans appreciate and understand the arts better than do most people in France.
5. The chief stimulants to basic institutions in France have come mainly from American ideas and doctrines.
6. American children are better mannered than French children.
7. The French people would benefit greatly if they adopted many aspects of the American culture.
8. Few French universities can match the intellectual standing of our American universities.
9. The French way of life seems crude when compared to ours.

9. *French-American Attitude Scale* (No reversed items)

*S*s were given a series of sixteen statements, with instructions similar to those accompanying the preceding list of forty-one statements, plus the following clarifying paragraph:

"French-Americans" means those French-speaking Americans who learn French in the home from French-speaking parents. For example, in Louisiana and Maine there are communities with a large proportion of French-speaking Americans, that is, "French-Americans."

1. French-Americans contribute to the richness of our society.
2. They have produced outstanding artists and writers.
3. The more I get to know the French-Americans, the more I want to be able to speak their language.
4. French-Americans are very democratic in their politics and philosophy.
5. By bringing the old French folkways to our society, they have contributed greatly to our way of life.
6. The French-Americans' undying faith in their religious beliefs is a positive force in this modern world.
7. The French-American has every reason to be proud of his race and his traditions.

8. If the United States should lose the French-American influence, it would indeed be a great loss.

9. French-Americans are much more polite than most Americans.

10. French-Americans are a very dependable people.

11. American children can learn much of value by associating with French playmates.

12. French-Americans set a good example for us by their family life.

13. We can learn better ways of cooking, serving food, and entertaining from the French-Americans.

14. French-Americans are generous and hospitable to strangers.

15. Americans should make a greater effort to meet French-American people.

16. It is wrong to try to force the French-American to become American in his habits.

10. *Motivational Intensity Scale*

*S*s were asked to answer the following questions by placing a check mark to the left of the statement which appeared most applicable to them. It was stressed that the questionnaire would not be seen by anyone in the school or by any of the school authorities and that only the directors of the research project would have access to answers. They were urged to be as accurate as possible.

1. Compared to the others in my French Class, I think I:
____ a. do more studying than most of them.
____ b. do less studying than most of them.
____ c. study about as much as most of them.

2. I think about the words and ideas which I learn about in my French classes:
____ a. once in awhile.
____ b. hardly ever.
____ c. very frequently.

3. If French was not taught in this school, I would **probably**:
____ a. not bother learning French at all.
____ b. try to obtain lessons in French somewhere else.
____ c. pick up French in everyday situations. (i.e., read French books and newspapers, try to speak it when possible, and go to French movies).
____ d. none of these (explain)_____

4. On the average, I spend about the following amount of time doing home study in French: (include all French homework)
____ a. four hours per week.
____ b. one hour per week.
____ c. seven hours per week.

_____ d. none of these. Give approximate number of hours per week: _____ hours.

5. Considering how I go about studying for French, I can honestly say that I:

_____ a. do just enough work to get along.

_____ b. will pass on the basis of sheer luck or intelligence because I do very little work.

_____ c. really try to learn French.

_____ d. none of these (explain) _____

6. After I finish high school, I will probably:

_____ a. try to use my French as much as possible.

_____ b. make no attempt to remember my French.

_____ c. continue to improve my French (e.g., daily practice, night school, etc.).

_____ d. none of these (explain) _____

11. *Desire to Learn French*

*S*s were asked to reply to the following questions:

1. Place a check mark anywhere along the line below to indicate how much you like French compared to all your other courses.

French is my		French is my
least preferred		*most* preferred
course	__: __: __: __: __: __: __:	course

2. When you have an assignment to do in French, do you:

_____ a. do it immediately when you start your homework.

_____ b. become completely bored.

_____ c. put it off until all your other homework is finished

_____ d. none of these (explain) _____

3. During French classes, I:

_____ a. have a tendency to daydream about other things.

_____ b. become completely bored.

_____ c. have to force myself to keep listening to the teacher.

_____ d. become wholly absorbed in the subject matter.

4. If I had the opportunity and knew enough French, I would read French newspapers and magazines:

_____ a. as often as I could.

_____ b. fairly regularly.

_____ c. probably not very often.

_____ d. never.

5. After I have been studying French for a short time, I find that I:

_____ a. have a tendency to think about other things.

___ b. am interested enough to get the assignment done.

___ c. become very interested in what I am studying.

6. It I had the opportunity to change the way French is taught in our school, I would:

___ a. increase the amount of training required for each student.

___ b. keep the amount of training as it is.

___ c. decrease the amount of training required for each student.

7. I believe French should be:

___ a. taught to all high school students.

___ b. taught only to those students who wish to study it.

___ c. omitted from the school curriculum.

8. I find studying French:

___ a. very interesting.

___ b. no more interesting than most subjects.

___ c. not interesting at all.

12. *Social Inquisitiveness Scale*

In this part of the questionaire, Ss were given descriptions of people about their own age. They were asked to read each section carefully and indicate how much they are like one of the people described. They were told that sometimes boys' names were used, sometimes girls' names, but that each S can think of him or herself as behaving like one of the persons even though not of the same sex as the one described in a particular example.

Responses to each section were to be:

I THINK OF MYSELF AS BEING:

___ 1. very much like A.

___ 2. more like A than B.

___ 3. more like B than A.

___ 4. very much like B.

1. A and B were both average in athletic ability at high school but not good enough to get on first teams. A was very content to watch the first teams when they played and was considered a regular fan. B didn't enjoy being a spectator very much and went out of his way to participate in games with neighborhood teams and to learn how to play many of the less popular sports.

2. A and B spent most of their summers at the same camp. They were both very happy at camp. A was always on the go, continually doing something new and had little time to write long letters home. B was very content to participate in the regular camp activities and she found more time to write home about all that was going on at camp.

3. A and B entered the armed services together right after high school and took their basic training together at the same camp. A spent most of his free evenings with a small group, and you could almost always find him at the same places with the same fellows, playing cards or out in front of the barracks exchanging stories with his friends. B would dress up right after supper and go into town where he had met some new friends, had joined a young people's group and was often seen reading up on something at the library.

4. A and B were close friends at school and once they took an organized tour of a large and interesting city quite a distance from their home. They both enjoyed the tour very much. A could be counted on to follow all that was explained and shown to the group. B would follow, too, but she'd stop and study the monument or displays mentioned by the tour leader or ask questions of the people who lived in certain districts they visited.

5. A and B were both good students at school and were happy to graduate from high school. A visited several cities rather distant from home to find a good position with a well-known company. He asked B to come with him because both could have had a job with the same company but B was more content to stay nearer home and, anyway, there were just as good jobs in their own town.

6. A and B were both very happy that a new neighbor had moved in next door, because they both liked people a great deal. A was sure that she'd meet the new neighbor sooner or later, but did not go out of her way to introduce herself. B had gone over the first thing, and within an hour knew everything about the new neighbors, where they had moved from, how long they were going to stay, etc.

7. A and B were both taking the technical course at high school and were both fairly good students. It was interesting to watch how they spent their Saturday afternoons. A had asked the manager of the local garage to let him learn more about mechanics by working without pay. B spent his free time getting his assignments well done.

8. A and B were both offered their choice of position after high school because they were both fairly good students and dependable. A was very happy to find a job that permitted her to settle down in one spot near people and places she knew well. B was very happy to take the job which gave her a good chance to travel, to train on the job for different positions even though it offered somewhat less security and pay than A's.

13. *Sensitivity for Others Scale*

*S*s were asked to indicate, by a check mark placed on the line below each of the following eight statements, how well each one applied to them. The line below the statements read:

Not like   Very much

me   __: __: __: __: __: __: __: me

1. I believe in treating *all* people with kindness and respect.

2. I'm often tempted to make fun of people who do things that I consider stupid. (Reversed.)

3. I often do things my own way without thinking about how it will affect others. (Reversed.)

4. It bothers me whenever I have been rude to someone.

5. I usually have a hard time anticipating how others will feel about what I am going to say. (Reversed.)

6. I sometimes enjoy laughing at the mistakes of others. (Reversed.)

7. Often I feel it is necessary to correct people without beating around the bush. (Reversed.)

8. I often listen to other people and do my best to understand their point of view.

14. *Parental Encouragement*

How much do your parents encourage you to study French?

Not at all   __ : __ : __ : __ : __ : __ : __   Very much

15. *Parents Favor Student Learning French*

Students were asked to reply to the following question: How do your parents feel about your learning French? Please explain their feelings. _____

16. *Parents' French Friends*

*S*s were asked to reply to the question: Have you ever had the opportunity to hear French used with friends of the family?____ Please give an example _____

17. *Student's French Acquaintances*

*S*s were asked to reply to the question: do you know any French-speaking people?_____About how many? _____

18. *Student's French Friends*

Immediately after the above question they were given the following:

Are any of these really good friends? _____

How friendly are you with them? _____

19-24. *Attitudinal Ratings*

The following instructions were given with regard to Variables 19 to 24:

"It is important that you make a separate and independent judgment of each item. Do not look back to check what you marked on earlier scales; try to keep your attention on the scale at hand. Work as rapidly as you can and do not worry or puzzle over individual items. It is your first impressions, the immediate 'feelings' about concepts, that are of interest. On the other hand, please do not be careless, because we are very interested in your true impressions.

Remember that this questionaire will not be seen by anyone in this school or by any of the school authorities. Only the directors of this research project will have access to your answers."

19. *French People from France*

Ss were asked to indicate their impressions of *French people from France* on the following 7-point evaluational scales:

1. Interesting	—: —: —: —: —: —: —	Boring
2. Prejudiced	—: —: —: —: —: —: —	Unprejudiced
3. Brave	—: —: —: —: —: —: —	Cowardly
4. Handsome	—: —: —: —: —: —: —	Ugly
5. Colorful	—: —: —: —: —: —: —	Colorless
6. Friendly	—: —: —: —: —: —: —	Unfriendly
7. Honest	—: —: —: —: —: —: —	Dishonest
8. Stupid	—: —: —: —: —: —: —	Smart
9. Kind	—: —: —: —: —: —: —	Cruel
10. Pleasant	—: —: —: —: —: —: —	Unpleasant
11. Polite	—: —: —: —: —: —: —	Impolite
12. Sincere	—: —: —: —: —: —: —	Insincere
13. Successful	—: —: —: —: —: —: —	Unsuccessful
14. Secure	—: —: —: —: —: —: —	Insecure
15. Dependable	—: —: —: —: —: —: —	Undependable
16. Permissive	—: —: —: —: —: —: —	Strict
17. Leader	—: —: —: —: —: —: —	Follower
18. Mature	—: —: —: —: —: —: —	Immature
19. Stable	—: —: —: —: —: —: —	Unstable
20. Happy	—: —: —: —: —: —: —	Sad
21. Popular	—: —: —: —: —: —: —	Unpopular
22. Hardworking	—: —: —: —: —: —: —	Lazy
23. Ambitious	—: —: —: —: —: —: —	Not Ambitious

They were also asked to rate the following concepts in the same manner as above: 20. *Me;* 21. *Americans;* 22. *Me, as I'd like to be;* 23. *French-Americans;* 24. *My French Teacher*

25. *Comparative Evaluation of European French and American English Voices* and 26. *Comparative Evaluation of French-American and American English Voices*

Ss were asked to rate the personalities of the speakers heard on each of the following traits:

Height	Very little ___: ___: ___: ___: ___: ___ Very much
Good Looks	Very little ___: ___: ___: ___: ___: ___ Very much
Leadership	Very little ___: ___: ___: ___: ___: ___ Very much
Thoughtfulness	Very little ___: ___: ___: ___: ___: ___ Very much
Sense of humor	Very little ___: ___: ___: ___: ___: ___ Very much
Intelligence	Very little ___: ___: ___: ___: ___: ___ Very much
Honesty	Very little ___: ___: ___: ___: ___: ___ Very much
Self-confidence	Very little ___: ___: ___: ___: ___: ___ Very much
Friendliness	Very little ___: ___: ___: ___: ___: ___ Very much
Dependability	Very little ___: ___: ___: ___: ___: ___ Very much
Generosity	Very little ___: ___: ___: ___: ___: ___ Very much
Entertainingness	Very little ___: ___: ___: ___: ___: ___ Very much
Nervousness	Very little ___: ___: ___: ___: ___: ___ Very much
Kindness	Very little ___: ___: ___: ___: ___: ___ Very much
Reliability	Very little ___: ___: ___: ___: ___: ___ Very much
Ambition	Very little ___: ___: ___: ___: ___: ___ Very much
Sociability	Very little ___: ___: ___: ___: ___: ___ Very much
Character	Very little ___: ___: ___: ___: ___: ___ Very much
General likability	Very little ___: ___: ___: ___: ___: ___ Very much

40. Other than School Experiences with French
Question:
Did you learn most of your French in school? (yes or no?) _____
If you learned French somewhere other than school, please explain where.

_____

41. Self-rating of French Skills
Students were asked to check those statements that best apply to themselves:
I speak French: not at all _____ a little _____ fairly well _____ fluently _____
I read French: not at all _____ a little _____ fairly well _____ fluently _____
I write French: not at all _____ a little _____ fairly well _____ fluently _____

42. Rating of Mother's French Skills
Ss were asked to rate their mother's French skills in the same manner as in (41) above.

43. Rating of Father's French Skills
Ss were asked to rate their father's French skills in the same manner as in (41) above.

II: PROCEDURES USED WITH FRENCH-AMERICAN STUDENTS

1. *Comparative Preference for English over French Acquaintances*
   Ss were asked to reply to the following questions, using 7-point scales:
   1. What is your general impression of the English-speaking people you know
as individuals? Please indicate your answer on the line below:

I like most of them very much	I don't particularly like any of them
__:__:__:__:__:__:__:	of them

I like most
of them
very much   __:__:__:__:__:__:__: of them

2. What is your general impression of the French-speaking people you know as
individuals? Please indicate your answer on the line below:

I like most
of them
very much   __:__:__:__:__:__:__: of them

2. *Desire for French Identity*
   The following questions were asked:
   1. Do you think there should be a French TV channel in your district?

Definitely
yes   __:__:__:__:__:__:__: need for one

2. Do you often think of yourself as being a French person, or a person of
French ancestry?

Very often   __:__:__:__:__:__:__: Never

3. Are you interested in seeing French-speaking Americans get ahead in
American business or politics?

Very
interested   __:__:__:__:__:__:__: at all

4. Are most of your close friends French or English-speaking?

Mostly
French   __:__:__:__:__:__:__: English

5. Would you prefer to work with French or English-speaking Americans?

Prefer French-speaking   Prefer English-speaking
     Americans   _____   Americans   _____

6. Do you want to marry someone who is French-speaking?

Definitely   Definitely
yes   __:__:__:__:__:__:__: no

7. Do you want your children to grow up speaking French?
Yes   No
8. Indicate along the line below how much you enjoy speaking French.

Enjoy it   Do not enjoy
very much   __:__:__:__:__:__:__: it at all

3. Self-rating of French Skills
Ss were asked the following questions:
1. How well do you *speak* French?
2. How well do you *read* French?
3. How well do you *write* French?
Ss were asked to indicate their degree of skill on the following scales:
not at all _____ a little _____ fairly well _____ fluently _____

4. Number of Years Studying English
1. Did you learn your English primarily at home or in school?
_____ Home   _____School
2. If your answer was "school," how many years have you studied English?

5. Thinking in French more than English
When you are thinking, do you think primarily in French or in English?
(Check one point along the scale where you feel you actually fall.)

Always in   Always in
French   __:__:__:__:__:__:__: English

6. Preferred Language
Which language do you prefer to speak? (Check one point along the scale
where you actually fall.)

English,   French,
definitely   __:__:__:__:__:__:__: definitely

7. Self-rating of English Skills
Students were asked the same question given for self-ratings of French skills.

8. *Word Completion*

"Following are four 2-letter sequences each of which is a commonly occurring beginning for words in either French or English. For each 2-letter beginning, you will be given *45 seconds* to write down as many words as you can which begin with these letters. Try your best to make both French and English words. For example, if you were given "vi" . . . . . you could make the words "ville," "victory," and many others. Don't turn to the next page yet. You will find the next page divided into 4 sections. You should start in the upper left, number A, and concentrate on it and write as many words as you can. When 45 seconds have passed, the examiner will say, "go on to B" and you should switch immediately to B and so on for C and D. Please do not go back after the time limit is up for that section and don't go ahead. Concentrate on the section you are working on.

Any questions? Don't turn the page until told to."

On the second page, divided into four sections, were the syllables:

li . . . . .   A   va . . . . .   B

su   C   te . . . . .   D

each followed by lines on which *S*s were to indicate the words constructed.

9. *Word Detection*

The Questionnaire included a two-page section, the first page as follows:

"Following are a series of long nonsense words which have small English and French words embedded in them. For example, in the nonsense word 'dansonodend' you can find the English words: on, no, nod, node, ode, end, etc., and also the French words: dans, ans, son, de, en, etc. We want you to find the small embedded words in some other examples. All parts of the word you find must be together as a unit, that is, you can't skip around to complete one word.

In the nonsense words on the next page, some of the hidden words will be long, some short. You will have one minute to find as many *English and French* words as you can in each nonsense word. Try to concentrate on each section for the minute and when told time is up, move immediately on to the next section. Don't go back or ahead.

Any questions? Don't turn the page until told to."

The second page contained, in its four sections:

A	B
pintonightresoisle	takinozzlesew
C	D
patomenestle	calmaisitueacheery

10. *Word Association*
*S*s were instructed as follows:
"You are now going to be presented a series of words, some in English, some in French. Think about the first word given you, and write down on the spaces provided all the words that come to mind as you think about the word given you. Any questions? Don't turn the page until told to." On pages 2 and 3, the following words, with spaces below each one, were given:
MAISON, IDEA, PAUVRE, HOUSE, IDEE, POOR

11. *Nationality When Asked by English-Speaking Person*
If an English-speaking individual asked you what nationality you were, what would you say? American _____ French _____ French-American or Franco-American _____

12. *Nationality When Asked by French-Speaking Person*
If a French-speaking individual asked you what nationality you were, what would you say?
American _____ French _____ French-American or Franco-American _____

13. *Reinforcements for Speaking European French*
1. If you spoke French *at home* the way the European French speak it, or as your teachers speak it, what would be the reactions of:
    a. your parents _____
    b. your brothers and sisters_____
    c. your close French-American friends_____
2. If you spoke French *at school* the way the European French speak, or as your teachers speak it, what would be the reactions of:
    a. your French teacher _____
    b. your French-speaking schoolmates _____
    c. your English-speaking schoolmates _____

14. *Desire to Live in France*
If you had the opportunity, would you like to live in France?
    a. For a short time:

definitely   definitely
would not   *would*
like it   __: __: __: __: __: __: __: like it

    b. Permanently:

definitely   definitely
would not   *would*
like it   __: __: __: __: __: __: __: like it

15. *Rating of Integrative Orientation to Learn English*

16. *Rating of Instrumental Orientation to Learn English*

17. *Phonetic Discrimination*

Appendix B

Correlation Tables

Table 1-B

Correlation Matrix for the *Louisiana* Study *

	1	2	3	4	5	6	7	8	9	10	11	12	13	14	15	16	17	18	19	20	21
1		38	26	31	07	-09	-03	04	08	-06	18	08	-01	-04	-19	-14	-23	-09	-20	-20	-10
2			33	37	13	-03	01	04	05	03	18	14	-06	-15	-10	-08	-14	-12	00	-25	16
3				32	18	19	-04	-02	19	21	15	-03	04	-12	-20	-03	-13	-19	-16	-06	-10
4					-03	01	-05	-16	06	27	-08	-10	07	-10	-10	-06	-14	-14	-21	-08	-11
5						51	03	-04	04	11	08	28	22	-14	-09	-09	-00	-01	-13	-03	-03
6							08	-07	02	15	20	35	17	03	-14	-08	02	-04	-14	01	10
7								46	28	-09	08	06	04	10	09	10	23	18	03	03	05
8									31	-29	13	11	-08	07	14	14	17	11	09	11	-10
9										-11	08	-06	23	20	03	08	04	04	09	06	-12
10											07	-14	17	03	13	-01	09	-18	-04	-00	-21
11												39	02	-14	-11	-02	-20	-15	20	-18	08
12													07	-12	-14	02	-18	-18	-14	-12	14
13														-06	02	-14	-14	-16	-12	11	05
14															40	41	40	45	17	24	10
15																43	49	43	15	45	20
16																	48	47	04	22	15
17																		53	10	44	21
18																			24	28	32
19																				07	06
20																					19

*(The names of the variables corresponding with the numbers are listed in Table 1 in the test.)

Table 1-B (Continued)

Correlation Matrix for the Louisiana Study

	22	23	24	25	26	27	28	29	30	31	32	33	34	35	36	37	38	39	40	41
1	-31	-08	01	-24	-15	-26	-12	05	-21	12	06	06	-10	-15	-16	07	00	-13	-13	02
2	-29	08	16	-26	-19	-29	-06	-10	-30	-13	-17	16	-00	-06	05	12	12	-04	-01	15
3	-13	10	13	-16	-07	-13	02	-15	-19	-21	-29	-13	04	-01	06	06	07	07	10	03
4	-19	-10	-03	-17	-16	-26	-19	-14	-21	03	-01	17	02	-18	-12	-06	05	-05	01	06
5	-02	-02	14	-09	-00	-16	08	-11	08	-15	-73	-24	07	-14	-01	-01	-16	-07	-05	09
6	-11	-09	09	-14	-18	-07	09	01	02	-33	-48	-07	00	-10	05	01	-01	-00	-05	09
7	18	-18	14	19	18	10	10	13	25	-06	-03	-03	-03	03	-06	-04	-07	02	01	-05
8	17	-03	29	37	29	38	21	12	40	-01	-05	01	-02	-05	-11	-03	-03	13	-00	-06
9	10	-02	30	22	24	12	10	05	16	-17	-05	-11	03	02	02	-03	07	10	00	01
10	04	-12	-29	03	08	01	06	-04	01	-09	-15	07	06	12	-03	01	12	11	07	12
11	06	11	14	-07	-01	-17	24	02	-07	-16	-14	10	05	05	05	-02	-04	02	08	04
12	-08	24	-05	-20	-20	-14	08	11	-12	-03	-22	-09	-08	-13	-03	-08	-06	-20	01	-02
13	-02	09	02	-05	10	-21	-08	04	-10	-05	-23	-05	-13	05	12	06	-01	01	-19	05
14	14	07	-04	33	29	34	-09	42	38	-18	16	08	29	10	15	21	10	39	03	15
15	31	10	10	46	49	51	07	38	39	-03	14	-07	21	29	31	36	22	35	36	07
16	34	25	11	49	49	42	-00	30	30	-16	21	01	06	07	15	20	33	25	34	03
17	29	-09	16	45	41	67	-07	41	54	-14	09	02	17	16	19	27	28	35	25	12
18	21	12	05	49	46	45	01	33	42	-09	13	09	11	07	20	28	24	32	33	16
19	23	23	25	24	33	16	18	15	16	-05	09	01	14	11	19	19	15	24	35	11
20	21	04	-02	32	32	42	-05	14	30	01	09	-17	30	21	19	25	22	33	35	11

Table 1-B (continued)

Correlation Matrix for the *Louisiana* Study

	22	23	24	25	26	27	28	29	30	31	32	33	34	35	36	37	38	39	40	41
21	17	18	04	39	36	22	-13	37	18	-08	-05	-08	20	08	27	26	23	19	24	04
22		-03	06	52	46	38	18	13	35	15	11	-03	10	07	-00	-04	-05	14	18	-17
23			01	26	20	03	23	03	-01	-11	-07	-26	-11	-14	05	03	18	04	07	-03
24				16	13	17	05	15	06	-09	-21	-01	05	07	08	10	26	05	07	-04
25					74	64	10	33	47	07	12	03	-12	04	11	20	25	26	34	-05
26						58	13	40	57	-02	13	-07	28	21	28	37	28	42	44	07
27							-01	34	53	05	19	01	11	23	17	22	27	30	34	-03
28								08	25	-09	-16	-32	-11	08	06	06	-05	06	05	-03
29									42	02	11	05	20	16	16	28	26	26	23	02
30										-07	04	-01	21	17	19	25	18	40	41	14
31											29	08	-17	-07	-27	-21	-18	-27	-20	-17
32												18	-02	19	03	03	12	06	07	05
33													13	06	-04	-00	14	01	03	10
34														64	74	72	41	72	72	60
35															72	71	48	46	55	39
36																88	54	61	68	52
37																	58	69	71	53
38																		48	54	47
39																			90	73
40																				74
41																				

Table 2-B

Correlation Matrix for the *Maine* Study *

	1	2	3	4	5	6	7	8	9	10	11	12	13	14	15	16	17	18	19	20	21
1		26	08	11	-25	-38	-16	-03	-27	-11	-21	-12	-10	-10	-00	-12	-13	-26	10	-02	09
2			39	33	07	09	-09	07	-14	03	-18	05	-23	-22	-14	-16	-13	-22	02	-05	06
3				38	02	06	-10	-00	-12	07	-20	07	-13	-05	-10	-11	-09	02	16	-13	04
4					-04	-01	-12	-06	-10	03	-23	08	-12	-11	-24	-20	-08	-16	04	04	12
5						45	-00	03	09	19	-14	16	16	02	-02	-00	-06	07	02	16	-05
6							19	21	27	18	-02	49	00	-07	-15	-01	-06	02	08	15	11
7								58	24	-03	20	08	10	16	08	26	27	09	27	03	-02
8									27	-06	-04	12	23	11	-04	10	19	-03	24	05	-02
9										-09	06	19	08	-05	-06	16	-02	12	24	-08	-05
10											-13	17	01	12	04	-09	-06	06	02	-06	-13
11												-01	-17	07	11	17	28	05	-06	-06	-04
12													-01	01	-11	02	-12	13	12	-10	03
13														-08	-12	-06	-12	-06	04	02	-11
14															41	23	39	46	18	13	-08
15																27	43	31	-06	22	19
16																	26	28	04	27	21
17																		37	10	23	04
18																			26	14	02
19																				06	-05
20																					44

* (The names of the variables corresponding with the numbers are listed in Table 2 in the text.)

Table 2-B (continued)

Correlation Matrix for the *Maine* Study

	22	23	24	25	26	27	28	29	30	31	32	33	34	35	36	37	38	39	40	41
1	11	07	15	05	-01	-14	-14	-13	10	17	24	16	45	28	-05	07	01	-06	04	-15
2	-10	04	02	-10	-09	-27	-33	-14	-14	-02	-10	03	-01	-16	-08	01	-06	-11	-09	-02
3	-08	19	-04	-00	-19	-22	-29	-19	01	04	-24	-11	-12	-16	-08	-03	03	05	-13	-14
4	01	16	-11	-09	-15	-20	-15	-16	16	09	-07	12	03	-02	-10	-07	03	-05	-13	-02
5	00	-02	-07	-10	-07	10	05	-11	-29	-15	-12	09	-52	-13	-15	-14	-11	-18	-09	-08
6	10	10	-03	-07	09	05	-11	-02	-30	-18	-13	-06	-60	-32	01	-09	-04	-09	-08	-01
7	-04	-03	13	14	23	04	19	38	-14	-19	-05	-11	-09	-25	09	23	05	12	19	19
8	-10	-04	16	12	18	02	02	40	-14	-22	-07	-02	-13	-40	04	01	-02	-01	11	11
9	-20	-09	-03	04	-06	18	-00	23	-09	-41	-08	-20	-17	-25	08	04	05	16	03	16
10	-12	-05	-15	-09	-08	-07	16	-09	-08	-01	03	08	-17	-07	-10	-29	-27	-27	02	-00
11	-06	-09	17	-01	23	04	16	22	-05	15	19	13	07	-19	09	19	05	10	14	20
12	-04	19	-09	-06	-01	-06	-04	-18	-16	-24	-15	-02	-25	-22	-18	-10	-08	-09	-13	05
13	-10	-03	-18	-08	-18	15	-11	-08	-16	-10	04	-08	02	-14	-14	-11	-14	-12	-04	-10
14	02	02	00	18	20	16	37	34	11	-06	01	-03	05	11	16	12	24	24	03	25
15	19	10	14	31	41	15	45	29	05	01	-01	09	06	11	47	35	35	37	29	33
16	09	17	35	44	35	-05	48	28	-04	-05	07	-09	01	-00	37	26	33	32	18	29
17	06	-06	18	30	53	08	43	59	02	01	-03	08	01	-03	25	31	26	25	16	28
18	03	05	07	27	15	01	30	24	-10	-17	-17	-18	-15	-00	13	09	22	26	12	20
19	-09	-02	-01	11	-05	-06	-13	15	-16	-15	-13	-34	-15	-06	-01	08	16	14	-02	21
20	47	29	13	16	19	03	11	20	-06	-04	11	07	-06	-02	18	11	28	23	09	17

Table 2-B (continued)

Correlation Matrix for the *Maine* Study

	22	23	24	25	26	27	28	29	30	31	32	33	34	35	36	37	38	39	40	41
21	60	54	30	36	27	-06	-00	09	01	02	04	01	-03	-09	20	11	26	22	01	17
22		42	21	16	16	02	03	-05	-04	18	16	21	01	08	16	-01	14	10	-04	23
23			16	24	07	-08	-02	-06	-05	-09	03	-02	09	09	10	-04	23	16	-07	20
24				54	44	08	22	32	-04	11	01	04	10	06	31	28	26	26	25	26
25					48	10	27	44	01	11	-07	-02	-02	03	46	31	41	35	27	30
26						13	38	62	-03	04	03	13	00	-08	42	32	30	37	19	29
27							10	13	05	05	-00	10	01	-04	22	08	26	22	30	29
28								31	15	12	17	10	16	20	28	28	15	11	24	17
29									03	-10	-08	01	01	-14	29	26	25	27	20	31
30										39	28	26	39	28	-09	-10	-12	-11	01	-23
31											41	43	34	38	15	-02	-09	-16	06	-03
32												39	41	34	-02	-03	-22	-15	08	-14
33													22	27	-03	-03	-07	-16	09	-10
34														45	10	00	-05	-04	12	03
35															06	-00	10	02	16	-05
36																49	63	46	43	42
37																	53	56	33	27
38																		70	37	40
39																			30	40
40																				31
41																				

Table 3-B

Correlation Matrix for the *Connecticut* Study*

	1	2	3	4	5	6	7	8	9	10	11	12	13	14	15	16	17	18	19	20	21
1		13	05	-06	00	-17	11	24	28	14	22	28	09	18	02	11	10	04	15	23	18
2			17	23	27	03	-04	03	14	-08	02	07	-21	-12	-10	-14	-16	00	-19	-04	-05
3				36	04	18	-10	-13	-02	-05	-06	13	-16	-29	-24	-18	-12	02	-02	03	-02
4					33	24	04	-06	01	-13	-06	-07	-10	-22	-14	-31	-05	03	-04	00	-10
5						29	06	-12	-02	-34	-07	03	-17	-19	-25	-17	-23	-05	-01	09	-11
6							08	-21	-21	-17	-19	-22	-24	-09	-15	-12	-25	-16	-12	-05	-29
7								-10	-01	02	-01	12	-06	-04	01	-11	-01	26	-11	-11	01
8									54	-04	24	26	24	13	08	14	25	24	18	13	30
9										01	06	19	17	30	12	16	22	28	15	17	08
10											11	-00	10	07	16	24	19	-06	21	21	18
11												12	-05	03	03	-04	12	-05	15	10	65
12													04	03	13	06	03	03	20	21	04
13														51	49	49	56	12	17	12	04
14															59	53	42	02	23	21	-00
15																53	36	16	10	08	04
16																	50	01	22	20	10
17																		24	19	12	21
18																			-19	-08	20
19																				80	12
20																					10

*(The names of the variables corresponding with the numbers are listed in Table 3 in the text.)

Table 3-B (continued)

Correlation Matrix for the *Connecticut* Study

	22	23	24	25	26	27	28	29	30	31	32	33	34	35	36	37	38	39	40	41
1	04	21	09	-10	19	-11	12	01	-07	-09	-02	17	16	12	15	20	-09	15	14	15
2	-23	-12	-18	04	-06	06	-15	-01	-04	-11	24	-10	-07	-13	-16	01	-03	-15	-16	-11
3	-20	-26	-20	-04	05	01	-13	-21	-10	05	-11	-12	01	-12	-06	07	-18	-20	-12	-06
4	-14	-23	-10	-03	06	05	-20	-19	-04	06	-04	-25	-20	-24	-19	-08	-10	-28	-20	-13
5	-26	-15	-12	20	03	-05	-33	-26	15	-10	04	-20	01	-30	-19	-08	04	-18	-19	-19
6	-04	-19	-11	38	03	-07	-16	-06	12	-06	06	03	01	-05	-07	02	14	-03	03	-04
7	-01	-02	-07	09	02	-06	07	00	-21	-01	-33	-19	02	-17	-15	-07	-13	-16	-09	-23
8	29	28	40	-03	30	18	10	43	06	01	02	27	21	15	29	22	18	32	38	27
9	25	19	26	04	39	-05	12	39	16	-04	-02	28	21	16	32	20	23	28	29	19
10	09	19	12	-09	03	12	21	01	-08	-05	07	05	-22	07	11	-04	-21	09	04	09
11	02	17	10	03	24	14	01	-07	-20	-10	-02	-03	20	05	18	12	-22	11	11	13
12	09	17	13	00	29	20	14	09	-01	-02	-10	01	24	01	12	15	-01	04	02	08
13	45	39	41	-33	08	02	61	35	02	-02	03	27	17	25	26	01	12	27	28	29
14	51	56	47	-01	17	06	59	44	12	02	11	50	31	45	46	29	29	54	59	59
15	45	44	50	-18	04	05	65	33	14	-09	07	43	28	38	49	19	20	48	41	41
16	51	49	62	-22	03	01	71	44	29	-14	16	39	25	33	38	19	26	42	39	39
17	55	43	55	-28	03	11	56	31	10	02	03	29	13	31	25	13	20	23	28	33
18	18	07	21	-12	02	02	-03	21	-14	-12	-15	-01	12	04	06	03	03	10	15	-11
19	30	35	30	14	34	11	16	-01	-04	10	-12	11	09	06	26	-09	-17	29	30	35
20	26	36	29	05	25	05	08	-07	-01	-04	-21	12	16	07	28	-07	-11	33	33	30

Table 3-B (continued)

Correlation Matrix for the *Connecticut* Study

	22	23	24	25	26	27	28	29	30	31	32	33	34	35	36	37	38	39	40	41
21	09	16	30	03	03	15	01	04	-10	-11	-04	05	17	16	16	11	-14	11	27	19
22		71	73	06	18	09	52	51	13	-07	07	49	27	42	43	20	42	44	49	41
23			65	06	21	08	44	40	-06	-12	-09	43	23	41	38	21	33	45	50	44
24				02	24	11	51	38	17	-20	-02	45	21	37	48	26	32	51	54	46
25					32	31	-31	02	02	-08	01	24	15	21	11	16	16	18	26	17
26						13	03	04	-14	-14	-21	28	13	17	41	26	06	30	31	28
27							04	08	-12	-02	09	21	22	25	27	15	11	26	35	30
28								40	16	-17	07	38	21	39	34	23	15	37	34	38
29									23	-01	09	44	32	43	29	29	38	35	40	29
30										03	36	20	10	-03	04	-06	29	01	03	10
31											13	04	-05	-23	-04	-02	-15	-27	-20	-11
32												12	-12	-06	03	-06	-04	00	-05	06
33													49	64	69	51	40	67	68	61
34														46	54	38	41	46	46	45
35															59	45	45	59	54	48
36																41	28	69	61	55
37																	20	36	35	44
38																		43	38	31
39																			84	65
40																				70
41																				

Table 4-B

Correlation Matrix for the *Louisiana French-American* Study*

	1	2	3	4	5	6	7	8	9	10	11	12	13	14	15	16	17	18	19	20	21
1		-04	25	05	13	48	-07	43	39	31	11	33	-12	09	11	13	05	12	15	10	36
2			11	23	37	-16	-05	04	-08	-10	-27	-11	14	-16	-31	-10	-20	-28	-11	-10	-08
3				33	15	39	10	20	21	13	11	17	-12	26	21	09	13	-04	02	30	17
4					24	02	07	-03	02	-10	-04	-14	08	-03	-04	-11	-26	-26	-13	-13	03
5						08	-10	00	-02	16	-16	01	03	-31	-20	-29	-16	-18	-05	-19	04
6							-21	24	29	07	05	39	-14	16	17	16	13	02	25	13	33
7								-08	-24	-03	13	06	-01	03	01	03	02	-09	-34	-03	-07
8									57	32	17	17	-11	05	14	12	04	00	03	18	21
9										30	23	32	-10	24	28	02	01	-01	15	17	12
10											01	03	-11	-07	08	-04	-07	17	03	17	17
11												14	-24	16	20	-07	07	06	00	18	14
12													-07	09	-01	07	14	-02	07	27	18
13														-08	-16	04	-23	-13	14	-11	-09
14															44	06	30	27	19	19	-14
15																15	40	21	18	44	-05
16																	27	06	10	27	02
17																		36	18	49	15
18																			12	24	14
19																				08	16
20																					18

*(The names of the variables corresponding with the numbers are listed in Table 4 in the text.)

Table 4-B (continued)

Correlation Matrix for the *Louisiana French-American* Study

	22	23	24	25	26	27	28	29	30	31	32	33	34	35	36	37	38	39	40	41
1	16	26	30	36	36	33	25	38	12	14	20	24	15	29	19	05	14	-15	-02	-19
2	-10	-07	-20	-25	-12	-03	-07	14	-33	16	-06	-17	-13	16	31	20	-27	-03	-20	07
3	04	10	33	14	21	20	40	27	20	12	23	15	10	11	02	03	17	33	06	12
4	04	-12	-12	-16	-11	-05	-03	05	-03	-09	21	04	-17	-06	-15	-08	08	29	03	-11
5	-01	09	02	-07	-06	01	10	35	-08	13	-09	10	03	23	15	03	-16	-10	-21	-17
6	24	12	22	44	34	26	17	43	17	-04	20	11	04	06	18	14	38	07	15	-16
7	16	-01	07	-02	-08	-23	04	05	17	19	27	19	30	08	-11	-06	08	08	12	12
8	06	10	25	33	27	36	30	35	19	11	19	05	09	16	12	16	28	-15	-17	-11
9	04	05	03	13	17	24	20	18	12	22	29	16	14	22	21	20	13	05	-07	07
10	10	23	27	19	23	22	31	15	05	19	06	21	21	08	10	34	-01	-12	-06	15
11	-10	-08	14	02	-03	-02	14	08	28	-12	20	11	25	01	-28	-33	30	23	10	08
12	18	31	20	16	28	17	15	18	01	17	16	05	08	-01	44	42	-01	-06	-16	-06
13	-05	-09	-08	-13	-07	-09	06	-12	-09	03	24	-10	01	-01	-06	01	-12	-05	00	-19
14	-08	-15	11	07	11	14	05	-05	04	-04	10	19	-00	-04	-18	-12	25	29	10	28
15	00	07	15	33	38	29	15	-16	17	-03	24	24	-01	-09	-21	-18	40	14	03	04
16	17	18	17	40	25	27	06	16	-05	06	-01	19	12	09	16	15	04	-02	13	-22
17	18	21	14	41	22	38	-03	-02	15	-06	06	18	12	32	16	-02	20	-04	-06	03
18	11	14	34	40	29	37	23	03	21	-04	-05	22	17	-06	-05	10	15	-13	-17	10
19	-12	07	26	33	29	22	17	06	-03	11	27	33	31	12	02	02	10	07	02	-06
20	14	34	34	37	46	48	29	-05	10	-00	20	20	17	-03	16	22	18	-05	-26	01

Table 4-B (continued)

Correlation Matrix for the *Louisiana French-American Study*

	22	23	24	25	26	27	28	29	30	31	32	33	34	35	36	37	38	39	40	41
21	46	35	24	32	24	39	15	26	36	00	23	31	19	08	11	02	02	-06	-03	-26
22		23	07	34	26	25	05	16	25	18	09	23	07	02	11	12	-02	-17	16	-10
23			19	30	35	35	10	23	06	09	06	15	11	17	38	22	-15	-21	-12	-28
24				62	49	33	78	27	32	38	25	53	54	34	-08	11	24	-03	-03	-07
25					74	58	39	32	20	27	20	38	37	28	08	08	31	-12	-03	-13
26						53	38	24	10	30	29	34	25	24	10	20	17	-05	-12	-09
27							29	20	20	11	15	31	11	17	23	21	06	-14	-22	-08
28								20	35	55	41	47	47	28	-17	08	21	-01	-19	00
29									09	27	12	23	20	35	25	15	17	-13	-02	-22
30										01	25	20	14	-04	-25	-27	25	-07	12	-09
31											36	46	49	43	13	28	-07	-11	-05	01
32												47	40	21	-15	-13	16	06	-05	-18
33													55	46	-03	03	14	10	-01	-17
34														35	-00	05	11	-07	-07	-03
35															16	06	-01	-17	04	-07
36																65	-32	-17	-02	-15
37																	-29	-19	-25	09
38																		11	-05	02
39																			21	11
40																				-08
41																				

Table 5-B

Correlation Matrix for the *Maine French-American* Study*

	2	3	4	5	6	7	8	9	10	11	12	13	14	15	16	17	18	19	20	21
1	70	-17	28	29	09	51	44	41	23	16	12	14	-06	08	-03	-27	-17	-09	11	-12
2		-06	30	33	23	45	31	25	26	20	01	05	-21	-02	-20	-36	-13	-18	-05	-14
3			14	05	37	-04	-08	-20	-26	-03	-18	-13	04	-18	-19	-18	-09	-05	-14	-12
4				46	41	52	21	12	07	03	02	-09	-15	-09	-25	-25	-16	-14	06	-25
5					49	34	17	09	13	-08	-15	-15	-09	-39	-27	-24	-27	-37	-06	-18
6						17	-02	-05	-05	-05	-47	-24	-10	-41	-41	-28	-31	-38	-21	-29
7							36	27	10	04	06	12	-15	-01	-04	-27	-14	-06	11	-19
8								69	32	26	32	17	-07	01	-05	10	-14	01	26	22
9									27	22	29	41	-04	06	-01	04	-18	05	24	19
10										03	34	-09	-01	-01	04	-08	02	12	14	07
11											20	04	-27	-16	21	10	08	22	27	17
12												15	-13	26	20	02	16	31	36	40
13													-01	18	14	01	-04	12	17	12
14														-03	05	02	-17	05	-42	-07
15															40	29	32	52	11	21
16																31	32	56	23	43
17																	28	29	16	33
18																		29	27	22
19																			24	23
20																				23

*(The names of the variables corresponding with the numbers are listed in Table 5 in the test.)

Table 5-B (continued)

Correlation Matrix for the *Maine French-American Study*

	22	23	24	25	26	27	28	29	30	31	32	33	34	35	36	37	38	39	40	41
1	-08	11	07	-17	-25	-19	-05	18	00	28	05	06	-04	06	04	-14	-19	03	21	09
2	-14	-03	-04	-09	-13	-11	-02	18	-20	25	-04	-02	-02	03	09	05	-28	04	30	08
3	-00	-14	-12	25	17	17	-18	-16	-15	-17	-21	-02	-03	-08	-10	14	04	-02	-07	-04
4	09	04	-02	04	04	05	-21	01	-15	-07	-21	00	-02	-14	-19	-00	-02	07	07	-04
5	-20	-05	-17	20	12	17	-26	12	-23	-04	-17	-12	04	-15	-22	-03	-24	08	05	-20
6	-42	-29	-34	42	32	33	-33	-26	-37	-24	-34	-13	-03	-13	-28	15	-05	23	-17	-25
7	13	19	14	-05	-01	-11	-16	07	-02	14	01	08	08	-12	00	-14	-14	05	18	-10
8	23	35	31	-24	-30	-21	15	17	26	16	13	15	30	28	09	-37	-21	-24	17	15
9	25	31	22	-25	-30	-24	21	16	30	08	20	17	43	46	07	-38	-04	-15	27	14
10	19	19	28	-17	-13	-24	10	15	03	15	05	-07	-08	04	01	-03	-16	-01	20	-02
11	23	35	25	-08	-15	-14	39	18	23	15	20	19	16	20	21	-17	-04	-16	02	13
12	55	55	63	-57	-50	-50	36	19	50	34	31	26	18	15	18	-27	03	-28	21	25
13	34	27	11	00	-04	-11	34	10	19	29	17	06	46	44	08	-05	09	-19	12	06
14	-04	-35	-06	13	07	11	-04	11	-11	-20	-16	-09	-12	-06	-05	06	12	-08	-11	-16
15	27	13	19	-21	-22	-26	18	09	22	11	12	23	06	11	26	-05	26	-02	04	25
16	24	26	39	-16	-02	-22	25	07	34	23	28	31	04	06	26	-01	27	01	05	27
17	14	32	18	-09	03	-03	27	11	37	03	11	13	01	12	21	01	28	-07	-09	11
18	19	27	25	-24	-04	-13	23	-07	21	05	23	09	02	00	28	28	07	-11	05	31
19	33	24	35	-26	-14	-26	34	-01	34	11	20	23	18	10	37	-07	31	-05	-01	19
20	35	42	33	-15	-08	-10	38	09	48	25	37	29	20	32	14	-22	-17	-19	05	18

Table 5-B (continued)

Correlation Matrix for the *Maine French-American Study*

	22	23	24	25	26	27	28	29	30	31	32	33	34	35	36	37	38	39	40	41
21	32	41	37	-36	-27	-28	43	21	46	31	37	29	20	28	12	-14	15	-22	09	29
22		62	65	-35	-23	-30	34	14	46	10	21	24	26	23	08	-23	13	-38	15	15
23			58	-37	-27	-34	38	12	55	31	41	33	31	27	17	-15	01	-25	16	26
24				-46	-33	-47	32	20	51	29	37	43	10	12	21	-17	01	-24	16	32
25					78	77	-17	-15	-29	-20	-22	-09	-12	-14	-05	19	-18	15	-10	-25
26						72	-06	-16	-24	-24	-19	-12	-17	-15	-01	11	-10	02	-10	-23
27							-18	-24	-24	-33	-25	-11	-15	-11	-08	14	-10	05	-11	-17
28								37	40	21	27	25	30	46	46	-04	09	-23	-10	13
29									05	27	08	07	-07	06	20	-07	-13	-25	07	08
30										31	50	53	21	22	10	-16	12	-23	17	30
31											57	37	10	13	13	14	-10	-00	27	22
32												61	16	19	15	10	-08	02	21	17
33													06	17	13	08	04	-08	04	19
34														60	-10	-23	11	-35	03	04
35															-08	-24	12	-20	-09	06
36																07	-05	06	-05	25
37																	05	23	02	03
38																		28	-25	-01
39																			-17	-09
40																				04

Table 11-B

Correlation Matrix for the *Value Orientation* Study*

	2	3	4	5	6	7	8	9	10	11	12	13	14	15	16	17	18	19	20	21
1	34	33	26	25	34	12	17	19	37	15	24	20	-10	10	-18	13	-07	-04	-01	-07
2		70	48	20	31	40	42	40	52	19	20	21	03	05	-19	-09	-09	-08	02	13
3			54	29	34	26	37	38	56	14	28	15	00	-07	-15	-09	-06	-09	-04	00
4				62	35	38	43	46	64	23	47	39	06	08	02	11	04	-04	-04	-14
5					32	27	30	36	51	19	31	25	03	00	09	09	00	-16	04	-20
6						28	37	32	35	14	14	07	-04	07	-15	-03	-13	-13	-04	-08
7							31	27	30	07	08	23	04	09	-11	-12	-02	-13	-20	01
8								75	50	20	30	15	-09	-03	-13	-11	-06	-08	10	-11
9									45	43	24	22	13	00	07	-04	00	-17	08	-12
10										31	43	25	-09	-07	-13	-01	-14	-11	16	-12
11											32	39	45	31	43	25	37	12	09	12
12												48	00	-20	-08	-05	07	-09	09	-06
13													21	04	02	-14	14	-12	09	12
14														26	51	12	56	31	09	17
15															37	26	35	21	04	18
16																40	37	26	05	16
17																	42	42	-03	-09
18																		26	15	14
19																			09	16
20																				09

.26 to 1.00 = .01 level
.21 to 0.25 = .05 level
.17 to 0.20 = .10 level

*(The names of the variables corresponding with numbers are listed in Table 11 in the text.)

Table 11-B (continued)
Correlation Matrix for the *Value Orientation Study*

	22	23	24	25	26	27	28	29	30	31	32	33	34	35	36	37	38	39	40	41
1	-01	-09	03	16	-11	06	11	02	04	26	44	34	35	-02	14	14	05	08	11	06
2	08	-07	02	-01	03	-22	-02	05	-06	31	40	37	50	19	47	35	00	16	22	29
3	12	-13	05	02	06	-23	10	02	05	36	38	31	48	16	66	38	14	33	40	15
4	03	-08	-04	-05	17	-08	15	-03	-04	35	32	38	50	27	57	43	20	38	36	39
5	04	-06	-11	-08	16	12	06	-05	-04	29	13	23	30	12	19	19	05	07	13	12
6	-03	-01	01	10	-01	-05	04	-05	11	21	14	30	25	22	32	11	02	00	04	12
7	25	-14	-04	07	11	-16	-13	11	03	12	13	23	21	20	10	05	-06	00	09	09
8	07	-04	-04	-01	01	12	-10	15	-04	29	29	32	41	12	40	21	13	12	28	28
9	02	-06	08	14	-12	05	04	08	-13	43	24	43	46	15	46	36	21	16	27	30
10	02	-08	-01	04	-01	-06	14	16	-15	38	42	43	48	25	47	36	20	15	26	28
13	-06	-20	01	05	-03	01	04	34	-16	49	17	29	32	33	32	25	26	14	16	19
11	-10	02	-01	-17	19	-08	18	18	-05	35	29	30	41	14	34	32	24	13	23	17
12	10	-03	-11	-16	18	-17	04	29	02	17	35	17	26	30	21	18	09	03	11	16
14	20	-15	-02	-09	-04	-02	-11	05	-22	18	-01	-03	-01	18	12	-05	16	03	-03	05
15	00	-06	-12	16	03	-05	-15	04	-11	14	08	04	16	26	05	04	03	08	13	08
16	-05	-05	-09	-07	02	25	-16	-02	-20	06	-11	02	11	12	-06	07	15	-02	03	-05
17	01	02	01	15	04	10	-13	04	04	15	04	-02	17	03	03	17	01	-09	00	-10
18	05	-06	-26	11	24	-06	06	21	10	26	03	-12	-03	06	-02	-05	07	-01	10	-01
19	14	-06	-24	-08	-01	-01	09	07	-05	-08	-04	-01	01	02	-05	-02	05	15	09	14
20	-11	-05	11	-08	-15	-16	36	25	10	13	06	03	-14	05	08	01	31	18	08	12

Table 11-B (continued)

Correlation Matrix for the *Value Orientation* Study

	22	23	24	25	26	27	28	29	30	31	32	33	34	35	36	37	38	39	40	41
21	13	-10	-23	-26	-20	-37	00	18	-07	-08	-04	-04	08	-02	-03	-05	04	00	00	06
22		11	-22	-27	-10	-27	-19	-14	-07	-18	17	-09	-04	11	01	-14	-05	-06	01	-01
23			-15	-19	11	-22	-09	-21	04	-03	09	03	06	-06	-03	-10	-08	-09	-06	-24
24				21	-31	-02	-19	-08	-14	04	-17	09	-09	-07	11	02	01	-03	-10	-03
25					-21	02	-24	00	03	02	-14	03	03	02	03	09	-18	04	-18	-04
26						-13	-16	01	08	09	09	-22	13	01	02	-01	-10	02	-02	-14
27							-15	05	-02	05	-12	-05	-07	-01	-11	08	05	-04	09	07
28								09	18	05	07	22	-11	-02	06	07	24	14	18	12
29									-12	19	11	10	12	07	-02	11	22	-05	-01	15
30										07	-08	-19	-10	-13	02	10	-16	11	07	01
31											22	22	39	15	48	38	29	26	32	24
32												30	42	26	33	28	14	21	21	15
33													43	13	35	31	20	20	30	15
34														14	51	56	18	25	31	20
35															23	14	26	27	36	28
36																54	35	46	43	48
37																	22	35	26	30
38																		46	43	50
39																			59	60
40																				64
41																				

Table 12-B

Correlation Matrix for the *Philippines* Study*

	1	2	3	4	5	6	7	8	9	10	11	12
1	—	.29	.32	.09	.02	.07	.05	.05	.00	.20	.16	.10
2		—	.03	.53	.20	.16	-.07	.07	.00	.04	.10	.37
3			—	.26	.20	-.06	.05	.07	.04	.01	-.01	-.17
4				—	.09	-.09	.00	.01	.02	.08	.04	.14
5					—	.07	-.02	-.06	-.19	-.12	-.09	.05
6						—	.03	-.00	-.16	-.03	-.03	.03
7							—	.12	.17	.29	.20	.06
8								—	.38	.12	.14	.25
9									—	.14	.22	.10
10										—	.64	.16
11											—	.33
12												—
13												
14												
15												
16												
17												
18												
19												
20												
21												
22												
23												
24												
25												
26												
27												
28												
29												
30												
31	(The names of the variables corresponding with the numbers are listed in Tabl
32	12 in the text.)
33	
34	
35-47	

Table 12-B (continued)

	13	14	15	16	17	18	19	20	21	22	23	24
1	-.05	-.26	-.07	.04	-.05	-.02	-.09	.16	.19	-.02	-.03	-.01
2	-.06	.21	.04	-.09	-.16	-.22	-.13	.04	.14	.02	.05	.20
3	-.08	.00	-.17	-.05	.06	.07	-.09	.15	.13	.04	.03	.06
4	-.01	.11	.10	-.11	-.01	-.08	-.10	.01	.13	-.02	-.11	.21
5	-.20	-.12	-.02	-.07	-.04	-.09	-.10	.17	.01	-.07	-.01	.14
6	.00	-.07	.01	.06	-.06	-.19	-.01	-.03	-.09	.04	-.01	-.05
7	.15	.25	.08	.06	.20	-.16	-.08	-.07	-.11	-.14	-.06	-.19
8	.12	.02	-.08	.09	.18	-.11	.23	.06	-.15	.08	-.02	-.04
9	.15	.10	.10	.26	.06	-.02	.10	-.01	-.14	-.10	-.06	-.07
10	.41	.37	.09	.26	.02	-.21	-.01	.00	-.08	-.02	.03	.10
11	.45	.45	.15	.17	-.08	-.42	-.13	-.23	-.09	.12	.03	.09
12	.30	.31	.14	.05	.00	-.24	-.02	-.08	-.07	.17	.07	.06
13	—	.21	.13	.27	.03	-.10	-.07	-.09	-.21	.03	.01	.05
14		—	-.01	.07	.03	-.20	.04	-.04	.08	.10	.08	.06
15			—	-.03	-.32	-.07	-.27	.09	-.09	-.14	-.02	-.03
16				—	.18	.01	.08	.03	-.16	.04	.19	-.06
17					—	.16	.32	-.08	-.05	.06	-.11	-.18
18						—	.27	.17	.02	.01	-.08	-.09
19							—	-.09	.07	.03	-.10	-.19
20								—	.02	-.07	.14	.21
21									—	.08	.02	.12
22										—	.27	.28
23											—	.17
24												
25												
26												
27												
28												
29												
30												
31												
32												
33												
34												
35-47												

Table 12-B (continued)

	25	26	27	28	29	30	31	32	33	34	35	36
1	.29	.29	-.18	.32	.17	.17	.16	.16	.14	.02	.15	-.04
2	.31	.27	.20	.22	.12	.15	.17	.03	.19	.06	.09	-.02
3	.04	-.02	.15	.01	.02	-.01	.04	.14	.09	.15	.12	.01
4	.09	.00	.09	.00	.01	.05	.08	.03	.05	.02	.00	.10
5	.02	-.03	.11	-.07	.12	.13	.11	.13	.22	.03	.04	.04
6	-.17	-.06	-.12	.07	.16	.05	.01	.01	-.07	-.04	-.22	.04
7	-.01	-.11	.01	-.03	.06	.08	.09	.04	.06	-.04	.11	.31
8	.00	-.13	-.08	.06	-.15	-.16	-.11	-.14	-.13	-.13	-.04	-.14
9	.00	-.08	-.08	.12	-.09	-.07	-.02	-.05	-.10	-.11	-.05	.07
10	.27	.01	.23	.17	.04	.07	.24	ı.12	.34	.19	.01	-.12
11	.20	-.02	.10	.04	.02	.05	.14	.12	.22	.18	.06	.11
12	.09	.14	.19	.05	.09	.12	.07	.08	.16	.01	.12	.01
13	.09	-.14	.08	-.17	.04	.06	.10	.16	.11	.04	-.02	.03
14	.18	.21	.13	.24	.17	.19	.11	.16	.19	.18	.14	.15
15	-.07	-.08	-.06	-.02	-.15	-.14	-.10	-.10	-.03	-.16	-.12	.15
16	.01	-.07	.02	.05	-.01	-.01	.06	.07	.03	.11	-.09	-.35
17	.02	-.11	-.09	.00	.05	.05	.05	.01	-.11	.03	-.12	.07
18	-.14	.08	-.06	-.06	-.06	-.07	-.07	-.12	-.16	-.11	-.11	-.07
19	-.17	-.09	.01	.14	-.08	-.09	-.18	-.10	-.12	-.07	-.17	-.22
20	.21	.29	.24	.18	.27	.26	.22	.22	.24	.14	.18	-.01
21	.22	.18	.28	.22	.10	.10	.13	.03	.24	.16	.11	.00
22	.19	.13	.23	-.06	.19	.18	.17	.10	.17	.24	.21	.12
23	.20	.15	.14	.07	.13	.14	.17	.17	.25	.27	.26	.08
24	.32	.30	.46	.03	.41	.42	.41	.36	.47	.44	.46	.15
25	–	.48	.62	.25	.47	.49	.54	.44	.64	.53	.47	.16
26		–	.56	.26	.43	.44	.47	.34	.49	.43	.42	.07
27			–	.32	.55	.56	.62	.50	.74	.56	.55	-.02
28				–	.19	.20	.17	.19	.24	.17	.00	-.18
29					–	.99	.87	.83	.72	.66	.59	.22
30						–	.88	.85	.74	.69	.60	.22
31							–	.73	.79	.67	.56	.10
32								–	.73	.72	.49	.14
33									–	.74	.55	.03
34										–	.50	.11
35											–	.31
36-47												–

Table 12-B (continued)

	37	38	39	40	41	42	43	44	45	46	47
1	.34	.02	.06	-.09	-.05	-.06	-.04	.01	.05	.05	.14
2	.15	.20	.21	.02	.09	-.11	-.08	-.08	.37	.27	.15
3	.15	-.16	-.03	.23	.01	.09	.14	.07	.05	-.03	.09
4	-.03	.04	.36	-.02	.21	.05	.03	-.11	.19	.22	.19
5	-.02	-.03	.14	-.19	-.07	-.08	-.15	-.15	.18	.21	.22
6	.18	-.04	-.21	-.21	.06	.02	-.10	-.01	-.04	-.13	-.17
7	-.08	.03	-.01	.07	-.22	-.09	.06	-.03	-.01	.08	-.06
8	.24	.24	.03	.05	-.01	.10	.19	.29	.02	.03	-.07
9	.20	.16	.01	.08	-.05	.03	.14	.23	.04	.04	-.12
10	.12	.10	.20	.16	-.04	-.14	-.10	-.06	.35	.45	.17
11	.07	.06	.08	.12	-.11	.01	-.13	-.12	.28	.36	.13
12	.05	.11	.14	.22	-.02	-.06	-.06	-.03	.29	.35	.23
13	-.20	.02	.02	.23	-.11	-.14	-.08	.00	.21	.24	.10
14	.19	.04	.31	.11	-.02	-.10	-.07	.02	.23	.30	.18
15	-.02	.08	.16	.30	-.14	-.02	-.09	-.10	-.04	.01	-.07
16	.02	.17	-.07	.20	.18	.07	.13	.12	.18	.14	.05
17	-.11	.05	-.08	-.05	.03	.02	.14	.20	-.05	-.07	-.10
18	.02	.03	.11	-.02	.06	.07	.29	.10	-.10	-.20	-.04
19	.18	.11	.06	-.04	.05	.08	.19	.40	-.02	-.08	-.08
20	.02	.05	.12	.06	-.02	.08	.00	-.15	.12	.13	.08
21	.07	-.09	.00	.09	-.04	-.13	-.05	-.07	.08	.15	.16
22	.14	-.15	-.10	-.10	-.16	-.19	-.16	-.20	.06	.01	.13
23	-.01	-.03	-.17	-.04	.04	.01	-.11	-.16	.19	.15	.13
24	.00	-.21	.15	.10	.09	-.07	-.09	-.30	.27	.27	.35
25	-.05	.00	.07	.00	-.04	-.11	-.24	-.21	.41	.42	.45
26	.13	.05	.00	.03	.00	-.02	-.03	-.10	.32	.32	.41
27	.14	-.01	.15	.18	-.13	-.33	-.20	-.23	.52	.51	.55
28	.34	.17	.06	-.11	.14	.00	-.01	.16	.31	.25	.06
29	.00	-.08	.05	.00	-.07	-.16	-.19	-.30	.39	.42	.52
30	-.02	-.07	.04	-.01	-.06	-.16	-.18	-.29	.42	.46	.55
31	.00	.02	.01	.00	-.05	-.18	-.17	-.31	.50	.55	.55
32	-.06	-.12	.02	-.04	.10	-.02	-.12	-.22	.43	.44	.57
33	-.02	-.07	.10	.09	-.05	-.23	-.18	-.30	.60	.65	.57
34	-.04	-.08	-.03	-.03	.06	-.06	-.11	-.34	.38	.45	.52
35	-.06	-.14	.10	.20	-.17	-.11	-.25	-.40	.14	.22	.47
36	-.17	-.18	.08	-.04	-.20	.14	-.30	-.31	-.18	.02	.12

Table 12-B (continued)

	37	38	39	40	41	42	43	44	45	46	47
37	–	.32	.22	.02	.00	-.12	.09	.12	.04	-.04	-.10
38		–	.25	.22	.02	.00	.19	.04	.11	.23	-.06
39			–	.26	.28	.01	.03	-.14	.15	.16	.04
40				–	-.05	-.25	-.04	-.33	.10	.06	.01
41					–	.52	.36	.22	.12	.02	-.03
42						–	.37	.38	-.07	-.03	-.10
43							–	.59	-.03	-.09	-.12
44								–	-.01	-.13	-.22
45									–	.79	.51
46										–	.60
47											–

Appendix C
Readings

Reading Number One: R. C. Gardner and W. E. Lambert. Motivational variables in second-language acquisition.

Reading Number Two: R. C. Gardner. Motivational variables in second-language acquisition.

Reading Number Three: M. Anisfeld and W. E. Lambert. Social and psychological variables in learning Hebrew.

Reading Number Four: W. E. Lambert, R. C. Gardner, H. C. Barik, and K. Tunstall. Attitudinal and cognitive aspects of intensive study of a second language.

Reading Number Five: Elizabeth Peal and W. E. Lambert. The relation of bilingualism to intelligence.

Reading Number Six : R. C. Gardner and W. E. Lambert. Language aptitude, intelligence, and second-language achievement.

Reading Number Seven: W. E. Lambert, R. C. Hodgson, R. C. Gardner, and S. Fillenbaum. Evaluational reactions to spoken languages.

READING NUMBER ONE

MOTIVATIONAL VARIABLES IN SECOND-LANGUAGE ACQUISITION[1]

ROBERT C. GARDNER AND WALLACE E. LAMBERT
McGill University

Most research on second-language acquisition has been concerned with the measurement of an "ability for languages," the assumption being that achievement is largely due to a linguistic aptitude. However, when measures of aptitude are correlated with grades in language courses, the validity coefficients show considerable variability from situation to situation even with tests developed through factor analytic methods (2), suggesting that variables other than linguistic aptitude are involved. Researchers have mentioned that motivation and interest probably play important roles in second-language acquisition (4, 5, 8, 16, 18), but perhaps because of difficulties in measuring them, these aspects have not been given systematic attention.

Theoretical attempts to explain how the child learns his first language have emphasized a particular type of motivation. Mowrer's theory (11) suggests that language acquisition is motivated by a desire to be like valued members of the family and, later, of the whole linguistic community. Ervin (6) has extended this view, suggesting that emotional dependence or respect for another individual may account for some instances of marked success in second-language achievement. Support for this extended interpretation has been found in recent studies where (*a*) fluency in the second language was found to depend upon an active interest in members of the other linguistic community (19); (*b*) both extent of bilingualism (10) and advanced level of language study (7) were associated with lower F-scores; (*c*) dominance in the acquired language was related to personal dissatisfactions with one's own group (9). In line with this latter finding, adults electing to study French conversational courses scored

---

[1]This research was supported by the Canadian Defence Research Board, Grant no. D77-94-01-10 and by a Ford Foundation Grant to D. O. Hebb. We are grateful to both Professor G. A. Ferguson (McGill) and Professor J. B. Carroll (Harvard) for their advice on statistical analysis. In particular, we want to thank J. T. McIlhone of the Catholic School Board of Montreal for his co-operation and kindness in permitting us to carry out this study.

higher on Srole's Anomie Scale (14) than students enrolled in the more grammatical courses, suggesting that adults dissatisfied with their position in their own cultural group are seeking to learn, as rapidly as possible, those aspects of the other language which will allow them to become members of a new group (7).

It is our contention then that achievement in a second language is dependent upon essentially the same type of motivation that is apparently necessary for the child to learn his first language. We argue that an individual acquiring a second language adopts certain behavior patterns which are characteristic of another cultural group and that his attitudes towards that group will at least partly determine his success in learning the new language. Our use of attitude as a motivational construct presupposes an intention on the part of students to learn the language with various aims in mind, and to pursue these aims with varying degrees of drive strength. Our test battery consequently included indices of motivational intensity and orientation. The "Orientation Index" classifies purposes in one of two ways: "integrative," where the aim in language study is to learn more about the language group, or to meet more and *different* people; "instrumental," where the reasons reflect the more utilitarian value of linguistic achievement. The "Motivational Intensity Scale" measures the amount of effort and enthusiasm students show in their attempt to acquire the language.

The present research was designed to determine the comparative importance of linguistic aptitude and certain motivational variables[2] in learning a second language. The intercorrelations of a battery of tests administered to high school students were analyzed to determine the factorial structure and to see how the criterion variable, skill in speaking and understanding French, related to this structure.

METHOD

Subjects

Forthy-three male and thirty-two female English-speaking Grade XI high school students acted as Ss. They had already completed an average of about 7 years of formal training in French.

Materials

Scores on the following tests were obtained:

(1) Achievement ratings: The French instructor of each class was asked to rate the students on each of two attributes: oral skills (ability to imitate French word sounds) and aural comprehension (understanding of spoken French). Ratings were made on a 5-point scale for poor (1) to excellent (5). Since these 2 ratings were highly correlated, they were combined, then standardized, to arrive at the achievement rating, Variable 1.

---

[2]Copies of these scales can be obtained from the authors at McGill University.

Variables 2-6 are the five sub-scales from Carroll's "Psi-Lambda Foreign Language Aptitude Battery" (3). They include: (2) number learning, (3) phonetic script, (4) spelling clues, (5) words in sentences, and (6) paired associates.

Variables 7 and 8 are two subscales from the A.C.E. College Entrance Examination, 1943 edition. Those used were: (7) same-opposites, and (8) verbal analogies.

(9) Orientation index: Ss were presented with four alternative reasons for studying French and asked to rank them as to their personal relevance. They indicated that a knowledge of French would: (1) be useful in obtaining a job, (2) be helpful in understanding the French-Canadian people[3] and their way of life, (3) permit meeting and conversing with more and varied people, and (4) make one a better-educated person. A fifth alternative, "any other personal reason," was supplied in case an individual thought the alternatives given were inadequate. Ss who ranked either alternative (2) or (3) as most relevant were classified as "integratively oriented." Those choosing alternatives (1) or (4) were classified as "instrumentally oriented." Those choosing alternative (5) were not classified.

(10) Attitude scale: Twenty positively worded statements about French-Canadians were presented and S was asked to indicate his degree of disagreement or agreement on a 7-point scale. A sample item is: "The French-Canadian has every reason to be proud of his race and culture."

(11) Motivational-intensity scale: Eight multiple choice statements were designed to measure intensity of motivation in terms of: work done for assignments, preference for and comparative ease of the course, opportunities taken to improve speaking and reading French, future intentions to study or make use of the language, and importance attributed to a knowledge of the language. Ss were asked to choose, in each case, the alternative most descriptive of themselves.

(12) California F-scale: Twenty-five items from forms 45 and 40 (1).

(13) Sex: This was included as a separate variable to account for sex differences.

(14) Audience sensitivity scale: This scale (13) is a measure of the typical anxiety responses made by the individual in a variety of social situations. It was included in the present battery because it was thought that such anxiety might deter a student from practicing the second language.

RESULTS AND DISCUSSION

Product-moment intercorrelations were computed for twelve of the tests, and the correlations of these twelve with variables 9 and 13 were computed as biserial correlation coefficients. The correlation between variables 9 and 13 is a *phi*-coefficient. The correlation matrix is given in Table I.

---

[3]The term "French-Canadian" instead of "French" was used to make Ss think in terms of the language group with which they come into contact in Montreal. Although the courses use Standard French with little or no reference to any French-Canadian modifications, the French learned in school can be used with no difficulty by English-speaking students in the province of Quebec. It may be true that a few Ss were motivated to learn French because of its possible value to them in the European French community and these Ss will tend to reduce the relationships of the orientation index and attitude scale (see below) with other measures.

TABLE 1

Correlation Matrix*

	1	2	3	4	5	6	7	8	9†	10	11	12	13‡	14
1. Achievement ratings	—	.22	.28	.28	−.01	.18	.16	.42	.34	.10	.40	.08	−.06	−.08
2. Number learning		—	.33	.04	.10	.25	.22	.41	−.24	−.18	.13	.03	−.18	−.07
3. Phonetic script			—	.47	.31	.58	.34	.44	.21	.13	.22	.15	.28	.05
4. Spelling clues				—	.29	.43	.48	.40	−.04	.23	.20	−.02	.08	−.08
5. Words in sentences					—	.13	.30	.21	.17	.15	.04	−.07	.22	.03
6. Paired associates						—	.37	.53	.08	.32	.22	.13	.43	.37
7. Same-opposites							—	.56	−.14	.16	.01	−.14	.24	.08
8. Verbal analogies								—	.14	−.05	.12	−.19	.12	.00
9. Orientation index									—	.42	.44	−.02	.01	−.04
10. Attitude scale										—	.44	.27	.28	−.03
11. Motivational-intensity											—	.24	.04	−.10
12. California F-scale												—	.31	.04
13. Sex													—	.14
14. Audience sensitivity scale														—

*It was not possible with the testing time given us to have Ss complete all parts of the Foreign Language Aptitude Test (Variables 2–6). A different test of the battery was omitted for each school class. Consequently, the total N is reduced by approximately 20 for all correlations involving these variables.

†Biserial correlations are positive if the integratively oriented Ss obtained a higher mean score on the continuous variables than did those instrumentally oriented.

‡Biserial correlations are positive if the females scored higher on the tests.

Four factors (see Table II) were extracted by Thurstone's centroid method (17). Graphical representations of these factors plotted two at a time indicated that no meaningful rotation could be obtained with the fourth factor, and this factor was subsequently omitted in the rotations. Examination of the plots of the first three factors suggested that an orthogonal solution was warranted, and that little could be gained with oblique rotations. The rotated factor loadings are given in Table III.

TABLE II

CENTROID FACTOR MATRIX

Measures	I	II	III	IV	Communalities
1. Achievement ratings	.47	.11	− .46	.20	.49
2. Number learning	.26	− .39	− .27	.30	.39
3. Phonetic Script	.70	− .17	.10	.13	.55
4. Spelling clues	.56	− .26	.18	− .16	.44
5. Words in sentences	.35	− .13	.16	− .09	.17
6. Paired associates	.76	− .22	.11	− .12	.65
7. Same-opposites	.50	− .40	.20	.10	.46
8. Verbal analogies	.60	− .41	− .24	.22	.64
9. Orientation index	.30	.46	− .26	− .25	.43
10. Attitude scale	.45	.48	.24	− .30	.58
11. Motivational-intensity	.50	.46	− .30	− .08	.55
12. California F-scale	.17	.40	.24	.26	.31
13. Sex	.34	.11	.55	.17	.46
14. Audience sensitivity scale	− .13	.09	.19	.42	.24

TABLE III

ROTATED FACTOR MATRIX
(ORTHOGONAL)

Measures	I	II	III	IV	Communalities
1. Achievement ratings	.30	.55	− .23	.20	.49
2. Number learning	.45	.00	− .31	.30	.39
3. Phonetic script	.66	.21	.24	.13	.55
4. Spelling clues	.60	.20	− .08	− .16	.43
5. Words in sentences	.36	.02	.20	− .09	.17
6. Paired associates	.73	.20	.24	− .12	.64
7. Same-opposites	.64	− .10	.18	.10	.46
8. Verbal analogies	.73	.15	− .19	.22	.64
9. Orientation index	− .05	.60	.03	− .25	.43
10. Attitude scale	.05	.47	.52	− .30	.59
11. Motivational-intensity	.10	.73	.06	− .08	.55
12. California F-scale	− .12	.26	.41	.26	.31
13. Sex	.19	.00	.62	.17	.45
14. Audience sensitivity scale	− .16	− .10	.16	.42	.24

The factor analysis indicates that two independent factors are related to achievement in French. Factor I has its highest loadings on Tests 1-8. Test 1 is the criterion, suggesting that the others measure some component related to achievement in French. Tests 7 and 8 are the two indices of verbal intelligence while Tests 2-6 are the subscales from the language aptitude battery. Factor I, therefore, is clearly a *linguistic aptitude* factor. It should be noted that the high loadings of the verbal intelligence tests on this factor lend support to the findings of Wittenborn and Larsen (20) that intelligence and language aptitude are factorially similar.

Factor II derives its highest loadings from Tests 1, 9, 10, and 11. Since the criterion is substantially loaded on this factor, the latter three variables must be considered important for the successful acquisition of a second language. Examination of these three variables suggests that Factor II should be defined as a *motivation* factor. It should be emphasized however that this denotes a motivation of a particular type, *characterized by a willingness to be like valued members of the language community*.

These results indicate, therefore, that two components are related to second-language achievement. That this is not an artifact of the factorial rotations is substantiated by examining those tests which produce the maximum multiple correlation with the criterion. Four tests (8, 11, 9, and 5) were selected by the Wherry-Doolittle test selection technique (15) which yielded the maximum multiple correlation of 0.558. These tests are equally divided between the two factors indicating the bidimensional character of the variables associated with second-language achievement.

In an exploratory study such as this, it is not advisable to pay too much attention to relatively small differences in the magnitude of specific factor loadings. The important result is that two factors, not one as previously presumed, are associated with second-language achievement. Furthermore, the variables constituting the "new" factor have an empirical as well as a theoretical basis. The significant positive correlation between the orientation index and achievement in French indicates that the integratively oriented students are generally more successful in acquiring French than those who are instrumentally oriented. Further, the students with the integrative orientation have more favorable attitudes towards members of the French group and are more strongly motivated to acquire their language. Although we favor the view that a strong motivation to learn a second language follows from a desire to be accepted as a member of the new linguistic community (cf. 12), the correlation technique does not permit us to be completely certain of such an interpretation. However, with the demonstration presented here of the importance of the "motivational factor," further study of the integrative orientation can incorporate experimental procedures to determine the actual causal sequence of events.

SUMMARY

Montreal high school students studying French as a second language completed a battery of tests including measures of linguistic aptitude, verbal intelligence, and various attitudinal and motivational characteristics. Analysis of the intercorrelations of these tests yielded two orthogonal factors equally related to ratings of achievement in French: a "linguistic aptitude" and a "motivational" factor. It was also found that maximum prediction of success in second-language acquisition was obtained from tests of: verbal intelligence, intensity of motivation to learn the other language, students' purposes in studying that language, and one index of linguistic aptitude.

REFERENCES

1. ADORNO, T. W., FRENKEL-BRUNSWIK, ELSE, LEVINSON, D. J., & SANFORD, R. N. *The authoritarian personality*. New York: Harper, 1950.

2. CARROLL, J. B. Summary of validity coefficients—foreign language aptitude battery. Harvard University, 1956 (mimeographed).

3. CARROLL, J. B., & SAPON, S. M. Supplement 1 to examiner's manual—Psi-Lambda foreign language aptitude battery. Harvard University, 1956 (mimeographed).

4. CARROLL, J. B. A factor analysis of two foreign language aptitude batteries. *J. gen. Psychol.*, 1958, *59* 3-19.

5. DUNKEL, H. B. *Second-language learning*. Boston: Ginn, 1948.

6. ERVIN, SUSAN. Identification and bilingualism. Harvard University, 1954 (mimeographed).

7. GARDNER, R. C. Social factors in second-language acquisition. Unpublished Master's thesis, McGill University, 1958.

8. HENMON, V. A. C. Prognosis tests in the modern foreign language. *Publications of the American and Canadian Committees on Modern Foreign Languages*, 1929, *14*, 3-31.

9. LAMBERT, W. E. Measurement of the linguistic dominance of bilinguals. *J. abnorm. soc. Psychol.*, 1955, *50*, 197-200.

10. LAMBERT, W. E., HODGSON, R. C., GARDNER, R. C., & FILLENBAUM, S. Evaluational reactions to spoken languages. *J. abnorm. soc. Psychol.*, (in press).

11. MOWRER, O.*Learning theory and personality dynamics*. New York: Ronald, 1950.

12. NEWCOMB, T. M. *Social psychology*. New York: Dryden, 1950.

13. PAIVIO, A. V., & LAMBERT, W. E. Measures and correlates of audience anxiety (stage fright). *J Pers.*, 1959, *27*, 1-17.

14. SROLE, L. Social dysfunction, personality and social distance attitudes. (Paper read before American Sociological Society, 1951 National Meeting, Chicago, Illinois.)

15. STEAD, W., SHARTLE, C. L., *et al. Occupational counseling techniques*. American Book Company, 1940.

16. SYMONDS, P. M. A modern foreign language prognosis test. *Publications of the American and Canadian Committees on Modern Foreign Languages*, 1929, *14*, 91-126.

17. THURSTONE, L. L. *Multiple factor analysis*. Chicago: Univer. Chicago Press, 1947.

18. TODD, J. W. The psychological fundamentals of linguistic achievement. *Publications of the American and Canadian Committees on Modern Foreign Languages*, 1929, *14*, 129-172.

19. WHYTE, W. F., & HOLMBERG, A. R. Human problems of U.S. enterprise in Latin America. *Human Organization*, 1956, *15*, No. 3, 1-40.

20. WITTENBORN, J. R., & LARSEN, R. P. A factorial study of achievement in college German. *J. educ. Psychol.*, 1944, *35*, 39-48.

READING NUMBER TWO

MOTIVATIONAL VARIABLES IN SECOND-LANGUAGE ACQUISITION[1]

ROBERT C. GARDNER

University of Western Ontario

The previous study by Gardner and Lambert (1959) indicated that both language aptitude and an integrative motive are important for successful acquisition of a second language. However, many questions remain unanswered by that study. Foremost among these is the matter of replicability. Would similar results be obtained if the study were repeated? Secondly, although only one criterion measure, a combination of teacher's ratings of oral skills and aural comprehension, was employed in that study, two independent dimensions were found to be related to it. This suggests that there were in fact two relatively independent aspects of French achievement included in the one rating. *A posteriori,* it seems reasonable to expect that the two factors, language aptitude and an integrative motive would facilitate the acquisition of different types of second-language skills, and that it should be possible to isolate the skills related to each. Finally, there is the question, raised in the basic study, of the cause-effect relation existing between the integrative motive and second-language achievement. Does the integrative motive facilitate achievement, or does achievement in the second language result in the development of an integrative motive?

---

[1]This reading is an abstract from R. C. Gardner's unpublished doctoral dissertation, "Motivational variables in second-language acquisition," McGill University, 1960.

The study reported here was designed to answer these questions. Partial replication was permitted by the use of a group of tests which overlapped those used in the previous study. Identification of second-language skills related to the aptitude and motivation dimensions was allowed by the use of a number of objective measures of specific second-language skills. Finally clarification of the cause-effect relations was sought by introducing into the correlation matrix a series of measures concerning the subject's attitude toward his present home environment as well as to his earlier home environment. In addition, a follow-up study was performed on the relation between the parent's attitudes and those of the student.

METHOD

Subjects (Ss)

Ninety grade 10 students were selected from six Montreal high schools[2] to act as *S*s. Within each school, fifteen students were chosen by the principal and French language teacher such that 5 were classified as "superior", 5 "average", and 5 "poor" students in French[3]. One further restriction on the selection of these students was that they came from English-speaking homes. Although the ninety students were screened by the school authorities on this variable, a personal history sheet completed by the students during the testing session revealed that seven students had one French-speaking parent and spoke French in the home. These students were not included in the data analysis; the resulting sample of 83 consisted of 39 boys and 44 girls.

The *S*s were tested in one three-hour session with a battery of tests that provided measures of the following variables:

1. *Reading Fluency.* Tape recordings of each student's reading of a passage of unfamiliar French prose were rated for fluency on a seven point scale by two French experts. Interjudge reliability was 0.87, thus the ratings were combined.
2. *Pronunciation Accuracy.* The same two judges rated each student's recording on a seven point scale for accuracy of French pronunciation. Interjudge reliability was 0.84, and the two ratings were combined.
3. *French Phonetic Discrimintation.* Part I of the French Listening Comprehension Test, Form A (Brooks, 1955). High scores on this test reflect the

---

[2]Three of these were high schools for boys and three for girls. They were chosen such that one school for each sex represented different socioeconomic regions of Montreal (i.e., the west, central and eastern parts of the city).

[3]This selection procedure was used in order to ensure a wide variance with respect to French achievement. Examination of the distributions of scores on the tests of French achievement indicated that they were continuous and approximately normally distributed.

ability to make auditory distinctions in consonant, vowel and nasal sounds, verb endings, linking, etc., in the aural comprehension of French.

4. *Grammer*. Part III of the Cooperative French Test (Advanced form).

5. *Vocabulary*. Part II of the Cooperative French Test (Advanced form).

6. *Accent*. Two judges classified each student's tape recording as manifesting either a French-Canadian or no French-Canadian accent. A "high" score on this test indicates the presence of a French-Canadian accent.

7. *Meaning Separation.* A combined semantic separation score (D_{ij}) (Osgood, Suci, and Tannenbaum, 1959) between translated equivalents for the three major semantic factors was calculated. The terms "me" "moi" "my friend" and "mon ami" were rated on the following semantic differential scales: good-bad, pleasant-unpleasant,   clean-dirty,   strong-weak,   large-small,   fast-slow, active-passive, and hot-cold. A high score indicates large separation between the translated equivalents.

8. *Automaticity.* The time taken to respond to each of a series of French and English directions on Lambert's (1955) Finger Key was obtained. The time scores were converted to ranks to remove the effects of speed of response and the mean rank of the English times was subtracted from the mean rank of the French times. A high score indicates English Dominance, a low score bilingual automaticity.

9. *Associations in French.* Ss were presented with the words petit, ami, maison, and libre and given 30 seconds to write down French associations for each. The score was the number of French words written.

The following three variables are subtests from Carroll's (1955) Psi-Lambda Foreign Language Aptitude Battery,

10. *Spelling clues.*

11. *Words in Sentences.*

12. *Paired Associates.*

13. *Orientation.* An *S's* orientation to the study of French was classified as integrative (1) or instrumental (0) according to his answers to the following questions:

(a) What advantages, if any, have you experienced by speaking French with your French friends?

(b) What disadvantages are there for not being able to speak French?

(c) What types of personal satisfactions, if any, have you had for speaking French.

Those *S*s who stated that the value of speaking French was that they could know French speaking people better, and become more friendly with them, were classified as integratively oriented: those who stressed that the major advantage of speaking French was the job opportunities it permitted, or the educational prestige or satisfaction it afforded, were classified as instrumentally oriented.

14. *Desire to learn French.* Ss rated on a seven point scale (from "not at all" (1) to "very much" (7) how much they wanted to learn French.

15. *Motivational Intensity Scale.* Seven multiple choice statements were presented which dealt with the student's motivation to acquire fluency in French. The statements attempted to ascertain the amount of effort he currently expended in attempting to perfect his French, the amount he thought he would expend if French were not a school subject, and his interest in continuing this training after school.

16. *French-Canadian Attitude Scale.* Twenty positively worded statements about French-Canadians were presented, and S indicated his degree of agreement or disagreement with each on a 7 point scale. A high score indicates a favorable attitude toward the French-Canadians.

17. *French-Canadian Evaluation.* S's ratings of the concept "French-Canadians" on three evaluative scales of the semantic differential (good-bad, pleasant-unpleasant, clean-dirty) were combined to provide an index of each S's attitude toward French-Canadians. A high score indicates an unfavorable evaluation.

18. *Ethnocentrism Scale.* This scale was adapted from Else Frenkel-Brunswick's (1949) Ethnocentrism Scale for Children. High scores indicate an ethnocentric attitude toward out-groups.

19. *California F-Scale.* All but the three sex items of Forms 40 and 45 of the F-Scale (Adorno, et al, 1950) were administered.

20. *Anomie Scale.* Srole's (1951) five item Likert scale designed to measure an individual's dissatisfaction with his role in society was administered.

21. *English-Canadian Evaluation.* S's ratings of the concept "English-Canadians" on three evaluative scales of the semantic differential (see 17, above) were combined to form a measure of attitudes toward English-Canadians. A high score indicates an unfavourable evaluation.

22. *English vs French-Canadian Identification.* The three concepts "me", "French-Canadians", and "English-Canadians" were rated on nine semantic differential scales (see 7, above). The semantic separation score (D_{ij}) for "me" vs "English-Canadians" was subtracted from that for "me" vs "French-Canadians" to yield a score which describes how similarly an S rates himself relative to the two ethnic groups. After the addition of a constant to eliminate negative values, a high score indicates that S perceives himself similar to English-Canadians, a low score reflects more perceived similarity with French-Canadians.

Variables 23, 24, and 25 were adapted from Schutz (1958) to measure an S's remembered characteristics of his early home environment.

23. *Attention.* A high score indicates a considerable amount of attention from the parents.

24. *Discipline.* A high score suggests a considerable amount of early discipline.

25. *Affection.* A high score is indicative of an abundance of affection in the home.

Variables 26, 27 and 28 are mean ratings on three evaluative scales of the semantic differential (see 17, above) for the following concepts: (In each instance a high score is indicative of a relatively negative evaluation).

26. *My mother.*

27. *My father.*

28. *Me*

29. *Associations in English.* Ss were presented with the words sad, garden, thought, and honor and given 30 seconds to write down English associations for each. The score was the number of associations.

30. *Sex.* In the correlation matrix, point biserial correlations involving sex are positive if girls tended to obtain higher scores than boys on the test in question.

RESULTS AND DISCUSSION

Table 1 presents the matrix of correlation coefficients. Since Variables 6 (Accent), 13 (Orientation), and 30 (Sex) are dichotomous measures, the correlations of these with other measures are point biserial coefficients, while the correlations among these three variables are phi-coefficients. All other entries are Pearson product-moment correlation coefficients.

The correlation matrix was factor analyzed using the Principal Axis solution and factoring was terminated after 91% of the common factor variance had been extracted. Nine factors were obtained (see Table 2), and these were rotated by means of the normalized Varimax solution (see Table 3).[4]

Factor I obtains high loadings from Variables 1-5 and 10-12, and lower, but appreciable, loadings from Variables 6, 13, and 14. The defining characteristic of this factor would seem to lie in the nature of the French achievement measures (Variables 1-5) included. Although this factor obviously defines a dimension of French achievement, the magnitude of the loadings of the achievement measures appear to reflect the extent to which these skills are stressed in the classroom situation. These students have had considerable prior training, hence their curriculum has undoubtedly involved training in oral reading (Variables 1 and 2), aural comprehension (Variable 3), and grammar and vocabulary (Variables 4 and 5). However, it is unlikely that specific attention was directed toward the development of those language skills measured by Variables 8 (Automaticity) and 9 (Associations in French), or whether a French-Canadian accent (Variable 6) was encouraged in the classroom. Factor I is thus best identified as a *School*

---

[4]The factor analysis contained in the original report was a principal component solution, subsequent rotations being performed by means of Carroll's biquartimin solution.

TABLE 1

CORRELATION MATRIX

	1	2	3	4	5	6	7	8	9	10	11	12	13	14	15
1		.84	.62	.51	.62	.43	.01	-.08	.33	.47	.40	.34	.40	.36	.?
2			.60	.51	.58	.56	-.03	-.07	.35	.49	.39	.34	.39	.42	.?
3				.58	.43	.29	-.16	-.07	.18	.42	.41	.28	.36	.34	.0
4					.52	.26	-.24	.06	.27	.46	.56	.46	.40	.39	.3
5						.25	-.12	-.30	.38	.49	.39	.37	.31	.37	.3
6							.16	-.14	.35	.18	.08	.01	.41	.30	.2
7								.07	-.09	-.10	-.16	-.16	-.16	-.27	-.0
8									.03	.25	.20	.08	-.24	-.23	-.1
9										.28	.09	.20	.08	.33	.3
10											.56	.51	.34	.26	.0
11												.51	.08	.25	.0
12													.10	.25	.1
13														.37	.2
14															.4
15															

See table 2 for the names of the variables.

TABLE 1 (continued)

CORRELATION MATRIX

	16	17	18	19	20	21	22	23	24	25	26	27	28	29	30
1	-.02	-.06	.00	.08	.03	.00	-.21	.26	.16	.20	-.11	-.18	-.09	.22	.08
2	.02	.04	-.05	-.04	-.11	.00	-.22	.24	.12	.15	-.09	-.09	-.06	.24	.00
3	.23	-.10	-.19	.00	-.11	-.14	-.24	.16	.10	.02	.08	-.15	-.08	.17	.06
4	.09	-.11	-.07	.04	-.14	-.04	-.30	.13	.03	.07	-.11	-.05	-.14	.17	.37
5	.10	-.05	.07	.13	.03	-.05	-.15	.13	-.04	.10	-.14	-.04	-.02	.28	.15
6	-.14	.20	-.04	-.25	-.03	-.04	-.14	.12	.06	.08	.22	.09	.05	.24	-.15
7	-.35	.40	.21	-.12	.08	-.02	.08	.24	-.11	.17	-.05	.05	.06	.03	-.32
8	-.04	.04	.14	.00	-.04	-.11	.07	.08	.02	.07	-.04	-.02	-.10	.15	.12
9	.19	-.11	.00	.15	.11	-.17	-.15	.02	.01	.13	-.14	.12	-.16	.69	-.19
10	.25	-.06	-.07	.08	-.05	-.15	-.18	.15	.01	.07	-.07	-.05	.06	.32	.10
11	.19	-.04	-.16	.04	-.13	.02	-.12	.10	.14	.03	.00	-.14	-.03	.18	.18
12	.23	-.22	-.08	.04	-.18	-.05	.00	.12	.07	.22	-.17	-.11	-.22	.11	.30
13	.12	-.01	.04	-.03	.18	.05	-.19	.11	.06	-.03	.19	.02	.00	-.06	.16
14	.23	-.25	-.16	-.07	-.25	.01	-.31	.15	.00	.17	-.11	-.21	-.14	.22	.22
15	.08	-.22	.07	.17	-.01	.02	-.18	.21	.03	.24	-.24	-.11	-.07	.10	.19

TABLE 1 (continued)

CORRELATION MATRIX

	16	17	18	19	20	21	22	23	24	25	26	27	28	29	30
16		-.54	-.14	.24	-.07	.06	-.27	-.08	.20	.05	-.19	-.06	-.14	.13	.15
17			.03	-.22	.10	.32	.28	.00	-.05	-.05	.41	.22	.52	-.01	-.07
18				.30	.27	-.16	.08	-.02	.00	.03	-.19	-.02	.05	-.07	.15
19					.54	.01	.01	-.07	-.02	-.06	-.31	-.10	.03	.06	.01
20						.06	.24	-.18	.08	-.24	.15	.05	.21	.09	-.10
21							-.18	.02	-.06	.05	.46	.21	.51	-.14	.26
22								-.15	-.07	.01	.08	.13	-.01	-.15	.05
23									.18	.68	-.19	-.29	-.07	-.05	.17
24										.20	.00	-.25	-.02	-.02	.09
25											-.25	-.32	-.21	-.01	.22
26												.39	.56	.02	-.06
27													.28	-.03	-.13
28														-.02	.03
29															-.30
30															

TABLE 2

PRINCIPAL COMPONENT FACTOR MATRIX

	I	II	III	IV	V	VI	VII	VIII	IX
1. Reading Fluency	.79	.23	.13	.16	-.07	.15	-.15	-.09	.05
2. Pronunciation Accuracy	.79	.31	.10	.17	.00	-.01	-.12	-.06	.04
3. French Aural Comprehension	.69	.12	-.07	-.07	.13	-.04	-.26	-.28	.13
4. Grammar	.75	.08	-.18	-.09	.12	.12	-.14	.15	.06
5. Vocabulary	.71	.18	.14	-.07	-.12	.14	-.10	.25	.08
6. Accent	.42	.53	.20	.25	-.07	-.30	-.07	-.10	-.19
7. Meaning Separation	-.23	.22	.33	.61	.10	.09	.04	.00	.29
8. Automaticity	-.06	-.18	.05	.09	.60	.32	.26	-.04	-.03
9. Associations (French)	.49	.06	.55	-.13	.03	-.21	.42	.17	-.24
10. Spelling Clues	.66	.07	.03	-.13	.41	.22	.03	-.04	.09
11. Words in Sentences	.57	.03	-.23	-.13	.45	.28	.03	-.07	.08
12. Paired Associates	.57	-.19	-.18	-.07	.30	.23	.02	.25	-.12
13. Orientation	.47	.33	-.09	-.12	-.33	.01	-.33	-.17	-.12
14. Desire to learn French	.64	-.02	-.13	-.06	-.26	-.33	.08	.16	-.06
15. Motivational Intensity Scale	.47	-.07	.11	.11	-.52	-.03	.17	.33	-.10

TABLE 2 (continued)

PRINCIPAL COMPONENT FACTOR MATRIX

	I	II	III	IV	V	VI	VII	VIII	IX
16. French Attitude Scale	.30	-.39	-.14	-.48	-.10	-.08	.32	-.25	.03
17. French-Canadians (Eval.)	-.27	.70	-.03	.33	.16	.23	.03	.07	-.04
18. Ethnocentrism Scale	-.11	-.07	.46	.12	-.20	.42	-.15	.05	.17
19. California F-Scale	.07	-.25	.39	-.39	-.31	.55	.11	-.02	.17
20. Anomie Scale	-.16	.21	.45	-.30	-.29	.52	-.02	-.20	-.20
21. English-Canadians (Eval.)	-.11	.44	-.47	-.10	-.28	.19	.44	.07	.20
22. Perceived Dissimilarity	-.37	.02	.12	.09	.18	.32	-.26	.28	-.59
23. Parental Attention	.31	-.14	-.16	.68	-.14	.15	.23	-.11	.08
24. Parental Discipline	.16	-.13	-.13	.14	-.11	.15	.13	-.64	-.44
25. Parental Affection	.27	-.28	-.14	.67	-.14	.12	.34	.07	-.14
26. Mother (Eval.)	-.24	.73	-.29	-.17	.07	-.04	.14	-.14	-.21
27. Father (Eval.)	-.24	.48	.04	-.29	.12	-.11	.07	.34	-.03
28. Me (Eval.)	-.24	.65	-.18	-.13	-.14	.27	.29	-.06	.15
29. Associations (English)	.35	.14	.51	-.13	.30	-.20	.49	-.03	-.08
30. Sex	.22	-.17	-.63	-.05	-.15	.36	.01	.29	-.21

TABLE 3

Rotated Factor Matrix

(Normalized Varimax Solution)

MEASURES	I	II	III	IV	V	VI	VII	VIII	IX
1. Reading Fluency	.77	.30	.16	.09	-.06	.23	.12	.11	-.09
2. Pronunciation Accuracy	.76	.30	.20	.13	-.02	.16	-.08	.19	-.08
3. Aural Comprehension	.69	.12	.26	-.17	-.06	.00	-.12	-.03	-.15
4. Grammar	.71	.09	.04	-.10	-.06	.01	-.07	.09	.29
5. Vocabulary	.67	.33	-.14	.02	-.03	.03	.14	.20	.11
6. Accent	.30	.30	.39	.30	.08	.04	-.18	.36	-.09
7. Meaning Separation	-.12	-.07	-.10	.51	.03	.25	.05	.05	-.32
8. Automaticity	-.04	.57	.02	-.06	.07	-.10	-.02	-.08	-.09
9. Associations (French)	.22	.12	.02	-.08	-.11	.02	.11	.81	.03
10. Spelling Clues	.70	-.22	.01	-.12	.01	.03	.00	.20	.04
11. Words in Sentences	.68	-.28	-.06	-.18	.05	.04	-.08	.00	.09
12. Paired Associates	.53	-.18	-.13	-.16	-.13	.11	-.06	.08	.33
13. Orientation	.37	.35	.43	-.03	.08	-.06	.05	-.01	.14
14. Desire to learn French	.35	.41	.06	.26	-.07	.13	-.22	.24	.21
15. Motivational Intensity Scale	.18	.49	-.06	-.04	-.09	.25	.14	.26	.29
16. Attitude Scale	.10	-.03	.04	-.74	-.05	.04	.03	.12	.04
17. French-Canadian (Eval.)	-.01	-.14	.04	.60	.50	.00	-.04	-.01	-.11
18. Ethnocentrism	-.08	-.01	-.01	.23	-.12	.07	.46	.00	.12
19. California F-Scale	.05	.01	-.15	-.26	-.05	.00	.72	.05	-.02
20. Anomie	-.07	-.02	.22	.07	.15	-.21	.72	.07	-.10
21. English-Canadian (Eval.)	-.05	.13	-.10	-.11	.75	.09	-.04	-.04	.12
22. Perceived Dissimilarity	-.20	-.26	.01	.35	-.07	-.14	.15	-.09	.15
23. Parental Attention	.15	.03	.07	.10	.02	.79	-.05	-.02	.02
24. Parental Discipline	.05	-.11	.36	-.17	-.03	.26	.05	-.05	-.02
25. Parental Affection	.02	-.01	-.01	.04	-.10	.79	-.13	.11	.20
26. Mother (Eval.)	-.03	-.05	.32	.14	.65	-.30	-.21	-.02	-.04
27. Father (Eval.)	-.10	.01	-.06	.19	.32	-.42	-.08	.14	.08
28. Me (Eval.)	-.02	.01	.00	.12	.76	-.10	.12	-.06	-.06
29. Associations (English)	.22	-.11	-.05	-.10	.01	-.03	.01	.75	-.24
30. Sex	.18	-.02	.01	-.14	.09	.17	.04	-.26	.60

TABLE 4

RELATION BETWEEN STUDENT ORIENTATION

AND PARENT'S INTERVIEW DATA

Variables	X^2*	d.f.	P
Mother's Orientation	6.73	1	<.01
Mother's Attitudes	4.30	1	<.05
Parent's French Friends	0.00	1	N.S.
Student's French Friends	3.17	1	<.10
Parent's French Skills			
Mother	0.10	1	N.S.
Father	0.04	1	N.S.

*Corrected for continuity. A negative X^2 would indicate that the distribution of frequencies in the 2 x 2 table was in the opposite direction to that predicted.

French Achievement factor. The loadings of the three language aptitude measures (Variables 10-12) and the measures of an integrative orientation (Variable 13) and the desire to learn French (Variable 14) suggest that these variables are related to school French achievement. Clearly language aptitude plays the dominant role. Where language achievement depends upon formal instruction, it is understandable that differences in verbal skills will account for differences in attainment. It is surprising however, that the orientation and desire variables also account for individual differences in achievement on these school taught skills. It would appear that a desire to learn French and an integrative orientation toward the French-Canadian community enable the student to profit from such instruction. It seems unlikely that this component operates to motivate the student to expend more energy in studying French since the measure of motivational intensity (Variable 15) is not represented on this factor. It seems more probable that the desire to learn the language for integrative reasons facilitates the incorporation of these language habits since it provides the student with a more accepting attitude toward the program of instruction.

Factor II is defined by eight measures; three indices of the integrative motive (Variables 13, 14, and 15), and five measures of French achievement (Variables 1, 2, 5, 6, and 8). This factor clearly describes the motivational component in second language acquisition; this motive being expressed in a desire to learn the language, with concomitant effort directed at perfecting the skills, for purposes of integrating with the other group. Unlike the findings of Gardner and Lambert (1959) this integrative motive is independent of favorable attitudes toward the French-Canadians (note Variables 16 and 17), and it seems likely that a desire for integration may not presuppose a favorable attitude toward the whole group (cf. Lambert, 1955). Whatever the underlying reasons for this integrative motive it is clear that it accounts for considerable individual differences in language achievement as evidenced by the appreciable loadings of the five measures of French proficiency. Furthermore, this factor subsumes a dimension of French achievement different from that described by Factor I. Whereas Factor I appears to involve a dimension of French achievement similar to Lambert's (1956) "vocabulary cluster", in that it appears to depend primarily on training, Factor II is more like Lambert's "cultural cluster". The dominant measure is bilingual automaticity (Variable 8) which appears to depend upon considerable active use of the two languages. Since these students are all native English speaking, it must be assumed that they acquired this second-language proficiency in the community in interaction with members of the French group. The loadings of the other French achievement measures support this interpretation. Those measures receiving appreciable loadings on this factor reflect oral proficiency (Variables 1, 2, and 6) and vocabulary knowledge (Variable 5), achievement in which would be enhanced by communicating with members of the other group. Similarly, the French achievement measures not receiving appreciable loadings on this factor appear primarily to be those which would not be improved, over the level developed in school, as a result of active use of the language. Factor II is thus considered to reflect the Integrative Motive which accounts for most of the variability in achievement on those bilingual language skills developed through active use of the language in a bicultural community. It is of interest to note that such an active drive for enculturation is at least slightly associated with a perceived similarity of the self and the French Canadians (Variable 22), as well as a relative inability with comples aspects of English achievement (Variables 10 and 11). It is as though extreme identification with the French group might slightly impair English language proficiency.

The factorial composition of the student's orientation (Variable 13) is indeed complex. Like the previous two factors, Factor III also receives appreciable loadings from Orientation as well as one measure of French achievement, Accent (Variable 6), and two home variables, recollections of early home discipline (Variable 24), and attitudes toward the mother (Variable 26). Thus, it is clear that some aspect of the integrative orientation is also related to the development of a French-Canadian accent. The loadings of the other two variables moreover suggest that this aspect is related to negative attitudes toward the mother and a feeling that the early home life was too disciplined, and it is therefore possible that one antecedent of an integrative orientation is feelings of dissatisfaction with the home situation. The total pattern suggests that this aspect of the integrative orientation, fostered by feelings of dissatisfaction with one's family life, leads to interaction with the other group such that their accent is acquired.

Factor IV is clearly a *French-Canadian Attitude* factor. Variables 16 and 17 are measures of positive and negative attitudes respectively, the opposite loadings reflecting this difference in scoring. Variable 22 measures *S's* ethnic group identification, its negative loading indicating that favorable attitudes toward the French-Canadians are associated with feelings that one is more like the French- than the English-Canadians. Two measures of French achievement are included on this factor. Positive attitudes are related to similar connotative reactions to translated equivalents (Variable 7) as well as to the absence of a French-Canadian accent (Variable 6). That favorable attitudes promote similar connotative reactions to the words used probably is due to the concepts included since they are of high personal relevance; nonetheless it is clear that attitudes toward an ethnic group can influence semantic differential ratings of words from that group's language. The other finding that favorable attitudes towards the French-Canadians are negatively related to the presence of a French-Canadian accent is difficult to interpret. Since these attitudes are independent of an integrative orientation they do not apparently reflect a desire to meet with members of the French-Canadian group and hence it is not surprising that they do not facilitate the acquisition of an accent. However, that they should impair its acquisition is peculiar. Variable 6 itself is so factorially complex moreover that interpreting it as a valid index of accent on each factor may be unwarranted.

Factor V is dominated by the loadings of two measures of word association. These tests required *S*s to write associations to common French (Variable 9) and English (Variable 29) words, and consequently this factor seems best defined as a verbal fluency dimension. The positive loading of Variable 6 (Accent) would appear to indicate that verbal fluency aids in the acquisition of a French-Canadian accent, however the factorial composition of this variable is so complex that any interpretation is highly speculative.

Factor VI is defined by five variables, the dominant one being sex (Variable 30). Clearly, therefore, this factor reflects a dimension on which girls excel boys. Examination of the remaining four variables suggests that girls are superior to boys on the Paired Associates test (Variable 12), French grammar (Variable 4), motivational intensity (Variable 15), and on maintaining similarity of connotative meaning of French-English translated equivalents (Variable 7). Each of these relationships is supported by the values in the correlation matrix (Table 1). One interpretation of this factor might be that girls are superior in paired associate learning and that when this skill is linked with a drive to learn French, their memory skills enable them to retain associations between translated equivalents, as well as grammatical rules.

Factor VII describes a dimension of attitudes toward the home environment. High positive loadings are obtained by measures of perceived attention (Variable 23) and affection (Variable 25) in the early home environment, while substantial negative loadings (reflecting favorable attitudes) are obtained by evaluations of the father and mother (Variables 27 and 26, respectively). The interpretation is obvious.

Factor VIII is defined by three measures of general attitudes, and would appear to be a dimension of authoritarian attitudes. The two highest loadings are obtained by the California F-Scale (Variable 19), and the Anomie scale (Variable 20); a somewhat lower loading is obtained by the Ethnocentrism scale (Variable 18). This component of authoritarianism would appear to involve dissatisfaction with one's roles in society as well as dislike and distrust of outgroups.

Factor IX is clearly a semantic differential factor. It is defined by the five variables (17, 21, 26, 27, and 28) which involved pure semantic differential ratings. Further interpretation of this dimension seems unwarranted since it appears to primarily reflect the variance associated with the semantic differential method.

In summary, the results of this study suggest that the integrative orientation serves to motivate the individual to acquire a second language. Because of this, additional data were obtained in this study, to determine what parental support there was for the student's orientation. Interviews with the mothers of each student were designed to determine:

(a) the mother's orientation towards language study (classified as integrative or instrumental);

(b) the mother's attitude towards the French-Canadian community (scored as pro-French, neutral, or anti-French);

(c) the number of French-speaking friends the parents had (classified as many, or few);

(d) the number of French-speaking friends the parent thought his child had (classified as many, or few); and

(e) the degree of French language skill each parent felt he or she possessed (classified as poor, or good command of the language).

Table 4 gives the X^2 values obtained for the relation between the student's orientation and each of the variables listed below. These data clearly suggest that a high school student's orientation is related to that of the parent. Integratively-oriented students tended to have an integratively-oriented parent, instrumentally-oriented students, an instrumentally-oriented parent ($X^2 = 6.73$, $p < .01$). Similarly, the student's orientation was positively related to the parent's attitude towards the French-Canadians. Integratively-oriented students came from homes where the attitudes were pro-French, while instrumentally-oriented students came from homes where the attitudes were either neutral or negative ($X^2 = 4.30$, $p < .05$).

While the data do not indicate any association between the student's orientation and the number of French friends his parents have (X^2 = 0.00), there is the suggestion that the parents of integratively-oriented Ss think that their children have more French-Canadian friends than do the parents of the instrumentally-oriented students (X^2 = 3.17, p <.10). Whether this is a statement of fact (i.e., that the integratively-oriented Ss do have more French friends) cannot be ascertained from the data. It is equally possible that this relation reflects the attitudes of the parents. That is, because they have favorable attitudes towards the French-Canadian community, the parents of the integratively-oriented students are willing to ascribe a number of French friends to their children, while parents of the instrumentally-oriented Ss, with their relatively unfavorable attitude, will not admit that their children associate with many French-Canadian children.

Finally, the student's orientation does not reflect an opportunity to use the second language in the home situation. Neither the mother's (X^2 = 0.10, df = 1, n.s.) nor the father's (X^2 = 0.14, df = 1, n.s.) proficiency in French is significantly related to the student's orientation.

Although, there is nothing in the data to definitely support the hypothesis that an integrative motive is dependent upon any antecedent conditions in the home, it is clear that an integrative orientation will not be maintained by the student unless it is reinforced by a similar orientation and favorable attitudes toward the other language group by members of his family.

The factor analysis of the correlations among the 30 measures obtained on the students revealed nine factors which accounted for the correlations. The interpretation of these factors suggested that they were best identified as describing respectively *School French Achievement, Integrative Motive, Orientation, French-Canadian Attitudes, Verbal Fluency, Sex, Attitudes Toward the Home Environment, Authoritarian Attitudes, and Semantic Differential Judgements.* Of major importance to this study are the composition of the first three factors since they help to clarify some of the interpretations suggested by the Gardner and Lambert (1959) study. First, the results support the generalization made in that study that two relatively independent factors are related to the successful acquisition of a second language, viz., language aptitude and an integrative motive. Second, they help to clarify just how these two factors operate.

Language aptitude appears to be of major importance in the acquisition of second-language skills acquired through direct instruction. Measures of language aptitude involve the assessment of verbal abilities which are directly related to the acquisition of second-language skills (Carroll, 1958). It seems reasonable to propose therefore that, in an instructional setting where there is specific material such as vocabulary items, grammatical constructions, correct pronunciations and auditory recognitions to be acquired, those students with the requisite abilities will achieve better than those students who are deficient in this regard. This interpretation is supported by the composition of Factor I. Moreover, it is clear that proficiency, even in these school-taught skills, is at least partially dependent upon motivational elements, probably because their incorporation depends upon an accepting attitude on the part of the student to make such skills part of his own language system.

An integrative motive, defined as a willingness or desire to acquire a second language for the purposes of integrating, or becoming part of the second-language community, seems important primarily for the development of communicational skills (Factor II). The psychological mechanism here would seem to be largely attitudinal. The student seeking to acquire language skills in order to become part of the other language community would be expected to work harder to acquire those skills which are important for communication. Undoubtedly verbal abilities would be a factor in determining achievement (as indicated by the fact that many of these skills are also included on Factor I), but an additional factor, and clearly an important one, is the integrative motive. It is important to note moreover that, in this study, the integrative motive does not necessarily imply favorable attitudes toward the other language community as it did in the Gardner and Lambert (1959) study. This could reflect sampling variations from that study to this, or could be due to situational and cultural factors operating at the time of the investigation, and could indicate that the basis of an integrative motive depends upon the individual, and the setting in which he finds himself. In an earlier study, Lambert (1955) described one individual, at least, whose superior second-language proficiency appeared dependent upon an integrative motive based, not on favorable attitudes toward the other language community, but more on a desire to withdraw himself from the cultural (and linguistic) community in which he currently found himself. In short, the results of this study suggest that an integrative motive is important for the successful acquisition of a second language; the bases for the integrative motive may be many, and may vary from one setting to another.

One additional finding of this study is that an integrative orientation in language study is related to feelings of dissatisfaction with the home environment (Factor III). This relationship is reminiscent of Lambert's (1963) hypothesis that feelings of anomie might direct an individual to seek membership in another culture, and consequently serve to motivate him to acquire another language. It is of interest to note that the anomie scale tends to be represented on Factor III, though the loading is not sufficiently great to justify its inclusion on the factor. Nonetheless there is the suggestion that an integrative orientation is related to, and possibly dependent upon, feelings of dissatisfaction with the home environment and to a lesser extent to feelings of anomie. Moreover, this orientation is clearly associated with the development of a French Canadian accent, and to a lesser extent to other French language skills (note particularly the loadings obtained from the measures of aural comprehension and pronunciation accuracy).

In summary, Factors I, II, and III all reflect a relation between an integrative orientation and various aspects of French language achievement, pointing to the educational relevance of this type of motivation. Moreover, the data obtained from the parents indicate some antecedents of this orientation. From the data gathered, it is clear that the student's orientation reflects that of his parents, and in particular that an integrative orientation is fostered by favorable attitudes on the part of the parents toward the other language community. These results are encouraging in that they make clear the value of pursuing this line of research as a means of understanding the motivational determinants of second-language achievement.

References

Adorno, T. W., Frenkel-Brunswik, Else, Levinson, D. J., and Sanford, R. N. *The authoritarian personality*. New York: Harper, 1950.

Brooks N. Cooperative French Listening Comprehension Test, Form A. Princeton, N.J., Cooperative Test Division, Educational Testing Service, 1955.

Carroll, J. B. A factor analysis of two foreign language aptitude batteries. *Journal of General Psychology,* 1958, *59,* 3-19.

———, and Sapon, S. M. *Psi-Lambda Foreign Language Aptitude Battery.* Copyright, J. B. Carroll, 1955.

Frenkel-Brunswik, Else. A study of prejudice in children. *Human Relations,* 1949, *1,* 295-306.

Gardner, R. C. and Lambert, W. E. Motivational variables in second-language acquisition. *Canadian Journal of Psychology,* 1959, *13,* 266-272.

Lambert, W. E. Measurement of the linguistic dominance of bilinguals. *Journal of Abnormal and Social Psychology,* 1955, *50,* 197-200.

———, W. E. Developmental aspects of second-language acquisition: III. A description of developmental changes. *Journal of Social Psychology,* 1956, *43,* 99-104.

Osgood, C. E., Suci, G. J., and Tannenbaum, P. H. *The measurement of meaning.* Urbana, University of Illinois Press, 1957.

Schutz, W. C. *FIRO: a three dimensional theory of interpersonal behavior.* New York: Rinehart, 1958.

Srole, L. Social dysfunction, personality, and social attitudes. Paper read before the American Sociological Society National meeting, Chicago, Illinois, 1951.

READING NUMBER THREE

SOCIAL AND PSYCHOLOGICAL VARIABLES IN LEARNING HEBREW[1]

MOSHE ANISFELD AND WALLACE E. LAMBERT

McGill University

The role of social attitudes in the learning of foreign languages has caught the attention of social scientists as well as language teachers (Nida, 1957-58; Vachon-Spilka, 1959; Whyte & Holmberg, 1956). Gardner and Lambert (1959) and Gardner (1960) have carried out empirical studies of this aspect of second language learning. The available findings indicate that the attitude of a student of a second language towards the other language community plays an important role in his acquisition of the other language. Students who hold sympathetic attitudes toward the other language community are found to be more successful in acquiring a second language than those holding unfavorable attitudes.

Several theoretical positions have been presented to account for these findings (Anisfeld, 1960; Ervin, 1954; Gardner, 1960). Our own theoretical scheme, presented in detail elsewhere (Anisfeld, 1960), emphasizes the generalization of attitudes developed toward a linguistic group to the language they speak (and vice versa). From this perspective, a language has potential positive or negative reinforcing value.

Since Hebrew is associated exclusively with the Jewish people, unlike many other languages that are spoken by various cultural groups, the generalization hypothesis seemed particularly appropriate for this language. The specific hypothesis was posed that the relation between attitudes toward the other language group and language achievement, found to hold for other languages,

[1]This research was supported by the Canadian Defence Research Board, Grant Number D77-94-01-10.

We are grateful to S. Cytrynbaum for his assistance in the administration and scoring of the tests, to D. Solomon (McGill) and L. Rosenberg, research director of the Canadian Jewish Congress, for their critical readings of a preliminary draft relating to the characterization of the various Jewish congregations in Montreal.

should be particularly prominent in the case of Jewish children learning Hebrew, in which their own language is learned as a second language. A favorable attitude towards belonging to the Jewish community should facilitate the children's acquisition of Hebrew. On the other hand, an attitude of marginality vis-à-vis the Jewish group should interfere with achievement in Hebrew.

Another related prediction follows from Gardner and Lambert's (1959) distinction between "integrative" and "instrumental" orientations towards the study of a foreign language. In their study, students' purposes for studying a foreign language were classified as integrative when the aim was to "learn more about the language group, or to meet more and *different* people," and as instrumental when the reasons reflected the "more utilitarian value of linguistic achievement" such as getting a better position, becoming better educated. In this study, we attempt to test, in the case of Hebrew, the findings of Gardner and Lambert (1959) and Gardner (1960) that integratively oriented students are better learners of a second language than are instrumentally oriented students.

The predictive power of the Psi-Lambda Foreign Language Aptitude Battery is also tested for the case of high school students studying Hebrew. Carroll (1960) mentions the use of this test with adults for predicting success in intensive courses of Hebrew with results similar to those found for other languages in similar training situations.

METHOD

Achievement Measures

Scores on the following tests were obtained:

1. *Teachers' ratings.* The Hebrew instructor of each class was asked to assign to his students the usual school marks for achievement in Hebrew with as much distribution as possible. In some cases, teachers were approached a second time and asked to rank those students who were given the same mark. Since most teachers tended to stress reading ability and understanding of written language, we asked them to pay special attention when assigning ratings to their students' ability to speak and comprehend Hebrew. In one class (Class A) which was at a sufficiently advanced level to enable the teacher to make a distinction between her students' comprehension of Hebrew and their oral skills in the language, she was asked to rate them separately on these two aspects of performance.

2-4. *Voice recordings.* For one school 2-minute tape recordings of the subjects' readings of a difficult Hebrew passage were obtained. These recordings were evaluated by two Hebrew experts on each of the following three aspects: Reading Fluency (2), Pronunciation Accuracy (3), Purity of Accent (4).   The score on each skill was taken as the combined ratings of both judges. The interjudge agreement was 88%.

Ability Measures

5. *Verbal Reasoning test.* This test, taken from the Differential Aptitude Tests (Bennett, Seashore, & Wesmen, 1959), was used as a measure of intelligence. Because of time limitations the time allowance for this test was shortened from 30 to 15 minutes.

6. *IQ*. Estimates of IQ were available for one class (Class A) only. These estimates were based on the Otis Self-Administering Tests of Mental Ability which had been administered by the Jewish Vocational Guidance Centre in 1958.

7. *Psi-Lambda Foreign Language Aptitude Battery, Short Form* (Carroll & Sapon, 1956). The tests used were: Spelling Clues, Words in Sentences (shortened from 15 to 10 minutes), and Paired Associates.

Attitude Measures

8. *Anti-Semitism (A-S) scale*. This scale is composed of seven items, of which six were selected from the California A-S scale (Adorno, Frenkel-Brunswik, Levinson, & Sanford, 1950) on the basis of their fitness for Jewish subjects. Minor changes in the wording of some items were introduced to make them appropriate for Canadian Jewish students. We employed this scale as a measure of Jewish "self-hatred."

9. *Orientation Index*. On the basis of preliminary discussions with Jewish educators and analysis of compositions written by Jewish pupils in Montreal on topics related to study of Hebrew and other languages, 14 possible reasons for learning Hebrew were composed. Nine judges were asked to classify these statements as either integrative or instrumental according to the definitions of Gardner and Lambert (1959). The criterion of inclusion in the scale was agreement of at least seven judges on the categorization of an item. Six items, three integrative and three instrumental, met this criterion and were finally used to make up the Orientation Index.[2] For each of these statements the subject was requested to state, along a three-point scale, the degree of importance the particular reason had for him.

The integrative and instrumental items were scored separately, and then the instrumental score was subtracted from the integrative score to obtain an index of the balance between the two orientations for each individual. Thus the Orientation Index measures how much more (or less) intense the student's integrative motive is than his instrumental motive for studying Hebrew.

Subjects

Although 11 classes in seven Jewish parochial schools in Montreal were contacted, for reasons described elsewhere (Anisfeld, 1960), only 7 classes were used for the final analysis. The main reason for not analyzing all classes was that the samples were so small. In this paper we report the results of 6 classes from three schools in different settings in Montreal. (Because of doubts regarding the validity of the achievement measures of the seventh class, it is not included in the present discussion.) The schools as well as the classes so obviously differed in level of training, experience required, and regularity of attendance, in addition to having different instructors, that it was appropriate to treat each class as a separate sample (Guilford, 1950, pp. 352-354). A description of each class is therefore in order.

---

[2]The integrative reasons were:

2. Hebrew is necessary to keep the Jewish people together.
4. I want to become more a part of the Jewish culture.
5. In order to be a good Jew I have to know Hebrew.

The instrumental reasons were:

1. One can enjoy a more successful life in the community with a knowledge of Hebrew.
3. In the future it may prove useful in getting a job.
4. I wish to enter a profession in which it is necessary to be familiar with Hebrew.

Class A (N = 16) is a Grade 9 class in an all-day Hebrew school. All children have attended the elementary branch of this school, so that when tested they were in their ninth year of experience in Hebrew studies. The children study the Hebrew language for 5 hours weekly in addition to their contact with the language in other Jewish subjects, such as Bible and Talmud study, and reading of prayers.

Class B (N = 11) is a Grade 8 class in another school. All students except for one have already gone through the all-day elementary branch of the school, and they now attend only Sunday and afternoon classes. They receive 3.5 hours of instruction in Hebrew subjects and 2.5 in Yiddish subjects during the week.

We also tested four classes in School C (N = 54) which is the largest and wealthiest Jewish afternoon school in Montreal. We will refer to these classes as *Class C (8a)*, *Class C (8b)*, *Class C (9a)*, and *Class C (9b)*, with the number denoting grade, *a* and *b* standing for the "better" and the "poorer" classes of students, respectively. In this school the children receive 4 hours of instruction in Jewish subjects during the week. Most pupils have been attending this afternoon school since Grade 1.

The students were divided into better and poorer classes when they completed Grade 2. We wanted to understand on what basis this classification was made. The classes were therefore compared on the following variables: Verbal Reasoning (Variable 5), and Anti-Semitism (Variable 8). The *t* tests indicate that only the differences in language aptitude are significant. The *t* values for the differences between the *a* and *b* classes on each grade level are significant beyond the .02 level (on two-tailed tests). It appears reasonable to conclude that the factor underlying the differences in achievement between the *a* and *b* classes is language aptitude.

RESULTS AND DISCUSSION

In order to test our hypotheses relating both ability and attitude to achievement in Hebrew, the correlations of these two classes of prediction variables with achievement measures were computed for each of our six subsamples.

The heterogeneity of the classes in our study not only called for statistical treatment of each group separately but also prevented us from averaging the coefficients to obtain a single estimate of the population correlation. Since some of the correlations of the prediction variables with achievement measures differed significantly from class to class, we found it unjustified to assume that "the several *r*'s did arise by random sampling from the same population," an assumption necessary to allow the averaging of coefficients (Guilford, 1950, p. 355). Furthermore, there is also other evidence, to be presented later, that suggests that the schools investigated represent samples from different populations.

Ability and Achievement

Table 1 presents the correlations of our two indices of ability (intelligence and linguistic aptitude) with achievement measures. Linguistic aptitude as measured by the Psi-Lambda battery correlates quite highly with achievement

TABLE 1

CORRELATIONS OF ABILITY VARIABLES
WITH ACHIEVEMENT MEASURES

Achievement measures	Ability measures		
	Psi-Lambda	Verbal Reasoning	IQ
Class A (N = 16)			
Fluency	.599**	.079	.244
Pronunciation Accuracy	.613**	.098	.164
Purity of Accent	.420	.093	.068
Comprehension (Teacher's ratings)	.667***	.492	.546*
Oral Skill (Teacher's ratings)	.432	.377	.321
Class B (N = 11)			
Teacher's ratings	.817***	.663*	
Class C (8a) (N = 13)			
Teacher's ratings	.532	.409	
Class C (8b) (N = 11)			
Teacher's ratings	.621*	.700***	
Class C (9a) (N = 14)			
Teacher's ratings	.417	−.245	
Class C (9b) (N = 11)			
Teacher's ratings	.647*	.774***	

* Significant at .05 level; two-tailed test.
** Significant at .02 level; two-tailed test.
*** Significant at .01 level; two-tailed test.

measures for all classes. We notice in the Class A rubrics in Table 1 that the correlations between Foreign Language Aptitude and Purity of Accent and Oral Skill do not reach significance. This appears to be in line with the findings of Gardner (1960) who reports insignificant correlations between each of the subtests of the Short Form Psi-Lambda battery (the same that was used in the present study) and accent characteristics. However, the Short Form does not include the Phonetic Script test which measures the "ability to 'code' auditory phonetic material in such a way that this material can be recognized, identified, and remembered over something longer than a few seconds.... [an ability which is important not only in] remembering phonetic material (words, forms, etc.) but also in mimicking speech sounds" (Carroll, 1960, pp. 46-47). The auditory coding ability and the ability to mimic are obviously necessary for speech production; it therefore seems that Gardner's conclusion is not justified. As a matter of fact, in Gardner's (1960) study the correlation between the Spelling Clues test, which gauges the ability to produce sounds, and accent comes very close to significance, as do also the correlations of the total Short Form with Accent and with Oral Skill in the present study (Table 1).

Turning to intelligence, we observe in Table 1 that for Class A (which is at a sufficiently advanced level of proficiency in Hebrew to make possible a distinction among several aspects of linguistic skill) both Verbal Reasoning and IQ show differences in their correlations among various aspects of performance in Hebrew. Both indices of intelligence correlate highly with Comprehension of Hebrew and with Oral Skill but not with Fluency, Pronunciation Accuracy, and Purity of Accent. This finding appears to support the view (Dunkel, 1948) that intelligence plays a differential role in various language domains, with success in the more cognitive tasks, represented by Comprehension, being more dependent on intelligence than success in tasks involving mainly oral production. The considerable magnitude of the correlations of Verbal Reasoning and of IQ with the Oral Skill ratings is probably due to the fact that these ratings were assigned by the teacher who, very likely, took into account to some extent the cognitive aspects of oral proficiency, such as the ideas a student expresses and the way he presents them.

Attitudes and Achievement

Table 2 summarizes the relations between each of the attitude variables and the measures of achievement. The correlations of the Anti-Semitism (A-S) scale and of the Orientation Index with achievement measures seem to be dependent upon the particular classes examined. For Classes A and B, the A-S scale is a reliable predictor of achievement in Hebrew whereas the Orientation Index is not; the reverse is generally true for the C classes. A possible explanation for this patterning is suggested by a consideration of the differential social characteristics of our samples. Classes A and B are located in and draw their students from a dwelling district in Montreal (Outremont and vicinity) which is lower in the socioeconomic class hierarchy than School C (located in the Westmount suburb).[3]

Briefly, the parents of our students in the Outremont district are first generation North Americans; they still bear revealing traces of their old-fashioned Jewish background which they apparently dislike and from which they strive to free themselves. The Outremont students are or have been day students for 7 or 8 years, and they are advanced enough in Hebrew that both the teachers' ratings and the objective tests of achievement can be regarded as reliable discriminators of their ability in the language. Consequently, our finding of a correlation between attitudes toward the Jewish group (A-S) and proficiency in Hebrew should be taken as encouraging support of our hypothesis. On the other hand, the failure to find the same relation for three of

---

[3]The following characterization of the Jewish residents of these districts is based to a great extent on a sociological study of Montreal Jewish areas by Seidel (1939) and draws on the theory of Tryon (1955).

the Westmount classes is not necessarily conflicting evidence. Because the Westmount students are at a very elementary level of Hebrew and the individual differences between the students in achievement are slight, it seems likely that the teachers, when asked to rank their students in Hebrew skill, resort to considerations of other classroom behaviors which actually differentiate these students. The Anti-Semitism variable does not seem to be one of these behaviors. It is difficult to imagine why Westmount Jews should be anti-Semitic. They are already second-generation North Americans, have adapted to the American culture to a considerable extent, and are economically and socially secure. The dimension of own-group devaluation is comparatively meaningless for Westmount Jews. It is our belief that they are relatively unconcerned with feelings of self-devaluation. It follows that the variation obtained on the A-S scale for the C classes may well be chance variance,[4] and the scale should not be regarded as measuring for the Westmount students a latent variable around which psychological processes are organized—a conception of attitudes presented by Green (1954).

The Orientation Index, measuring a desire to integrate in the Jewish culture, also seems to manifest differential sensitivity from class to class. The Outremont children apparently take their Jewishness as a matter of obvious fact and are not concerned with problems of integration in the Jewish culture. For them the variance on the Orientation Index is presumably chance variance and consequently this index does not predict achievement in Hebrew. In contrast, the problem of understanding what being Jewish means, of establishing a cultural identity, is of major concern to our Westmount students and their parents. It would not be surprising, therefore, if the Westmount teachers in evaluating a student's standing in the Hebrew language, a major subject in the Hebrew school, took into account the degree a student exhibits a willingness to integrate in the Jewish culture through the Hebrew school. Furthermore, to the extent that the teachers' ratings do reflect true individual differences in Hebrew *achievement*, the integration dimension would be a salient one for the Westmount students and therefore contribute to differences in success in Hebrew. These two explanations may account for the correlations of the Orientation Index found in the Westmount school.

Two of the three significant correlations of the Orientation Index with teachers' ratings are negative. We predicted a positive correlation between the Orientation Index and achievement, indicating that the integrative motive—which expresses a desire to become better integrated in the Jewish culture—is more conducive to success in Hebrew than the instrumental motive.

---

[4]The two districts do not differ in mean scores and variances on either the A-S scale or the Orientation Index.

TABLE 2

CORRELATION OF ATTITUDE VARIABLES
WITH ACHIEVEMENT MEASURES

Achievement measures	Attitude measures	
	Anti-Semitism	Orientation[a]
Class A (N = 16)		
Fluency	−.504*	−.329
Pronunciation Accuracy	−.488	−.143
Purity of Accent	−.438	−.078
Comprehension (Teacher's ratings)	−.589**	.203
Oral Skill (Teacher's ratings)	−.495*	−.054
Class B (N = 9)		
Teacher's ratings	−.682*	−.405
Class C (8a) (N = 15)		
Teacher's ratings	−.576*	−.612**
Class C (8b) (N = 11)		
Teacher's ratings	−.084	.632*
Class C (9a) (N = 15)		
Teacher's ratings	−.160	−.514*
Class C (9b) (N = 11)		
Teacher's ratings	−.075	−.371

[a] Correlation is positive if "integrative" orientation is related to achievement; correlation is negative if "instrumental" orientation is related to achievement.
* Significant at .05 level; two-tailed test.
** Significant at .02 level; two-tailed test

This discrepancy suggests a reconsideration of the integrative-instrumental distinction as defined by our index. It seems that in the case of Hebrew the instrumental items really indicate a greater desire to integrate in the Jewish culture than the integrative items. Wanting to get a job requiring knowledge of Hebrew (an instrumental reason for studying Hebrew) actually means becoming a rabbi, a Hebrew teacher, or engaging in other Jewish professions which involve more participation in the Jewish culture and community than the more idealistic and vague purposes of becoming "more a part of the Jewish culture" (an integrative reason). The situation is different for English-speaking children in Catholic schools in bilingual Montreal where Gardner and Lambert (1959) and Gardner (1960) found that the integrative orientation led to superior achievement than did the instrumental orientation. In Montreal there are positions requiring knowledge of French which are clearly instrumental and do not imply any integrative feelings towards the French-Canadians. Our results may suggest that the reasons for studying a language, whether instrumental or integrative are not important in themselves: a particular orientation influences language acquisition only to the extent that it is indicative of attitudes towards the language community.

Interrelations among Prediction Variables

This discussion suggests that for a student to do well in Hebrew, and probably in other languages as well, he needs to possess intelligence, language aptitude, and a proper attitude toward the language community. Inspection of the intercorrelations among these variables indicates that some of the correlations between the prediction variables and the achievement measures may be artificially high. The correlations of Psi-Lambda with Verbal Reasoning for the six classes under our consideration range from .47 to .83 with only one exception of a correlation of .19. (Similar results with a different intelligence test are documented by Gardner & Lambert, 1959.) Partialing out the intercorrelation from either of these variables would certainly reduce their correlations with achievement measures. Though much lower in magnitude, there is also some relation between A-S and Psi-Lambda. The correlations for Classes A, B, C (*8a*), C (*8b*), C (*9a*), and C (*9b*) are −.27, −.48, .09, −.84, .01, and .01, respectively. A partial correlation between Psi-Lambda and achievement measures and between A-S and the same measures would lower some of the correlations reported in this paper. However, the present study has demonstrated the relevance of attitudes to the acquisition of a new language, but because of the smallness of samples and inequality of *N*s for different variables it is impossible to determine more precisely the role of each variable through factor analysis or partial correlations.

The relation between Psi-Lambda and A-S warrants interest apart from its possible influence on the correlations of these variables with achievement. There appear to be at least two plausible cause-effect interpretations of this finding. The causal relation may rest between language aptitude and anti-Semitism. The ability of a pupil to master the Hebrew language is a prerequisite to whatever success he may have in Hebrew school. The Hebrew school plays a central role in the Jewish community, and whatever attitudes a student develops toward the Hebrew school hold for the Jewish community at large. The student with language aptitude would find it easier to learn Hebrew, and consequently do well in Hebrew school, be rewarded for his achievement and come to attach positive value to the Hebrew school and the Jewish community—an indirect source of reinforcement. His favorable attitude to the Jewish cultural group could express itself as a low score on the A-S scale. In comparison, students who lack language aptitude would find it more difficult to learn Hebrew; possibly they associate the Hebrew language and school with frustrating experiences which, when generalized as an attitude to the Jewish community, would yield high scores on the A-S scale. Such an explanation is consonant with our generalization hypothesis, suggesting that the generalization process works not only from a community to its language but also from a language to the language community. An alternative interpretation is that the negative correlations between anti-Semitism and Psi-Lambda are due to the influence of some common factor. Since the F Scale (which is highly related to A-S) does not correlate with the Psi-Lambda tests (Gardner, 1960; Gardner & Lambert, 1959), it is difficult to speculate about the nature of such a common factor.

SUMMARY

A study was conducted with Jewish eighth and ninth grade students learning Hebrew. Measures of achievement in the Hebrew language were correlated with scores on two groups of tests: attitude tests which measure their reasons for learning Hebrew and their attitudes toward the Jewish culture and community, and ability measures including intelligence and language aptitude tests. The results support our predictions about the relation of both ability and attitude to success in learning Hebrew. However, whereas, intelligence and linguistic aptitude are relatively stable predictors of success, the attitude measures are less stable and vary in their relationship to achievement from school to school and from class to class. We attempted to explain these differences through considerations of the sociopsychological characteristics of the Jews in the various districts of Montreal where the schools are located.

REFERENCES

ADORNO, T. W., FRENKEL-BRUNSWIK, ELSE, LEVINSON, D. J., & SANFORD, R. N. *The authoritarian personality*. New York: Harper, 1950.
ANISFELD, M. Social and psychological variables in learning Hebrew. Unpublished master's thesis, McGill University, 1960.
BENNETT, G. K., SEASHORE, H. G., & WESMEN, A. G. *Manual for the differential aptitude tests*. New York: Psychological Corporation, 1959.
CARROLL, J. B. The prediction of success in intensive foreign language training. Prepared for a symposium on Training Research, University of Pittsburgh, 1960. (Final rev. Harvard University, 1960 [Mimeo]).
CARROLL, J. B., & SAPON, S. M. Supplement 1 to examiner's manual—Psi-Lambda foreign language aptitude battery. Harvard University, 1956. (Mimeo)
DUNKEL, H. B. *Second-language learning*. Boston: Ginn, 1948.
ERVIN, SUSAN. Identification and bilingualism. Harvard University, 1954. (Mimeo)
GARDNER, R. C. Motivational variables in second-language acquisition. Unpublished PhD thesis, McGill University, 1960.
GARDNER, R. C., & LAMBERT, W. E. Motivational variables in second-language acquistion. *Canad. J. Psychol.*, 1959, *13*, 266-272.
GREEN, B. F. Attitude measurement. In G. Lindzey (Ed.), *Handbook of social psychology*. Vol. I. Cambridge, Mass.: Addison-Wesley, 1954. Pp. 335-369.
GUILFORD, J.. *Fundamental statistics in psychology and education*. (2nd ed.) New York: McGraw-Hill, 1950.
NIDA, E. A. Some psychological problems in language learning. *Lang. Learning*, 1957-58, *8*, 7-16.

SEIDEL, JUDITH. The development and social adjustment of the Jewish community in Montreal. Unpublished master's thesis, McGill University, 1939.

TRYON, R. C. Identification of social areas by cluster analysis. A general method with an application to the San Fransisco Bay area. *U. Calif. Pubn. Psychol.*, 1955, *8*(1), 1-100.

VACHON-SPILKA, IRENE. Communication aux membres de l'Association Canadienne de Linguistique. Saskatoon, 1959. (Mimeo)

WHYTE, W. F., & HOLMBERG, A. R. Human problems of U. S. enterprise in Latin America. *Hum. Organization*, 1956, *15*, 1-40.

READING NUMBER FOUR

ATTITUDINAL AND COGNITIVE ASPECTS OF INTENSIVE STUDY OF A SECOND LANGUAGE[1]

WALLACE E. LAMBERT, R. C. GARDNER,[2] H. C. BARIK, AND K. TUNSTALL

McGill University

Students attending a 6-week French Summer School were examined for attitudes toward French people and culture, their orientations toward learning a 2nd language, and their feelings of anomie at the start and end of the course. Attention was also given to modification in the meanings of French and translated-equivalent English concepts. Students at 2 levels of skill in French were compared. Results supported the theory that learning a 2nd language efficiently depends on an appropriate pattern of attitudes toward the other cultural group and a particular orientation toward language study. Anomie increased for both groups of students during the course. Students utilized the semantic features of both their languages and permitted the 2 to interact. This linguistic interdependence correlates positively with achievement.

If one views the learning of a foreign language from a social-psychological standpoint, the process takes on a significance which might otherwise be overlooked. Psychological questions then come to mind, such as: What motivates people to learn another language? Is there anything unique about the learning process involved in language study? Recent research carried out in our laboratory (Anisfeld & Lambert, 1961; Gardner, 1960; Gardner & Lambert, 1959) has focused on such questions, and various findings have increased our confidence in a psychological theory of second-language learning. This theory states that an individual successfully acquiring a second language gradually adopts various features of behavior which characterize another linguistic and, as is often the case, another cultural group. The learner's ethnocentric disposition

---

[1]This research was supported by a Canadian Defence Research Board grant (9401-10) to the first author. A recent subvention from the Carnegie Corporation of New York has made various facilities available to us which assisted in this work. We are particularly grateful to J. Launay and A. Rigault of McGill's French Department for their cooperation, encouragement, and assistance at various stages of the study. Moshe Anisfeld and Robert Olton have given us various helpful suggestions for interpretation and analysis of results.

[2]Now at the University of Western Ontario.

and his attitude toward the other group are believed to influence his success in learning the new language. His motivation to acquire the language is considered to be determined both by his attitudes toward the other group and by his orientation toward learning a second language. The orientation takes an "instrumental" form if the purposes of language study reflect the more utilitarian value of linguistic achievement such as getting ahead in one's work, and an "integrative" form if the student is oriented toward learning more about the other cultural community, as if he were eager to be a potential member of the other group. Furthermore it is argued that some individuals may be prone to learn another language as a means of potential acceptance in another cultural group because of dissatisfactions experienced in their own group, while others may be as seriously interested in another culture as they are in their own. As one becomes proficient in a second language he may find that his place in his own membership group changes at the same time as the other linguistic-cultural group becomes more than a reference group for him. It may become a second membership group for him. His new position may become a marginal one, accompanied by feelings of chagrin or regret as he loses ties in one group coupled with the fearful anticipation of entering another. The term "anomie" (Durkheim, 1897; Srole, 1951; Williams, 1951, pp. 479 ff.) refers to the feelings of social uncertainty or dissatisfaction which characterize not only the socially unattached person but also, it appears, the bilingual or even the serious student of a second language and culture.

Another set of psychological questions arises when one realizes that learning a second language brings a new verbal system into contact with one which is (usually) already well established, setting the stage for interaction and potential interference. We have examined the consequences of this interaction among bilinguals (Jakobovits & Lambert, 1961; Lambert, Havelka, & Crosby, 1958) and have studied means of reducing interlingual interference (Lambert & Witelson, 1961; Wimer & Lambert, 1959). The little evidence at hand suggests that if the two languages are learned and used in culturally distinctive contexts, rather than within a single cultural or linguistic setting, they function relatively independently, and the connotative meanings of translated-equivalent words in the two languages are comparatively distinctive—two factors which reduce interlingual interference. When two artificial languages are learned simultaneously in a common laboratory context (Lambert & Witelson, 1961), translated equivalents do become semantically close and yet interlingual interference does not play in important inhibitory role in two-language learning apparently because subjects pay close attention to cues which distinguish words in one language from words in the other. The Wimer and Lambert study indicates that the "direct" method of learning a second language (where foreign words are associated directly with their referents rather than, as in the "indirect" method, by being paired with their word equivalents in the native language) is more effective because actual referents to which the new words are associated are more distinctive than are other words. It is this distinctiveness characteristic of the direct method which apparently reduces interlingual interference and promotes faster learning of a new vocabulary. However, the generalizability of these findings obviously needs to be investigated using actual language learning situations. Young adults learning a second language may develop other means of dealing with the potential interference of their two languages.

The present study was designed to examine more extensively both the attitudinal and cognitive correlates of second-language learning among students attending the McGill French Summer School where, for 6 weeks, students are required to follow full-day course work in French (a second language for all attending) and to use only French at all other times during the period, i.e., to follow a direct method, par excellence. This concentrated experience appeared to us particularly likely to highlight the attitudinal and motivational features of language learning as well as the phenomenon of interaction of two language systems. Our notions about second-language learning are based on studies conducted with Canadian students in a multilingual community where bilingual skill is so common that students can sense its potential value for them. The present study permits us to test our theoretical ideas with American students, since the large majority of those attending the Summer School are from the United States. It also permits an examination of the reactions of older students than those studied in the Montreal school systems. Most of the Summer School students are at the college or university level and many are specializing in French at the undergraduate or postgraduate level.

Although this is viewed as a pilot study which calls for methods of analysis, such as factor analysis, which will tease our trends and patterns, we also predicted certain outcomes, as is apparent from the introduction and the choice of procedures.

1. Favorable attitudes toward the other linguistic-cultural group, including a nonethnocentric outlook, should promote greater achievement in language learning.

2. An integrative orientation toward language learning should be more effective than an instrumental orientation for language learning.

3. Those at a relatively elementary level of training should contrast with those seriously specializing in French study. The more advanced group should be more involved with feelings of anomie.

4. In a concentrated period of study such as that afforded by the Summer School, all students should show evidence by the end of the course of a conflict in making bicultural identifications.

5. The direct learning context of the Summer School's course should engender interlingual semantic distinctiveness and thereby reduce bilingual interference.

METHOD

Subjects

The subjects were 192 students attending the McGill French Summer School for the years 1959 and 1960,[3] the large majority of whom were from the United States. The directors of the Summer School take care to place each student in courses designed for his level of attainment in French by interviewing each before registration and suggesting which of three levels would be most appropriate for him. Because the different sections are kept fairly well homogeneous and since the levels represent differences in attainment (particularly the introductory group compared to the other two), we decided to maintain the school's sectional groupings of students and consider the resultant differences in the group's patterns of behavior as due to differences in level of skill.

Since French is theoretically the only language used at the school, students are required to have a working knowledge of the spoken language even at the introductory level. Applicants for the *Introductory* section should have completed one semester of French at the college level following at least 2 years of French in high school. *Intermediate* level students normally have completed 2 or 3 years of college or university training with French as a major or continuation subject. They are expected to speak with some fluency, to write correct grammatical French, and to read French at a fair speed. The *Advanced* level students have typically graduated (or are about to) with French as their major subject and with teaching or graduate work in French as an aim or actual profession. It was decided to work with two groups for our purposes, calling the Introductory level *Elementary* and combining the Intermediate and Advanced to make one comparably large group and calling them *Advanced*. Comparisons of Elementary and Advanced students will be made throughout this report.

Materials

Students were asked to voluntarily participate in the present study by the director of the school who mentioned his interest in, and the anticipated value of, the project. The subjects were given questionnaires to complete in group settings at the beginning and at the end of the 6-week course. Only those students who completed both questionnaires are included in the analysis.

Scores on the following tests were obtained:

California F Scale. Ten items were taken from Forms 45 and 40 (Adorno, Frenkel-Brunswik, Levinson, & Sanford, 1950). This scale is designed to measure antidemocratic and ethnocentric prejudice of an authoritarian nature which we felt would reflect a dimension of suspicion-acceptance of foreign peoples in general.

Anomie Scale. This scale was designed to measure feelings of normlessness, social dissatisfaction or dysfunction, or group alienation. It is made up of nine items, five of which come from Srole's (1951) Anomie Scale and four of which were developed specifically for this research. Sample items are: "These days a person doesn't know whom he can count on" (from Srole) and "Having lived my life in this culture, I'd be happier moving to some other country now" (our own item).

Francophilia Scale. Eight statements about French people and the French culture were presented and subjects were asked to indicate their degree of disagreement or agreement on a seven-point scale. A sample item is: "Compared to the French, the North Americans are an

---

[3]A preliminary study was carried out in the Summer of 1958. On the basis of the analysis of the results of the 1958 study, the procedures and content of certain questionnaires were modified to the form presented here.

unimaginative people." This test is a direct measure of one's positive or negative attitudes toward French people and customs compared to one's own people and customs.

Orientation Index. Subjects were presented with eight alternative reasons "typically given" for studying French, and asked to indicate the one (or more) which best describes their reasons for studying the language. These alternatives were:

1. Usefulness in work situations.
2. Enables one to gain friends more easily among French-speaking people.
3. Because no one is really educated unless he is fluent in the French language.
4. To better understand the French way of life.
5. One needs a good knowledge of at least one foreign language to merit social recognition.
6. Because I hope to live in France some day.
7. I need the training in French for college credits.
8. To enable me to begin to think and behave as the French do.
9. "Any other personal reason."

Alternative 9 was supplied in case an individual thought the alternatives given were inadequate. Those choosing Alternatives 1, 3, 5, or 7 were classified as "instrumentally" oriented in their approach to language learning. Those choosing Alternatives 2, 4, 6, or 8 were classified as "integratively" oriented. Responses to Alternative 9 were classified by two judges as instrumental or integrative if both judges agreed.

Distinctiveness of English and French meanings, at the start of the course ($E_1 F_1$). Seven English words and their translated equivalents in French were presented to subjects in the form of concepts to be rated on standard seven-point semantic differential scales (Osgood, Suci, & Tannenbaum, 1957). The concepts were: friend, literature, truth, church, elegance, family, and me, and their French translated equivalents. The eight semantic scales were in English for English concepts and in French for French concepts. The semantic differential was developed to measure the connotative meaning of concepts. The technique permits one to compare the degree of similarity of connotative meaning of any two concepts by utilizing the "general distance formula" (D) presented in Osgood et al. In the present case the similarity of semantic profiles of each pair of concepts rated at the start of the course (e.g., friend and *ami*), calculated on eight different semantic scales, was determined for each subject and then an average similarity of meaning was calculated for all seven pairs of concepts.

Distinctiveness of English and French meanings, at the end of the course ($E_2 F_2$). This score refers to the separation of French and English meanings after the 6-week course of study in French.

Relative change in French meanings during the course of study when compared to English meanings ($F_1 F_2 - E_1 E_2$). In this case the difference in French semantic patterns at the start and end of the course are compared with the changes in the English semantic patterns for the same concepts.

Achievement in French. Only those students who registered for at least the average number of courses in the school and took examinations in each were retained in the samples. Our measure of achievement was the average grade each student was assigned in his four or five courses. The typical set of courses for all students would involve training in speaking, reading, and writing as well as literature or French civilization courses. Because each instructor undoubtedly used quite different criteria for grading, all grades were transformed to z scores and averaged to determine each subject's final achievement score. Unfortunately there was not enough time available to us to obtain measures of achievement based on standardized examinations of French skills. We are aware that the final average includes various literary and academic skills other than purely linguistic ones.

In addition to these eight variables, several other combination or difference scores derived from these eight variables will be examined. For example, at one point we will discuss changes in attitudinal measures from the start to the end of the course, such as changes in Francophilia or in anomie, and the changes in English meanings from the start to the end of the course (E_1 E_2) or in French (F_1 F_2) meanings will be discussed.

Two questions were asked of those students attending the 1960 Summer School. These dealt with the extent to which the student spoke only French outside of the classroom and the extent to which translation was made from English before speaking French (as opposed to thinking exclusively in French). The analysis of the responses to these questions will be discussed separately below.

Finally, two control groups of subjects were used to determine the test-retest stability of certain attitude and meaning measures. These are introduced and described at appropriate points in the discussion section.

RESULTS AND DISCUSSION

Pattern Analyses

Attention is directed first to analyses of patterns of interrelations among the variables measured. The intercorrelations of the eight main measures for both the elementary and the advanced groups are presented in Table 1.[4] All coefficients listed are product-moment correlations except for those involving the Orientation Index. This index is scored dichotomously for integrative or instrumental orientations; point-biserial correlations were computed between this and all other variables. The correlations are positive if integratively oriented subjects obtained a higher mean score on the continuous variables than did those who were instrumentally oriented. The tables of intercorrelations were subjected to factor analyses using a centroid solution. The rotated factor matrices are displayed in Table 2. The factor analysis reflects attitudinal differences between

---

[4]The correlations given are small in magnitude, but two comments should be made about them. First, the same correlational trends as presented here were found in both the 1959 and 1960 samples and thus they appear reliable. Furthermore in the 1958 pilot study with French Summer School students, we were able to administer an objective French achievement test (Cooperative French Test) at the start of the course. The correlation between a preliminary form of the Orientation Index and the achievement test scores was significant for the elementary group ($r = .44$, p .01), but not for the advanced group ($r = .03$). In the 1958 study, attitudes toward Europeans were measured instead of attitudes toward the French and, as is the case here, these attitudes were significantly related to anomie for the advanced group ($r = .33$, p .01), but not for the elementary group ($r = .16$, ns). However, the relation of orientation to actual grades was much lower and not significant ($r = .18$ for the elemntary and .14 for the advanced groups). The correlation of French grades with French achievement test scores was .70 and .59 for the elementary and advanced groups, respectively. Thus some variables other than French skills are involved in the grades assigned. We feel therefore that the relations presented here are reliable and their smallness is attributable in part to the poor estimate of pure language skills derived from teachers' grades alone.

The multiple correlation of the Orientation and Francophilia scales with grades in the present case is .33, significant at the .01 level.

TABLE 1

CORRELATION MATRICES

Test	1	2	3	4	5	6	7	8
Elementary group[a]								
1. F Scale		.44	.31	−.25	.19	.02	−.09	−.05
2. Anomie			.15	−.21	.00	.05	−.20	−.09
3. Francophilia				.08	.09	.02	.26	.23
4. Orientation					.13	−.05	.14	.25
5. E_1F_1						.27	.07	−.12
6. E_2F_2							−.12	−.16
7. $F_1F_2 - E_1E_2$								.18
8. Achievement								
Advanced group[b]								
1. F Scale		.40	.58	−.08	.03	.04	.29	−.04
2. Anomie			.40	.13	.05	.04	.09	−.11
3. Francophilia				.10	.06	.11	.17	−.21
4. Orientation					.08	−.06	.01	−.09
5. E_1F_1						.45	.36	−.19
6. E_2F_2							.05	−.23
7. $F_1F_2 - E_1E_2$								−.11
8. Achievement								

[a] Total N varied around 89, slightly less for cases where the data were incomplete. Correlations of .21 are significant at the .05 level, .25 at the .02 level, and .27 at the .01 level.
[b] Total N varied around 103. Correlations of .20 are significant at the .05 level, .24 at the .02 level, and .26 at the .01 level.

TABLE 2

ROTATED FACTOR MATRICES

Test	I	II	III	h^2
Elementary group				
1. F Scale	.00	.68	.22	.51
2. Anomie	−.11	.62	.12	.40
3. Francophilia	.56	.34	.15	.45
4. Orientation	.38	−.32	.03	.25
5. E_1F_1	.06	−.10	.63	.41
6. E_2F_2	−.17	−.04	.42	.20
7. $F_1F_2 - E_1E_2$	.45	−.17	−.04	.23
8. Achievement	.49	.00	−.22	.29
Advanced group				
1. F Scale	.15	.76	−.14	.61
2. Anomie	.53	.34	.04	.41
3. Francophilia	.46	.63	.00	.60
4. Orientation	.27	−.06	.12	.09
5. E_1F_1	−.11	.19	.70	.53
6. E_2F_2	.02	.06	.59	.36
7. $F_1F_2 - E_1E_2$	−.15	.46	.23	.29
8. Achievement	−.12	−.14	−.36	.16

Note.—Orthogonal rotations.

the elementary and advanced groups as well as group similarities in cognitive reactions to the Summer School experience. For the elementary students, one pattern of attitudes appears to be important for achievement in French: students with favorable attitudes toward France, a willingness to identify with French people, and a capacity to modify meanings of French concepts are more likely to do well in the French course. This pattern is very similar to the "social motivational" factor found by Gardner and Lambert (1959) for English-Canadian high school students who were questioned about their attitudes toward French-Canadian people and culture. The fact that a group of American students displays the same pattern of attitudes toward a quite foreign cultural group, one which is related to achievement in the other group's language, is of particular interest. A second attitudinal pattern is not associated with achievement: an authoritarian disposition, feelings of anomie coupled with both favorable attitudes toward France and instrumental orientations toward the study of French. The measures of meaning indicate that elementary students do poorly in the course if they maintain semantic distinctiveness between English and French translated-equivalent concepts.

The factors for the advanced students indicate that the attitudinal variables show no relation to French achievement. The orientations toward the study of French are not related to attitudes as was the case for the elementary students. Two factors for the advanced group indicate that favorable attitudes toward France are associated with anomie but not with integrative orientations toward

TABLE 3

COMPARISONS OF ELEMENTARY AND
ADVANCED GROUPS

Variable	df	Elementary		Advanced		t
		M	Variance	M	Variance	
F Scale	190	36.74	94.30	35.95	85.79	.57
Anomie	190	23.16	59.93	22.17	49.03	.93
Francophilia	184	32.04	42.77	32.04	58.06	.00
E_1F_1	183	2.75	1.31	2.32	0.96	2.74*
E_2F_2	183	2.19	0.91	2.00	0.50	1.54
E_1E_2	183	3.35	1.28	2.84	0.76	3.45*
F_1F_2	183	3.48	1.16	3.06	1.03	2.73*
$F_1F_2 - E_1E_2$	183	0.13	0.43	0.22	0.38	.93

Note.—Scores of 40, 36, and 32 indicate neutrality of attitudes on the F, Anomie, and Francophilia scales, respectively. The higher the respective scores, the more the attitudes are authoritarian, anomic, and favorable toward French people and culture.

The semantic differences between English and translated French equivalents (E_1F_1) are given in the form of group means. In the first case, the elementary group shows a reliably greater semantic separation between English and French words than does the advanced group, 2.75 units compared to 2.32. The larger the difference score, the greater the differences in connotative meanings. These units are D scores based on differences of semantic ratings on eight scales for all of the seven French-English pairs. In the case of English (or French) words rated at the start and the end of the course (E_1E_2 or F_1F_2) the D scores are based on the comparisons of semantic ratings of the same seven words made at the different times.
* $p \leq .01$.

learning the language. In fact, Francophile attitudes are positively related to anomie for the advanced group but not for the elementary. The patterning of attitudes suggests that favorable attitudes toward the other culture which are linked to anomie bear no relation to achievement in the language. As was the case with the elementary group, maintenance of separate or distinctive French and English meaning patterns also hampers achievement in the Summer School course for the advanced students.

Attitudinal and Meaning Changes during the Course of Study

The data on attitude and meaning changes from the beginning to the end of the course reveal mainly similarities between the elementary and advanced groups (Tables 3 and 4). The two groups manifest the same degrees of authoritarianism, anomie, attitudes toward France, and orientations toward the study of French at the start of the course. On the last point, approximately 25% of both groups give integrative reasons, 60% give instrumental reasons, and 15% cannot be classified unambiguously. Both groups become clearly more anomic (actually, less nonanomic) during the course and the elementary group also becomes reliably more authoritarian. Neither group changes its attitudes toward

France. The advanced subjects become somewhat less instrumental in their orientations to language study during the course (29% are integrative, 46% instrumental, and 25% cannot be classified). These findings strongly support the notion that students in a concentrated course of foreign language study may become psychologically marginal between two linguistic-cultural groups.

Correlations of the attitude changes during the course with achievement ratings are given in Table 5. (Because the Orientation Index is a dichotomous variable, difference scores could not be assigned.) The only change in attitudes related to achievement is an increase in pro-French attitudes among the advanced students, which is positively related to achievement. Since the increases in anomie and authoritarianism are not associated with doing poorly in French, one cannot argue that such changes are a product of frustration generated by poor achievement in the course. Instead, the findings suggest that concentrated immersion in the study of a second language possibly evokes invidious comparisons between the other culture and one's own social group, thereby increasing feelings of anomie. (It should be noted that the mean anomie scores are below the neutral point of the scale, and consequently our statements about increases in anomie actually reflect a reduction in social satisfaction—the opposite of anomie.)

There are reliable increases in the similarities of English and French meanings during the course of study for both elementary and advanced groups. This *rapprochement* of meaning systems of the two languages is of interest in view of the fact that all instruction and a large part of outside-class conversations were carried out in French. It appears that students at this age and level of training in French do make use of their first language and permit it to interact with the French that is being learned. We have already commented on the fact that the more the two languages do interact the better are the achievement ratings in French. There is further evidence of language interaction in the correlations between changes in English meaning (E_1 E_2) and changes in French meanings (F_1 F_2) during the study period: the correlations of E_1 E_2 with F_1 F_2 are .82 and .80 for the elementary and advanced groups, both highly significant.

A control group of 32 senior students at McGill who were not taking French instruction was administered the same English and French concepts as used here to be rated on the same semantic scales twice during a 6-week period. Since nearly all these students were from Montreal, they would have had about 6 or 7 years of high school training in French and possibly a year at the university level. When one examines the separation between meanings for English and French concepts for the control group there is no *rapprochement* of French and English meanings from one testing period to the other; the t test for the difference between E_1 F_1 and E_2 F_2 is −.48 which is clearly not significant.

For the advanced group there are reliably greater changes in French than in English meanings (F_1 $F_2 < E_1$ E_2) but this pattern is not quite significant for the

TABLE 4

ATTITUDINAL AND MEANING CHANGES DURING THE COURSE OF STUDY

Variable	df	M (Before)	Variance	M (After)	Variance	t
Elementary group						
F Scale	88	36.74	94.30	38.31	87.70	-2.20*
Anomie	88	23.16	59.93	24.88	65.21	-2.51**
Francophilia	85	32.04	42.77	32.63	47.86	$-.96$
E_1F_1 versus E_2F_2	84	2.75	1.31	2.19	0.91	4.07***
F_1F_2 versus E_1E_2 M	84	(F_1F_2) 3.48	1.16	(E_1E_2) 3.35	1.28	1.83
Advanced group						
F Scale	102	35.95	85.79	36.95	77.23	-1.74
Anomie	102	22.17	49.03	24.21	54.69	-3.21***
Francophilia	97	32.04	58.06	31.55	70.66	.86
E_1F_1 versus E_2F_2	99	2.32	0.96	2.00	0.50	3.54***
F_1F_2 versus E_1E_2 M	99	(F_1F_2) 3.06	1.03	(E_1E_2) 2.84	0.76	3.55***

* $p < .03$.
** $p < .02$.
*** $p < .01$.

TABLE 5

CORRELATIONS OF ATTITUDE CHANGES (during course)
WITH ACHIEVEMENT

	Elementary group[a]				Advanced group[b]			
	1	2	3	4	1	2	3	4
1. F Scale (After-Before)		.37	.34	.12		.26	.22	.06
2. Anomie (After-Before)			.27	.05			.25	.06
3. Francophilia (After-Before)				−.14				.20
4. Achievement								

[a] Total N varied around 89, slightly less for cases where the data were incomplete. Correlations of .21 are significant at the .05 level, .25 at the .02 level, and .27 at the .01 level.
[b] Total N varied around 103. Correlations of .20 are significant at the .05 level, .24 at the .02 level, and .26 at the .01 level.

elementary group. Apparently the summer school experience does effect greater changes in French than English meanings, particularly for the more advanced students.

One reason for the less pronounced changes in French relative to English meaning changes for the elementary subjects is the fact that they show more change in both their English (E_1 E_2) and French meanings (F_1 F_2) than do the advanced students. (These findings indicate that relative to their English meaning changes, the elementary students show less French meaning changes than the advanced students.) Thus elementary students manifest a general semantic malleability or instability in comparison to the advanced group.

The elementary students show more distinctiveness or separation of English and French meanings at the start of the summer course than the advanced, but this difference does not appear at the end of the course, suggesting that as one progresses from the elementary to the advanced level of skill he reduces the degree of linguistic separation between his two languages.

Personal Estimates of Concentration on French during the Course

Students of the 1960 session were asked how often they had spoken in English outside of class and how much they had thought in French when speaking French. The elementary students used English more frequently than did the advanced students ($t = 2.98$, $p<.01$). However, there is no reliable difference between groups in the extent of thinking in French when speaking French ($t = .93$, ns). Apparently, the summer course has a common effect on students at both levels with respect to their own evaluations of the amount of thinking done in French. This variable was measured on a five-point scale ranging from "always thought in English before speaking French" (rated as 1) to "always thought in French before speaking French" (rated as 5). Both groups

TABLE 6

CORRELATES OF USE OF ENGLISH AND THINKING IN
FRENCH FOR ELEMENTARY AND ADVANCED GROUPS[a]

Variable	Elementary group		Advanced group	
	Degree of use of English	Degree of thinking in French	Degree of use of English	Degree of thinking in French
F Scale (Before)	.04	−.04	−.02	.09
F Scale (After)	.24	.18	.10	.07
Changes in F Scale	.33	.32	.15	−.04
Anomie (Before)	−.29	−.33	.28	.05
Anomie (After)	.17	.04	.37	−.11
Changes in Anomie	.54	.40	.13	−.17
Francophilia (Before)	−.05	−.13	.16	.12
Francophilia (After)	.13	−.09	.13	.15
Changes in Francophilia	.24	−.04	−.05	.07
Orientation Index (Before)	−.09	−.09	.09	−.41
Orientation Index (After)	−.06	−.25	.14	−.42
E_1F_1	−.27	−.07	−.23	.09
E_2F_2	−.23	−.10	−.10	−.04
$F_1F_2 - E_1E_2$	−.22	−.14	.06	.31
Achievement	−.33	.35	.07	−.02
Degree of using English		.25		−.40

[a] These data are for the 1960 Summer School samples only. The N for the elementary group varies around 32 and for the advanced group 46. For the elementary group, an r of .36 is significant at the .05 level. For the advanced group, an r of .31 is significant at the .05 level.

fall about at Point 3 which was defined as "thought primarily in English at the start of the course but more in French at the end of the course." The mean scores were 2.95 for the advanced students and 2.71 for the elementary. These results are quite consistent with the previously mentioned finding that students use both their languages for cognitive activities.

The correlates of speaking English outside of class are presented in Table 6. For the elementary group, there is a marked relation between increases in feelings of anomie during the course period and the use of English outside of class. A similar finding is noted for the advanced group: those who were more anomic, especially at the end of the course, are prone to use English. These findings give strong support to the hypothesis that students revert to English (even though they thereby break their pledges to speak only French) because of a conflict based on anomie. One cannot be certain of the causal nature of this relation with these data. However, it is logically clearer to suggest that reverting to English follows from an uncomfortable feeling of anomie rather than the converse.

The two groups differ when consideration is given to the correlates of thinking in French. For the elementary group, thinking in French is also associated with feelings of anomie, but because there is an insignificant correlation between using English and thinking in French, the pattern suggests

that elementary subjects become anomic as they commence to think in French
and then use English more frequently when anomie reaches a certain strength.
Furthermore, there is a trend for those elementary subjects who use English to
do poorly in the course and for those who think more frequently in French to
do well in the course.

For the advanced subjects, neither using English nor thinking in French is
related to achievement in French. Thinking in French does not appear to involve
the advanced students in a conflict based on feelings of anomie as did the use of
English. Rather, those advanced subjects who think most regularly in French are
those who are clearly instrumentally oriented toward learning French ($r = -.41$
between the Orientation Index on the first testing and thinking in French, and r
$= -.42$ for the second test results of the Orientation Index).

The first interpretive task is to account for the differences in attitudes of
elementary and advanced groups. The advanced students are older, more
advanced in the study of French, and are concentrating in French at college or
university levels of training or actually teaching French at high school or college
levels. A careful examination of the responses to the Orientation Index indicates
that the advanced subjects are more professionally oriented in their approach to
French study. Table 7 presents a more complete analysis of the Orientation
Index scores for both groups. The advanced students apparently want to learn
about the French way of life more so than do the elementary but not because
they are more eager to live in France, to study or visit in France, to gain French
friends, or to communicate with the language, but because they clearly are more
interested in teaching or improving their teaching of the language, a response
which would be categorized as "instrumental." This more professional orientation indicates that the advanced students have a definite and immediately
accessible goal which may likely maintain a strong degree of motivation in
language study. Our previous studies indicated that favorable attitudes and
orientations toward the other language contributed to a strong motivation to
learn the other group's language and consequently correlated with achievement
measures. In the present case, even the instrumentally oriented advanced
students have strong motivations to learn the language, thereby reducing the
relation of Orientation Index scores to achievement.

The data also indicate that the advanced students do not exhibit the
particular syndrome of attitudes which has been found to be related to
achievement in language training. That is, their Francophilia is accompanied by
anomie and authoritarianism to a much more marked degree than is the case
with the elementary students. This finding could mean that the advanced
students are unable to exhibit a patterning of attitudes which will relate to
achievement because of the strong relation of anomie and Francophilia. Several
lines of evidence support the contention that both groups experience a conflict
based on anomie. Both groups increase their anomie during the course, and for

TABLE 7

GROUP COMPARISONS OF ORIENTATIONS TOWARD LEARNING FRENCH

Category	Elementary students		Advanced students	
	Before	After	Before	After
A Useful in work situations	23	21	18	12
B To gain friends more easily among French people	4	5	5	2
C No one really educated without French skill	9	9	7	7
D To better know French way of life	7	7	15	16
E Need French to merit social recognition	4	3	5	2
F I hope to live in France some day	6	3	2	3
G I need it for college credits	8	7	4	4
H To begin to think and behave as French people do	2	0	0	1
I Personal reasons[a]				
Love, enjoy, fascinated by (beauty of) the French language	10	14	18	18
General usefulness	0	0	2	2
General knowledge about literature, theatre, history of France	3	5	6	5
Desire to use (communicate with) the language	3	3	3	6
To study in or visit France	3	2	0	0
Research purposes or to major in French	3	1	2	2
To teach (or improve teaching of) the language	2	1	16	16
Personal satisfaction with learning languages	2	5	0	1
No answer or multiple response	0		0	6
Total	89	89	103	103

[a] The "personal reasons" responses were categorized as instrumental or integrative in terms of other responses which were given along with these responses if no clear placement was indicated in the personal reason itself. When no certain placement could be made the response was called "uncertain."

both groups the extent of use of English outside of class is related to anomie. The nature of the conflict may well differ for the two groups. For elementary students, the use of English and the tendency to think in French, although unrelated themselves, are both related to anomie. This is not the case for the advanced students for whom thinking in French is not related to anomie but rather to instrumental orientations toward the learning of the language. It is only with the advanced students that favorable attitudes toward France correlate highly with anomie. One can interpret these findings to mean that as a student progresses in specialization of French, as an avocation in a non-French culture, he develops invidious comparisons of American and French cultures such that the more appreciation he develops for the French language and culture the more socially dissatisfied he is, or conversely, the more anomic he becomes, the more he appreciates the French culture. The elementary student is not committed to the study of French as a professional specialization and can appreciate a new culture without the involvement of anomic feelings. It is clear that he, too, will encounter a conflict centering around feelings of anomie, however, as he concentrates in the study of the new language and culture. The evidence is too sparse to extend the discussion to strategies employed to manage anomie, but the overall findings point to the value of further research on this matter.

We were interested in checking on the test-retest stability of the attitude scales used, even though published studies, such as Smith's (1955), have demonstrated that these or related scales are reliable. We administered the F Scale, anomie, and Francophilia items to a group of 30 McGill students 5 weeks before and at the end of the school year, to approximate the "end of school" feature of the second test for the French Summer School students. The respective first and second test means for the control group are: authoritarianism, 41.41 and 39.66; anomie, 28.21 and 27.58; and Francophilia, 28.90 and 30.20; none of these changes is significant.

However, the control students are highly significantly more anomic, significance levels being .01 and .001 when compared with elementary and advanced groups, respectively, at the start of the course (cf. Table 4). There are no reliable differences between control and either of the student groups at the end of the course. These findings suggest that serious students of a second language *as a group* are less socially dissatisfied at the start of the course than control students who are not specializing in language training. The present findings indicate that the Summer School population of students, on the average, apparently find dual cultural membership satisfying, as though their experience with a second cultural-linguistic group has been enriching for them. The conflict around feelings of anomie which has been mentioned actually involves attitudinal changes from relatively nonanomic towards more anomic feelings during the course of the Summer School.

The second major trend is the *rapprochement* of meanings of concepts in the students' two languages during the course of study. It is assumed that the large majority of both the elementary and advanced students have learned their French mainly in an American setting and that French concepts have been learned through the use of English concepts, i.e., that they enter the Summer School with compound French and English linguistic systems. Furthermore, it would be more difficult to develop a coordination of French concepts in such a short period as the Summer School than to make efficient use of a well-established compound system. The Montreal setting would not likely be distinctively French enough in any case to facilitate the development of a separate language learning context for French especially since most of the students' time is spent with other American students.

The findings indicate that both groups of students manifest an increase in semantic similarity of French and English concepts during the summer course. Furthermore, maintenance of semantic distinctiveness of French and English concepts apparently leads to poor achievement in the course. In addition, the more that semantic change occurs in one language, the more change is also noted in the other language. Modifications occur in both French and English concepts, indicating that training in French has affected both languages. These findings are of interest because they suggest that these American students, taught by the direct method, do not keep their two languages functionally separated. Rather they tend to permit the two languages to interact, and this is to their advantage in the learning of the second language. It is hypothesized that these students develop generalized super-linguistic concepts which incorporate the unique semantic features of the concepts in each of their two languages. Rather than encountering difficulty because of the interaction of their languages, these students are better able to acquire French by making use of interacting or compound linguistic systems.

REFERENCES

ADORNO, T. W., FRENKEL-BRUNSWIK, ELSE, LEVINSON, D. J., & SANFORD, R. N. *The authoritarian personality.* New York: Harper, 1950.

ANISFELD, M., & LAMBERT, W. E. Social and psychological variables in learning Hebrew. *J. abnorm. soc. Psychol.*, 1961, 63 524-529.

DURKHEIM, E. *Le suicide.* Paris: F. Alcan, 1897.

GARDNER, R. C. Motivational variables in second-language acquisition. Unpublished doctoral dissertation. McGill University, Redpath Library, 1960.

GARDNER, R. C., & LAMBERT, W. E. Motivational variables in second-language acquisition. *Canad. J. Psychol.*, 1959, *13*, 266-272.

JAKOBOVITS, L. A., & LAMBERT, W. E. Semantic satiation among bilinguals. *J. exp. Psychol.*, 1961, *62*, 576-582.

LAMBERT, W. E., HAVELKA, J., & CROSBY, C. The influence of language-acquisition contexts on bilingualism. *J. abnorm. soc. Psychol.*, 1958, *56*, 239-244.

LAMBERT, W. E., & WITELSON, SANDRA. Concurrent and consecutive orders of learning two "languages." Montreal: McGill University, 1961. (Mimeo)

OSGOOD, C. E., SUCI, G. J., & TANNENBAUM, P. H. *The measurement of meaning.* Urbana: Univer. Illinois Press, 1957.

SMITH, H. P. Do intercultural experiences affect attitudes? *J. abnorm. soc. Psychol.*, 1955, *51*, 469-477.

SROLE, L. Social dysfunction, personality and social distance attitudes. Paper read at American Sociological Society, Chicago, 1951.

WILLIAMS, R. M., JR. *American society: A sociological interpretation.* New York: Knopf, 1951.

WIMER, CYNTHIA, & LAMBERT, W. E. The differential effects of word and object stimuli on the learning of paired associates. *J. exp. Psychol.*, 1959, *57*, 31-36.

READING NUMBER FIVE

Vol. 76, No. 27   Whole No. 546, 1962

Psychological Monographs: General and Applied

THE RELATION OF BILINGUALISM TO INTELLIGENCE[1]

ELIZABETH PEAL AND WALLACE E. LAMBERT

McGill University

Psychologists and linguists have wondered whether bilingualism affects intellectual functioning since as early as the 1920s when Saer (1923) and Smith (1923) reported research on the topic. Numerous studies since then have attempted to determine whether monolingual and bilingual young people differ in intelligence as measured by standard tests. A large proportion of investigators have concluded from their studies that bilingualism has a detrimental effect on intellectual functioning. The bilingual child is described as being hampered in his performance on intelligence tests in comparison with the monolingual child. A smaller proportion of the investigations have found little or no influence of bilingualism on intelligence, in that no significant difference between bilinguals and monolinguals on tests of intelligence was apparent. Only two empirical studies were encountered which suggest that bilingualism may have favorable intellectual consequences.

    An attempt will be made to understand these seemingly contradictory findings by critically reviewing representative studies reporting each type of effect. The studies will be evaluated mainly in terms of how well other relevant

---

[1]This research was carried out with the financial support of the Carnegie Corporation of New York, through a subvention to W. E. Lambert. The authors are grateful to G. Barbeau and T. Boulanger of the Catholic School Commission of Montreal and to the principals and teachers of the six schools used in this study for their assistance and cooperation during the testing programs in their schools. Special thanks are expressed to Irene Vachon-Spilka for her assistance in translation and administration of the tests. The writer is indebted to R. C. Gardner (McGill) and R. M. Olton (McGill) for writing the necessary programs for the IBM 650 computer, without which the statistical analysis would not have been possible. Thanks are also due to G. A. Ferguson (McGill) for his advice on statistical matters.

variables were controlled, particularly certain personal characteristics which are known to be related to intelligence and which should be taken into account when the effect of bilingualism on intelligence is examined.

In the design typically used, where two groups of subjects are being compared on intelligence, it is necessary to match the groups on as many features known or suspected to correlate with intelligence as possible so that the difference between the groups, if any, may be attributed to linguality itself. This model requires a clear definition of monolingualism and bilingualism in order that the two can be objectively determined without risk of overlap or confusion. Socioeconomic status has been repeatedly found to be related to intelligence and linguistic development (Jones, 1960; McCarthy, 1954). McCarthy states that "there is considerable evidence in the literature to indicate that there exists a marked relationship between socioeconomic status of the family and the child's linguistic development" (p. 586). From past research it is well established that girls are more advanced than boys in language development, especially in the early years. They have a larger vocabulary and are more skilled in the use of words. Since most intelligence tests draw heavily on verbal skills, it would be advisable to have approximately equal numbers of boys and girls in the groups to be compared. Furthermore, groups should also be matched for age. The educational background of children may also affect their performance on standardized tests of intelligence. This variable could be approximately controlled by using subjects from the same schools or school system. The intelligence tests should be constructed and standardized on a population similar to the one being tested, especially with respect to language. A translation of a test from one language to another, without standardization, might bias the results for or against one group. Also, the tests should be given in the language in which the bilinguals are most proficient.

Studies Supporting the Detrimental Effects of Bilingualism on Intelligence

The studies in this category may be arbitrarily divided into two subgroups. The first of these consists of those which found that monolingual groups performed better than bilingual on *both* verbal and nonverbal intelligence tests. Can the depressed scores of the bilinguals be attributed to bilingualism itself, or were there uncontrolled variables which might account for the obtained differences between groups?

After testing 1,400 children in Wales, Saer (1923) reported a statistically significant inferiority of rural bilingual children when compared with rural monolingual children on the Stanford-Binet scale. This inferiority became consistently greater in degree with each year from 7 to 11 years of age. Saer attempted to explain this trend in terms of the "mental confusion" encountered by the bilingual children. When urban children only were compared he found no significant difference between monolinguals and bilinguals. It should be noted that socioeconomic class was not controlled in this research and that a Welsh translation of the Stanford-Binet test was used.

Pintner (1932) administered the Pintner Language and Nonlanguage tests to monolingual and bilingual groups in each of three schools in New York City. The results obtained are inconclusive in the sense that in one school monolinguals were superior on both tests while in another they were inferior and in the third, there was no difference between the groups. There was no control for socioeconomic class in this study and bilingualism was determined by looking at the child's name!

The most important study in this grouping was the one by Jones and Stewart (1951). After surveying the studies done prior to 1951 in Wales, they concluded that bilingual and monolingual groups differed little in nonverbal intelligence tests and that monolingual groups were usually superior to bilingual groups in verbal tests. The design of their experiment was based on these conclusions. A verbal test and a nonverbal test were given to monolingual and bilingual groups in rural districts. The children were between 10-6 and 11-6 years of age. The monolinguals were found to score significantly higher on both types of tests. The two groups were equated statistically, by the analysis of covariance, on nonverbal IQ and the differences between them on verbal IQ were then noted. "It was therefore concluded that the bilingual children were significantly inferior to the monolingual children, even after full allowance has been made for the initial difference in the nonverbal intelligence tests" (Jones & Stewart, 1951). It could be argued that the bilinguals may have encountered greater difficulties because for them the tests were translated into Welsh, their vernacular, but not standardized in the Welsh culture. This may have lowered their scores on the verbal test. However, this would not account for the original difference in nonverbal IQ. After further investigations, Jones later conceded that the significant difference in nonverbal test scores observed in all his studies may have arisen from occupational rather than linguistic variations between the groups. Thus the complete work of Jones and his collaborators has, according to James (1960), "drawn attention to the influence of socioeconomic factors in comparisons between groups of monolingual and bilingual children and has emphasized the importance of such factors in the correct interpretation of test results."

In his most recent article, Jones (1960) criticized a study published by Lewis (1959) for the inadequate treatment given to socioeconomic class. Lewis had reported a statistically significant difference in favor of the monolinguals corresponding to about 8 IQ points on a nonverbal intelligence test. Apart from his failure to control socioeconomic class, his method of selecting his groups was an improvement over previous studies. He assessed the linguistic background of 10-year-old children by means of a language questionnaire and attempted to make each group as homogeneous as possible.

Several studies (Graham, 1925; Mead, 1927; Rigg, 1928; Wang, 1926) have found that monolingual American groups performed better than children with various foreign backgrounds on intelligence tests. All these studies lacked controls for age and socioeconomic class, and in some bilingualism was not adequately measured.

The second subdivision of studies showing the unfavorable effect of bilingualism encompasses those which reported that monolinguals scored better than bilinguals on verbal tests, but the bilinguals scored better or as well as monolinguals on performance or nonverbal tests.

A rather well-controlled study by Seidl (1937) found that monolinguals were superior to bilinguals on all verbal tests, but bilinguals were superior to monolinguals on performance measures. The 1916 Stanford-Binet scale and the Arthur Point Scale of Performance were the tests used. The two groups of subjects, whose linguality was determined by a questionnaire, were matched on sex and age. However, the mean occupational level of the monolinguals' parents was in the laboring class while the bilinguals' was semiskilled labor. This difference in social class may partly account for the results. Seidl, however, concluded that the language handicap of the bilinguals interfered with their verbal IQ scores.

Pintner and Keller (1922) gave the Stanford-Binet and the Pintner Non-language Group Test to two groups, one English-speaking and the other of foreign background, and found that the latter group received lower scores on the Stanford-Binet than on tests in which a minimum of English was required. The authors concluded that these children were penalized because the Stanford-Binet was used. However, no measures of bilingualism were used and no mention was made of the social status of the children's families. .

Darcy (1946) reported on research carried out with 212 American preschool children of Italian parentage. In this study, the relevant variables were quite well controlled. The subjects were classified as bilingual or monolingual by a rating scale; the groups were matched for age, sex, and social class. The Stanford-Binet (1937 Revision) was used as the verbal measure, and the Atkins Object-Fitting Test as the nonverbal. Darcy found that the monolingual group scored significantly higher than the bilingual on the Stanford-Binet, but lower on the Atkins test. She concluded that the bilingual subjects of her investigation suffered from a language handicap in their performance on the Stanford-Binet scale. However, the subjects were so young (from 2-6 to 4-6 years) that it would not be advisable to draw any general conclusions from this study. Even if the bilinguals suffered from a language handicap at this age, they might overcome it later. Also the intelligence of infants and pre-school children is known to be somewhat difficult to determine accurately and depends more on performance items than on verbal.

Another study from which generalizations should not be drawn is that by Altus (1953) since both groups used were "dull" school children. They may have been classed as dull for various reasons. The groups were equated on age, sex, and the Performance IQ of the Wechsler Intelligence Scale for Children (WISC). Differences in IQ on the Verbal scale averaged 17 points in favor of the monolingual group. Altus suggests that linguistic difficulties interfered with normal functioning in the bilingual group.

An important technique for objectively measuring bilingualism was introduced by Johnson (1953). His Reaction Time Test, derived from the earlier work of Saer (1931), was a measure of linguistic balance obtained by dividing the number of words produced in English in 5 minutes, by the number of words produced in Spanish in 5 minutes. The subjects for his experiment were 30 Spanish-English bilingual boys in the United States between the ages of 9 and 12 years. The Goodenough IQ for these children was about average for the total population, but the Otis IQ was considerably below average. Johnson's Test of Bilingualism was found to correlate negatively with the Otis (a verbal test) and positively with the Goodenough Draw-A-Man Test (a performance test). The more bilingual the subjects were the better they did on a performance test and the poorer on a verbal test.

Levinson (1959) tested American-born Jewish preschool monolingual and bilingual children of similar socioeconomic level and found them to perform alike on the Goodenough test and most subscales of the WISC. However, on the Stanford-Binet and the WISC Arithmetic, Vocabulary, and Picture Arrangement subtests the monolinguals scored higher.

Many of these studies of the detrimental effects of bilingualism lacked important controls. Taking this into account, the weight of evidence so far presented seems to support the contention that there is no significant difference between monolinguals and bilinguals on nonverbal intelligence, but the bilinguals are likely to be handicapped on verbal intelligence measures. The need for further research with more complete controls becomes evident.

Studies Supporting the Favorable Effects of Bilingualism on Intelligence

The paucity of studies that have found a favorable intellectual effect accruing from bilingualism would seem to suggest that bilingualism may not be as advantageous as has been thought by many language teachers and educators. In a study conducted in London, England, Davies and Hughes (1927) reported the superiority of Jewish over non-Jewish children in arithmetic, English, and general intelligence. However, no measure of bilingualism was used and the Jewish children were assumed to be bilingual. Other controls such as age, sex, and social class were notably absent, as they were in the study by Stark (1940), who found that at 10 and 11 years of age, bilinguals were superior to monolinguals on one form of a test. At a later age, this trend was reversed, but the measurement was made on a different form of the test. Stark concluded that children of "innate verbal facility" may find early bilingualism an asset to their mental development.

Studies Finding No Effect of Bilingualism on Intelligence[2]

From his study of Japanese and American children, Darsie (1926) concluded that the differences in general mental capacity between the two groups were slight. On some tests, the Japanese subjects were inferior while on others the Americans were inferior. However, the social class of these two groups was not comparable and no measure of bilingualism was employed.

The best controlled study in this category is that of Hill (1936) with Italian-American children. Bilingualism was determined by a questionnaire and on the basis of language background. The two groups were matched on sex, age, IQ, socioeconomic class, and mental age. No reliable differences were found in scores on verbal, nonverbal, and performance tests between monolinguals and bilinguals. However, it should be kept in mind that since the two groups were matched on mental age and IQ, only minor differences between them could be expected on intelligence subtests. Thus, there may have been a selection of brighter Italian-American children in this instance.

Pintner and Arsenian (1937) gave the Hoffman Bilingual Schedule to 459 Jewish children in New York City; all the children were Yiddish-English bilinguals. The 20% receiving the highest scores on the Hoffman test constituted a high bilingual group, and the 20% receiving the lowest scores, a low bilingual group. The mean verbal and nonverbal IQs of these two bilingual groups were compared, and no difference was found between them. The authors concluded that the relationship between intelligence and bilingualism is "practically zero" ($r = -.059$).

Spoerl (1944) tested all the bilingual freshmen enrolled at an American college. These were matched with a group of monolingual freshmen for sex, age, intelligence, and social class. A student was considered bilingual if he had learned two languages before school entrance. No differences were found between monolinguals and bilinguals on the 1937 Stanford-Binet or Purdue Placement Test. A slight inferiority was shown by the bilingual students on five of the verbal items of the Stanford-Binet scale. It is interesting to note, however, that the bilinguals had done consistently better in school work than the monolinguals even though their IQs did not differ significantly. Spoerl mentioned that a compensatory drive arising from a feeling of environmental insecurity may have been contributing cause of the superiority of the bilinguals in academic achievement.

[2]Several studies (Arthur, 1937; Bere, 1924; Feingold, 1924; Hirsch, 1926) which have reported that bilingualism has no effect on intelligence lack too many important controls to be worth considering in detail here.

Arsenian's (1937) experiments with American-born Italian and American-born Jewish children were well controlled from the point of view of age, sex, socioeconomic class, and measurement of bilingualism. However, Darcy (1953) questions the adequacy of the tests used (Pintner Nonlanguage Test, and the Spearman Visual Perception Test), as measures of intelligence. The Spearman test was not even standardized. Furthermore, there were no tests of verbal intelligence. Several different combinations of subjects were used in the analysis; and in the comparison between bilinguals and monolinguals, the number of subjects (38 of each group) was too small to permit definite conclusions. The findings are nevertheless of interest and of some importance. The extent of bilingualism did not vary from 9 to 14 years. There was only a very slight relation between intelligence and socioeconomic class. There was no difference between the two language groups as to intelligence or age-grade status. Arsenian concluded: "it may be stated that . . . there was discovered no retardation or acceleration in the mental development of children from ages 9 to 14 in the groups studied, which might be attributable to bilingualism as such" (p. 120).

In summary, it becomes apparent that it is necessary to control certain variables in this type of study before any conclusions can be drawn. The important variables to control seem to be socioeconomic class, sex, degree of bilinguality, age, and the actual tests used. In view of the weaknesses of the studies reviewed, the best general conclusion is that there is little evidence to suggest that bilinguals differ from monolinguals on nonverbal intelligence, but that there may be differences in verbal intelligence as measured by intelligence tests. At a certain stage in the learning of the second language, a bilingual may suffer from a "language handicap."

Theoretical Considerations

Theoretically, what would be the expected effects of bilingualism on intelligence or mental development? Few of the psychologists who have studied this problem have attempted any explanation beyond rather vague references to a "language handicap" or "mental confusion."

An inquiry into the effects of the learning of two languages on mental development demands a serious consideration of the broader question of the relation between language and thought, and modern psychology has generally eschewed this question. The apparent belief of many is that at least partial answers to the broad question may appear from the study of the interrelation of language and intelligence. Arsenian (1937), after examining various theories of language and thought, hypothesized that language and intelligence are not identical. In line with this hypothesis, he maintained that:

the influence of bilingualism, whatever for the moment we may suppose it to be, does not extend to the whole area of thinking or intelligence, but to that particular section where linguistic symbolism and schemata are involved in the thinking process.

Susanne Langer (1942) made a distinction between speech and thought. She argued that: "It [speech] is the normal terminus of thought. . . . But in fact, speech is the natural outcome of only one kind of symbolic process" (p. 45). Assuming then, that language and thought are not isomorphic, how would the learning of two languages influence scores on intelligence tests, which obviously require thought?

Several writers, assuming a lack of identity between language and thought, suggest that the learning of two languages from childhood has favorable effects on the thinking process. Two writers in particular have made this point. Leopold (1949), after extensive observations of the mental development of his own child, felt that the bilingual child learns early to separate the sound of a word from its referent. He writes:

I attribute this attitude of detachment from words confidently to the bilingualism. Constantly hearing the same things referred to by different words from two languages, she had her attention drawn to essentials, to content instead of form (p. 188).[3]

S. J. Evans of Wales (1953) also argues that the:

teaching of Welsh along with English does what the efficient study of any two languages must do: it frees the mind from the tyranny of words. It is extremely difficult for a monoglot to dissociate thought from words, but he who can express his ideas in two languages is emancipated (p. 43).

These arguments, suggesting that a bilingual has an intellectual advantage over a monolingual because his thinking is not restricted by language, give support to those few studies which found favorable effects of bilingualism on intelligence and mental development. In view of these arguments, it also seems possible that the type of benefit that comes from bilingualism might not become apparent on standard intelligence tests. It could be argued that the studies finding no difference or a deficit for bilinguals were simply using inappropriate measures.

O'Doherty (1958) suggests that it is necessary in any consideration of the influence of bilingualism on intelligence to distinguish between two types of bilinguals for whom the effects may differ—the pseudo-bilingual and the genuine bilingual. The pseudo-bilingual knows one language much better than the other and does not use his second language in communication. The true bilingual masters both at an early age and has facility with both as means of communication. O'Doherty states that there can be no question that bilingualism of the genuine kind is an intellectual advantage. "The pseudo-bilingual is the real problem, since very often he fails to master either language, while the bilingual by definition has mastered both" (p. 285). Thus, O'Doherty's writings lend additional support to the notion that "genuine" bilingualism may be an asset.

---

[3]From *Speech development of a bilingual child*, Vol. 3, by W. F. Leopold. Copyright 1949, Northwestern University Press. Used by permission.

Can we find any theoretical support for the detrimental effects of bilingualism on intelligence? Weinreich (1953) makes the point that any individual who speaks two or more languages will experience interference due to the contact between them. That is, a bilingual's speech in each language will be different than it would have been had he only learned one language. The extent of the interference in any particular case will depend in part on certain linguistic differences between the two language systems.

The more numerous the mutually exclusive forms and patterns in each, the greater is the learning problem and the potential area of interference. But the mechanisms of interference ... would appear to be the same whether the contact is between Chinese and French or between two subvarieties of English (pp. 1-2).

The language handicap reported for bilinguals could thus be attributed to interlingual interference. The effect of this interference would show up on verbal tests, but could be expected to influence performance on nonverbal tests only insofar as these depend on verbal skills.

It could be hypothesized that bilingualism might affect the very structure of intellect. Such a hypothesis could be developed from a current conceptualization of intellect as consisting of factors. Guilford (1956) and others propose that intelligence is composed of a general factor and many different specific factors, each of which may be isolated by factor analytic methods. Ferguson (1954) has put forth the thesis that human abilities are learned. Stated another way, a large proportion of an individual's intellectual ability is acquired though experience and its transfer from one situation to another. The "factors of intellect" are gradually developed through a series of learning situations. This learning process may proceed in different ways for different individuals depending on their experiences. Thus the structure of intellect will very likely vary from one individual to another. The developmental process for monolinguals and bilinguals is certainly different in respect to language, and the learning of abilities depends greatly on language. Bilinguals could have different and more complex contexts for learning than monolinguals. Arsenian (1937) states that, "The two different words in two different language systems for the same referent may carry different connotations and put the bilingual person in contact with two worlds of experience." We could, therefore, hypothesize that the structure of the intellect of monolinguals and bilinguals might differ in various aspects. Guilford (1956) states: "to the extent that factors [of intellect] are developed by experience, they would appear at such ages as the effects of experience have sufficiently crystallized" (p. 287). That is, the emergence of an intellectual factor is dependent on the accumulation of experiences. From this notion, it seems reasonable to propose that such factors would appear at different ages in monolinguals and bilinguals, since their linguistic and cultural experiences are quite different. It may therefore be important to discover the nature of the effects of bilingualism on intellectual functioning.

Some recent studies have emphasized the importance, for second language learning, of an individual's attitude toward the second language community. Using a language involves personal participation in a second culture, Christophersen (1948) has made the point that a bilingual person belongs to two different communities and possesses two personalities which may be in conflict if the two language communities are in social conflict. Changes in the bilingual's attitude toward a language community may account for the variation in his efficiency in the use of that language which could even effect his performance on intelligence tests. Arsenian (1937) mentions that, "National, religious, and political sympathies or antipathies determine the affective tone or the *attitude* of a bilinguist toward the second language, and they introduce, therefore, important differences among bilinguists." The studies of Lambert, Hodgson, Gardner, and Fillenbaum (1960), and Anisfeld, Bogo, and Lambert (1961) suggest that certain community-wide negative stereotypes toward speakers of a particular language may have a negative influence on a bilingual who uses that language. He may be aware, for example, of the ridicule coming from others when he uses that language and this may constitute an intellectual interference in that language for him. This could have a detrimental effect for a bilingual when functioning in one of his languages if he had associations of inferiority or shame with that language. However, a bilingual even in Montreal's bicultural community could have favorable attitudes toward the use of both his own and the other language. The fact that an individual becomes bilingual in a bicultural community may be attributable to a favorable disposition toward both the linguistic communities, whereas the monolingual may be retarded in his acquisition of a second language because of his unfavorable attitudes toward both the other culture and its language.

STATEMENT OF THE PROBLEM

The present research was designed to examine more extensively the effects of bilingualism on the intellectual functioning of children and to explore the relations between bilingualism, school achievement, and students' attitudes to the second language community.

In line with previous findings, it was predicted that two groups of subjects, one monolingual and the other bilingual, should not differ significantly on nonverbal IQ, but might differ on verbal IQ as measured by intelligence tests standardized in the native language of both the monolinguals and bilinguals. The monolinguals were expected to perform significantly better than the bilinguals on the verbal tests. The groups were matched on socioeconomic class, sex, and age. They were selected from the same school system and where possible the same school. Several measures of degree of bilingualism were employed to determine objectively the bilingualism of each subject.

It was further predicted that the attitudes of the monolinguals would likely be less favorable to the other language group than those of the bilinguals, and that individual differences in these attitudes would be related to school achievement in the second language. For this purpose, several measures of attitude were used.

It was also thought that a relationship might be found between bilingualism and school grade. This idea stemmed from the work of Morrison (1958) who found that bilinguals were as much as 1½ years behind their age norms in school.

In line with the hypothesis that the structure of intellect might be different for the two groups of subjects, we used a wide variety of measures of different types of intelligence. It was predicted that bilinguals and monolinguals would perform differently on various types of subtests of intelligence. This is, in effect, an attempt to investigate the *nature* of the effect of bilingualism on intelligence.

METHOD

Subjects

The subjects were 10-year-old school children from six French schools under the jurisdiction of the Catholic School Commission of Montreal. Three of these schools were located in the western region of Montreal, and the remainder in the extreme eastern region of the island. All were roughly classified as middle class schools by the School Commission. In each school all the 10-year-olds available were tested, regardless of school grade.

Procedure

The testing took place in the classroom and was divided into five sessions of 1 hour each, spaced about a week apart. All instructions to the children were given in French by native speakers of French, except for the test of English vocabulary which was administered by a native speaker of English.

In the first session, all the 10-year-olds were administered a questionnaire and several tests to determine degree of bilingualism. The questionnaire sought general information about the child and his family, specific information about his language history, and details about his father's occupation. Three tests were used to determine whether the child was a *balanced bilingual* that is, equally skilled in French and English, or whether he was a monolingual. His own self-ratings of his ability in English were also taken into account.

Criteria for Selection of Subjects

Word Association Test. The first test of bilingualism was based on an association fluency technique developed by Lambert (1956). Modifications were introduced to make the technique appropriate for use with children in a group setting. French and English words were presented alternately and the children were asked to write down as many words as they could think of in the same language as the stimulus which seemed to "go with" or "belong with" that word. An interval of 60 seconds was allowed for association to each word. For each subject the sum of the associations to all the French words was calculated (NF). The same was done for the associations to the English words (NE). These two sums were used to form a balance score:

$$\text{Balance} = \frac{NF - NE}{NF + NE} \times 100$$

A zero score indicates perfect balance between the two languages, a plus score means French dominance, and a minus score English dominance.

Word Detection Test. This test was also a modification of one developed by Lambert, Havelka, and Gardner (1959). It was postulated that bilingualism would express itself in the facility of finding short embedded English and French words in a series of letters such as DANSONODEND. The subjects were given four such series and allowed 1½ minutes to work on each. Approximately equal number of English and French words were embedded in each group of letters. A balance score was obtained here, similar to the one described above.

Peabody Picture Vocabulary Test. This test, derived from Dunn (1959), was used because it made possible a distinction between oral and graphic language skills. It was thought that there might be bilinguals who were not able to read or write English, but who would nevertheless be balanced bilinguals in the oral sense. Such bilinguals might be at a disadvantage on the two previous tests which required some knowledge of written English. The test consists of a series of plates, each of which has four pictures of objects or actions numbered 1-4. The examiner says one English word aloud and the subject has to point to the picture corresponding to the word. To adapt this for use with a group, we flashed each plate on a screen by means of an epidiascope, and an examiner pronounced the word in English. The children wrote down the number of the picture which corresponded to the English word pronounced. In this way, no graphic skills in English were required of the subjects. Twenty-one plates of increasing difficulty were presented. A score of the number of correct responses out of 21 was obtained for each child.

Subjective Self-Rating Score. The subjects were asked to rate their ability to speak, read, write, and understand English on 4-point scales ranging from "not at all" (scored 1) to "very fluently" (scored 4). For each subject an oral self-rating score was obtained by summing his weights on "speak" and "understand," and a graphic score by doing the same on "read" and "write." The maximum possible score was 8 on each (oral and graphic scores).

On the basis of these tests, the entire sample of 364 subjects originally contacted was divided into three groups: one group composed of monolinguals, a second group of bilinguals, and a third group which could not be unambiguously classified as either monolingual or bilingual. Only the first two of these groups were further tested. The third group was not used again.

The criteria used in the classification of subjects were as follows: (*a*) Monolinguals—Word Association Test, a balance score of at least +75; Word Detection Test, a balance score of at least +75; Peabody Picture Vocabulary, a score of not more than 6; Subjective Self-Rating, a score of not more than 7 in oral and graphic skill in English (combined). (*b*) Bilinguals—Word Association Test, a balance score of 0 ±30; Word Detection Test, balance score of 0 ± 30; Peabody Vocabulary, a score of at least 15 out of 21; Subjective Self-Rating, a score of at least 13 out of a possible 16 in oral and graphic English (combined).

Two judges consulted on the classification of each subject. In some cases where the different criteria were in disagreement, more weight was given to the Vocabulary score than to the others.

Our selected sample was composed of 164 subjects: 75 monolinguals and 89 bilinguals; 96 boys and 68 girls. These subjects were tested four additional times.

Measures of Intelligence[4, 5]

Lavoie-Laurendeau (1960) Group Test of General Intelligence (Variables 6-9; Variables 16-23). Previous studies pointed to the importance of using a test of intelligence standardized in the native language of the subject and preferably prepared for use in that language community. The Lavoie-Laurendeau test, standardized by psychologists at the University of Montreal on a Monteal French-speaking school population, seemed to meet these requirements. It is based on several other well-developed tests (Wechsler-Bellevue, WISC, Barbeau-Pinard) using those sections which could best be adapted for group testing. The nonverbal and verbal sections of this test were administered to each group. Nonverbal, verbal, and total IQ scores were calculated for each subject. A ratio score was obtained by dividing the verbal IQ by the nonverbal IQ and multiplying by 100.

Raven (1956) Progressive Matrices Test (Variable 10). The colored form of this (Sets A, Ab, and B) was administered as a group test. This was included as a measure of basic intelligence (pure "g"). A total raw score was obtained for each subject (maximum 36).

Thurstone (1954) Primary Mental Abilities (Variables 11-15). An attempt was made to select those subtests from the Primary Mental Abilities which draw least directly on verbal skills. The following five were chosen and administered in French: Space, Figure-Grouping, Perception, Number, and Verbal Meaning. This test was translated by a linguist at McGill.

Measures of Attitude

In the final testing session, the children were given a booklet containing a number of different measures of attitude. The complete versions of these are presented in Appendix C.

Attitude-to-English Scale (Variable 33); Attitude-to-French Scale (Variable 34). The first measure was an attitude questionnaire, devised especially for use with children in the Montreal setting, answers to which purportedly reflect social attitudes toward either English Canadians or French Canadians. Two scales were derived from this questionnaire. Each question was defined as belonging either to the Attitude-to-English scale or to the Attitude-to-French scale. Responses to each question were scored on a three-point scale, from favorable to unfavorable. All the responses to the questionnaire belonging to the Attitude-to-French scale were scored and summed, a high score indicating a favorable attitude to French and a low score an unfavorable attitude. The Attitude-to-English scale was scored in the same manner.

Parents' Attitudes to English Canadians (Variable 38); Parents' Attitudes to French Canadians (Variable 39). The questionnaire contained items relating to the parents' attitudes toward the French and the English communities. These were scored in the same way as Variables 33 and 34.

Evaluation of Moi *(Me) (Variable 35); Evaluation of French Canadians (Variable 36); Evaluation of English Canadians (Variable 37)*. A second series of measures made use of the Semantic Differential (Osgood, 1957) as a technique for determining the subjects' attitudes to various groups. The subjects rated several concepts on 18 bipolar scales, each with seven

---

[4]Appendices A-D have been deposited with the American Documentation Institute. Order Document No. 7308, from ADI Auxiliary Publications Project, Photoduplication Service, Library of Congress; Washington 25, D. C., remitting in advance $2.25 for microfilm or $5.00 for photocopies. Make checks payable to: Chief, Photoduplication Service, Library of Congress.

[5]The numbering in the following sections refers to the number assigned to that variable for the analysis and is consistent throughout the rest of the paper. For names and numbering of subtests of intelligence, see Appendix B.

points. The concepts used in the analysis of the data were: Me, *les canadiens francais*, and *les canadiens anglais*.

Variables 35, 36, and 37 were obtained by summing the ratings assigned by a given subject to each of the concepts on all 18 scales. A high score on these variables indicates a high evaluation of the concept and a low score a low evaluation.

Differential Evaluation of French Canadians (Variable 40); Differential Evaluation of French Canadians and English Canadians (Variable 41); Differential Evaluation of Me and English Canadians (Variable 42). This measure was obtained by subtracting the evaluation of the concept listed second from the evaluation of that listed first. A high score indicates the first concept was evaluated more unfavorably than the second. A low score shows the opposite. A differential evaluation score was calculated between French Canadians and Me (Variable 40), between French Canadians and English Canadians (Variable 41), and between Me and English Canadians (Variable 42).
(Variable 41), and between Me and English Canadians (Variable 42).

Identification of French Canadians and Me (Variable 43); Identification of French Canadians and English Canadians (Variable 44); Identification of Me and English Canadians (Variable 45). Osgood Ds were calculated between the subject's ratings of each pair of concepts. These constitute scores on Variables 43, 44, and 45. A high score (D) indicates greater semantic distance between the two concepts or less similarity between them. A low score shows closer identification of the two concepts as discussed by Lazowick (1955).

Voice Study (Variable 46). In an attempt to get at stereotypes which the subjects might hold about French Canadians and English Canadians, a study was carried out using tape recordings of the voices of children reading a passage in French and an English translation of the same passage—an adaptation of a study by Lambert et al. (1960). There were four speakers, each one reading twice, once in each language. The subjects were unaware that they were rating the personality characteristics of only four speakers who were perfectly bilingual. English and French voices were presented alternately, the two voices of any one speaker being maximally separated on the tape. The subjects were asked to rate what they thought each speaker must be like as a person from the sound of her voice. The ratings were made on 15 traits, each one having a 5-point scale. For each subject on each of the traits, the sum of his ratings for all the English voices was subtracted from the sum of his ratings for all the French voices, yielding a measure (D) of the direction of the difference between his ratings of the two. In this case a constant of five was added to all scores. A score of 5 would mean there was no difference perceived between the two guises. A score greater than 5 would mean that the English were perceived more favorably than the French and a score lower than 5 would indicate that the French were perceived more favorably than the English.

Achievement Measures

From the teachers, ratings were obtained of how well each child did in school in relation to the others in his class. The teacher rated each child along a five-point scale in terms of his achievement in general (Variable 24), in French (Variable 25), and in English (Variable 26) if this happened to be one of his subjects. We also obtained the marks in French that each subject received in *dictée* (Variable 27), *lecture* (Variable 28), and *composition* (Variable 29) at midterm.

The following measures were based on information from the original questionnaire filled out by each subject.

Sex (Variable 1); School Grade (Variable 4); Number of Years Speaking English (Variable 5); French Skills of Parents (Variable 30). Each subject rated the ability of his father and mother to speak, read, write, and understand French. These were scored in the same manner as his self-ratings of his English ability. The scores for mother and father were summed.

English Skill of Parents (Variable 31). This variable was derived in the same way as above, using the items about English in place of those about French.

Balance between English and French Skills of Parents (Variable 32). The score on Variable 30 was subtracted from the score on Variable 31 and a constant of 100 added. A score of 100 on this variable indicates that the parents are equally skilled in French and English. A score of less than 100 means that the parents are more skilled in English than in French, and vice versa.

Socioeconomic Class (Variable 3). Realizing the relevance of socioeconomic class to language learning, we decided 'to investigate its role in detail. On the basis of information received from the child, the school records, the school principal, and the parents themselves when necessary, we placed each child into one of the seven categories outlined by Warner, Meeker, and Eells (1949). A small sample of 110 children was selected from the large sample so that there were equal numbers of bilinguals and monolinguals in each of the seven classes.

RESULTS AND DISCUSSION

Comparisons were made between the performance of the monolinguals and bilinguals on the various measures employed. Table 1 presents the means, *t* values, and associated probability levels for each comparison for the entire sample of subjects (large sample). The original statement of the problem required that the two groups be matched for socioeconomic class since previous studies had indicated the importance of this variable. Although the subjects in both groups were drawn from the same school system and in many cases the same school, all of which were considered middle class by the school commission, there was a significant difference between the two groups on socioeconomic level (Table 1, Variable 3). Because of this discrepancy, a small sample having equal numbers of bilinguals and monolinguals in each of seven socioeconomic status categories was analyzed separately. Table 2 shows the means, *t* values, and probability levels for this small sample. The general pattern of results for the two samples was highly similar.

For purposes of correlational analysis, 38 out of the 48 variables were chosen and intercorrelated for the bilingual group and the monolingual separately. Thirty-one variables were selected on the basis of their appropriateness for factor analysis. That is, total IQ measures were eliminated and only subtests kept, ratio and balance scores were eliminated because they were composed of two other measures, and only two of the nine rating scales of attitudes were kept, to reduce the possibility of built-in correlations. Each 31 by 31 variable correlation matrix was factor analyzed by Thurstone's (1947) centroid solution and seven factors were extracted. The factors were rotated using the normal varimax rotation program developed at McGill.

The correlation matrices and factor matrices (centroid solution) are presented in Appendix A. The rotated factor matrices appear later in the Discussion section. In these analyses, the large sample was used, with socioeconomic status left free to vary in order that the extent of its influence could be determined.

TABLE 1

MEANS, t VALUES, AND PROBABILITY LEVELS FOR
MONOLINGUAL AND BILINGUAL GROUPS ON
ALL MEASURES, LARGE SAMPLE

Name of Variable	Bi-lingual M	Mono-lingual M	t value [a]
1. Sex	—	—	—
2. Linguality	—	—	—
3. Socioeconomic class	4.27	3.31	3.71***
4. School grade	4.86	4.42	5.61***
5. Number of years speaking English	5.68	.71	14.44***
6. Lavoie-Laurendeau (L-L) Nonverbal IQ	109.43	95.40	5.78***
7. L-L Verbal IQ	116.26	103.14	6.06***
8. L-L Total IQ	115.01	99.45	6.75***
9. L-L Ratio Score	106.60	110.34	−1.46
10. Raven Progressive Matrices	27.48	22.40	5.44***
11. Primary Mental Abilities (PMA) Verbal Meaning	26.91	24.94	3.13***
12. PMA Space	15.96	14.33	2.48**
13. PMA Figure-Grouping	19.21	17.49	2.62***
14. PMA Perception	22.32	20.19	2.07*
15. PMA Number	36.38	33.13	2.58**
16. L-L Picture Arrangement	8.55	6.19	4.80***
17. L-L Figure Manipulation	10.58	8.77	3.57***
18. L-L Dissimilarities	9.33	8.03	3.57***
19. L-L Picture Completion	10.10	8.43	3.58***
20. L-L Vocabulary	12.74	10.52	4.08***
21. L-L Comprehension	6.23	5.23	3.32***
22. L-L Similarities	9.08	7.70	3.93***
23. L-L Information	12.67	9.44	6.19***
24. Achievement in General	3.43	3.04	2.85***
25. Achievement in French	3.37	3.10	1.86
26. Achievement in English	4.16	2.63	7.61***
27. Marks in French *dictée*	73.65	71.14	1.02

Table 1—Continued

Name of Variable	Bi-lingual M	Mono-lingual M	t value [a]
28. Marks in French *lecture*	78.78	75.22	1.97
29. Marks in French *composition*	74.93	73.03	1.18
30. French skills of parents	22.15	23.26	−2.34*
31. English skills of parents	21.59	16.36	7.05***
32. Balance between Variables 30 and 31	100.74	106.92	−7.19***
33. Attitude-to-English scale	52.75	38.85	8.91***
34. Attitude-to-French scale	26.71	31.31	−5.46***
35. Evaluation of self	111.18	105.12	2.11*
36. Evaluation of French Canadians (FC)	109.27	110.07	−.34
37. Evaluation of English Canadians (EC)	104.34	95.24	2.87***
38. Parents' attitude to EC	5.00	4.06	5.86***
39. Parents' attitude to FC	4.95	5.40	−2.92***
40. Differential Evaluation of FC—Me	511.58	485.25	2.36**
41. Differential Evaluation of FC—EC	477.75	425.80	2.83***
42. Differential Evaluation of Me—EC	466.55	441.26	1.38
43. Identification of FC and Me	37.55	39.40	−.23
44. Identification of FC and EC	56.63	82.75	−1.53
45. Identification of Me and EC	54.22	90.98	−2.06*
46. Voice Study	4.98	4.65	3.38***

[a] Positive entries indicate that the mean for the bilingual group is higher than the mean for the monolingual group. Negative entries indicate the reverse.
* $p < .05$.
** $p < .02$.
*** $p < .01$.

TABLE 2

MEANS, t VALUES, AND PROBABILITY LEVELS FOR
MONOLINGUAL AND BILINGUAL GROUPS ON
ALL MEASURES, SMALL SAMPLE [a]

Name of Variable	Bi-lingual M	Mono-lingual M	t value [b]
1. Sex	—	—	—
2. Linguality	—	—	—
3. Socioeconomic class	3.80	3.83	.11
4. School grade	4.87	4.48	4.77***
5. Number of years speaking English	5.36	.72	11.24***
6. Lavoie-Laurendeau (L-L) Nonverbal IQ	110.26	95.85	4.84***
7. L-L Verbal IQ	114.98	104.43	4.08***
8. L-L Total IQ	114.62	100.60	5.11***
9. L-L Ratio Score	104.80	111.62	− 2.13*
10. Raven Progressive Matrices	27.15	22.12	4.40***
11. Primary Mental Abilities (PMA) Verbal Meaning	26.94	25.35	2.23*
12. PMA Space	15.80	14.31	1.90
13. PMA Figure-Grouping	19.46	17.58	2.39**
14. PMA Perception	22.06	20.33	1.29
15. PMA Number	35.92	33.29	1.65
16. L-L Picture Arrangement	8.50	6.15	4.00***
17. L-L Figure Manipulation	10.42	8.96	2.37**
18. L-L Dissimilarities	9.69	8.08	3.64***
19. L-L Picture Completion	10.35	8.50	3.21***
20. L-L Vocabulary	12.63	10.73	2.99***
21. L-L Comprehension	6.02	5.22	2.17*
22. L-L Similarities	8.77	7.80	2.21*
23. L-L Information	12.81	10.02	4.62***
24. Achievement in General	3.38	3.04	1.97
25. Achievement in French	3.35	3.11	1.29
26. Achievement in English	4.00	2.68	5.24***
27. Marks in French *dictée*	72.73	71.51	.40
28. Marks in French *lecture*	79.04	75.73	1.46
29. Marks in French *composition*	75.09	72.49	1.29

Table 2—Continued

Name of Variable	Bi-lingual M	Mono-lingual M	t value [b]
30. French skills of parents	22.50	23.10	− 1.09
31. English skills of parents	21.13	17.08	4.27***
32. Balance between Variables 30 and 31	101.38	106.05	− 4.75***
33. Attitude-to-English scale	51.76	38.85	7.12***
34. Attitude-to-French scale	26.57	31.65	− 5.00***
35. Evaluation of self	110.55	105.82	1.24
36. Evaluation of French Canadians (FC)	108.89	110.58	− .60
37. Evaluation of English Canadians (EC)	101.04	98.28	.76
38. Parents' attitude to EC	4.88	4.09	4.11***
39. Parents' attitude to FC	5.14	5.48	− 2.03*
40. Differential Evaluation of FC—Me	510.04	492.42	1.24
41. Differential Evaluation of FC—EC	462.94	432.42	1.40
42. Differential Evaluation of Me—EC	453.26	439.66	.63
43. Identification of FC and Me	42.36	35.42	.74
44. Identification of FC and EC	70.64	64.98	.32
45. Identification of Me and EC	66.78	73.93	− .39
46. Voice Study	4.95	4.63	2.33*

[a] Equated for socioeconomic status.
[b] Positive entries indicate that the mean for the bilingual group is higher than the mean for the monolingual group. Negative entries indicate the reverse.
* $p < .05$.
** $p < .02$.
*** $p < .01$.

The main findings of the study will be presented in summary. Following this, each one will be examined separately in more detail. Finally, an attempt will be made to integrate all the findings.

The first hypothesis, that the two groups would not differ significantly on nonverbal IQ, was not supported. The results (Table 2) show that the bilingual group performed significantly better than the monolingual on the Raven Progressive Matrices, and the Lavoie-Laurendeau Nonverbal IQ, and most of the subtests of the nonverbal type.

The finding that the bilinguals also scored significantly higher than the monolinguals on the Lavoie-Laurendeau Verbal IQ, and on all the verbal subtests, is in direct contradiction to the original prediction.

The monolingual and bilingual groups performed differentially on subtests of intelligence, as was expected. On certain subtests of the nonverbal type there were no significant differences between the groups, while on others, both nonverbal and verbal, the bilinguals performed better in differing amounts. However, on none of the subtests did the monolinguals exceed the bilinguals.

The predicted relation between attitudes to English and school achievement in English was found. For example, in the monolingual case, there is a significant correlation $(-.51)$ between achievement in English (Variable 26) and the degree of perceived similarity between Me and English Canadians (Variable 45).

Morrison's observation that bilinguals were often behind in school grade was not borne out in this study. Quite to the contrary, the results show that bilingual subjects who were of the same age as the monolinguals (10 years), were in a higher grade in school, even for the sample which was matched on socio-economic class.

The attitudes of the bilinguals toward English Canadians were significantly more favorable than those of the monolinguals, as indicated by the means on the Attitude-to-English scale. These attitudes appear to be related to socioeconomic class, however, since in the larger sample where the bilinguals were of a higher social class, their favorable attitudes to English became evident on more variables measuring attitudes. It should also be noted that the monolinguals held more favorable attitudes to the French Canadians than the bilinguals.

No significant differences were found between the group means (small sample) for: achievement in general, achievement in French, evaluation of self, and most of the remaining attitude measures, although these do relate differentially to the other variables.

Performance on Nonverbal Intelligence Measures

The finding that a group of bilingual children scored higher on nonverbal intelligence tests than did a group of monolinguals runs counter to most previous findings in this area and to the original expectation of this study. It raises the question as to why the bilinguals scored higher on nonverbal tests.

This problem may be viewed from two perspectives. One may ask whether the more intelligent children, as measured by nonverbal intelligence tests, are the ones who become bilingual, or whether bilingualism itself has a favorable effect on nonverbal intelligence.

In support of the first notion, one could argue that the more intelligent child would be more able to pick up English from his playmates and his schooling than the less intelligent child, given the same opportunities. Previous studies have shown a correlation between intelligence and language aptitude (Gardner & Lambert, 1959; Wittenborn & Larsen, 1944). When a frequency distribution is made of the scores obtained by the two groups on a nonverbal test (such as the Raven) we find that the distribution of bilinguals' scores is negatively skewed. That is, though there were some children of low intelligence who became bilingual, most of the bilinguals scored higher on this intelligence test. Also, there were a few monolinguals who did as well as the bilinguals on the test, but the majority was found near the middle or at the lower end of the distribution. This shape of distribution implies that at least some minimum level of intelligence is necessary to become a really balanced bilingual, at least to meet the requirements for bilingualism set in this study.

In a bilingual community such as Montreal, it is a very great asset and at times a necessity for French Canadians to know English. These advantages may be realized more fully by parents of higher intelligence who may be more inclined to encourage their children to learn English. Parents of higher intelligence may be expected to have more intelligent children. This notion is supported by the following facts. The bilinguals reported significantly more than the monolinguals that their parents encouraged them to learn to speak English and the parents themselves had more skill in English than did the parents of the monolingual children ($p < .01$) who apparently either failed to see the benefits of knowing English or reacted negatively to the English-Canadian community. The more intelligent children may themselves realize the value of knowing English and therefore seek opportunities to learn it. When they do show progress in learning English, one could predict that they would receive parental encouragement for so doing. Even if the less intelligent child should see the advantages, he might encounter difficulties in attempting to learn English and might give up more readily, being accustomed to failure in other areas. Furthermore, he does not receive encouragement from his parents. But for the bright child who is ahead in school, the opportunity to learn anything new may present a challenge, which he is capable of meeting.

An alternative explanation of these results is that bilingualism may in some way influence nonverbal intelligence. It may be that knowing two languages from an early age gives a child an advantage in his performance on nonverbal tests. If this is the case, why did the bilinguals not do better on all the different nonverbal subtests? In her chapter on Performance and Nonlanguage tests, Anastasi (1961) writes:

An important question to consider regarding non-language tests concerns the extent to which they depend upon spatial and perceptual functions, as contrasted to the symbolic manipulation of abstract relations, concepts, and factual information. The latter functions would seem to resemble more closely those required in the traditional verbal tests of "intelligence" ... Some tests ... stress spatial and perceptual factors almost to the exclusion of other functions ... Other non-language tests employ a greater proportion of items calling for ideational or symbolic responses (p. 253).[6]

The nonverbal tests in this study can be subdivided conveniently into two groups in the fashion suggested by Anastasi. The Primary Mental Abilities Space and Perception tests both draw more on spatial and perceptual processes than on symbolic manipulation. The Number test of the Primary Mental Abilities is composed of simple addition questions which do not involve much mental "manipulation." Because this is a timed test, the important requirement is perceptual speed. In the Primary Mental Abilities Figure-Grouping, the Raven, and the Lavoie-Laurendeau Dissimilarities tests the subjects must form a concept or discover relations between elements which cannot be done without cognitive reorganizations. The Lavoie-Laurendeau Figure-Manipulation and the Lavoie-Laurendeau Picture Arrangement tests require reorganizations of relations and concepts. Thus, the different nonverbal tests do logically fall into two categories: (a) those with spatial-perceptual requirements: Primary Mental Abilities Space, Perception, and Number; and (b) those with symbolic reorganization requirements: Primary Mental Abilities Figure-Grouping, Raven Progressive Matrices, Lavoie-Laurendeau Dissimilarities, Figure-Manipulation, and Picture Arrangement. The Picture Completion test is difficult to categorize, a priori. Further support for the division of nonverbal or performance tests into two subtypes comes from an abstract of a study conducted by Ahmed (1954):

A factorial analysis study demonstrating that spatial visualization and mental manipulation are independent abilities ... The author tentatively describes this ability as if it consisted of *mental flexibility* [italics added] which is involved in the process of mentally reorganizing the elements of a problem or situation.

Reference to Table 2 reveals that on the spatial-perceptual type of test, the two groups performed similarly whereas on the mental reorganization type there is a significant difference between them. The bilinguals therefore perform better only on the type of nonverbal tests involving concept-formation or symbolic "flexibility."

Several hypotheses will be proposed as to why bilinguals might have an advantage on these tests. People who learn to use two languages have two symbols for every object. From an early age, bilinguals may be forced to conceptualize environmental events in terms of their general properties without reliance on their linguistic symbols. This would be particularly relevant in the case of those bilinguals who are "compound" (Lambert, Havelka, & Crosby,

---

[6]From *Psychological testing*, by Anne Anastasi. Copyright 1961, Macmillan Company. Used by permission.

1958), that is, bilinguals who learned their two languages in the same setting and therefore have two words for the identical referent. Most of our bilinguals have learned both their languages in Montreal and would likely be compound. Leopold (see the introduction) noted that his bilingual child learned to separate the sound of the word from the thing itself. This ability to think in terms of abstract concepts and relations, independent of the actual word, apparently is required in the symbolic reorganization type tests. The monolinguals may never have been forced to form concepts or abstract ideas of things and may be more likely to think mainly in terms of concretes. They could not be expected, therefore, to be as agile at concept-formation as the bilinguals and they might appear handicapped comparatively. S. J. Evans (1953) implies that monolinguals may be at a disadvantage in that their thought is always subject to language. In summary, it is proposed that bilinguals, because of their training in two languages, have become more adept at concept formation and abstract thinking than the monolinguals, and that this accounts, in part, for their superiority on the symbolic reorganization type tests.

The second hypothesis is that bilinguals may have developed more flexibility in thinking. Compound bilinguals typically acquire experience in switching from one language to another, possibly trying to solve a problem while thinking in one language, and then, when blocked, switching to the other. This habit, if it were developed, could help them in their performance on tests requiring symbolic reorganization since they demand a readiness to drop one hypothesis or concept and try another. Morrison (1958) gives an example of a Gaelic-speaking boy of 11, who had just taken the Raven Matrices test. When asked whether he had done his thinking in Gaelic or in English he replied, "Please, sir, I tried it in the English first, then I tried in the Gaelic to see would it be easier; but it wasn't, so I went back to the English" (p. 288). The monolinguals of course could not have developed a habit of alternating languages, and therefore, of making use of two different perspectives. One might thus expect them to be more rigid or less flexible than the bilinguals on certain tests. This might account for the significant difference between the two groups on these tests. This hypothesis could be more directly tested by giving groups of monolinguals and bilinguals tests of rigidity to see if rigidity-flexibility is a dimension on which they actually do differ.

Nonlanguage or performance tests depend, to a certain extent, on prior exposure to and familiarity with materials similar to those used in the test. The broader a child's experience, the higher the probability that he will have come into contact with the type of ideas and situations that will assist him in his performance. The bilingual child has been exposed to a wider range of experiences than the monolingual, because his experiences stem from two different cultures. This enriched environment may benefit him on nonverbal tests.

The bilingual's contact with the English culture should have put him in an advantageous position on the Primary Mental Abilities Test which is basically an English style test translated into French for present purposes. However, the fact that this was the test on which the bilinguals performed relatively the poorest would seem to justify our use of a translation; that is, it apparently did not give the bilinguals an advantage.

Performance on Verbal Intelligence Measures

The next finding to be discussed is that bilinguals also performed better on verbal tests. We had anticipated that the monolinguals would excel. Why this complete reversal? The superior performance of the bilinguals on the verbal tests may simply be a reflection of their overall superior intelligence. This seems to be the case for the small sample. An analysis of covariance (Table 3) showed that when the two groups were matched statistically on nonverbal intelligence, there was no significant difference between them on verbal intelligence. (The Lavoie-Laurendeau Nonverbal and Verbal IQs were used in this analysis.) For the large sample, this does not hold up (see Table 4). There is still a significant difference ($p = .01$) between the groups in favor of the bilinguals on verbal, even after they have been matched on nonverbal. Arguing from the large sample results, it appears that our bilinguals, instead of suffering from "mental confusion" or a "language handicap" are profiting from a "language asset." A partial explanation of this may lie in our method of choosing the bilingual sample. Those suffering from a handicap may unintentionally have been eliminated. We attempted to select bilinguals who were balanced, that is equally fluent in both languages. However, when the balance measures used did not give a clear indication of whether or not a given child was bilingual, more weight was attached to his score on the English vocabulary test. Thus some bilinguals who might be balanced, but whose vocabulary in English and French might be small, would be omitted from our sample. The less intelligent bilinguals, those who have not acquired as large an English vocabulary, would not be considered "bilingual" enough for our study. In O'Doherty's terms, we may have included mainly genuine bilinguals, as opposed to pseudo-bilinguals. The genuine bilingual, having mastered both languages, is believed by O'Doherty (1958) to be clearly in an advantageous position intellectually. But this study does not include information about the other type of bilingual.

The superiority of the bilinguals on the verbal measures might be considered from another point of view. Bilinguals have a more extended total vocabulary than have monolinguals in the sense that they have learned both English and French symbols for most referents in their environment. The overlap of English and French vocabularies is considerable, so that an English-French bilingual may actually be helped when functioning in either language by the positive transfer derived from the other. The difference in the amount of overlap between two

TABLE 3

ANALYSIS OF COVARIANCE OF PERFORMANCE OF
TWO GROUPS OF SUBJECTS, SMALL SAMPLE

Source	df	X^2	XY	Y^2
Between groups	1	3998.51	3365.39	2832.52
Within groups	103	34207.89	21629.28	41040.82
Total	104	38206.40	24994.67	43873.34

Source	Analysis of Covariance SS of errors of estimate	df	MS	F
Total	27521.80	103		
Within groups	27364.86	102	268.28	
Adjusted means	156.94	1	156.94	.584

Note.—Sums of squares and cross products for 2 groups of subjects (monolingual and bilingual) on Lavoie-Laurendeau Nonverbal IQ (X) and Lavoie-Laurendeau Verbal IQ (Y).

TABLE 4

ANALYSIS OF COVARIANCE OF PERFORMANCE OF
TWO GROUPS OF SUBJECTS, LARGE SAMPLE

Source	df	X^2	XY	Y^2
Between groups	1	8284.89	6864.76	5687.94
Within groups	145	32361.41	14500.34	26389.26
Total	146	40646.30	21365.10	32077.20

Source	Analysis of Covariance SS of errors of estimate	df	MS	F
Total	20847.00	145		
Within groups	19892.06	144	138.14	
Adjusted means	954.94	1	954.94	6.91*

Note.—Sums of squares and cross products for 2 groups of subjects (monolingual and bilingual) on Lavoie-Laurendeau Nonverbal IQ (X) and Lavoie-Laurendeau Verbal IQ (Y).
* Indicates significance at the 1% level of confidence.

languages may, in part, explain the discrepancy between the results reported here and those reported previously from Wales. French and English have many more words derived from common roots than do Welsh and English. A Welsh-English bilingual would not benefit from as much positive transfer in vocabulary as would a French-English bilingual.

Differential Performance on Intelligence Measures

It was suggested in the introduction that bilinguals and monolinguals might be found to perform differently on various types of intelligence subtests and that this performance difference might somehow be related to a difference in the structure of the intellect of the typical students in the two groups. Reference to the factor analyses (Tables 5 and 6) shows that the bilinguals seem to have a greater number of separate or independent abilities on which to draw in completing these tests in contrast to the monolinguals who have fewer. That is, the bilinguals have more independent factors defined by intelligence variables than the monolinguals. For the bilinguals, Factor IV is clearly defined as a verbal intelligence factor. There are several nonverbal intelligence factors—III, V, VI, VII—which are defined by the intelligence measures, but also have loadings of achievement and attitude variables on them. Factor I also has some loadings of intelligence tests on it. For the monolinguals, on the other hand, most of the intelligence variables, both verbal and nonverbal, load together on Factor I which is clearly a general intelligence factor. Factor VI for the monolinguals is roughly equivalent to the verbal factor (IV) for the bilinguals, but it is not so pure and clear. Similarly, Factor VII (monolinguals) has high loadings of both intelligence and achievement in English. The remaining loadings of the intelligence variables on other factors do not play an important role for the monolinguals. Thus some support is given to the notion that bilinguals have developed more independent abilities and skills at an earlier age through their experiences and their learning of a second language. In summary, the structure of intellect of the bilinguals appears to be more diversified than that of the monolinguals. Thus, Guilford's (1956) belief that different experiences might cause different factors of intellect to appear at varying times for different individuals receives support here. Further research on this structure for monolinguals and bilinguals, including a greater number of different types of measures of intelligence, might prove extremely useful in current attempts to define the nature of intelligence. It would also be interesting to investigate whether the monolinguals eventually develop similar factors, or whether the basic structure remains different.

It is important to realize that it is not possible to ascertain from the present study whether the more diversified structure of intelligence of the bilinguals is attributable to their bilinguality or simply to the fact that they are more intelligent. Perhaps a higher degree of intelligence means more diversified abilities and aptitudes.

TABLE 5

Rotated Factor Matrix for Monolinguals

Variable	I	II	III	IV	V	VI	VII	h^2
3. Socioeconomic class	.03	-.04	.57	.20	.01	.25	.15	.46
4. School grade	.14	-.07	.51	.08	.04	.52	.09	.57
10. Raven Matrices	.71	.24	-.06	.20	-.02	.06	.19	.64
11. Primary Mental Abilities (PMA) Verbal Meaning	.47	.11	.08	.23	.28	.22	-.10	.43
12. PMA Space	.29	.06	-.01	.32	.15	.26	.40	.44
13. PMA Figure-Grouping	.40	.05	.06	-.04	.13	.15	.58	.54
14. PMA Perception	.35	.20	-.06	.31	.09	.45	.33	.59
15. PMA Number	.04	.40	-.07	.25	-.05	.49	.16	.50
16. Lavoie-Laurendeau (L-L) Picture Arrangement	.74	.17	.09	.02	-.08	.06	.04	.59
17. L-L Figure Manipulation	.57	.22	.17	.21	.11	.16	.24	.54
18. L-L Dissimilarities	.13	.19	.09	.04	.34	.24	.46	.45
19. L-L Picture Completion	.64	.09	.15	-.17	-.01	.30	.21	.60
20. L-L Vocabulary	.50	-.07	.25	-.00	.20	.54	.02	.64
21. L-L Comprehension	.19	.19	.19	-.05	.29	.68	.10	.66
22. L-L Similarities	.38	.03	.28	-.05	.35	.11	.04	.37
23. L-L Information	.21	-.01	.30	.18	.08	.74	-.09	.73
24. Achievement in general	.26	.88	-.02	.14	.07	-.05	.08	.88
25. Achievement in French	.15	.87	.03	.09	.01	.12	.15	.82
26. Achievement in English	.11	.48	.08	.13	.79	.06	.32	.99
27. Marks in French *dictée*	.08	.85	.12	.01	.09	.14	.12	.78
28. Marks in French *lecture*	.15	.67	.03	-.07	.38	-.07	-.13	.65
29. Marks in French *composition*	.10	.74	-.15	-.28	.36	.11	.00	.80
30. French skills of parents	.12	.22	.25	.10	-.11	.09	.30	.24
31. English skills of parents	.12	-.04	.76	.15	.03	-.02	.21	.66
33. Attitude-to-English scale	-.03	.03	.42	-.35	.21	.17	.30	.47
34. Attitude-to-French scale	.10	-.08	.03	.52	.02	.13	-.04	.31
38. Parents' attitude to English Canadians (EC)	.09	.01	.34	-.05	.13	.07	-.02	.14
39. Parents' attitude to French Canadians (FC)	-.04	.09	.22	-.02	.24	.16	-.07	.14
43. Identification of FC and Me	-.00	-.14	-.12	-.63	-.19	-.03	-.19	.50
45. Identification of Me and EC	-.01	-.11	.02	.14	-.58	-.10	-.12	.39
46. Voice Study	-.04	-.06	-.36	.04	.12	-.01	.19	.19

TABLE 6

ROTATED FACTOR MATRIX FOR BILINGUALS

Variable	I	II	III	IV	V	VI	VII	h²
3. Socioeconomic class	−.05	.07	.07	−.06	−.05	.06	.47	.24
4. School grade	.14	.19	−.26	.58	.26	−.11	.08	.54
10. Raven Matrices	.32	.16	.54	.14	−.08	.39	.11	.61
11. Primary Mental Abilities (PMA) Verbal Meaning	.27	.03	.18	.75	.13	.09	−.01	.69
12. PMA Space	.09	.02	.24	.26	.41	.29	.40	.54
13. PMA Figure-Grouping	.18	.14	.41	.15	.06	.50	−.02	.50
14. PMA Perception	−.05	−.20	.11	.22	.56	.21	.02	.47
15. PMA Number	.22	.05	−.11	.07	.48	−.11	−.02	.32
16. Lavoie-Laurendeau (L-L) Picture Arrangement	.03	.12	.49	.31	.12	.06	.15	.40
17. L-L Figure Manipulation	.29	−.08	.32	.16	.10	.38	.32	.47
18. L-L Dissimilarities	.03	.08	−.02	−.05	.04	.60	.08	.38
19. L-L Picture Completion	−.17	−.14	.32	.43	.17	−.09	.15	.40
20. L-L Vocabulary	.21	−.20	.10	.68	.04	.11	.05	.58
21. L-L Comprehension	.11	−.08	.08	.41	−.02	.08	−.13	.22
22. L-L Similarities	−.02	−.05	.15	.36	−.02	.40	−.22	.37
23. L-L Information	.42	−.22	.07	.44	.22	−.08	.15	.50
24. Achievement in general	.78	.02	.07	.15	.10	.25	.15	.74
25. Achievement in French	.83	−.07	.10	.20	.09	.16	.00	.78
26. Achievement in English	.19	.26	.13	.12	.62	.05	−.08	.53
27. Marks in French dictée	.75	−.05	.01	.19	−.09	−.03	.02	.61
28. Marks in French lecture	.62	−.34	.06	.08	.42	−.05	−.20	.73
29. Marks in French composition	.71	−.04	.06	.07	.19	.21	−.27	.67
30. French skills of parents	−.13	−.42	−.16	.27	−.22	−.54	.11	.64
31. English skills of parents	−.38	.34	.11	.06	−.07	.14	−.06	.30
33. Attitude-to-English scale	−.10	.69	.02	−.13	.14	.21	.13	.58
34. Attitude-to-French scale	−.01	−.73	.09	.05	−.09	−.04	.01	.55
38. Parents' attitude to English Canadians (EC)	−.13	.67	.04	.09	−.19	.12	.11	.54
39. Parents' attitude to French Canadians (FC)	.03	−.49	−.33	.14	−.32	.10	−.09	.49
43. Identification of FC and Me	−.28	.35	.09	−.09	.36	−.36	−.19	.51
45. Identification of Me and EC	−.06	−.03	−.07	−.13	.13	−.42	−.29	.30
46. Voice Study	−.10	.38	.15	−.13	−.04	−.26	.06	.27

Attitudes to English and French

For all the measures of attitudes used, the means for the bilingual group were in the direction of being more favorable to English Canadians, while the means for the monolingual group were more favorable to the French Canadians. A comparison of Tables 1 and 2 shows that the differences between means reached significance on more of the relevant attitude variables for the large sample than for the small sample. These results present a clear picture of the bilingual group being more favorably disposed to English Canadians, and less to French Canadians than the monolingual group.

Several possible explanations of these findings come to mind. The greater contact which the bilinguals have with English Canadians and English culture may account in part for their more favorable attitudes. The very fact that they have succeeded in becoming bilingual indicates that getting to know the English and their language must have been a goal or value for them. This goal, which may have been engendered by parents (Gardner, 1960), led them to seek more contact with the English community. These contacts may well have been positively reinforcing thereby increasing the desire for further interactions. Support for the notion of the influence of the parents comes from our data. The bilingual children report that their parents' attitudes toward English Canadians are favorable. Their parents' skill in English is also significantly higher than that of the monolinguals' parents. The correlation (.48) between the bilinguals' attitudes to EC and the attitudes they reported that their parents held may indicate that the Parents' Attitude-to-English scale was just a reflection of how the children themselves feel. This in no way diminishes the importance of it as a measure. It is a child's *perception* of the attitudes his parents hold that to a great extent influences his behavior and thinking, whether or not this perception is in line with reality. For the monolinguals, the correlation between Attitude-to-English scale and the Parents' Attitude-to-English is lower (.27). Attitudes toward the English may not be salient for monolingual families and therefore less frequently discussed.

Because the bilinguals held more favorable attitudes toward English Canadians, does this necessarily mean they had to hold less favorable attitudes to French Canadians? The scales devised to measure these two attitudes were composed from the same questionnaire and had some overlapping items (e.g., My best friend is English Canadian? French Canadian? or other?) which might suggest that there is a built-in negative relation between the Attitude-to-English scale and the Attitude-to-French scale. If we examine the correlations between these two scales (Variables 33 and 34), we find that for the monolinguals the *r* is only −.11 which clearly suggests that the relation between attitudes to French and attitudes to English is not inherent in the nature of the scales. The correlation of −.48 for the bilinguals therefore needs some explanation. The fact that they have learned English indicates that they must have identified, to some extent at least, with the English Canadians. This tendency is reflected in the measure of Identification with English Canadians (Variable 45) on which the bilinguals identify with English Canadians more closely than do the monolinguals. It is psychologically difficult to belong to two communities at once, to identify to the same extent with two groups which are culturally different. It appears that the bilinguals have resolved this "conflict" by clearly identifying with the English Canadians rather than with the French Canadians. The closer identification with English Canadians is supported by the higher means for bilinguals on the Differential Evaluation measures where a higher score indicates that the second concept is evaluated more favorably than the first. This strong identification with the English seems to require the bilinguals to identify less with the French Canadians.

On the reactions to spoken language (Variables 46), the mean score for the bilinguals was 4.98, which suggests that the stereotypes they hold of French Canadians and English Canadians are of a similar degree of favorableness. This variable measures stereotypes and does not correlate with the attitude scores. The monolinguals' evaluations indicate that they hold more favorable stereotypes of the French Canadians than of the English Canadians.

Many of the monolinguals and bilinguals in our sample live in the same districts and have approximately the same opportunities to learn English. Why did the one group take advantage of these occasions for interaction while the other group did not? One could suggest that the less favorable attitudes of the monolinguals toward English Canadians and the lack of encouragement from their parents on this matter have had a powerful negative effect. This will be dealt with more fully in the following discussion of the relation between attitudes to English and achievement in English.

Attitude and English Achievement

If we examine the correlation and factor tables to determine which variables are related to achievement in English, we discover that the attitude variables are important for the monolinguals, but not for the bilinguals. The bilinguals as a group appear to have more clearly defined attitudes which are favorable to the English, and which have ceased to present a problem for them. To the extent that there is consensus among the bilinguals there would be less variance and less chance for correlation. For the bilinguals, Achievement in English is related more to intelligence than to attitude. The only significant relation for them between attitude and achievement is the negative relation between Achievement in English and Attitude-to-French scale ($-.42$) which indicates that the more unfavorable attitudes to French the bilingual holds, the better he does in English. For the monolinguals on the other hand, attitudes play as important a role as intelligence. Factor V obtains its highest loadings from achievement in English. The high loading of the Identification of moi and English Canadians on this factor (−.58) indicates the importance of attitudes for English achievement for monolinguals. Correlations of −.51, −.52, and −.54 between Achievement in English and Identification of Me and English Canadians, of French Canadians and Me, and of French Canadians and English Canadians, respectively, suggest that a monolingual does better in English if he sees all these three as being similar, that is, French Canadians, English Canadians, and himself. Apparently it is necessary for him to identify with both groups in order to do well in English. This attempt at dual identification may well constitute a conflict for him and possibly hinder him from becoming bilingual. If he fails to identify with both, he does poorly in English.

It appears, then, that the attitude an individual holds toward the other language community plays a vitally important role in his learning the other group's language in school, as is particularly the case with our monolingual sample. If he views the other community with favor, he is more likely to do well in his attempts to learn the language, and vice versa. It also becomes evident that for those who have already practically mastered a second language, (e.g., our bilinguals) their attitudes to the second language community, of which they are in some way not a part, no longer play as important a role in their continued achievement in that language as do factors such as intelligence. The hypothesis that those with more favorable attitudes toward the English community would do better in learning English has received substantial support.

Bilingualism and School Grade

Previous studies had pointed out that bilinguals suffered from a language handicap and possibly because of it were behind in school. In the present study, where no handicap became evident, one should not expect bilinguals to be retarded in school. Indeed, the bilinguals as a group were significantly more advanced in school grade than were the monolinguals, and this, undoubtedly, can be attributed to their higher intelligence. For the bilinguals, school grade loads on the intelligence factors, expecially the verbal intelligence factor (IV), suggesting that it is the verbal skills of the bilinguals that help them do well in school. Their bilingualism apparently gives them an advantage in those skills which depend on verbal fluency. For the monolinguals the picture is somewhat different. Grade in school loads about equally on Factor VI (intelligence) and Factor III (essentially an attitude factor). It is related to such variables as Space, Perception, Figure Manipulation, but not to Verbal Meaning or Vocabulary. Thus the monolinguals draw more on nonverbal than verbal abilities for their advancement in school grade, in contrast to the bilinguals. Socioeconomic class also seems to be a powerful determinant of how well monolinguals will do in school ($r = .46$). The implications of the correlates of achievement in school such as the contribution of socioeconomic class to school grade advancement for the monolinguals but not for the bilinguals, will not be fully considered in this thesis. In fact, many of the ramifications of the factor structures in general have not been fully explored. They constitute the start of the next phase of this research.

CONCLUSION

This study has found that bilinguals performed better than monolinguals on verbal and nonverbal intelligence tests. These results were not expected because they constitute a clear reversal of previously reported findings. How can we account for this difference in intelligence between the two groups? An attempt will be made here to integrate the explanations presented above into a description of the differences between the groups which may partially account for their differences in intellectual functioning.

The picture that emerges of the French-English bilingual in Montreal is that of a youngster whose wider experiences in two cultures have given him advantages which a monolingual does not enjoy. Intellectually his experience with two language systems seems to have left him with a mental flexibility, a superiority in concept formation, and a more diversified set of mental abilities, in the sense that the patterns of abilities developed by bilinguals were more heterogeneous. It is not possible to state from the present study whether the more intelligent child became bilingual or whether bilingualism aided his intellectual development, but there is no question about the fact that he is superior intellectually. In contrast, the monolingual appears to have a more unitary structure of intelligence which he must use for all types of intellectual tasks.

Because of superior intelligence, these bilingual children are also further ahead in school than the monolinguals and they achieve significantly better than their classmates in English study, as would be expected, and in school work in general. Their superior achievement in school seems to be dependent on a verbal facility. Those monolinguals who do poorly in their English study apparently fail to identify either with the English or the French cultural groups, In contrast, those monolinguals who do well in English, have closely identified themselves with both communities. Their failure to become bilingual may be attributed in part to the difficulties they may encounter in making a dual identification with both cultural groups, coupled with their acceptance of their own group (i.e., French Canadians) as being superior. The attitudes of the bilinguals are quite different. They hold more favorable attitudes towards the English than towards the French. Their clear identification with one group may contribute to their mastery of English. It is interesting to note that in the Voice Study, which attempts to tap stereotypes, the bilinguals evaluate the personalities of French and English speakers in a similar manner while the monolinguals evaluate the French more favorably than the English.

The pattern of attitudes that emerges for the two groups is distinctively different and these attitude differences might be expected to influence performance on intelligence tests, but this is not the case. There are no significant correlations between attitude and intelligence for either group. Nevertheless it is worthwhile examining the group differences in attitude patterns since they throw light on the possible reasons why some students become bilingual while others remain monolingual. This can best be done by comparing Factor III for the monolinguals with Factor II for the bilinguals. Factor III, for the monolinguals reflects a family-wide attitude to English Canadians, while Factor II for the bilinguals reflects a family-wide attitude to English Canadians versus French Canadians. The bilingual factor is bipolar in the sense that it has positive loadings of attitude variables favorable to English as well as negative loadings of attitude variables favorable to French. That is, the bilinguals, very likely through parental influence, are favorable toward the English community and at the same time unfavorable to the French.

Factor III for the monolinguals is a unitary factor. It indicates that the monolingual children of higher socioeconomic class, even though they hold positive attitudes to the English as do their parents, still have more favorable stereotypes of the French than of the English. This tendency to see the French as better may partly explain why the children have remained monolingual. Possibly children from these families of higher social class have developed positive attitudes to the English and yet feel a pressure to remain French. It is possible that some conservative nationalistic sentiment for the retaining of the French language exists among these children and prevents them from identifying sufficiently with the English community to be psychologically set to learn the language and thus they remain monolingual. And yet the higher social class families may admire and emulate the English Canadians as instrumentally valuable models in spheres of activity which contribute to maintaining higher social class standing, such as economic and social situations. Factor III also affords a second description of the monolingual family. In this case, the lower social class monolingual family has the following characteristics: the parents have little skill in English and hold negative attitudes to the English, although they do endorse favorable stereotypes of the English. The children are comparatively retarded in school grade. This pattern suggests that those French-Canadian families of lower socioeconomic class may become envious of the English Canadians and, perhaps through places of residence and type of work, culturally isolated and remain monolingual.

Thus a picture emerges of monolingual and bilingual children as representatives of two distinct groups, differing in intellectual structure, attitude patterns, achievement in school, and achievement in languages. The results of this study indicate the value of shifting emphasis from looking for favorable or unfavorable effects of bilingualism on intelligence to an inquiry into the basic nature of these effects. Perhaps further research may profit from this different emphasis.

SUMMARY

The effects of bilingualism on intellectual functioning are explored in this study. A group of monolingual and a group of bilingual 10-year-old children from six Montreal French schools were administered verbal and nonverbal intelligence tests, and measures of attitudes to the English and French communities. Contrary to previous findings this study found that bilinguals performed significantly better than monolinguals on both verbal and nonverbal intelligence tests. Several explanations are suggested as to why bilinguals have this general intellectual advantage. It is argued that they have a language asset, are more facile at concept formation, and have a greater mental flexibility. The results of factor analyses applied to the data supported the hypothesis that the structures of intellect for the two groups differ. The bilinguals appear to have a more diversified set of mental abilities than the monolinguals. The correlations of the attitude measures with other variables are also discussed.

REFERENCES

AHMED, M. A.-S. Mental manipulation. *Egypt. Yearbk. Psychol.*, 1954, *1*, 23-88.

ALTUS, GRACE T. WISC patterns of a selective sample of bilingual school children. *J. genet. Psychol.*, 1953, *83*, 241-248.

ANASTASI, ANNE. *Psychological testing.* (2nd ed.) New York: Macmillan, 1961.

ANISFELD, M., BOGO, N., & LAMBERT, W. E. *Evaluational reactions to accented English-speech.* McGill University, 1961. (mimeo)

ARSENIAN, S. Bilingualism and mental development. *Teach. Coll. Contr. Educ.*, 1937, No. 712.

ARTHUR, G. The predictive value of the Kuhlmann-Binet Scale for a partially Americanized school population. *J. appl. Psychol.*, 1937, *21*, 359-364.

BERE, M. *A comparative study of mental capacity of children of foreign parentage.* New York: Teachers College, Columbia University, 1924.

CENTRAL ADVISORY COUNCIL FOR EDUCATION (Wales). *The place of Welsh and English in the schools of Wales.* London: Her Majesty's Stationery Office, 1953.

CHRISTOPHERSEN, P. *Bilingualism.* London: Methuen, 1948.

DARCY, NATALIE T. The effect of bilingualism upon the measurement of the intelligence of children of preschool age. *J. educ. Psychol.*, 1946, *37*, 21-44.

DARCY, NATALIE T. A review of the literature on the effects of bilingualism upon the measurement of intelligence. *J. genet. Psychol.*, 1953, *82*, 21-57.

DARSIE, M. L. The mental capacity of American-born Japanese children. *Comp. Psychol. Monogr.*, 1926, *3*, 1-18.

DAVIES, M., & HUGHES, A. G. An investigation into the comparative intelligence and attainments of Jewish and non-Jewish school children. *Brit. J. Psychol.*, 1927, *18*, 134-146.

DUNN, L. M. *Peabody Picture Vocabulary Test.* Tennessee: American Guidance Service, 1959.

EVANS, S. J. Address of the Conference of Headmasters of Grammar Schools, Wales, 1906. In Central Advisory Council for Education (Wales), *The place of Welsh and English in the schools of Wales.* London: Her Majesty's Stationery Office, 1953.

FEINGOLD, G. A. Intelligence of the first generation immigrant groups. *J. educ. Psychol.,* 1924, *15,* 65-82.

FERGUSON, G. A. On learning and human ability. *Canad. J. Psychol.,* 1954, *8,* 95-112.

GARDNER, R. C. Motivational variables in second-language acquisition. Unpublished doctoral dissertation, McGill University, 1960.

GARDNER, R. C., & LAMBERT, W. E. Motivational variables in second-language acquisition. *Canad. J. Psychol.,* 1959, *13,* 266-272.

GRAHAM, V. T. The intelligence of Italian and Jewish children. *J. abnorm. soc. Psychol.,* 1925, *20,* 371-376.

GUILFORD, J. P. The structure of intellect. *Psychol. Bull.* 1956, *53,* 267-293.

HILL, H. S. The effects of bilingualism on the measured intelligence of elementary school children of Italian parentage. *J. exp. Educ.,* 1936, *5,* 75-79.

HIRSCH, N. D. A study of natio-racial mental differences. *Genet. Psychol. Monogr.,* 1926, *1,* 231-407.

JAMES, C. B. E. Bilingualism in Wales: An aspect of semantic organization. *Educ. Res.,* 1960, *2,* 123-136.

JOHNSON, G. B. Bilingualism as measured by a reaction-time technique and the relationship between a language and a non-language intelligence quotient. *J. genet. Psychol.,* 1953, *82,* 3-9.

JONES, W. R. A critical study of bilingualism and nonverbal intelligence. *Brit. J. educ. Psychol.,* 1960, *30,* 71-76.

JONES, W. R., & STEWART, W. A. Bilingualism and verbal intelligence. *Brit. J. Psychol.,* 1951, *4,* 3-8.

LAMBERT, W. E. Developmental aspects of second-language acquisition: I. Associational fluency, stimulus provocativeness, and word-order influence. *J. soc. Psychol.,* 1956, *43,* 83-89.

LAMBERT, W. E., HAVELKA, J., & CROSBY, C. The influence of language-acquisition contexts on bilingualism. *J. abnorm. soc. Psychol.,* 1958, *56,* 239-244.

LAMBERT, W. E., HODGSON, R. C., GARDNER, R. C., & FILLENBAUM, S. Evaluational reactions to spoken languages. *J. abnorm. soc. Psychol.,* 1960, *60,* 44-51.

LANGER, SUSANNE. *Philosophy in a new key.* Cambridge: Harvard Univer. Press, 1942.

LAVOIE, G., & LAURENDEAU, MONIQUE. *Tests collectifs d'intélligence générale.* Montreal, Canada: Institut de Recherches Psychologiques, 1960.

LAZOWICK, L. M. On the nature of identification. *J. abnorm. soc. Psychol.,* 1955, *51,* 175-183.

LEOPOLD, W. F. *Speech development of a bilingual child.* Vol. 3. Evanston: Northwestern Univer. Press, 1949.

LEVINSON, B. M. A comparison of the performance of bilingual and monolingual native born Jewish preschool children of traditional parentage on four intelligence tests. *J. clin. Psychol.,* 1959, *15,* 74-76.

LEWIS, D. G. Bilingualism and non-verbal intelligence: A further study of test results. *Brit. J. educ. Psychol.,* 1959, *29,* 17-22.

MCCARTHY, DOROTHEA. Language development in children. In L. Carmichael (Ed.), *Manual of child psychology.* New York: Wiley, 1954.

MEAD, M. Group intelligence and linguistic disability among Italian children. *Sch. Soc.*, 1927, *25*, 465-468.

MORRISON, J. R. Bilingualism: Some psychological aspects. *Advanc. Sci.*, 1958, *56*, 287-290.

O'DOHERTY, E. F. Bilingualism: Educational aspects. *Advanc. Sci.*, 1958, *56*, 282-286.

OSGOOD, C. E., SUCI, G. J., & TANNENBAUM, P. H. *The measurement of meaning*. Urbana: Univer. Illinois Press, 1957.

PINTNER, R. The influence of language background on intelligence tests. *J. soc. Psychol.*, 1932, *3*, 235-240.

PINTNER, R., & ARSENIAN, S. The relation of bilingualism to verbal intelligence and school adjustment. *J. educ. Res.*, 1937, *31*, 255-263.

PINTNER, R., & KELLER, R. Intelligence tests of foreign children. *J. educ. Psychol.*, 1922, *13* 214-222.

RAVEN, J. C. *Coloured Progressive Matrices: Sets A, Ab, B*. London: Lewis, 1956.

RIGG, M. Some further data on the language handicap. *J. educ. Psychol.*, 1928, *19*, 252-257.

SAER, D. J. The effects of bilingualism on intelligence. *Brit. J. Psychol.*, 1923, *14*, 25-38.

SAER, HYWELA. Experimental inquiry into the education of bilingual peoples. In, *Education in a changing commonwealth*. London. New Education Fellowship, 1931. Pp. 116-121.

SEIDL, J. C. G. The effect of bilingualism on the measurement of intelligence. Unpublished doctoral dissertation, Fordham University, 1937.

SMITH, F. Bilingualism and mental development. *Brit. J. Psychol.*, 1923, *13*, 270-282.

SPOERL, DOROTHY, T. The academic and verbal adjustment of college-age bilingual students. *J. genet. Psychol.*, 1944, *64* 139-157.

STARK, W. A. The effect of bilingualism on general intelligence: An investigation carried out in certain Dublin primary schools. *Brit. J. educ. Psychol.*, 1940, *10*, 78-79.

THURSTONE, L. L. *Multiple factor analysis.* Chicago: Univer. Chicago Press, 1947.

THURSTONE, L. L., & THURSTONE, THELMA G. *Primary Mental Abilities: Ages 7 to 11*. Chicago: Science Research Associates, 1954.

WANG, S. L. A demonstration of the language difficulty involved in comparing racial groups by means of verbal intelligence tests. *J. appl. Psychol.*, 1926, *10*, 102-106.

WARNER, W. L. MEEKER, MARCHIA, & EELLS, K. *Social class in America*. Chicago: Science Research Associates, 1949.

WEINREICH, U. *Languages in contact*. New York: Linguistic Circle of New York, 1953.

WITTENBORN, J. R., & LARSEN, R. P. A factorial study of achievement in college German. *J. educ. Psychol.*, 1944, *35*, 39-48.

LANGUAGE APTITUDE, INTELLIGENCE, AND SECOND-LANGUAGE ACHIEVEMENT[1]

R. C. GARDNER   W. E. LAMBERT

University of Western Ontario   *McGill University*

This study demonstrates that measures of intelligence are relatively independent of both language aptitude and 2nd-language achievement, and moreover, that different 2nd-language skills are related to different abilities. A factor analysis of 24 variables (N = 96 high-school students) yielded 7 orthogonal factors. 4 of these were composed primarily of indexes of 2nd-language skills suggesting relatively independent dimensions of achievement. Each of these factors also included 1 different measure of language aptitude indicating that these dimensions of language achievement were dependent upon different abilities. A 5th factor appeared to describe much of the variance common to the measures of language aptitude but included measures of language achievement and reasoning skills. 2 additional factors defined as "intelligence" and "verbal knowledge" were orthogonal to the other factors.

To date very little research has been concerned with the relations among measures of language aptitude, intelligence, and second- (or foreign-) language achievement. Most previous studies have shown instead that grades in a foreign-language course correlate higher with measures of language aptitude than with intelligence (Carroll & Sapon, 1959; Henmon, 1929), but there has been little attempt to determine the degree of interdependence of measures of language aptitude and intelligence or to isolate just what second-language skills could be predicted. One exception was a study by Wittenborn and Larsen (1944) in which the factor structure of measures of language aptitude, intelligence, and second-language achievement was determined. However, that study was incon-

[1]This study was sponsored by the Language Development Section of the United States Office of Education under Title VI of the National Defense Education Act, Section 602, Public Law 85-864, and was conducted while the senior author was a research associate at McGill University. We extend our gratitude to Irene Vachon-Spilka for the linguistic analysis of the speech samples, and to Janine Lambert and Nicole Deschamps who rated each student's oral reading for accuracy of pronunciation, reading fluency, and type of accent. We sincerely thank Roy Miles of Lafayette, Louisiana, for his assistance in carrying out the testing program, and the principals and teachers of the high schools in which the study was conducted.

clusive, showing only that much of the variance common to the language-aptitude measures included in their matrix was related to intelligence but not to second-language achievement.

In a factor-analytic study specifically designed to determine the nature of language aptitude, Carroll (1958) analyzed correlation matrices obtained from batteries of tests administered to two different samples of Air Force personnel enrolled in a 1-week trial course in Mandarin Chinese. Although the test batteries were not identical for the two samples, there was sufficient similarity between the factor structures to permit a cross-identification of six factors. The one criterion, grades in the course, received substantial loadings on three factors in each sample, suggesting that achievement in the course was related to three abilities: linguistic interest, associative memory, and an inductive language-learning ability. Multiple-regression analyses performed on each sample indicated that the remaining factors also were represented in tests which predicted achievement, though to a lesser extent. Since no measure of intelligence, and only one criterion was included in the matrices, however, this study provides only limited information concerning the relation of language aptitude to intelligence or to specific second-language skills. What was clear was that a simple criterion like grades in a course is indeed factorially complex.

Some data have been obtained on the relation of language aptitude to intelligence. Carroll (1962) reports significant correlations between total scores on the American Council Psychological Examination (ACE) and three of four language-aptitude subtests. Using an experimental version of the Modern Language Aptitude Test (MLAT) developed by Carroll and Sapon (1959), Gardner and Lambert (1959) found that language aptitude was factorially similar to intelligence (as defined by two ACE verbal subtests). This finding may be spurious, however, since the factor matrix also contained many measures of attitudes and motivation which, because of their low correlations with the aptitude and intelligence variables, could artificially enhance the factorial similarity of language aptitude and intelligence. In addition, the use of verbal measures of intelligence would be expected to increase this similarity. What is obviously required is a study relating language aptitude to a multifactor measure of intelligence, thus allowing for a clearer delineation of the specific intellectual variables (if any) actually related to language aptitude.

Although Carroll (1958) has shown that numerous abilities comprise an aptitude for languages, little research has subsequently been done to relate these abilities to specific second-language skills. In one study, Carroll (1962) correlated instructors' ratings of students' attainments on a number of second-language skills with subtests from the MLAT. Most of these correlations were significant, however, and the differential magnitudes are generally not sufficient to allow for a clear statement of the relevance of the abilities measured to specific skills. Moreover, as Carroll (1962) states, ". . . it is hard to know whether to take the ratings themselves at face value, since there is no way of guaranteeing that an instructor would be able to separate the several aspects of behavior even conceptually [p. 115]." Using objective measures of second-language skills, Gardner (1960) obtained two relatively independent factors of second-language achievement. One, which characterized second-language skills specifically taught in the classroom situation, received substantial loadings from the language-aptitude measures (MLAT) indicating the importance of language aptitude for the learning of such skills. The other factor, which appeared to describe second-language skills developed outside the classroom in interaction with members of the other language community, was, however, virtually independent of language aptitude. The importance of this to the present study is the finding that although second-language achievement involves the acquisition of an integrated set of skills, it is nonetheless possible to use factor-analytic techniques to isolate different aspects of this total skill. That only two major factors of language achievement were isolated in the Gardner (1960) study probably is due to the heterogeneous collection of tests included in the matrix rather than to the fact that only these two elements of achievement can be empirically isolated. By careful choice of measuring instruments, it should be possible to isolate relatively independent second-language skills (cf. Lado, 1961, pp. 25-26), and, in fact, Lambert (1956) has demonstrated that different language skills help to differentiate degrees of bilinguality.

The purpose of the present study is to determine the factorial structure of a battery of tests designed to measure these attributes, in order not only to clarify the relationship of intelligence to language aptitude and second-language achievement, but also to delineate the specific second-language skills associated with specific language-learning abilities.

METHOD

Subjects

A total of 96 boys and girls studying French I and II at high schools in Lafayette, Louisiana, were tested. Students were selected if the school records indicated that they came from English-speaking homes and had no previous regular experience with the French language.

Materials

The tests described in this study were administered in conjunction with a larger battery of tests (see Lambert, Gardner, Olton, & Tunstall, 1961). Of the tests to be described below, the language-aptitude battery was administered in early December 1960, while the measures of French achievement were obtained in late April 1961. Intelligence-test scores and school grades were obtained from the school records.

Variables 1-5 are the subtests from Carroll and Sapon's (1959) Modern Language Aptitude Test (MLAT). The descriptions of the subtests are adapted from Carroll and Sapon (1959):

1. Number Learning: this test measures both a memory component and a general auditory-alertness factor.

2. Phonetic Script: this test is a measure of both memory for speech sounds and the ability to learn correspondence between speech sounds and orthographic symbols.

3. Spelling Clues: scores on this test are dependent upon a student's knowledge of English vocabulary as well as the "sound-symbol association ability" described in 2, above.

4. Words in Sentences: this test measures a student's sensitivity to grammatical structure. Although it is obvious that knowledge of English grammar is important for achievement on this test, grammatical terminology is not used, hence it would appear that high scores on the test require more than memory for specific grammatical terminology.

5. Paired Associates: this test is a measure of the student's rote-memory ability.

Variables 6-10 are five of the tests from Thurstone and Thurstone's (1941) Primary Mental Abilities (PMA) test battery. The tests included are:

6. Verbal Meaning
7. Space
8. Reasoning
9. Number
10. Word Fluency

Variables 11-14 are subtests from the Cooperative French Listening Comprehension Test, Form A (Brooks, 1955). The total test consists of four parts, each of which involves a different type of listening situation. The description of the subtests is adapted from Brooks (1955):

11. Phonetic Discrimination: a low score on this test indicates that the student is poor in making auditory distinctions in consonant sounds, vowel sounds, nasal sounds, verb endings, linking, etc., in the aural comprehension of French.

12. Answering Questions: this test is a measure of the student's comprehension of isolated questions asked in French.

13. Completion of Statements: this test measures the student's ability to complete French sentences presented aurally.

14. Comprehension of Passages: this test measures the student's ability to comprehend and retain impressions that are described in a series of aurally presented, related French sentences.

Variables 15-17 are the subtests from the Cooperative French Test, Elementary Form Q (Greenberg & Spaulding, 1940). The tests, presented in printed form, include:

15. Reading: incomplete French sentences are given, and, in each case, the subject is required to select the alternative which most reasonably completes the sentence.

16. Vocabulary: 50 French words are presented, and, for each word, the subject chooses the English equivalent.

17. Grammar: the subject is presented a series of English sentences, each followed by an incomplete French translation. The subject is required to choose the word, word ending, or phrase which best completes each sentence.

The remaining measures were either developed for this study (Variables 18-21) or were obtained from the school records (Variables 22-24):

18. French Free Speech: two flash cards were used, one bearing the phrase, "*Je vais,*" the other, "*Si nous,*" and, in each case, the student was required to complete the sentences. Responses were tape-recorded and subsequently analyzed by a linguist in terms of "complexity of response pattern" and "correctness."

19. French Reading Fluency: each student read a standard passage of French dialogue into a tape recorder. Two experts in French subsequently rated each oral production on a 7-point scale in terms of fluency. The two ratings were totaled to produce an estimate of the student's reading fluency.

20. French Pronunciation Accuracy: the above passage was also rated by the same judges on a 7-point scale in terms of the accuracy with which words were pronounced in context. Emphasis for this rating was on the total impression each student gave while reading, rather than on the accuracy of pronouncing key words.

21. Standard French Accent: the judges rated each student's reading on the extent to which it evidenced a Franco-American accent (1) or a European-French accent (7). Seven categories were used, the middle one (4) representing no trace of either accent.

22. Midterm French Grade: the grades obtained by each subject in the French course in December 1960 were standardized for each class to remove the effects of differences in teachers' grading standards.

23. Final French Grade: the grades obtained by each subject in the French course at the end of the academic year were standardized for each class to remove the effects of differences in teachers' grading standards.

24. Academic Average: the student's final grades in all academic school courses except French were averaged to obtain an estimate of his academic proficiency.

RESULTS AND DISCUSSION

Pearson product-moment correlation coefficients were computed among the 24 variables. Before the correlations were computed all scores were standardized within the two levels of French achievement in order to eliminate the differential effects of training. The correlation matrix (see Table 1) was factor analyzed using the Centroid method (Thurstone, 1947), and factoring was continued until it was obvious from observation that the residual matrix contained little more common variance. Seven factors were extracted (see Table 2) and were rotated by use of the normalized Varimax rotation solution (Kaiser, 1958). The rotated orthogonal factor matrix is presented in Table 3.[2]

Factor I receives substantial loadings from the five MLAT subtests (Variables 1-5), a measure of reasoning ability (Variable 8), and three measures of French achievement (Variables 11, 15, and 17). That all of the language-aptitude measures share variance in common is to be expected since Carroll (1958) has already demonstrated that four of these tests (among others) formed a factor labeled "Linguistic Interest" which appeared to describe "an increment of test performance ascribable to a specific motivation, interest, or facility with respect to unusual linguistic materials [p. 12]." The results of the present study suggest that this Linguistic Interest reflects mostly a *facility* with unusual linguistic materials since it is clear that reasoning skills (note Variable 8) are important for achievement on these tests. Because of this it appears reasonable to define Factor I as a *Linguistic Reasoning* factor,[3] thus emphasizing the role that reasoning skills play in the language-aptitude measures.

---

[2]All calculations were performed on the 4,000-word IBM 650 at the McGill Computing Center. Appreciation is expressed to Robert Olton for writing the correlation-matrix program. The factor analysis and rotation programs were written by the senior author.

TABLE 1

CORRELATION MATRIX

	1	2	3	4	5	6	7	8	9	10	11	12	13	14	15	16	17	18	19	20	21	22	23	24
1	—	.40	.41	.40	.45	.35	.11	.37	.30	.23	.24	.10	.14	.07	.33	.28	.34	.12	.49	.46	.30	.38	.36	.39
2		—	.43	.49	.43	.38	.10	.29	.24	.27	.45	.20	.30	.10	.46	.49	.51	.22	.44	.43	.11	.38	.38	.35
3			—	.48	.47	.25	.10	.22	.20	.25	.22	.15	.34	.25	.49	.49	.42	.37	.33	.33	.09	.30	.35	.34
4				—	.53	.35	.19	.43	.30	.23	.44	.21	.29	−.09	.45	.41	.67	.30	.40	.38	.14	.54	.51	.47
5					—	.22	.06	.27	.30	.32	.28	.32	.21	.12	.49	.46	.45	.18	.33	.36	.13	.42	.43	.38
6						—	.42	.29	.39	.48	.11	.31	.20	.07	.38	.49	.40	.28	.40	.42	.23	.35	.33	.42
7							—	.44	.30	.14	.06	.34	−.03	−.12	.13	.16	.11	.18	.15	.13	.17	.24	.22	.23
8								—	.39	.31	.17	.21	.19	−.07	.23	.22	.25	.11	.27	.25	.10	.34	.27	.26
9									—	.27	.20	.29	.03	.11	.29	.26	.28	.36	.20	.24	.04	.30	.24	.30
10										—	−.03	.16	.11	.02	.22	.38	.22	.20	.28	.22	−.01	.23	.24	.28
11											—	.19	.21	.04	.32	.32	.42	.18	.38	.41	.20	.30	.26	.17
12												—	.17	.18	.39	.36	.22	.20	.21	.28	.06	.18	.12	.11
13													—	−.03	.52	.46	.38	.07	.31	.38	.06	.35	.30	.22
14														—	.26	.20	.03	.20	.07	.11	−.01	−.01	−.03	−.06
15															—	.74	.64	.36	.41	.51	.15	.47	.38	.36
16																—	.58	.29	.52	.55	.14	.57	.53	.42
17																	—	.34	.40	.45	.06	.52	.54	.50
18																		—	.26	.34	.12	.23	.26	.40
19																			—	.85	.57	.51	.54	.43
20																				—	.56	.53	.52	.50
21																					—	.26	.28	.22
22																						—	.83	.61
23																							—	.70
24																								—

The presence of three measures of French achievement on Factor I indicates that *Linguistic Reasoning* is related to second-language achievement, particularly where such achievement is measured by the student's skill in recognizing significant linguistic elements. Note that in each of these measures of French achievement, the student's success depends in part on his ability to choose the correct alternative from subtle variations in speech sounds (Variable 11), contextual meaning (Variable 15), and grammatical forms (Variable 17).

All but one of the variables receiving high loadings on Factor II are measures of French achievement; the dominant component seemingly being *French Vocabulary Knowledge*. Although it is obvious that all measures of French achievement require knowledge of vocabulary, the relative magnitudes of the loadings on this factor seem to reflect the extent to which vocabulary knowledge alone would account for scores on these tests. The tests yielding the three highest loadings (Variables 16, 15, and 13) generally involve the selection of one-word alternatives, and it seems clear that vocabulary knowledge alone would often yield the correct answer. This same interpretation is suitable for the other measures of achievement which receive moderate loadings on this factor. Inspection of the items comprising Variables 17, 12, 20, and 11 suggests that

---

[3] Since the PMA reasoning test is heavily saturated with an Inductive Reasoning factor (Thurstone & Thurstone, 1941, p. 6), this factor might be referred to as Inductive Language Learning. However, Carroll (1962, p. 130) uses this term in a different context, hence that label was not used.

TABLE 2
CENTROID FACTOR MATRIX

Variables	I	II	III	IV	V	VI	VII	h^2
1 Number learning	.56	−.09	−.06	−.07	−.14	−.33	−.10	.47
2 Phonetic script	.63	.06	.18	.10	−.04	−.22	.08	.50
3 Spelling clues	.59	.18	.15	.11	−.26	−.12	−.12	.51
4 Words in sentences	.69	.05	−.05	.31	.15	−.29	−.13	.70
5 Paired associates	.61	.12	.09	.14	−.08	−.22	−.09	.48
6 PMA verbal meaning	.60	.19	−.26	−.22	−.08	.15	.18	.57
7 PMA space	.32	.17	−.43	−.20	.29	.09	.14	.47
8 PMA reasoning	.47	.14	−.33	−.05	.28	−.26	.12	.51
9 PMA number	.47	.27	−.28	−.15	.10	.03	−.17	.44
10 PMA word fluency	.41	.25	−.19	−.07	−.29	−.04	.31	.45
11 Phonetic discrimination	.45	−.08	.24	.05	.23	−.19	−.12	.37
12 Answering questions	.40	.30	.10	−.24	.25	.16	.06	.41
13 Completion of statements	.43	−.05	.32	.20	.14	.06	.22	.40
14 Comprehension of passages	.13	.20	.28	−.20	−.23	.14	−.15	.27
15 Reading	.73	.18	.38	.06	.09	.23	−.07	.78
16 Vocabulary	.76	.11	.28	.07	−.08	.23	.26	.80
17 Grammar	.71	.07	.12	.35	.06	.04	−.11	.66
18 French free speech	.45	.16	−.04	−.07	−.09	.20	−.32	.39
19 French reading fluency	.72	−.45	.09	−.32	−.08	−.10	.10	.86
20 French pronunciation accuracy	.76	−.43	.16	−.33	−.02	.07	−.05	.91
21 Standard French accent	.34	−.47	−.05	−.36	−.02	−.06	−.08	.48
22 Midterm French grade	.73	−.29	−.18	.30	.09	.18	.09	.79
23 Final French grade	.71	−.35	−.20	.34	−.08	.18	.07	.83
24 Academic average	.65	−.17	−.30	.20	−.21	.20	−.12	.68

knowledge of French vocabulary, either in terms of correct word meanings, appropriate word endings, or recognition of familiar words would account for some of the variability on these tests. Variable 22, the teacher's midterm evaluation, is a composite rating, but it is conceivable that part of this evaluation is dependent upon the student's knowledge of French vocabulary. The five remaining measures of French achievement do not receive substantial loadings on this factor, and inspection of them strongly suggests that they involve second-language skills which are much more complex than mere vocabulary knowledge.

The only nonachievement variable which contributes substantially to Factor II is the Phonetic Script test (Variable 2). Carroll (1962) has stated that this test measures "... the ability to code auditory phonetic material in such a way that this material can be recognized, identified, and remembered over something longer than a few seconds [p. 128]." Individuals low in this ability, he suggests,

TABLE 3
Rotated Factor Matrix
(Orthogonal)

Variables	I	II	III	IV	V	VI	VII	h^2
1 Number learning	.52	−.02	.14	.36	.06	.13	.18	.47
2 Phonetic script	.53	.34	.12	.18	.08	.08	.20	.50
3 Spelling clues	.52	.17	.19	.08	.34	.02	.23	.51
4 Words in sentences	.71	.21	.31	.07	−.04	.23	−.02	.70
5 Paired associates	.58	.19	.18	.11	.16	.11	.14	.47
6 PMA verbal meaning	.10	.15	.24	.20	.20	.50	.39	.57
7 PMA space	−.03	.03	.12	.07	−.08	.66	.10	.47
8 PMA reasoning	.36	.05	.07	.11	−.20	.56	.11	.52
9 PMA number	.24	−.03	.16	.06	.23	.53	.05	.42
10 PMA word fluency	.16	.08	.12	.03	.08	.25	.58	.45
11 Phonetic discrimination	.44	.30	.03	.23	.03	.08	−.18	.38
12 Answering questions	.07	.36	−.07	.06	.26	.44	.02	.41
13 Completion of statements	.21	.57	.14	.09	−.02	−.02	.04	.40
14 Comprehension of passages	.02	.09	−.11	.05	.48	−.06	.09	.27
15 Reading	.34	.62	.22	.11	.44	.18	−.01	.79
16 Vocabulary	.24	.66	.29	.16	.27	.14	.31	.79
17 Grammar	.51	.40	.43	.01	.17	.13	−.01	.65
18 French free speech	.19	.03	.27	.08	.46	.23	−.02	.38
19 French reading fluency	.27	.25	.20	.80	.05	.11	.18	.86
20 French pronunciation accuracy	.21	.32	.26	.79	.22	.13	.03	.90
21 Standard French accent	.05	−.04	.11	.67	.01	.07	−.04	.47
22 Midterm French grade	.25	.34	.69	.26	−.11	.21	.05	.78
23 Final French grade	.25	.26	.76	.28	−.08	.09	.13	.82
24 Academic average	.24	.03	.71	.22	−.15	.17	.16	.69

"will have trouble not only in remembering phonetic material, words, forms, etc., but also in mimicking speech sounds [p. 129]." The present data support this interpretation but suggest further that this ability is not specific to oral-aural skills. Since all aspects of vocabulary knowledge are related to this ability, it would seem that this "phonetic-coding" ability enables the individual to impose a meaningful code on incoming linguistic material thus ensuring its retention. It would seem that complete vocabulary knowledge, as distinct from simple knowledge of English equivalents of foreign words, is not dependent upon a passive rote-learning ability (note the contributions of Variables 1 and 5 to this factor), but rather upon a higher cognitive skill in which the individual actively seeks to impose a meaningful code on the material.

Five variables define Factor III, the three dominant ones being Final French Grade (Variable 23), Academic Average (Variable 24), and Midterm French

Grade (Variable 22), indicating that teachers' evaluations of French achievement are often confounded with school achievement in general. Factor III is thus labeled *School French Achievement*. The presence of Variable 17 (Grammar) on this factor indicates that in this school system at least, teachers' evaluations emphasize knowledge of French grammar and that other variables are only minimally involved. The one nonachievement variable which receives a substantial loading on this factor is the Words in Sentences test (Variable 4), suggesting that the student who is aware of grammatical distinctions in English will do well in French courses where the emphasis is on grammar.

The three variables which receive high loadings on Factor IV are measures of the student's skill in reading aloud a standard French passage fluently (Variable 19), with accurate pronunciation (Variable 20), and with a European-French accent (Variable 21). This factor clearly represents an *Oral French Reading Skill* which is independent of aural French skills (note Variables 12-14) and, possibly because it is more complex, the ability to speak French spontaneously (Variable 18). The one nonachievement variable receiving a substantial loading on this factor is the Number Learning test (Variable 1). Since this test presumably measures both memory skills and auditory alertness (Carroll & Sapon, 1959), these results suggest that in order to orally reproduce foreign-language material, students must not only be alert to phonemic differences, but must also be able to retain them for subsequent use. It is significant that it is a measure of auditory memory which shares variance in common with oral reading skills whereas a measure of rote memory (Variable 5) does not.

The definition of Factor V is not clear, and any interpretation must be highly speculative. Three measures of French achievement obtain high loadings on this factor: comprehension of French discussion (Variable 14), accurate spontaneous speech (Variable 18), and Reading (Variable 15). The element common to the first two tests appears to be one of facility in understanding and speaking French at a fairly sophisticated level since each of these tests requires a considerable knowledge of French. This interpretation may not appear suitable to Variable 15; however, its loadings on Factors I and II indicate that it is factorially complex. It is conceivable, therefore, that a further component of variance of the reading test reflects a relatively high level of achievement in French. Factor V is thus tentatively defined as a *Relative French Sophistication* factor since the characteristic common to the three measures appears to be the ability to perform as though one understood the language with a minimum of translation to the more familiar English.

The one aptitude measure which receives substantial loadings on Factor V is the Spelling Clues test (Variable 3). It has been suggested (Carroll & Sapon, 1959) that scores on this test reflect the student's English vocabulary knowledge as well as a sound-symbol association ability. However, such an interpretation seems unwarranted from these data. As shall be seen ultimately, Factor VII in this study defines a Verbal Knowledge dimension, and the Spelling Clues test receives minimal loadings on that factor. Similarly, an important component of Factor II is the Phonetic Script test, another measure of sound-symbol association ability, and the Spelling Clues test shares little variance in common with that dimension. The Spelling Clues test itself requires the individual to find the English equivalent of a word which is spelled phonetically. Thus, one characteristic tapped by this test is the ability to infer the correct meaning from relatively complex material. This same characteristic appears common to the three measures of French achievement which obtain high loadings on this factor. We have defined Factor V as a *Relative French Sophistication* factor since it seemingly described a rather complex skill for beginning students. To the extent that this interpretation is valid, it would suggest that such sophistication in a minimum of training is dependent upon an ability to quickly infer meaning from relatively complex material.

Two additional factors were isolated in this study. However, since they do not involve the language-aptitude or French-achievement measures to any great extent, they are of little interest. Factor VI is composed of four of the PMA subtests (Variables 6-9), indicating that this is basically an *Intelligence* factor. That these four relatively factorially pure tests collapse onto one dimension is probably due to the absence of other reference variables in the correlation matrix which would serve to more accurately delineate them. It is nonetheless clear that these four measures do have considerable variance in common and that they share little in common with measures of French achievement of language aptitude. The one exception to this statement is Variable 12, a measure of the student's understanding of French questions. It is difficult to decide whether this test has a high intelligence component or whether this aspect of French achievement is itself dependent upon intelligence. It is nevertheless clear that despite significant correlations between indexes of intelligence and measures of language aptitude and French achievement, it is unnecessary to postulate any relation between intelligence and these two attributes other than that to be expected due to considerable variation in intelligence.

Factor VII is defined by the Word Fluency test of the PMA (Variable 10), and by the Verbal Meaning test of the same battery (Variable 6) suggesting that this is a *Verbal Knowledge* factor. The positive loading of the French Vocabulary test (Variable 16) on this dimension is consistent with this interpretation, realizing, of course, that this ability transcends both French and English. Since this factor is orthogonal to Factor II (*French Vocabulary Knowledge*), it is clear that verbal knowledge plays little role in acquiring a meaningful French vocabulary, and that, if anything, it is important only in vocabulary-translation situations as characterized by the Vocabulary test (Variable 16).

REFERENCES

BROOKS, N. *Cooperative French Listening Comprehension Test—examiner's manual.* Princeton, N. J.: Educational Testing Service, 1955.

CARROLL, J. B. A factor analysis of two foreign language aptitude batteries. *Journal of General Psychology*, 1958, *59*, 3-19.

CARROLL, J. B., The prediction of success in intensive foreign language training. In R. Glaser (Ed.), *Training research and education.* Pittsburgh: Univer. Pittsburgh Press, 1962. Pp. 87-136.

CARROLL, J. B., & SAPON, S. M. *Modern Language Aptitude Test, Form A, manual.* New York: Psychological Corporation, 1959.

GARDNER, R. C. Motivational variables in second-language acquisition. Unpublished doctoral dissertation, McGill University, 1960.

GARDNER, R. C., & LAMBERT, W. E. Motivational variables in second-language acquisition. *Canadian Journal of Psychology*, 1959, *13*, 266-272.

GREENBERG, J., & SPAULDING, GERALDINE. *Cooperative French Test, Elementary Form Q.* Princeton, N. J.: Educational Testing Service, 1940.

HENMON, V. A. C. Prognosis tests in the modern foreign languages. *Publications of the American and Canadian Committees on Modern Foreign Languages*, 1929, *14*, 3-36.

KAISER, H. F. The varimax criterion for analytic rotation in factor analysis. *Psychometrika*, 1958, *23*, 187-200.

LADO, R. *Language testing.* London: Longman, Green, 1961.

LAMBERT, W. E. Developmental aspects of second-language acqustion. *Journal of Social Psychology*, 1956, *43*, 83-104.

LAMBERT, W. E., GARDNER, R. C., OLTON, R., & TUNSTALL, K. A study of the roles of attitudes and motivation in second-language learning. Montreal: McGill Univer., 1961. (Mimeo)

THURSTONE, L. L. *Multiple factor analysis.* Chicago: Univer. Chicago Press, 1947.

THURSTONE, L. L., & THURSTONE, THELMA G. *The Chicago tests of Primary Mental Abilities, ages 11 to 17, manual.* Washington, D. C.: American Council on Education, 1941.

WITTENBORN, J. R., & LARSEN, R. P. A factorial study of achievement in college German. *Journal of Educational Psychology*, 1944, *35*, 39-48.

READING NUMBER SEVEN

EVALUATIONAL REACTIONS TO SPOKEN LANGUAGES[1]

W. E. LAMBERT, R. C. HODGSON,[2] R. C. GARDNER, AND S. FILLENBAUM[3]
McGill University

Spoken language is an identifying feature of members of a national or cultural group and any listener's attitude toward members of a particular group should generalize to the language they use. From this viewpoint, evaluational reactions to a spoken language should be similar to those prompted by interaction with individuals who are perceived as members of the group that uses it, but because the use of the language is one aspect of behavior common to a variety of individuals, hearing the language is likely to arouse mainly generalized or stereotyped characteristics of the group. Thus, when one hears a radio broadcast of an international meeting and encounters passages of a foreign language, one's evaluational reactions to the communication are attributable, in part, to the language used and likely reflect generalized attitudinal reactions to the group that uses it.

The purpose of the present investigation was to determine the significance spoken language has for listeners by analyzing their evaluational reactions to English and French. Since we were interested in reactions that are attributable primarily to the language itself, we attempted to minimize the effects of both the voice of the speaker and his message by employing bilingual speakers reading the same message in two languages. In view of previous studies (see Licklider & Miller, 1951, p. 1070f) which have shown that evaluations of personality based solely upon voice have little or no reliability, it was predicted that the

[1] This research was supported by the Canadian Defence Research Board, Grant Number D77-94-01-10, and by a Ford Foundation grant to D. O. Hebb. We are grateful to Henri Barik for his computational assistance.

[2] Now with the Aluminum Company of Canada.

[3] Now at the University of North Carolina.

differences in the favorableness of any S's evaluations of the French and English guises of speakers would reflect his attitude toward members of his own and members of the other language group. The study was carried out with Ss living in Montreal, a community whose history centers largely in a French-English schism which is perhaps as socially significant for residents of the Province of Quebec as that between the North and the South is for Southerners in the United States.

METHOD

Procedure

A 2½ min. passage of French prose of a philosophical nature was translated into fluent English and tape recordings were made of the voices of four male bilinguals each of whom read both French and English versions of the passage. Recordings were also made of the voices of two other men, one reading the passage in English, the other in French. There were, then, 10 taped voices, four of which were "matched," each speaker using both languages, and two used as "filler" voices and for practice. The 10 voices were presented to Ss in alternating French-English order starting with the two filler voices and allowing the maximum possible interval between successive presentations of the English and French guises of any speaker. Evaluational reactions to the matched voices only were examined.

The study was introduced as an experimental investigation of the extent to which peoples' judgments about a speaker are determined by his voice and Ss were reminded of the common phenomenon of having a voice on the radio or telephone summon up a picture in the listener's mind of the person speaking. Ss were *not* told that they were going to hear some of the voices twice, but rather that they would hear 10 recorded male voices, all reading the same passage, five in French and five in English. The two languages, it was said, were being used to give greater scope to the experiment. In this regard, Ss were given copies of the French and English versions of the text they were to hear so that they could be acquainted with the message and the languages and be better prepared to pay attention only to the voices of the speakers. There was no indication that any S became aware of the fact that bilingual speakers were used.

The Ss were also given a response sheet for each voice which directed them to rate each of 14 traits on 6 point scales ranging from "very little" (*fort peu*, for French Ss) to "very much" (*beaucoup*). The traits used were: height (*taille*), good looks (*attrait physique*), leadership (*apte à diriger*), sense of humor (*sens de l'humour*), intelligence (*intelligence*) religiousness (*pieux*), self-confidence (*confiance en soi*), dependability (*digne de confiance*)[4], entertainingness (*jovialité*), kindness (*bonté*), ambition (*ambition*), sociability (*sociabilité*), character (*caractère*) and general likeability (*est-ce qu'il est sympathique?*). Each voice was played once and Ss rated that voice on the scales both while it was playing and during the 90 sec. interval between voices. At the bottom of each response sheet Ss were asked to indicate in what occupation this man would likely be found.

Attached to the back of the 10 response sheets, facing down and covered by a blank sheet, were several questionnaires to be completed. This packaging of questionnaires and response sheets discouraged Ss from looking ahead in the booklet and also permitted them to answer all items anonymously. Ss were asked only their age, place of birth and religious

---

[4]*Digne de confiance* translates to both "dependable" and "trustworthy."

affiliation. After the ratings were obtained on all voices, Ss were directed to turn to the first questionnaire.

Importance ranks of traits. The list of traits used to describe each voice was presented again and Ss were asked to rank the traits in terms of their desirableness in friends. It was felt that this information would offer a more personally relevant set of traits for analysis.

Prejudice scale. In view of its wide use as an index of generalized prejudice and ethnocentrism, we incorporated Forms 40 and 45 of the California F Scale (Adorno, Frenkel-Brunswik, Levinson, & Sanford, 1950) as one of the independent measures of attitude toward outgroups.

Attitude scales. Ss were asked to complete 14 incomplete sentences designed to elicit attitudes toward both their own and the other language group. Examples are: English Canadians think . . .; Children of French Canadian parents . . . ; The more I get to know French Canadians . . . ; French Canadians . . . ; English Canadians . . . ? and The more I get to know English Canadians. . . . The items were translated into French for the French speaking Ss. Two separate scores were assigned each S on the basis of his completions: an "attitude toward English group" score and an "attitude toward French group" score each comprising the number of favorable statements made minus the number of unfavorable statements made about each group. Two judges independently scored the items for each sample and the interjudge reliabilities are, for the English sample, $r = .69$ and $r = .86$ for attitudes toward English and French respectively and for the French sample $r = .75$, and $r = .80$.

Preference scale. Ss indicated their preference for English or French Canadians as: marital partners, friends, neighbors, tenants, colleagues, and political candidates, by ranking which they would rather have for each case. Preference scores were the sum of differences in ranks given to French and English Canadians for all items.

Degree of bilingualism. We reasoned that differences in evaluational reactions to the English and French guises would be less pronounced for those Ss who had experience with both languages and presumably both linguistic communities as well. Ss checked their degree of facility in the use of the other group's language by indicating how well they would speak, read, and write, and whether they could do so: not at all, a little, fairly well, or fluently. An index of bilingualism was computed for each S by assigning zero to "not at all" entries, and 3 to "fluently." We doubled the score for ability to speak the language on the assumption that speaking experience was most important for the purpose of the study. A maximum score would be 12. A bimodal distribution of scores was obtained from both samples and both were split at the same point so that Ss with scores 0 to 7 are categorized as being less bilingual and those with scores 8 to 12 as being more bilingual.

Subjects

The English speaking sample comprised 64 students, taking the first course in Psychology at McGill University, who volunteered to participate. The average age for the group was 18.8 years and both sexes were approximately equally represented.[5] The introduction and

---

[5]Thirty-two Ss indicated that their religion was Jewish, and, to determine their comparability with the rest of the sample, a separate analysis was carried out for Jewish and non-Jewish Ss. For both subgroups, correlations were calculated between each of the four attitude measures and the comparative favorableness of evaluations of the English and French guises considering all traits as well as those most desirable for friends. The comparison of correlations indicated that there were no statistically significant differences between the two subgroups at any point and therefore the Jewish and non-Jewish Ss were combined.

procedures were presented to the group by the first two authors in English. All Ss used English as their school and primary social language, and all but nine who were born in Europe learned English as their first language.

The French speaking sample was made up of 66 male students in their final year at a classical French *collège* in Montreal who were at approximately the same educational level as the English sample, with an average age for the group of 18.2 years. The study was presented to the students by a professor of the *collège* and the first author, in French. The experiment took the place of a regular lecture. All but one of these Ss were born in Canada and all but four in the province of Quebec. All used French as their home, school, and primary social language. The faculty and students speak grammatically correct French, of course, but in general they have a distinctive French Canadian accent.

Speakers

Much care was taken to select appropriate speakers who could take on both French and English guises (in the sense of habitual manners of speaking). We chose from acquaintances in the English speaking community three bilinguals (Bla, Cou, and Leo) who spoke faultless English and yet were trained in French schools in Canada through the graduate level and used French in their homes, or, in the case of Leo, in social or work situations. Several recordings had to be made of each speaker to have errorless readings and in the case of Bla to perfect the pronunciation of a few English words. The final recordings of all four speakers were judged to be spoken in perfect French and English by three bilingual judges. The judges agreed that speakers Bla and Cou spoke with French Canadian accents and that Leo spoke with a marked French Canadian accent characteristic of those who work "in the bush" where, in fact, his style of pronunciation was acquired. The fourth speaker, Tri, spoke French with an accent that was judged as indistinguishable from that used in France. It was felt that these variations in accent and style would not only make the task more interesting for Ss but would also lead to new aspects of the problem for further study, e.g., the reactions of both samples to Parisian French (Tri) and to caricatured French Canadian French (Leo). However, since the present study was not designed to deal comprehensively with variations in accent, attention will be mainly given to over-all comparisons of French and English languages until the final section where accent differences will be discussed.

RESULTS

Favorableness of reactions: English Ss' judgements. For each S on each of the 14 traits the difference (D) between the evaluations of the English and French guises of each speaker was noted, with account taken of the direction of the difference. These D values were then summed over the 4 speakers and over Ss and the departure of the D scores from zero was examined. As can be seen in the over-all column of Table 1, the English Ss evaluated the following seven traits significantly more favorably for the English than for the French guises: Height, Good looks, Intelligence, Dependability, Kindness, Ambition, and Character.[6] There were no significant differences in evaluations of Leadership, Religiousness,

---

[6]Although a rating toward the upper end of the scale does not necessarily indicate favorableness in the cases of "height" or "ambition," the term "favorableness" is a meaningful description for the majority of the judgements.

TABLE 1

t VALUES FOR SIGNIFICANCE OF DIFFERENCES IN EVALUATIONS OF ENGLISH AND FRENCH GUISES OF SPEAKERS

Trait	English Ss' Judgment of Speakers					French Ss' Judgments of Speakers				
	Cou	Bla	Leo	Tri	Over-all	Cou	Bla	Leo	Tri	Over-all
Height	8.63**	4.67**	4.05**	2.59*	8.83**	5.50**	2.32*	2.41*	1.04	4.58**
Good Looks	7.16**	4.10**	2.66**	-.90	5.78**	7.50**	6.00**	7.26**	1.73	9.77**
Leadership	1.72	.69	1.41	-1.82	1.20	4.05**	9.32**	12.10**	.82	11.06**
Sense of Humor	-.58	-.14	2.25*	-3.48**	-2.16*	2.67**	.58	.64	-.30	1.40
Intelligence	1.44	.11	2.25*	1.98*	2.40*	4.54**	9.17**	11.73**	1.00	10.22**
Religiousness	-.67	-.33	-.26	1.81	.27	-1.79	-3.11**	-1.60	-1.14	-2.94**
Self-confidence	-.50	-.47	1.13	-1.33	-.69	5.37**	7.56**	10.00**	-2.00*	8.23**
Dependability	1.61	-.15	3.51**	2.74**	3.11**	2.89**	4.36**	7.50**	1.89	6.44**
Entertainingness	1.77	1.67	.00	-4.44**	-.84	.44	-.27	-.81	.22	-.21
Kindness	2.40*	2.47*	1.67	.74	3.37**	.10	-4.12**	-2.65*	-.74	-2.96**
Ambition	.45	2.43*	2.33*	.84	2.83**	3.06**	4.64**	7.53**	-1.53	5.89**
Sociability	.24	-.16	-.17	-4.13**	-1.44	3.44**	2.10*	3.47*	.29	3.72**
Character	3.07**	1.00	3.17**	.12	3.08**	3.95**	6.81**	8.68**	.31	8.51**
Likability	2.38*	.26	1.38	-1.21	1.22	1.83	.80	2.05*	.79	2.00*

Note.—Positive entries indicate that English guises are evaluated more favorably than French, and minus entries indicate a more favorable evaluation for French guises. This is so for both French and English Ss' judgments.

* Significant at .05 level.

** Significant at .01 level, two-tailed tests.

TABLE 2
t VALUES FOR SIGNIFICANCE OF MEAN DIFFERENCES
IN EVALUATIONS, ENGLISH VS. FRENCH JUDGES

Trait	English Guises	French Guises
Height	3.76**	0.30
Good Looks	1.78	4.59**
Leadership	−2.55*	6.19**
Sense of Humor	0.62	3.10**
Intelligence	−2.87**	2.82**
Religiousness	2.44*	−0.15
Self-confidence	−3.02**	4.85**
Dependability	−1.32	1.97*
Entertainingness	−0.52	−0.42
Kindness	1.82	−3.18**
Ambition	−0.57	2.28*
Sociability	−1.87	2.14*
Character	−1.22	3.60**
Likability	−1.34	−0.31

Note.—Positive entries indicate that English judges evaluated
a particular trait more favorably on the average than did French
judges; minus entries indicate more favorable evaluation for
French than English judges.
  * indicates a *t* is significant at the .05 level, on two-tailed tests.
 ** indicates a *t* is significant at the .01 level, on two-tailed tests.

Self-confidence, Entertainingness, Sociability, and Likability. The French guises were evaluated significantly more favorably on Sense of Humor, but this finding is not clearcut since for one speaker the English guise was evaluated significantly more favorably on this trait. There was considerable consistency in the data for three of the four voices but the fourth (Tri) differed from the others on a number of traits.

Ss had ranked the 14 traits for their desirability in friends. For each S two D scores were obtained, one for the three traits judged most desirable and one for the three traits judged least desirable, by noting the difference in evaluations of the English and French guises for each set of traits. English Ss evaluated the English guises significantly more favorably both for desirable traits (t_{55df} = 2.13) and the less desirable traits (t_{53df} = 4.33). There was no difference between the most and least desirable traits with regard to this preference (t_{49df} = 1.72).

Favorableness of reactions: French Ss' judgements. A similar analysis was carried out for the French Ss. They evaluated the English guises of the speakers significantly *more* favorably than the French guises for the following 10 traits: Height, Good looks, Leadership, Intelligence, Self-confidence, Dependability, Ambition, Sociability, Character, and Likability (Table 1). There was no difference in evaluations with regard to Sense of Humor and Entertainingness, and the French guises were evaluated significantly more favorably on Religiousness and Kindness. The results for three of the four speakers were consistent and

TABLE 3
RELATION OF ATTITUDINAL MEASURES TO OTHER VARIABLES; ENGLISH SAMPLE

	1	2	3	4	5	6
Prejudice (F scale)	X	.29*	-.22	-.01	.20	.19
Preference (Bogardus)		X	-.40**	.17	.13	.13
Attitudes to French (incomplete sentences)			X	-.18	-.04	-.08
Attitudes to English (incomplete sentences)				X	.26*	.25
Favorableness of evaluations (English over French; all traits)					X	.77**
Favorableness of evaluations (English over French; desirable traits)						X

Note.—The N's vary around 55 for all entries except Variable 6 where they drop to around 50.
* Significant at .05 level.
** Significant at .01 level.

TABLE 4
RELATION OF ATTITUDINAL MEASURES TO OTHER VARIABLES; FRENCH SAMPLE

Variables	1	2	3	4	5	6
Prejudice (F scale)	X	.17	.03	-.07	-.05	-.11
Preference (Bogardus)		X	.38**	-.45**	.26*	.27
Attitudes to French (incomplete sentences)			X	-.43**	.25*	.45**
Attitudes to English (incomplete sentences)				X	-.21	-.20
Favorableness of Evaluations (French over English; all traits)					X	.72**
Favorableness of Evaluations (French over English; desirable traits)						X

Note.—The N's vary around 55 for all entries except Variable 6 where they drop to around 35.
Since the French Ss in general showed more favorableness to English than French guises, Variables 5 and 6 mainly represent degrees of nonfavorableness to English guises.
* Significant at .05 level.
** Significant at .01 level.

again speaker Tri was the exception. The English guises were evaluated significantly more favorably both for the three most desirable traits (t_{37} = 7.17) and for the three least desirable traits (t = 7.58) and, as in the case of the English Ss, there was no difference between the most and least desirable traints (t 1).

Favorableness of reactions: English Ss' vs. French Ss' judgements. The evaluations of the English guises given by the English judges were compared with the evaluations of the English guises given by the French judges, and a similar analysis was carried out for the evaluations of the French guises by the two groups of Ss. Table 2 shows that for the English guises the English Ss evaluated Height and Religiousness significantly more favorably than did the French Ss. There were no differences between English and French Ss with regard to: Good Looks, Sense of Humor, Dependability, Entertainingness, Kindness, Ambition, Sociability, Character, and Likability, and the French Ss evaluated the English guises significantly more favorably than did the English Ss on Leadership, Intelligence, and Self-confidence. The comparisons with respect to the French guises are also given in Table 2. It can be seen that the English Ss evaluated the French guises significantly *more* favorably than did the French Ss on the following nine traits: Good looks, Leadership, Sense of Humor, Intelligence, Self-confidence, Dependability, Ambition, Sociability, and Character. There were no differences in evaluations for: Height, Religion, Entertainingness, and Likability, and the French Ss evaluated the French guises significantly more favorably than did the English Ss on Kindness.

Attitudinal measures. The correlations between the various measures of attitude and the comparative favorableness of evaluations of guises are given in Table 3 for the English Ss. It is striking that none of the attitude measures correlate with the degree of favorableness of reactions to English and French guises, with the exception of attitudes to their own group as reflected in responses to the incomplete sentences, a measure that just meets significance requirements.

Although the pattern of correlations is also low for the French Ss, the comparative favorableness of evaluations of guises for this sample is somewhat more clearly related to both attitudes toward and preference for own group. It should be noted that the French Ss on the average clearly showed more favorableness to English than French guises, in fact only 14% of the Ss showed the expected trend of more favorable reaction to French over English versions. This was not the case for either the preference or attitude measures where the majority of Ss (85% and 62%, respectively) preferred and showed more favorable attitudes toward the French over the English group. The significant correlations in Table 4 therefore indicate that the more the French Ss show preference for and favorable attitudes toward their own group the less they overrate English guises.

The relation of bilingualism to other variables. Ss categorized as having a high degree of bilingualism were compared with those having little experience or skill in the other group's language on all attitudinal variables as well as the comparative favorableness of evaluations to the spoken languages. For the English sample, the more bilingual subgroup had a reliably lower mean F score than did the less bilingual group, $t_{60} = 2.20$, a finding consistent with another study (Gardner & Lambert, 1958) on the relation of bilingualism to attitudes. The two bilingual groups did not differ reliably on any other variable, however. For the French sample, the only significant difference between the more and less bilingual subgroups was on the modified Bogardus scale: the more bilingual group showed reliably less own group preference than did those with little facility in English, $t_{52} = 2.43$.

DISCUSSION

Evaluational reactions. It is not unexpected that English speaking Ss should show more favorableness to members of their linguistic group, but the finding that French Ss also evaluate English guises more favorably is as unexpected as the finding that these Ss judge French guises less favorably than do the English Ss.

The traits given to Ss for evaluation included several of those commonly considered necessary for social and economic success (e.g., looks, leadership, confidence, ambition), but we attempted to balance these with personality characteristics generally considered of greater value such as likability and kindness. It is possible that we were biased in the selection of traits and, through ignorance, presented a list which omitted characteristics which have value for French speaking Canadians. However, the French sample chose dependability, intelligence, and kindness as the most desirable traits for friends of those given them for consideration, and two of these were rated more favorably with the English guises, a fact which argues against the view that no opportunity was given the French sample to evaluate the speakers on culturally important traits.

In view of the greater probability of finding English people in more powerful social and economic positions in the Montreal community, both samples of Ss might more likely think of an English speaker as having higher status and then evaluate the English voice of the putative lawyer as having more ambition, intelligence, etc., than the French voice of the putative store employee. If the French Ss had a greater tendency to do so, this might account in part for their evaluational reaction pattern. Data were available to test this notion in an indirect fashion by making use of Ss' estimations of each speaker's likely occupation in his French and English guises. These occupational assignments were categorized as either professional or nonprofessional by two judges working independently. For the English sample, the ascribed status of English guises was markedly higher than for French guises, $X^2 = 38.14$ with 1 df. For the French sample, the same trend was noted but was much reduced in magnitude, $X^2 = 5.38$. The fact that the French Ss ascribe higher status to a larger proportion of French guises (44%) than do English Ss (33%) and also evaluate the French guises less favorably than do English Ss argues against an interpretation in terms of differences in perceived status of the two groups.

The findings can also be interpreted as meaning that the French Ss actually perceive members of the English speaking group as having various desirable personality traits. The characteristics ascribed to the English speakers are generally the same as those ascribed by the English Ss to the same guises with the exception of the English-French conflict over which group is more kind. The French Ss may well regard themselves as members of an inferior group, one that is nonetheless kind and religious. Several recent studies (Adelson, 1953; Sarnoff, 1951; Steckler, 1957) which document the manner in which minority groups sometimes adopt the stereotyped values of majority groups indicate that a parallel process may be taking place in the French Canadian community (cf. Stewart & Blackburn, 1956).

An examination of the common descriptions given by the French Ss in the open-ended questionnaire suggests that they have ambivalent feelings about both French Canadians and English Canadians, an interpretation that is analogous to the attitude of American Jews toward both Jews and non-Jews as described by Lewin (1948, p. 145ff). The French Ss describe their own group as progressing and having a potential (18 occurrences); feeling inferior or without confidence (16); having good qualities and being likable (16); being uninformed or uneducated (16); being intelligent or as intelligent as English Canadians (14); being individualistic or disunited (11); lacking ambition (11); and as being prejudiced or narrow-minded (10). They describe the English Canadians as being likable, good, or nice (27); thinking badly of French Canadians (19); feeling superior to French Canadians (13); being too Americanized (12); lacking knowledge of or appreciation for French Canadians (11); and as being less mannered or more rude (11).

The findings presented here take on somewhat more significance in view of two pilot studies using other samples of Ss which show essentially the same results. In the first study, 17 English speaking college students listened to three of the four speakers used in the present study. In this case, English guises were evaluated more favorably on all five traits presented. In the second study, 22 male and 25 female French speaking members of Catholic religious orders were Ss and three of the four speakers and 12 of the 14 scales used in the present study were administered. Ss evaluated the English guises significantly more favorably on most traits except for kindness (*bonté*) on which French guises were more favorably evaluated. Speaker Tri, as in the present study, was not subject to this trend.

Attitude data. The general trend of correlations indicates that certain measures of attitude, particularly attitudes toward one's own group, are associated with the favorableness of evaluational reactions to the spoken languages, but this relation is clearly not a marked one, especially for the English Ss. Furthermore, the prediction was not supported that more skill with the other group's language, which would permit more intimate interaction, would lead to smaller differences in favorableness of evaluational responses to the guises.

In view of the striking tendency for both English and French speaking Ss to evaluate the English guises more favorably, a possible reason for the generally low correlations may be that generalized characteristics of French speaking and English speaking people are so widely accepted in the Montreal community that even those English Ss with positive attitudes toward French may still perceive them as inferior on many traits. Likewise, French Ss with negative attitudes toward English speaking people may still perceive them as superior in many respects. That is, both French and English Ss regardless of their attitude may have come to believe that English speaking Canadians are taller and possibly more "intelligent" in the sense that they have more educational opportunities. To this extent, the attitude factor would be submerged by powerful community-wide stereotypes. This argument is limited, however, in that attitudes would certainly be expected to play the dominant role when the two guises are compared on such traits as good looks or character. To check this possible interpretation, correlations for the English sample were computed between the comparative favorableness of reactions to the guises and attitudes toward English Canadians for *each* trait examined separately. The correlations for character, intelligence, and dependability reach significance at about the .05 level but none of the others do, even those for good looks or kindness which would also be expected to reflect an attitude factor. We conclude, therefore, that the comparatively unfavorable perception of French speakers is essentially independent of the perceivers' attitudes toward French and English groups. The correlations for the French sample are not large or consistent enough to make French Ss an exception to this generalization. Furthermore, experience with both groups, as inferred from the degree of skill in using both languages, also appears to be independent of the tendency to downgrade French speaking individuals. Further research is necessary to determine the influence of community-wide stereotypes and majority-minority feelings of members of the two language groups in Montreal.

Although the findings may be considered consistent and reliable, the generality of the results will become clear only after extensions to other samples of Ss and a larger sample of speakers. It will be recalled that the four speakers used here were chosen to represent different linguistic communities: three speakers were educated in French Canadian universities but Leo spoke more naturally with a caricatured French Canadian accent. Only speaker Tri spoke French with a Parisian accent. A comparison of the evaluational reactions made to these speakers suggests that further study of accent differences of speakers from different linguistic communities may well extend the usefulness of the technique developed here. It can be seen in Table 1 that speaker Tri was not downgraded by the French Ss when speaking French as were the other speakers; in fact he was considered significantly more self-confident in French than in English. Nor do the English Ss treat him adversely in French, for they perceive him as having reliably more humor, entertainingness, and sociability in French than English. Clearly more than one speaker with a Parisian speech style is needed to test this notion, but the data suggest that the Montreal community may differentiate between Parisian and Canadian French in their attitudes. Note also in Table 1 that speaker Leo, the caricatured French Canadian, is particularly downgraded in his French guise by both English and French Ss, if we interpret the size of t values as an index of differential favorableness of evaluation.

SUMMARY

Samples of French speaking and English speaking Montreal students were asked to evaluate the personality characteristics of 10 speakers, some speaking in French, others in English. They were not made aware that actually bilinguals were used as speakers so that the evaluational reactions to the two language guises could be matched for each speaker. The comparative favorableness of evaluations of the two guises was correlated with various measures of attitudes toward French and English Canadians for both samples of Ss.

The results indicate that English Ss evaluate the English guises more favorably on most traits. French Ss not only evaluate the English guises more favorably than French guises, but their evaluations of French guises are reliably less favorable than those of English Ss. This finding is interpreted as evidence for a minority group reaction on the part of the French sample.

The correlations between comparative favorableness of English and French guises and measures of attitude toward own and other groups were generally low and insignificant, especially for the English sample. The essential independence of evaluational reactions to spoken languages and attitudes is interpreted as a reflection of the influence of community-wide stereotypes of English and French speaking Canadians.

REFERENCES

ADELSON, J. B. A study of minority group authoritarianism. *J. abnorm. soc. Psychol.*, 1953, *48*, 477-485.

ADORNO, T. W., FRENKEL-BRUNSWIK, E., LEVINSON, D. J., & SANFORD, R. N. *The authoritarian personality*. New York: Harper, 1950.

GARDNER, R. C., & LAMBERT, W. E. Social-motivational aspects of second-language acquisition. 1958. (Mimeo.)

LEWIN, K. *Resolving social conflicts*. New York: Harper, 1948.

LICKLIDER, J. C. R., & MILLER, G. A. The perception of speech. In S. S. Stevens (Ed.) *Handbook of experimental psychology*. New York: Wiley, 1951.

SARNOFF, I. Identification with the aggressor: Some personality correlates of anti-semitism among Jews. *J. Pers.*, 1951, *20* 199-218.

STECKLER, G. A. Authoritarian ideology in Negro college students. *J. abnorm. soc. Psychol.*, 1957, *54*, 396-399.

STEWART, J., & BLACKBURN, J. Tensions between English-speaking and French-speaking Canadians. *Contributions à l'Etude des Sciences de l'Homme*, 1956, *3*, 145-167.

References

Adorno, T. W., Else Frenkel-Brunswick, D. J. Levinson, and R. N. Sanford. *The Authoritarian Personality.* New York: Harper, 1950.

Anisfeld, M., and W. E. Lambert. "Social and Psychological Variables in Learning Hebrew." *Journal of Abnormal and Social Psychology*, 63 (1961), 524-29.

Anisfeld, M., N. Bogo, and W. E. Lambert. "Evaluational Reactions to Accented English Speech." *Journal of Abnormal and Social Psychology.* 65 (1962), 223-31.

Anisfeld, Elizabeth, and W. E. Lambert. "Evaluational Reactions of Bilingual and Monolingual Children to Spoken Language." *Journal of Abnormal and Social Psychology*, 69 (1964), 89-97.

Brooks, N. *Cooperative French Listening Comprehension Test, Form A.* Princeton, N.J.: Cooperative Test Division, Educational Testing Service, 1955.

Brown, W. F., and W. H. Holtzman. *Survey of Study Habits and Attitudes.* New York: The Psychological Corporation, 1953.

Carroll, J. B. *Summary of Validity Coefficients--Foreign Language Aptitude Battery.* Cambridge, Mass.: Harvard University, 1956, mimeo.

———."A Factor Analysis of Two Foreign Language Aptitude Batteries." *Journal of General Psychology,* 59 (1958), 3-19.

———. "The Prediction of Success in Intensive Foreign Language Training," in R. Glaser (ed.) *Training Research and Education.* Pittsburgh: University of Pittsburgh Press, 1962.

———, and S. M. Sapon. *Modern Language Aptitude Test, Form A.* New York: The Psychological Corporation, 1959.

Child, I. L. *Italian or American? The Second Generation in Conflict.* New Haven: Yale University Press, 1943.

Christie, R., and Florence Geis. *Studies in Machiavellianism.* New York: Academic Press, 1970.

Cliff, N., and C. D. Hamburger. "The Study of Sampling Errors in Factor Analysis by Means of Artificial Experiments." *Psychological Bulletin,* 68 (1967), 430-45.

Cook, S. W. "Motives in a Conceptual Analysis of Attitude-related Behavior," in W. J. Arnold and David Levine (eds.) *Nebraska Symposium on Motivation.* Lincoln: University of Nebraska Press, 1969.

Cooke, Madelaine A. "A Study of the Development of Positive Attitudes toward Native Speakers of Spanish." Diss. Ohio State University, 1969.

Cronbach, L. J. *Essentials of Psychological Testing.* New York: Harper & Row, 1970.

Delaunay, A. "L'Apprentissage precoce des languages vivantes par la methode naturelle." *L'Education Enfantine,* 1970, September, October, November, and December.

Dunkel, H. B. *Second-language Learning.* Boston: Ginn, 1948.

Durkheim, E. *Le Suicide.* Paris: F. Alcan, 1897.

Farwell, G. *Mask of Asia: The Philippines Today.* New York: Praeger, 1967.

Feenstra, H. J., and R. C. Gardner. *Aptitude and Motivation in Second-language Acquisition.* Department of Psychology, The University of Western Ontario, 1968, mimeo.

Fishbein, M. *Readings in Attitude Theory and Measurement.* New York: Wiley, 1967.

Fruchter, B. *Introduction to Factor Analysis.* New York: Van Nostrand, 1954.

Gardner, R. C. "Motivational Variables in Second-language Acquisition." Diss. McGill University, 1960.

———. "Motivational Variables in Second-language Learning." *International Journal of American Linguistics,* 32 (1966), 24-44.

———, and W. E. Lambert. "Motivational Variables in Second-language Acquisition." *Canadian Journal of Psychology,* 13 (1959), 266-72.

———, and W. E. Lambert. "Language Aptitude, Intelligence and Second-language Achievement." *Journal of Educational Psychology,* 56 (1965), 191-99.

———, D. M. Taylor, and H. J. Feenstra. "Ethnic Stereotypes: Attitudes or Beliefs." *Canadian Journal of Psychology,* 24 (1970), 321-34.

Gough, H. G. *California Psychological Inventory.* Palo Alto: Consulting Psychologists Press, 1956.

Greenberg, J., and G. Spaulding. *Cooperative French Test, Elementary Form Q.* Princeton, N.J.: Educational Testing Service, 1940.

Halili, A. "Listening Comprehension Test for Secondary School Freshmen." Diss. Phillipine Normal College, July, 1965.

Hayes, A. S., W. E. Lambert, and G. R. Tucker. "Evaluation of Foreign Language Teaching." *Foreign Language Annals,* 1 (1967), 22-44.

Hebb, D. O., W. E. Lambert, and G. R. Tucker. "Language, Thought and Experience." *The Modern Language Journal,* 55 (1971), 212-22.

Hunt, J. McV. *Intelligence and Experience.* New York: Ronald, 1961.

Jones, F. E., and W. E. Lambert. "Attitudes toward Immigrants in a Canadian Community." *Public Opinion Quarterly,* 23 (1959), 537-46.

———. "Occupational Rank and Attitudes toward Immigrants." *Public Opinion Quarterly* 29 (1965), 137-44.

———. "Some Situational Influences on Attitudes toward Immigrants." *British Journal of Sociology,* 18 (1967), 408-24.

Jones, W. R. "Attitude towards Welsh as a Second Language. A Preliminary Investigation." *British Journal of Educational Psychology* 19 (1949), 44-52.

———. "Attitude towards Welsh as a Second Language, a Further Investigation." *British Journal of Educational Psychology,* 20 (1950), 117-32.

Kaiser, H. F. "The Varimax Criterion for Analytic Rotation in Factor Analysis." *Psychometrica,* 23 (1958), 187-200.

Kanungo, R. N., and S. Dutta. "Retention of Affective Material: Frame of Reference or Intensity." *Journal of Personality and Social Psychology*, 4 (1966), 27-35.

———. "Effects of Emotional Involvement on the Perceived Intensity of Affect and Retention." Paper given at the Eastern Psychological Association meeting in Philadelphia, 1969.

Kluckhohn, F., and F. Strodbeck. *Variations in Value-orientations.* Evanston, Ill.: Rowe, Peterson, 1961.

Lambert, W. E. "Measurement of the Linguistic Dominance of Bilinguals." *Journal of Abnormal and Social Psychology*, 50 (1955), 197-200.

———. "A Social Psychology of Bilingualism." *Journal of Social Issues*, 23 (1967), 91-109.

———, J. Havelka, and R. C. Gardner. "Linguistic Manifestations of Bilingualism." *The American Journal of Psychology*, 72 (1959), 77-82.

———, R. C. Hodgson, R. C. Gardner, and S. Fillenbaum. "Evaluational Reactions to Spoken Languages." *Journal of Abnormal and Social Psychology*, 0 (1960), 44-51.

———, R. C. Gardner, H. C. Barik, and K. Tunstall. "Attitudinal and Cognitive Aspects of Intensive Study of a Second Language." *Journal of Abnormal and Social Psychology*, 66 (1962), 358-68.

———, and W. W. Lambert. *Social Psychology.* Englewood Cliffs, N.J.: Prentice-Hall, 1964.

———, and O. Klineberg. *Children's Views of Foreign Peoples: A Cross-national Study.* New York: Appleton, 1967.

———, H. Frankel, and G. R. Tucker. "Judging Personality through Speech. A French Canadian Example." *The Journal of Communication*, 16 (1966) 305-21.

———, M. Anisfeld, and Grace Yeni-Komshian. "Evaluational Reactions of Jewish and Arab Adolescents to Dialect and Language Variations." *Journal of Personality and Social Psychology*, 2 (1965), 84-90.

Lemaire, H. B. "Franco-American Efforts on Behalf of the French Language in New England," in J. A. Fishman (ed.) *Language Loyalty in the United States.* The Hague: Mouton, 1966.

Lott, B. E. and A. J. Lott. "The Formation of Positive Attitudes toward Group Members." *Journal of Abnormal and Social Psychology*, 61 (1960), 297-300.

Mackey, W. F. *Bilingualism as a World Problem.* Montreal: Harvest House, 1967.

McClelland, D. C. *The Achieving Society.* Princeton, N.J.: Van Nostrand, 1961.

———, and D. G. Winter. *Motivating Economic Achievement.* New York: Free Press, 1969.

Miller, N. E., and J. Dollard. *Social Learning and Imitation.* New Haven: Yale University Press, 1941.

Morris, C. *Varieties of Human Value.* Chicago: The University of Chicago Press, 1956.

Mowrer, O. H. *Learning Theory and Personality Dynamics.* New York: Ronald, 1950.

Nida, E. A. "Motivation in Second-language Learning." *Language Learning*, 7 (1956), 11-16.

Otis, A. S. *Self-administering Intelligence Test.* New York: World, 1954.

Padilla, A. M., and K. K. Long. "An Assessment of Successful Spanish-American Students at the University of New Mexico." Paper presented to the annual meeting of the AAAS, Rocky Mountain Division, Colorado Springs, 1969.

Parsons, T. *The Social System.* Chicago, Ill.: Free Press, 1951.

Peal, Elizabeth, and W. E. Lambert. "The Relation of Bilingualism to Intelligence." *Psychological Monographs*, 76 (1962), whole No. 546.

Pimsleur, P. "Testing Foreign Language Learning," in A. Valdman (ed.) *Trends in Language Teaching.* New York: McGraw-Hill, 1966.

Plaza, M. "An Achievement Test in English Grammar for Freshmen in Government Normal Schools." Diss. Phillipine Normal College, October, 1964.

Preston, M. S. "Evaluation Reactions to English Canadian French and European French Voices." Diss. McGill University, Redpath Library, 1963.

Read, W. A. *Louisiana-French.* Baton Rouge: Louisiana State University Press, 1963.

Roe, Anne. "A New Classification of Occupations." *Journal of Counseling Psychology* 1 (1956), 215-20.

Skinner, B. F. *Science and Human Behavior.* New York: Macmillan, 1953.

Smith, E. E. "Methods for Changing Consumer Attitudes." Project Report, Quartermaster Food and Container Institute for the Armed Forces, (PRA Report 61-2), February, 1961.

Spaulding, G., and P. Vaillant. *Cooperative French Test, Elementary Form Q.* Princeton, N.J.: Educational Testing Service, 1940.

Srole, L. "Social Dysfunction, Personality and Social Distance Attitudes." Paper read before the American Sociological Society, 1951, National Meeting, Chicago, Ill., mimeo.

Staats, W. W., and Carolyn Staats. "Attitudes Established by Classical Conditioning." *Journal of Abnormal and Social Psychology*, 57 (1958), 37-40.

Tisch, Joseph L. *French in Louisiana: A Study of the Historical Development of the French Language of Louisiana.* New Orleans: A. F. Laborde, 1959.

Thom, Stanley. Personal communication, with reference to work with Sister Ruth Jones: A matched classroom approach to the teachin of French in the elementary grades. Office of Education Contract OEC-3-061944-1891, continuing 1971.

Thurstone, L. L., and Thelma G. Thurstone. *Primary Mental Abilities.* Chicago: Science Research, 1954.

———. *SRA Test of Educational Ability, Grades 9-12.* Chicago: Science Research, 1958.

Triandis, H. C. *Attitude and Attitude Change.* New York: Wiley, 1971.

Tucker, G. R. "Judging Personality from Language Usage: A Filipino Example." *Philippine Sociological Review*, 16 (1968), 30-39.

Vogt, E. Z. *Modern Homesteaders.* Cambridge, Mass.: Belknap Press, 1955.

Whyte, W. F., and A. R. Holmberg. "Human Problems of U.S. Enterprise in Latin America." *Human Organization* 15 (1956), 1-40.

Zimbardo, P. G., and E. B. Ebbesen. *Influencing Attitudes and Changing Behavior.* Reading, Mass.: Addison-Wesley, 1969.

———, H. Weisenberg, I. Firestone, and B. Levy. "Communicator Effectiveness of Producing Public Conformity and Private Attitude Change." *Journal of Personality*, 33 (1965), 233-56.

Subject Index

Author Index